The Matthew J. and Arlyn Bruccoli COLLECTION OF
F. Scott Fitzgerald
at the University of South Carolina

The Matthew J. and Arlyn Bruccoli COLLECTION OF F. Scott Fitzgerald
at the University of South Carolina

An Illustrated Catalogue

Compiled by Park Bucker

From Initial Cataloguing by the Staff of
the Department of Rare Books and Special Collections
Thomas Cooper Library, University of South Carolina

Published in Cooperation with the Thomas Cooper Library

UNIVERSITY OF SOUTH CAROLINA PRESS

© 2004 University of South Carolina

Published in Columbia, South Carolina,
by the University of South Carolina Press

Manufactured in the United States of America

08 07 06 05 04   5 4 3 2 1

Library of Congress Cataloging-in-Publication Data

Thomas Cooper Library.
  The Matthew J. and Arlyn Bruccoli Collection of F. Scott Fitzgerald at the University of South Carolina : an illustrated catalogue / compiled by Park Bucker ; initial cataloguing by the staff of the Department of Rare Books and Special Collections, Thomas Cooper Library, University of South Carolina.
  p. cm.
  Includes index.
  ISBN 1-57003-556-3 (alk. paper)
  1. Fitzgerald, F. Scott (Francis Scott), 1896–1940—Bibliography—Catalogs. 2. Fitzgerald, F. Scott (Francis Scott), 1896–1940—Manuscripts—Catalogs. 3. Fitzgerald, F. Scott (Francis Scott), 1896–1940—Library—Catalogs. 4. Fitzgerald, F. Scott (Francis Scott), 1896–1940—Pictorial works—Catalogs. 5. Manuscripts, American—South Carolina—Columbia—Catalogs. 6. Fitzgerald, Zelda, 1900–1948—Bibliography—Catalogs. 7. Fitzgerald, Zelda, 1900–1948—Manuscripts—Catalogs. 8. Graham, Sheilah—Bibliography—Catalogs. 9. Graham, Sheilah—Manuscripts—Catalogs. 10. Thomas Cooper Library—Catalogs. I. Bruccoli, Matthew Joseph, 1931– II. Bruccoli, Arlyn. III. Bucker, Park. IV. Thomas Cooper Library. Dept. of Rare Books and Special Collections V. Title.
  Z8301.2.T47 2004
  [PS3511.I9]
  016.813'52—dc22

2004013610

For
Scottie
—M. B. J.

For
Henrietta Harsh Boylan Bucker
(1913–2003)
—P. B.

CONTENTS

Introduction   ix
Matthew J. Bruccoli

Compiler's Note   xv
Park Bucker

    I. Books and Collections by F. Scott Fitzgerald (Including Copies Inscribed by Him) / 1

   II. First Book Appearances by F. Scott Fitzgerald / 114

  III. Periodical Appearances by F. Scott Fitzgerald / 145

  IV. Keepsakes and Exhibition Catalogues / 169

   V. F. Scott Fitzgerald Manuscripts / 176

  VI. Correspondence
      A. From F. Scott Fitzgerald / 184
      B. To F. Scott Fitzgerald / 198
      C. Concerning F. Scott Fitzgerald / 201

 VII. Selected F. Scott Fitzgerald Documents and Other Literary Documents / 208

VIII. Inscriptions
      A. Books Inscribed to the Fitzgeralds / 215
      B. Books by Other Authors Inscribed or Annotated by F. Scott Fitzgerald / 220
      C. Books from F. Scott Fitzgerald's Library / 228

  IX. Screenplays and Movie Work by F. Scott Fitzgerald: Mimeographs and Xeroxes / 230

   X. Selected Graphic Material
      A. Photographs / 235
      B. Movie Posters and Promotional Material / 237
      C. Lois Moran Items / 242

  XI. Princetoniana / 245

XII. Memorabilia / 249

XIII. Zelda Fitzgerald Collection
    A. Books by Zelda Fitzgerald / 251
    B. Zelda Fitzgerald Manuscripts / 255
    C. Zelda Fitzgerald Correspondence / 255
    D. Zelda Fitzgerald Artwork / 257
    E. First Book and Periodical Appearances of Zelda Fitzgerald / 259
    F. Zelda Fitzgerald Documents / 261

XIV. Sheilah Graham Material
    A. Books by Sheilah Graham / 263
    B. Sheilah Graham Correspondence / 266
    C. Fitzgerald-Related Periodical Appearances of Sheilah Graham / 267

XV. Blurbs by F. Scott Fitzgerald / 269

    Supplement / 272

Index / 279

INTRODUCTION

The first F. Scott Fitzgerald volume I bought was a Grosset & Dunlap reprint of *The Great Gatsby* in a Times Square bargain bookstore in spring 1949. The first book I bought at Yale in fall 1949 was *The Portable F. Scott Fitzgerald*. In college I unsystematically acquired what I called "different copies" of *Gatsby*, but I couldn't explain why. Shortly before graduation I bought a copy of the 1925 Scribners edition of *Gatsby* in Whitlock's basement. I don't know whether it was a first printing because I didn't know how to identify a first printing. None of my teachers at Yale encouraged me to collect books.

In fall 1954 I met John Cook Wyllie, curator of Rare Books at the University of Virginia, the best bookman I've ever known. He trained me. These were some of his principles:

1. The purpose of building an author collection is to provide evidence for a bibliography.
2. There is no such thing as a duplicate copy until it is proven to be one by bibliographical examination; but you ought to have multiple copies anyhow. Mr. Wyllie taught me how to differentiate concealed printings.
3. A proper bibliographical description includes evidence for the history of the production, publication, reception, and reputation of the book.
4. The aim of collecting an American or English author is to acquire every printing of every edition of every work in the English language. This rationale serves two main functions: to provide evidence of the textual transmission of the works, and to document the writer's career. My Fitzgerald collection holds probably two hundred translations; but I stopped acquiring them because no translation can reproduce an author's style, language, tone.
5. There is no substitute for handling books—thousands and thousands of them. Mr. Wyllie granted me the freedom of his rare-book stacks.

Everything I have done as a bookman I owe to John Cook Wyllie's tutelage and example. One of the things he inadvertently taught me was to buy books and then worry about how to pay for them. As a Scotsman and a veteran of the Depression, he was unable to acquire books he couldn't pay for. That is not the right way to get books. This is said with respect, for I cherished Mr. Wyllie. Frazer Clark later taught me that acquiring books you can't pay for is the right way to do it.

The University of Virginia was the center for American bibliographical scholarship at that time. Linton Massey exposed me to his William Faulkner collection, but he cautioned me to collect an author I would be able to afford on a professor's pittance. Of the procession of bookmen who came to UVa for library events, the one who made the strongest impression on me was Charles E. Feinberg, the great Whitman collector and patron of scholarship. He told me how he had started buying Whitman with money earned shining shoes. Charlie provided me with two rules:

1. If you've never seen a book before, you may never see another copy. Buy it.
2. Books cost more today than they did yesterday, but tomorrow they'll cost even more. Buy them.

UVa was the fiefdom of Fredson Bowers, the greatest bibliographer who ever lived. He directed my dissertation on "The Composition of *Tender Is the Night*." Yet Fred did not collect books, and he thought that book collectors were a little crazy. He collected stamps.

I began my serious booking in New York, and Mr. Wyllie sent me to the best place in America: the Seven Gables Book Shop at 3 West 46th, owned by John S. Van E. Kohn and Michael Pappantonio. Seven Gables functioned as a book club where collectors, curators, researchers, and dealers assembled. A student with five or ten bucks was treated respectfully; and John Kohn, the American literature partner, enjoyed encouraging young collectors. Both John and Mike were good to me, although they regarded my Fitzgerald interest as an aberration. Later my main source for Fitzgerald was Henry Wenning in New Haven. He allowed me to pay for my purchases on time. My first jacketed *Gatsby* cost thirty or thirty-five dollars: fifteen dollars down and the balance in installments. The book in jacket now brings up to $150,000.

I remained a book buyer until my marriage in 1957, when I became a serious collector. My Arlyn understood my bibliographical ambitions, although she insisted that Jane Austen was a better novelist than F. Scott Fitzgerald. She once blew our eating money on a ten-dollar copy of *Taps at Reveille* in jacket. The collection bears her name as co-proprietor because she let me do it. No Arlyn, no books.

As the collection grew, civilians asked, "Where did you get them?" The answer is that books are where you find them and that you get them one at a time. I was very fortunate in my timing. In the Fifties and into the Sixties, a lot of Fitzgerald was available, and the prices were low. Some dealers took umbrage at my Fitzgerald endeavors. A prominent autograph dealer told me: "If I got a Fitzgerald letter I'd burn it." I found Fitzgerald in basements, attics, junk shops, book barns, as well as in used or secondhand-book shops. Dealers' catalogues still flourished before the Internet, and it was possible to find sleepers in them. Much of my education came from reading book catalogues. I learned more in bookshops and from catalogues than I learned in classrooms. During my grad-student years, I was spending my father's money. He regarded reading books as a waste of time and buying them as a waste of money, but he bankrolled me.

A year in Cambridge, Massachusetts, provided many finds. On Saturdays I went booking with five dollars and came back with books. That was more than forty years ago, and I still lament two of the books I didn't buy because I couldn't pay for them. The only ones you regret are the ones you don't buy. Gentle Jack Neiburg would save fifty-cent treasures for me and try to give them to me—including the only jacketed copy of the Bantam *Gatsby* I'd ever seen.

Book dealers provided tutelage: They handle more books than collectors do, and the good ones remember the books. Columbus was a bibliographical Sahara, but Cleveland and Peter Keisogloff were ninety miles away. Peter sold me books, gave me books, bought me lunch, and told me book stories. One of the functions of book collecting is to discover and preserve rare or previously unrecognized items. When there were many kinds of used-book establishments—from skid-row junk shops to big-ticket dealers—it was possible for collectors to make discoveries. Since there was then no reliable Fitzgerald bibliography, almost every find was a discovery. Nothing replaces seeing the books and touching them. That process has become increasingly difficult as the shops have disappeared; nonetheless, collectors can still work closely with knowledgeable antiquarian dealers.

After Mr. Wyllie and Arlyn, the two people who exerted the greatest influence on my Fitzgerald work were C. E. Frazer Clark, Jr., and Scottie Fitzgerald. Fraze and I met in 1962 when I was assisting Fredson Bowers in editing the Centenary Edition of Nathaniel Hawthorne, and Fraze was starting as a Hawthorne collector. While he was building the best Hawthorne collection, he abetted my Fitzgerald collecting by finding items and by teaching me a new kind of arithmetic. I was in debt most of the time we worked together, but we got the books. The only thing that matters is to get the books. Fraze was an inspired book-hunter. His chief rule was "Pay attention." We formed Bruccoli Clark Publishers to produce reference books and limited editions generated by our collections. Fraze was my luck.

I met Scottie on 9 October 1964, at an auction for the benefit of the Baltimore Symphony. She had donated two books I wanted: a copy of *Death in the Afternoon* inscribed by Hemingway to Fitzgerald and a *Gatsby* inscribed by Fitzgerald to his mother. By trying to get both, I got neither. There was a third book—not donated by Scottie—an inscribed *Taps at Reveille* that I tried to buy so as to not leave empty-handed. As the bidding rose to $250 I discovered that I was bidding against Scottie—to whom I had introduced myself earlier in the evening—and I dropped out. She took it at $275, wrote a gracious note in the book, and gave it to me. She later explained that she was troubled because I had missed out on the other books. That response defined Scottie. I fell in devotion to her; for the rest of her life she encouraged and inspired my Fitzgerald work. We collaborated on eight "Daddy books," four of which give her title-page credit. At some point around 1970 my Fitzgerald collection became a celebration of Scottie. She gave me Daddy items at Christmas. After her death I received a box of Fitzgerald books she had selected during her last days and arranged to be sent to cheer me up after she died. The best thing I got out of F. Scott Fitzgerald was Scottie Fitzgerald.

It was always my intention to keep the collection together in a library. Mr. Wyllie taught me that. Serious collectors collect for others. The ones who destroy their collections by disposing of them piecemeal are speculators or conspicuous consumers. Having seen what happened after the deaths of collectors who failed to make proper provisions for their books, I set about finding the right repository for my Fitzgerald Collection and my other collections. The Fitzgerald Collection was worth about two million dollars. I wanted some money to spend on more books; the rest would be a gift. Arlyn concurred. At that time USC was out of the question. I approached four major research libraries: two of them wanted the collection gratis, and the other two wanted to cherry-pick it. Duplication! The word triggers terror in library schools and other asylums. Then George Terry became Dean of Libraries at the University of South Carolina. He was the fifth major figure in my Fitzgerald saga: Mr. Wyllie, Arlyn, Fraze, Scottie, and George. George—who was not a library-school product—approached me with the right deal for the maintenance and growth of the collection. The collection was transferred to the Thomas Cooper Library in 1994 and has been augmented by a thousand items.

The dumbest question I am asked about the Fitzgerald Collection is: "What do you do with it?" You use it to make more books—that's what you do with it. It is not a show collection. It is a working collection for reference, research, and teaching. I use it; good teachers use it; visiting scholars use it; students use it. The collection began as a resource for my Fitzgerald bibliography. I have written or edited thirty-nine books and two journals from the collection. A scholar needs a working library. I don't trust self-proclaimed scholars who do whatever they claim to do without their own books. A scholar builds a collection for his own research and then places it in an institution to keep it together and make it accessible.

Research begets research. Books beget books. A collection can never be used up. The second dumbest question I am asked is: "What are you going to do now that you've stopped collecting Fitzgerald?" This stupidity is particularly aggravating when asked by a bookdealer. A bookman never stops being a bookman. You never stop looking and acquiring. A collection is never completed. Another dumb question is: "Don't you miss the books?" My father believed that you don't own something until you give it away. Placing a collection in the right library is a way of keeping it. There are no bookshelves in a coffin.

The collection now stands at 3,000 books; 500 periodicals; 18 Fitzgerald manuscripts or typescripts; at least 120 Fitzgerald letters, wires, and postcards; 26 letters to Fitzgerald; memorabilia, graphic material, and photos. It is impossible to identify the items that are most valuable (in money or research utility). I can only note some of my favorites: Fitzgerald's "Thoughtbook" (1910–11) from Scottie; the only set of the unrevised galleys of *Trimalchio;* one of the two known copies of the printed acting script for *Fie! Fie! Fi-Fi!*—and the only one with additional Fitzgerald lyrics inserted; a photo of Hemingway inscribed to Fitzgerald; *For Whom the Bell Tolls* inscribed to Fitzgerald; *Ulysses* with a note from Joyce to Fitzgerald pasted in and with Fitzgerald's annotations; 40 of his own books inscribed by Fitzgerald; 35 books by other writers inscribed or annotated by Fitzgerald; 24 books inscribed to the Fitzgeralds by their authors; 10 books from Fitzgerald's library; contracts for Fitzgerald's Scribner books; Fitzgerald's tax returns, 1920–39; *The Portable Fitzgerald* annotated by Kenneth Millar and *Gatsby* marked by Sylvia Plath; 3 copies in dust jackets for the first British printing of *The Great Gatsby*—2 with remainder prices; the partial carbon copy for "The Romantic Egoist" with Fitzgerald's rejected preface; Fitzgerald's briefcase, which brought a higher price than a pickled piece of Christopher Columbus at the same auction; the revised typescripts for "The Swimmers," "The Kingdom in the Dark," "The Count of Darkness," "Home to Maryland," and "Lo, the Poor Peacock!"—which provide lessons in how Fitzgerald edited himself. Francis Cugat's preliminary work and his duplicate painting of the final dust jacket art for *The Great Gatsby* are owned by Arlyn Bruccoli. Items that generate more interest than they should are 2 of Fitzgerald's engraved flasks. The Fitzgerald Collection includes 68 items related to Zelda Fitzgerald: printed material, manuscripts, correspondence, and 7 works of art from the Arlyn Bruccoli Collection.

Since the Brits read English, and since the standings of American authors are frequently influenced by their British critical receptions, the collection includes all the U.K. Fitzgerald material I could find. The first time I went booking in England in 1966, dealers claimed ignorance of F. Scott Fitzgerald and offered me *The Rubáiyát*. 'Struth. But Anthony Rota became a Fitzgerald supplier, and Freddie Zentner is a generous provider of movie-related material.

A research collection keeps enlarging itself. My Fitzgerald collection is not restricted to F. Scott Fitzgerald. It encompasses Fitzgerald's times and places, his literary friends, and the books in his life. There are ancillary collections for Ernest Hemingway, John O'Hara, Ring Lardner, Edmund Wilson, Donald Ogden Stewart, Budd Schulberg, H. L. Mencken, Thomas Wolfe, Maxwell Perkins, John Hall Wheelock, Princetoniana, the expatriate American writers and publishers in Paris, the Twenties, and the House of Scribner. These satellite collections of another 2,000 items are not included in this catalogue. Some of these collections have become stand-alones. The impossible goal is to provide at the Thomas Cooper Library all the sources for Fitzgerald study-research-teaching. I can justify almost any acquisition as a Fitzgerald item. Everything connects. My quest for the two Fitzgerald Armed Services Editions volumes—*Gatsby* and *The Diamond as Big as the Ritz and Other Stories*—led to my endeavor to assemble a complete Armed Services Editions collection. The Thomas Cooper Library now has 1,309 of the 1,322 ASE titles.

The Fitzgerald Collection is a working collection—not a display collection, although it generates exhibitions. It is accessible to anyone with clean hands who is not wearing a baseball cap. Researchers have come from Britain, France, Germany, Italy, Taiwan, and Japan. The Thomas Cooper Library Fitzgerald Centenary Web site averages 500,000 hits a month.

A research collection can never be used up. Serious Fitzgerald people will make use of this material for as long as literature matters. The "virtual library"—virtual lunacy—cannot replace or obviate the real thing. Librarians and administrators come and go; the books matter.

Book collecting is not a game or a hobby: it is a way of life. What did I get from book collecting? I got my education. I got my publications. I got most of my closest friends. I got Fraze. I got Scottie.

MATTHEW J. BRUCCOLI

Tools

Matthew J. Bruccoli. *F. Scott Fitzgerald: A Descriptive Bibliography, Revised Edition.* Pittsburgh: University of Pittsburgh Press, 1987; "F. Scott Fitzgerald: A Descriptive Bibliography, Supplement (2001)" in *Dictionary of Literary Biography Yearbook: 2001* (Detroit et al.: Bruccoli Clark Layman / The Gale Group, 2002), pp. 399–425, also distributed as an offprint.

———. *Some Sort of Epic Grandeur: The Life of F. Scott Fitzgerald.* New York: Harcourt Brace Jovanovich, 1981. Revised edition, London: Cardinal, 1991; New York: Carroll & Graf, 1993. Second revised edition, Columbia: University of South Carolina Press, 2001.

———, ed. *F. Scott Fitzgerald's The Great Gatsby: A Documentary Volume.* Detroit: Bruccoli Clark Layman / Gale, 2000. Reprint, *F. Scott Fitzgerald's The Great Gatsby: A Literary Reference.* New York: Carroll & Graf, 2002.

———, with George Parker Anderson, eds. *F. Scott Fitzgerald's Tender Is the Night: A Documentary Volume.* Detroit: Bruccoli Clark Layman / Thomson / Gale, 2003.

———, Scottie Fitzgerald Smith, and Joan P. Kerr, eds. *The Romantic Egoists: A Pictorial Autobiography from the Scrapbooks and Albums of F. Scott and Zelda Fitzgerald.* New York: Scribners, 1974. Reprint, Columbia: University of South Carolina Press, 2003.

F. Scott Fitzgerald Centenary Exhibition: The Matthew J. and Arlyn Bruccoli Collection, the Thomas Cooper Library. Columbia: University of South Carolina Press for the Thomas Cooper Library, 1996.

Fitzgerald, F. Scott. *Trimalchio: A Facsimile Edition of the Original Galley Proofs for "The Great Gatsby."* Edited by Matthew J. Bruccoli. Columbia: University of South Carolina Press in Cooperation with Thomas Cooper Library, 2000.

A catalogue for the Matthew J. and Arlyn Bruccoli Collection of F. Scott Fitzgerald can be accessed online at: http://www.sc.edu/uscan; Select: **Rare Books & Special Collections - T. C. Library**; Select: **Author,** then enter search term **"Fitzgerald F Scott"**

The University of South Carolina's F. Scott Fitzgerald Centenary Web site can be accessed at: http://www.sc.edu/fitzgerald/index.html

COMPILER'S NOTE

This catalogue provides a comprehensive list of the major components in the Matthew J. and Arlyn Bruccoli Collection of F. Scott Fitzgerald at the Thomas Cooper Library, University of South Carolina. The Department of Rare Books and Special Collections staff initially catalogued the collection in MARC format for the university's online catalogue, USCAN. The USCAN entries drew on Professor Bruccoli's *F. Scott Fitzgerald: A Descriptive Bibliography, Revised Edition* (Pittsburgh: University of Pittsburgh Press, 1987) and his "F. Scott Fitzgerald: A Descriptive Bibliography, Supplement" in *Dictionary of Literary Biography Yearbook: 2001*, ed. Bruccoli with the assistance of George Parker Anderson (Detroit et al.: Bruccoli Clark Layman/Gale Group, 2002), pp. 399–425, to which citations are given both in USCAN and here. USC Computer Services kindly provided database downloads of the USCAN entries for preparation of this hard-copy catalogue. The downloaded entries have been checked, revised, reformatted, and augmented by Professor Bruccoli and me, with additional information on specific copies and inscriptions, as detailed below.

Items are arranged chronologically except where noted. The catalogue is divided into the following sections:

Section I lists all separately published books, including proofs and review copies, by Fitzgerald, corresponding to A items in the Bruccoli bibliography. The section also lists books by Fitzgerald inscribed by him. The section concludes with collections of Fitzgerald's work that do not include material published by Fitzgerald for the first time (Bruccoli AA items). All printings for the first editions of books by Fitzgerald are identified.

Section II lists works in which writing by Fitzgerald appears for the first time in a book or pamphlet written or edited by someone else (Bruccoli B and BB items).

Section III lists first periodical appearances by Fitzgerald (Bruccoli C items). Magazine and newspaper serialization of the novels are also listed here.

Section IV lists keepsakes with material by Fitzgerald (Bruccoli D items) and exhibition catalogues.

Section V lists Fitzgerald manuscripts (MS), typescripts (TS), and revised typescripts (RTS).

Section VI lists correspondence from and to Fitzgerald, as well as correspondence concerning him.

Section VII lists Fitzgerald documents (certificates, contracts, royalty reports, etc.) as well as literary documents relating to Fitzgerald's career and reputation.

Section VIII lists books inscribed to the Fitzgeralds, or books by other authors inscribed or annotated by Fitzgerald. The section also lists books known to have been in Fitzgerald's library.

Section IX lists printed material related to Fitzgerald's movie work (Bruccoli J items).

Section X lists selected graphic material from the collection, including photographs, movie posters, and promotional material, as well as items related to the career of actress Lois Moran.

Section XI lists Fitzgerald-related Princetoniana.

Section XII lists Fitzgerald memorabilia including personal items owned by Fitzgerald and his family.

Section XIII lists Zelda Fitzgerald items, including her published works, manuscripts, correspondence, artwork, documents, and periodical appearances (Bruccoli ZF items).

Section XIV lists Sheilah Graham items related to Fitzgerald, including books, correspondence, and periodical appearances.

Section XV lists blurbs written by Fitzgerald.

Each entry conforms to the following format:

(Item #) Title.
- Subtitle (when necessary).
- Author or Editor (when necessary).
- Publisher and date of publication.
- Physical description.

NOTES: (When necessary).
- Call number or "On deposit" for items that have not yet been catalogued or not yet donated.
- Duplicate items in collection (when necessary).

The title rubric for a book does not attempt to duplicate the volume's title-page typography; titles have been regularized. The first line of the notes cites the item's listing in the Bruccoli Fitzgerald bibliography, if one exists (Bruccoli A11.1.a identifies the first printing (a) of the first edition (1) of Fitzgerald's eleventh book.) This rubric also provides information to differentiate copies of the same printing. All books are clothbound unless otherwise described. Inscriptions or annotations are recorded; all inscriptions by Fitzgerald are quoted in full or facsimiled. Cross references have been restricted to cases where confusion might otherwise result.

The F. Scott Fitzgerald material in this catalogue is limited to writings by Fitzgerald published and unpublished, association items, and memorabilia. Hundreds of foreign-language editions; adaptations of Fitzgerald's work; and published works about Fitzgerald, his literary associates, and the literary and social history of his times are omitted here. The entire collection/archive and satellite collections for his literary friends included in the Thomas Cooper Library catalogue is available online via www.sc.edu/library. The records are best consulted in the enhanced "long" entry format, which gives copy-specific notes.

Acknowledgments: Judith S. Baughman; Elizabeth Sudduth, Dean Paul Willis, and Professor Patrick G. Scott, Thomas Cooper Library; USC Computer Services; Keith McGraw, Distance Education and Instructional Support; Joseph M. Bruccoli, photographer; Danielle Lake, proofreader; Mary Jo Tate, indexer; and Patricia Callahan, designer; Bill Adams, managing editor, and Curtis Clark, director, University of South Carolina Press.

PARK BUCKER

The Matthew J. and Arlyn
Bruccoli COLLECTION OF
F. Scott Fitzgerald
at the University of South Carolina

1 Books and Collections by F. Scott Fitzgerald (Including Copies Inscribed by Him)

This section lists all separately published books, including proofs and review copies, by Fitzgerald, corresponding to A items in the Bruccoli bibliography, as well as copies of Fitzgerald books inscribed by him. It concludes with collections of Fitzgerald's work that do not include material published by Fitzgerald for the first time (Bruccoli AA items).

Fie! Fie! Fi-Fi! (1914)

1. "Fie! Fie! Fi-Fi!".
   - [Princeton University: Triangle Club, 1914].
   - 2 parts; wrappers.
   NOTES: Bruccoli A1. First edition, only printing.
       Acting script: "For the use of Cast Candidates exclusively". Laid in: 5 additional printed leaves with song lyrics by FSF.
       Previously owned by Joshua B. Everett, who performed the role of Dr. Blossom in the original production.
       With: 24 October 1964 letter from Everett to MJB, discussing FSF.
   - PS3511.I9 F45

2. *Fie! Fie! Fi-Fi!*
   - A Musical Comedy in Two Acts Presented by the Princeton University Triangle Club Season of 1914–1915.
   - [Philadelphia: E. A. Wright, 1914].
   - Wrappers.
   NOTES: Program: "Lyrics by F. Scott Fitzgerald, 1917".
   With: Programs for *The Pursuit of Priscilla* and *The Evil Eye.*
   - PS3511.I9 F445 1914

3. *Fie! Fie! Fi-Fi!*
   - A Musical Comedy in Two Acts Presented by the Princeton University Triangle Club.
   - Dialogue and characters by Walker M. Ellis; plot and lyrics by F. Scott Fitzgerald; music by D. D. Griffin, A. L. Booth, and P. B. Dickey.
   - Cincinnati: John Church Co., 1914.
   - Wrappers; vocal score.
   NOTES: Bruccoli A2. First edition, only printing.
   - PS3511.I9 F45 1914

4. *Fie! Fie! Fi-Fi!*
   - A Facsimile of the 1914 Acting Script and the Musical Score.
   - Edited with Introduction by Matthew J. Bruccoli.
   - [Columbia]: University of South Carolina Press for the Thomas Cooper Library, [1996].
   NOTES: Bruccoli Supplement A48.
   - PS3511B.I9 F46 1996

The Evil Eye (1915)

5. *The Evil Eye.*
   - A Musical Comedy in Two Acts Presented by the Princeton University Triangle Club 1915–1916.
   - Book by E. Wilson, Jr.; lyrics by F. Scott Fitzgerald; music by Paul B. Dickey and F. Warburton Guilbert.
   - [Cincinnati, New York, & London]: The John Church Co., [1915].
   - Wrappers; vocal score.

   NOTES: Bruccoli A3. First edition, only printing.
   - PS3511.I9 E9 1915

6. *The Evil Eye.*
   - A Musical Comedy in Two Acts Presented by the Princeton University Triangle Club Season of 1915–1916.
   - [Trenton: Smith Press, 1915].
   - Wrappers: "Cincinnati Thursday, December 23, 1915".

   NOTES: Program: "Lyrics by F. Scott Fitzgerald, 1917"; "F. Scott Fitzgerald, 1917, composer of the Lyrics for 'The Evil Eye,' and One of Last Year's Attractive 'show girls'.", p. [14].

   With: programs for *The Pursuit of Priscilla* and *Fie! Fie! Fi-Fi!*
   - PS3511.I9 E89 1915
   - Another copy: "Pittsburgh Friday, December 31, 1915".

Safety First (1916)

7. *Safety First .*
   - A Musical Comedy in Two Acts Presented by The Princeton University Triangle Club 1916–1917.
   - Book by J. F. Bohmfalk and J. Biggs; Lyrics by F. Scott Fitzgerald; music by P. B. Dickey, F. Warburton Guilbert, and E. Harris.
   - Cincinnati, New York, & London: The John Church Co., [1916].
   - Vocal score; wrappers.

   NOTES: Bruccoli A4. First edition, only printing.
   - PS3511.I9 S25 1916

8. *Safety First .*
   - A Futurist Farce In Two Acts Presented by the Princeton University Triangle Club.
   - New York: Burr Printing House, [1916?].
   - Wrappers.

   NOTES: Program: "Season of 1916–1917"; "This souvenir program presented with the compliments of The Triangle Club"; "All lyrics by F. Scott Fitzgerald, '17," p. 17.
   - PS3511.I9 S251 1916

This Side of Paradise

9. *This Side of Paradise.*
   - New York: Charles Scribner's Sons, 1920.
   - Dust jacket.
   NOTES: Bruccoli A5.1.a. First edition, first printing.
   - PS3511.I9 T49 1920

10. *This Side of Paradise.*
    - New York: Charles Scribner's Sons, 1920.
    NOTES: Bruccoli A5.1.a. First edition, first printing.
     "I have transcribed all the notes in F's own copy of TSOP into this copy. MJB".
    - PS3511.I9 T49 1920 C.2

11. *This Side of Paradise.*
    - New York: Collectors Reprints, [1990].
    - Dust jacket: "F.E.L." [First Edition Library]. Slipcase.
    NOTES: Bruccoli Supplement A5.1.a, Note 4.
     "This facsimile of the first edition of the work is published by Collectors Reprints Inc., N.Y., N.Y. by arrangement with Charles Scribner's Sons, a division of Macmillan Inc."
    - PS3511.I9 T49 1990

12. *This Side of Paradise.*
    - New York: Charles Scribner's Sons, 1920.
    NOTES: Bruccoli A5.1.b. First edition, second printing.
     Signature of Lionel Trilling; bookplate of Lionel & Diana Trilling.
    - PS3511.I9 T49 1920b
    - Another copy (without signature and bookplate).

13. *This Side of Paradise.*
    - New York: Charles Scribner's Sons, 1920.
    NOTES: Bruccoli A5.1.c. First edition, third printing.
     One of possibly 500 copies with tipped-in glossy leaf with "The Author's Apology," signed by FSF. These were prepared for a meeting of the American Booksellers Association.
    - PS3511.I9 T49 1920c C.1

14. *This Side of Paradise.*
    - New York: Charles Scribner's Sons, 1920.
    NOTES: Bruccoli A5.1.c. First edition, third printing.
    - PS3511.I9 T49 1920c C.2

15. *This Side of Paradise.*
    - New York: Charles Scribner's Sons, 1920.
    NOTES: Bruccoli A5.1.d. First edition, fourth printing.
    - PS3511.I9 T49 1920d

4 *Books and Collections*

16. *This Side of Paradise.*
    - New York: Charles Scribner's Sons, 1920.
    NOTES: Bruccoli A5.1.e. First edition, fifth printing.
    - PS3511.I9 T49 1920e
    - Another copy.

17. *This Side of Paradise.*
    - New York: Charles Scribner's Sons, 1920.
    - Dust jacket.
    NOTES: Bruccoli A5.1.f. First edition, sixth printing.
    - PS3511.I9 T49 1920f

18. *This Side of Paradise.*
    - New York: Charles Scribner's Sons, 1920.
    NOTES: Bruccoli A5.1.g. First edition, seventh printing.
    - PS3511.I9 T49 1920g

19. *This Side of Paradise.*
    - New York: Charles Scribner's Sons, 1920.
    NOTES: Bruccoli A5.1.h. First edition, eighth printing.
    Inscribed by FSF to Faith Thomas.
    - PS3511.I9 T49 1920h

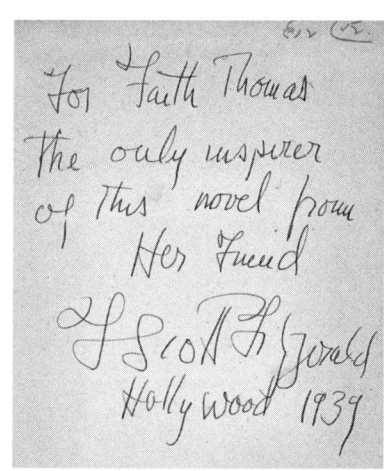

20. *This Side of Paradise.*
    - New York: Charles Scribner's Sons, 1920.
    NOTES: Bruccoli A5.1.i. First edition, ninth printing.
    Inscribed by FSF to Harry Nardini, his California doctor.
    - PS3511.I9 T49 1920i C.2
    - Another copy (without inscription).

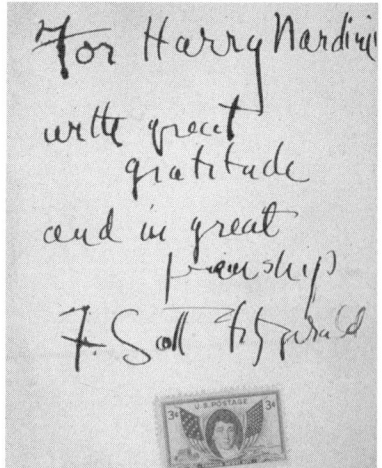

21. *This Side of Paradise.*
    - New York: Charles Scribner's Sons, 1920.
    - Scribners dust jacket: "FIFTH LARGE PRINTING".
    NOTES: Bruccoli Supplement A5.1.d. Scribners sheets of the fourth printing in binding of Whitcombe & Tombs [Auckland, New Zealand].
    - PS3511.I9 T49 1920j

22. *This Side of Paradise.*
    - New York: Charles Scribner's Sons, 1921.
    NOTES: Bruccoli A5.1.k. First edition, eleventh printing.
    - PS3511.I9 T49 1921c

23. *This Side of Paradise.*
    - New York: Charles Scribner's Sons, 1921.
    NOTES: Bruccoli A5.1.l. First edition, twelfth printing.
    - PS3511.I9 T49 1921d

24. *This Side of Paradise.*
    - New York: Charles Scribner's Sons, 1922.
    NOTES: Bruccoli A5.1.m. First edition, thirteenth printing. Inscribed by FSF to songwriter Gene Buck.
    - PS3511.I9 T49 1922
    - Another copy (without inscription).

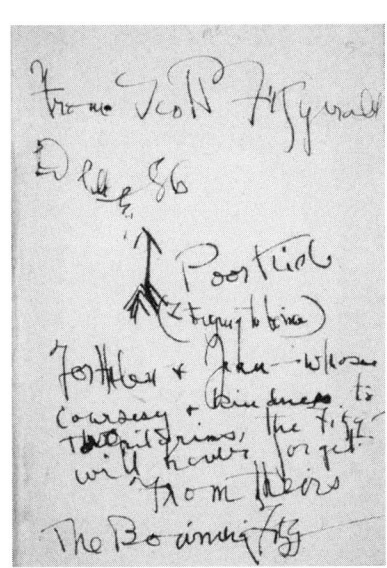

25. *This Side of Paradise.*
    - New York: Charles Scribner's Sons, 1922.
    NOTES: Bruccoli A5.1.n. First edition, fourteenth printing.
    - PS3511.I9 T49 1922b

26. *This Side of Paradise.*
    - New York: A. L. Burt, 1923.
    - Dust jacket.
    NOTES: Bruccoli A5.1.o. First edition, fifteenth printing?
    - PS3511.I9 T49 1923

27. *This Side of Paradise.*
    - New York: A. L. Burt, 1923.
    NOTES: Bruccoli A5.1.o. First edition, fifteenth printing?
    Inscribed by FSF to actress Carmel Myers.
    - PS3511.I9 T49 1923

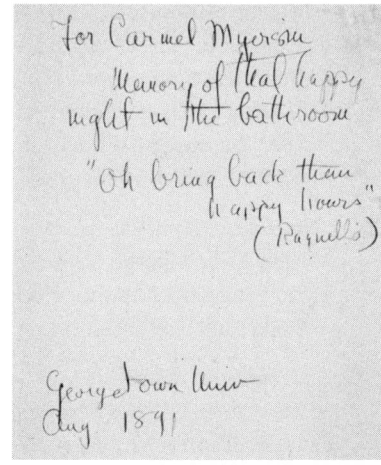

28. *This Side of Paradise.*
    - New York: Charles Scribner's Sons, 1925.
    NOTES: Bruccoli A5.1.p. First edition, sixteenth printing?
    Inscribed by FSF to actress Lois Moran.
    - PS3511.I9 T49 1925

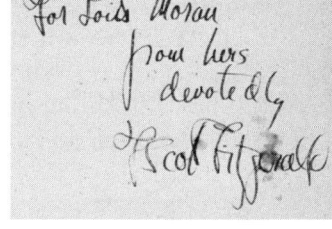

29. *This Side of Paradise.*
    - New York: Charles Scribner's Sons, 1925.
    NOTES: Bruccoli A5.1.p. First edition, sixteenth printing?
    Inscribed by FSF to John Biggs, who became the executor of the Fitzgerald Estate.
    - PS3511.I9 T49 1925 C.2.

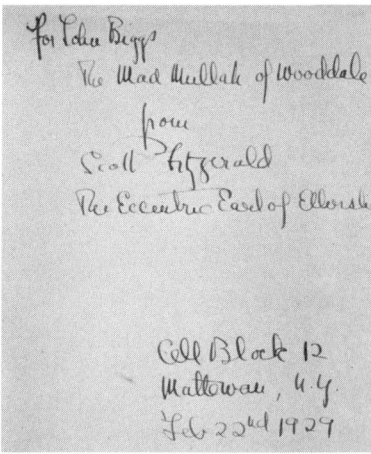

30. This Side of Paradise.
    - New York: Charles Scribner's Sons, 1931.
    NOTES: Bruccoli A5.1.q. First edition, seventeenth printing?
    Inscribed by FSF to Dorothy Williamson, his nurse.
    - PS3511.I9 T49 1931

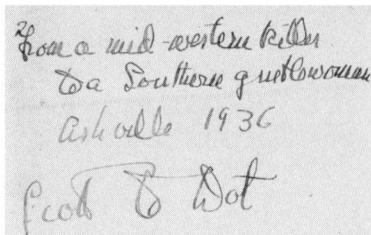

31. *This Side of Paradise.*
    - New York: Grosset & Dunlap, [1947].
    - Dust jacket.
    NOTES: Bruccoli A5.1.r.
    - PS3511.I9 T49 1947
    - Another copy.

32. *This Side of Paradise.*
    - New York: Charles Scribner's Sons, 1951.
    NOTES: Bruccoli A5.1.s.
    - PS3511.I9 T49 1951

33. *This Side of Paradise.*
    - New York: Charles Scribner's Sons, [1957].
    - Dust jacket.
    NOTES: Bruccoli A5.1.v.
    - PS3511.I9 T49 1957

34. *This Side of Paradise.*
    - New York: Charles Scribner's Sons, [1959].
    - Dust jacket.
    NOTES: Bruccoli A5.1.x.
    - PS3511.I9 T49 1959

35. *This Side of Paradise.*
    - New York: Charles Scribner's Sons, [1968].
    - Dust jacket.
    NOTES: Bruccoli A5.1.x.
    - PS3511.I9 T49 1968

36. *This Side of Paradise.*
    - London: Collins, [1921].
    NOTES: Bruccoli A5.2.a. First English edition, first printing. Inscribed by FSF to F. R. Henderson. Typed and printed reviews pasted on front endpapers.
    - PS3511.I9 T49 1921

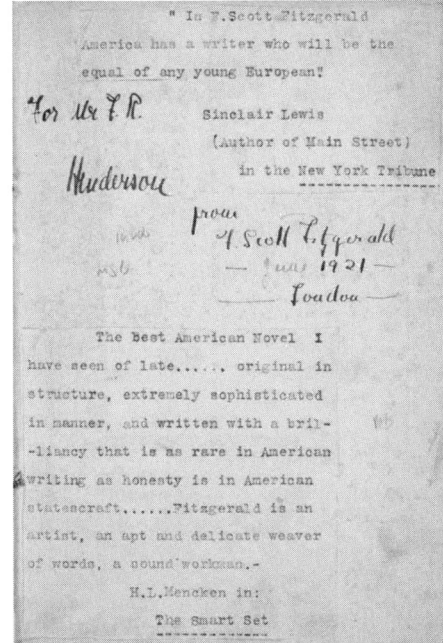

37. *This Side of Paradise.*
- London: Collins, [1921].
NOTES: First English edition, first printing. Bruccoli A5.2.a. Ownership inscription: "Among the books 'Keith' left me—Edward Pine's temporarily. (Keith reviewed it for G.K.'s Weekly in 1921)". "G.K." refers to G. K. Chesterton.
- PS3511.I9 T49 1921 C.2
- Another copy (without inscription).

38. *This Side of Paradise.*
- London: Collins, [1921].
- Dust jacket: "COLLINS' 2'6 NET. NOVELS".
NOTES: Bruccoli Supplement A5.2.a. First English edition, first printing.
- PS3511.I9 T49 1921 C.4

39. *This Side of Paradise.*
- London: Collins, [1923].
NOTES: Bruccoli A5.2.b. First English edition, second printing. Inscribed by FSF to Theodora Gager.
- PS3511.I9 T49 1923b
- Another copy (without inscription).

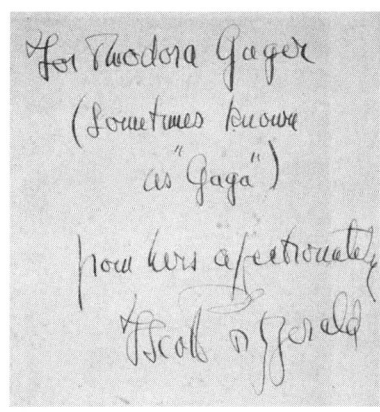

40. *This Side of Paradise.*
- London; Glasgow; Sydney; Auckland: Collins, [1927?].
- Dust jacket: "2' - NET".
NOTES: Bruccoli A5.2.c.
- PS3511.I9 T49 1927
- Another copy.

41. *This Side of Paradise.*
- [London]: Grey Walls Press, [1948].
- Dust jacket.
NOTES: Bruccoli A5.3. Second English edition, first printing.
- PS3511.I9 T49 1948

42. *This Side of Paradise.*
- [London]: Grey Walls Press, [1950].
NOTES: Bruccoli A5.3. Second English edition, second printing.
- PS3511.I9 T49 1950

43. *This Side of Paradise.*
    - [New York]: Dell, [1954], #D140.
    - Wrappers.
    NOTES: Bruccoli A5.4. Second American edition.
    - PS3511.I9 T49 1954

44. *This Side of Paradise.*
    - New York: Charles Scribner's Sons, [1962], #SL60.
    - Wrappers.
    NOTES: Bruccoli A5.5.b. Third American edition. First printing. "RESET OCTOBER, 1960"; "A-8.62[C]".
    - PS3511.I9 T49 1962

45. *This Side of Paradise.*
    - New York: Charles Scribner's Sons, [1965].
    - Wrappers.
    NOTES: Bruccoli A5.5.b. Third American edition. "E-2.65[Col]".
    - PS3511.I9 T49 1965b

46. *This Side of Paradise.*
    - New York: Charles Scribner's Sons, [1968].
    - Wrappers.
    NOTES: Bruccoli A5.5.b. Third American edition. "H-10.68[Col]".
    - PS3511.I9 T49 1968

47. *This Side of Paradise.*
    - New York: Charles Scribner's Sons, [1980].
    - Dust jacket.
    NOTES: Bruccoli A5.5.c. Hudson River Editions.
    - PS3511.I9 T49 1980

48. *This Side of Paradise.*
    - New York: Charles Scribner's Sons, [1982?].
    - Wrappers.
    NOTES: Bruccoli A5.5.d. Scribner Classics.
    - PS3511.I9 T49 1982

49. *This Side of Paradise.*
    - [Harmondsworth, England]: Penguin Books, [1963], #1867.
    - Wrappers.
    NOTES: Bruccoli A5.7. Fourth English edition.
    - PS3511.I9 T49 1963

50. *This Side of Paradise.*
    - [Harmondsworth, England]: Penguin Books, [1965], #1867.
    - Wrappers: "55c" label.
    NOTES: Bruccoli A5.7. Fourth English edition. Distributed in Australia.
    - PS3511.I9 T49 1965c

10 *Books and Collections*

51. *This Side of Paradise.*
    - [Harmondsworth, England]: Penguin Books, [1970], #1867.
    - Wrappers.
    NOTES: Bruccoli A5.7. Fourth English edition.
    - PS3511.I9 T49 1970

52. *This Side of Paradise.*
    - [Harmondsworth, England]: Penguin Books, [1985], #1867.
    - Wrappers.
    NOTES: Bruccoli A5.7. Fourth English edition.
    - PS3511.I9 T49 1985

53. *This Side of Paradise.*
    - Edited with Introduction and Notes by Makoto Nagai.
    - [Tokyo?]: Aoyama, [1970].
    - Wrappers.
    NOTES: Bruccoli A5.9. English-language edition.
       Includes "Spires and Gargoyles," "The Egotist Considers," and "Narcissus off Duty." Text in English; introduction and notes in Japanese.
    - PS3511.I9 T49 1970c

54. *This Side of Paradise.*
    - New York: Collier Books, [1986].
    - Wrappers.
    NOTES: A Scribner Classic. Tenth printing.
    - PS3511.I9 T49 1986

55. *This Side of Paradise.*
    - New York: Scribner Paperback Fiction, [1995?].
    - Wrappers.
    NOTES: New edition, first printing.
       On front endpaper: "When I recommended adding material to this book ... Mark Gomperts [Gompertz?] told me that the only thing he cared about was the cover. He picked the cover. MJB".
    - PS3511.I9 T49 1995

56. *This Side of Paradise.*
    - New York: Scribner Paperback Fiction, [1995?].
    - Wrappers.
    NOTES: New edition, first printing.
       Annotated by MJB on front cover: "I voted against this cover—MJB".
    - PS3511.I9 T49 1995 C.2

57. *This Side of Paradise.*
    - Edited by Ruth Prigozy.
    - New York: Washington Square Press, 1995.
    NOTES: Enriched Classic.
    - PS3511.I9 T48 1995c

58. *This Side of Paradise.*
    - [New York]: Scribner Classics, [1996], #9606.
    - Dust jacket.
    - PS3511.I9 T49 1996

59. *This Side of Paradise.*
    - New York; London: Dover, [1996].
    - Wrappers.
    NOTES: Dover Thrift Editions.
    - PS3511.I9 T49 1996d

60. *This Side of Paradise.*
    - Introduction by Jay Parini.
    - [New York]: Signet Classic, [1996], #CE2610.
    - Wrappers.
    - PS3511.I9 T49 1996e

61. *This Side of Paradise.*
    - Edited and with an introduction and notes by Patrick O'Donnell.
    - [New York & London]: Penguin, [1996].
    - Wrappers.
    NOTES: Penguin Twentieth-Century Classics. First printing.
    - PS3511.I9 T49 1996f

62. *This Side of Paradise.*
    - Edited and with an introduction and notes by Patrick O'Donnell.
    - [New York & London]: Penguin, [1996].
    - Wrappers.
    NOTES: Penguin Twentieth-Century Classics. Second printing.
    - PS3511.I9 T49 1996f C.2

63. *This Side of Paradise.*
    - New York: Modern Library, [1996], #9607.
    - Dust jacket.
    - PS3511.I9 T49 1996f 813

Flappers and Philosophers (1920)

64. *Flappers and Philosophers.*
    - New York: Charles Scribner's Sons, 1920.
    - Dust jacket.
    NOTES: Bruccoli A6.1.a. First edition, first printing.
    - PS3511.I9 F55 1920
    - Another copy without jacket.

65. *Flappers and Philosophers.*
    - New York: Charles Scribner's Sons, 1920.
    NOTES: Bruccoli A6.1.a . First edition, first printing.
       Australasian binding of first American printing in binding of Whitcombe & Tombs [Auckland, New Zealand].
    - PS3511.I9 F55 1920d

66. *Flappers and Philosophers.*
    - New York: Charles Scribner's Sons, 1920.
    NOTES: Replica Classics. 2001. Facsimile of the first edition.
    - PS3511.I9 F54 1921a

67. *Flappers and Philosophers.*
    - New York: Charles Scribner's Sons, 1920.
    NOTES: Bruccoli A6.1.b. First edition, second printing.
       Signature of Lionel Trilling; bookplate of Lionel & Diana Trilling.
    - PS3511.I9 F55 1920b

68. *Flappers and Philosophers.*
    - New York: Charles Scribner's Sons, 1920.
    NOTES: Bruccoli A6.1.b. First edition, second printing.
       Laid in: TLS from Katherine Fessenden to MJB, 12 March [1968], concerning her friendship with FSF.
    - PS3511.I9 F55 1920b C.2

69. *Flappers and Philosophers.*
    - New York: Charles Scribner's Sons, 1920.
    NOTES: Bruccoli A6.1.c. First edition, third printing.
       Inscribed by FSF to Marion Hennion.
    - PS3511.I9 F55 1920c

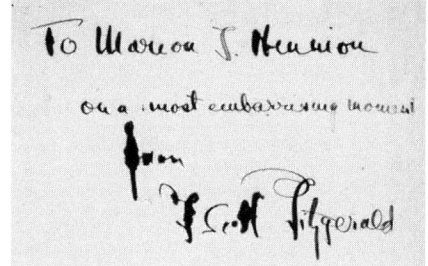

70. *Flappers and Philosophers.*
    - New York: Charles Scribner's Sons, 1920.
    - Partial dust jacket: "SECOND LARGE PRINTING".
    NOTES: Bruccoli A6.1.c. First edition, third printing.
    - PS3511.I9 F55 1920c C.2

71. *Flappers and Philosophers.*
    - New York: Charles Scribner's Sons, 1921.
    NOTES: Bruccoli A6.1.d. First edition, fourth printing.
    - PS3511.I9 F55 1921

72. *Flappers and Philosophers.*
    - New York: Charles Scribner's Sons, 1921.
    NOTES: Bruccoli A6.1.e. First edition, fifth printing.
    - PS3511.I9 F55 1921b

73. *Flappers and Philosophers.*
    - New York: Charles Scribner's Sons, 1922.
    NOTES: Bruccoli A6.1.f. First edition, sixth printing. Inscribed by FSF to Dorothy [Williamson].
    - PS3511.I9 F55 1922b

74. *Flappers and Philosophers.*
    - New York: Charles Scribner's Sons, 1922.
    NOTES: Bruccoli A6.1.f. First edition, sixth printing. Ober Agency office file copy. Label: "HAROLD OBER" on free front endpaper.
    - PS3511.I9 F55 1922b

75. *Flappers and Philosophers.*
    - London: Collins, [1922].
    NOTES: Bruccoli A6.2.a. First English edition, first printing. "REVIEW COPY" blindstamped on title page.
    - PS3511.I9 F55 1922 C.1

76. *Flappers and Philosophers.*
    - London: Collins, [1922].
    NOTES: Bruccoli A6.2.a. First English edition, first printing.
    - PS3511.I9 F55 1922 C.2
    - Another copy.

77. *Flappers and Philosophers.*
    - London: Collins, [1925].
    - Dust jacket: "2/-NET."
    NOTES: Bruccoli A6.2.b. First English edition.
    - PS3511.I9 F55 1925 C.1
    - Another copy (without jacket).

78. *Flappers and Philosophers.*
    - New York: Charles Scribner's Sons, [1959].
    - Dust jacket.
    NOTES: Bruccoli A6.3.a. Second American edition.
    - PS3511.I9 F55 1959

79. *Flappers and Philosophers.*
    - New York: Charles Scribner's Sons, [1972], #SL371.
    - Wrappers.
    NOTES: Scribner Library. "A.8.72(C)".
    - PS3511.I9 F55 1972

80. *Flappers and Philosophers.*
    - New York: Collier Books/Macmillan, [1987].
    - Wrappers.
    NOTES: Scribner Classic.
    - PS3511.I9 F55 1987

The St. Paul Daily Dirge (1922)

81. *The St. Paul Daily Dirge.*
    - St. Paul, Minnesota: [n.p.] 1922.
    - Broadside.
    NOTES: Bruccoli A7.1.a.
    - PS3511.I9 S26 1922

82. *The St. Paul Daily Dirge.*
    - *Fitzgerald Newsletter* [Columbus, Ohio]: 1968.
    - Portfolio.
    NOTES: Bruccoli A7.1.b.
        Facsimile of Bruccoli A7.1.a; one of 200 copies.
    - PS3511.I9 S26 1922

The Beautiful and Damned (1922)

83. *The Beautiful and Damned.*
    - New York: Charles Scribner's Sons, 1922.
    - Dust jacket: title in white.
    NOTES: Bruccoli A8.1.a. First edition,
        first printing.
        Laid in: Promotional postcard.
    - PS3511.I9 B4 1922 C.3

84. *The Beautiful and Damned.*
    - New York: Charles Scribner's Sons, 1922.
    - Dust jacket: title on front in white.
    NOTES: Bruccoli A8.1.a. First edition,
        first printing.
        Inscribed by Fitzgerald to
            bookseller A. L. Sugarman.
    - PS3511.I9 B4 1922

85. *The Beautiful and Damned.*
- New York: Charles Scribner's Sons, 1922.
NOTES: Bruccoli A8.1.a. First edition, first printing.
Signature of FSF pasted on front pastedown endpaper.
- PS3511.I9 B4 1922 C.2

86. *The Beautiful and Damned.*
- New York: Charles Scribner's Sons, 1922.
NOTES: Bruccoli A8.1.a. First edition, first printing.
Inscribed by Shane Leslie with inserted letter from FSF to Leslie transcribed by Leslie.
- PS3511.I9 B4 1922 C.4

87. *The Beautiful and Damned.*
- New York: Charles Scribner's Sons, 1922.
NOTES: Bruccoli A8.1.a. First edition, first printing.
Ober Agency office file copy. Label: "HAROLD OBER ASSOCIATES" on free front endpaper.
- PS3511.I9 B4 1922 C.6

88. *The Beautiful and Damned.*
- Toronto: Copp Clark, 1922.
NOTES: Bruccoli A8.1.a$_b$. Canadian issue of American sheets.
- PS3511.I9 B4 1922b

89. *The Beautiful and Damned.*
- New York: Charles Scribner's Sons, 1922.
- Dust jacket: "F•E•L" on rear flap. Slipcase.
NOTES: Bruccoli Supplement A8.1.a, Note seven.
Facsimile of the first printing produced by First Edition Library (Shelton, Conn., 1995); identified on copyright page.
Laid in: Publisher's note.
- PS3511.I9 B4 1995b

90. *The Beautiful and Damned.*
- New York: Charles Scribner's Sons, 1922.
NOTES: Replica Classics, 2001? Facsimile of the first edition.
- PS3511.I9 B4 2001

91. *The Beautiful and Damned.*
- New York: Charles Scribner's Sons, 1922.
- Dust jacket: title in black on front.
NOTES: Bruccoli A8.1.b$_1$. First edition, second printing, first state, with advertisement leaf.
- PS3511.I9 B4 1922e

92. *The Beautiful and Damned.*
- New York: Charles Scribner's Sons, 1922.
NOTES: Bruccoli A8.1.b$_1$. First edition, second printing, first state. Inscribed by James Dickey to MJB.
- PS3511.I9 B4 1922e C.2

93. *The Beautiful and Damned.*
- New York: Charles Scribner's Sons, 1922.
NOTES: Bruccoli A8.1.b$_2$. First edition, second printing, second state, with 2 leaves cancelled after p. 66.
- PS3511.I9 B4 1922f

94. *The Beautiful and Damned.*
- New York: Charles Scribner's Sons, 1922.
NOTES: Bruccoli A8.1.d. First edition, fourth printing. Scribners sheets in binding of A. L. Burt.
- PS3511.I9 B4 1922h

95. *The Beautiful and Damned.*
- New York: Charles Scribner's Sons, 1922.
NOTES: Bruccoli A8.1.e. First edition, fifth printing. Scribners sheets in binding of A. L. Burt.
- PS3511.I9 B4 1922i

96. *The Beautiful and Damned.*
- London: Grey Walls Press, [1950].
- Dust jacket.
NOTES: Bruccoli A8.1.f.
- PS3511.I9 B4 1950

97. *The Beautiful and Damned.*
- London: Grey Walls Press, [1954].
- Dust jacket.
NOTES: Bruccoli A8.1.f. "2nd impression 1954".
- PS3511.I9 B4 1954

98. *The Beautiful and Damned.*
- New York: Charles Scribner's Sons, [1958].
- Dust jacket.
NOTES: Bruccoli A8.1.g. "AA 2–58[MH]".
- PS3511.I9 B4 1958

99. *The Beautiful and Damned.*
- New York: Charles Scribner's Sons, [1963].
- Dust jacket.
NOTES: Bruccoli A8.1.h. "D-3.63[MH]".
- PS3511.I9 B4 1963

100. *The Beautiful and Damned.*
- New York: Charles Scribner's Sons, [1964], #SL90.
- Wrappers.
NOTES: Bruccoli A8.1.i. Scribner Library. "A-1.64[MCOL]".
- PS3511.I9 B4 1964

101. *The Beautiful and Damned.*
- New York: Charles Scribner's Sons, [1965], #SL90.
- Wrappers.
NOTES: Bruccoli A8.1.i. Scribner Library. "C-10.65[MCOL]".
- PS3511.I9 B4 1965

102. *The Beautiful and Damned.*
- New York: Charles Scribner's Sons, [1966], #SL90.
- Wrappers.
NOTES: Bruccoli A8.1.i. Scribner Library. "D-8.66[MCOL]".
- PS3511.I9 B4 1966

103. *The Beautiful and Damned.*
- New York: Charles Scribner's Sons, [1968], #SL90.
- Wrappers.
NOTES: Bruccoli A8.1.i. Scribner Library. "F-12.68[MCOL]".
- PS3511.I9 B4 1968

104. *The Beautiful and Damned.*
- New York: Charles Scribner's Sons, [1977?].
- Dust jacket.
NOTES: Bruccoli A8.1.j. Hudson River Editions.
    Laid in: TLS, 5 December 1985, from Charles Scribner III to MJB.
- PS3511.I9 B4 1977

105. *The Beautiful and Damned.*
- New York: Charles Scribner's Sons, [1980?].
- Wrappers.
NOTES: Scribner Library. Seventeenth printing.
- PS3511.I9 B4 1980

106. *The Beautiful and Damned.*
- New York: Charles Scribner's Sons, [1983?].
- Wrappers.
NOTES: Bruccoli A8.1.k. Scribner Classics.
- PS3511.I9 B4 1983

107. *The Beautiful and Damned.*
- London: Collins, [1922].
NOTES: Bruccoli A8.2.a. First English edition, first printing.
    Review copy, blindstamped on title page.
- PS3511.I9 B4 1922c C.1

108. *The Beautiful and Damned.*
- London: Collins, [1922].
NOTES: Bruccoli A8.2.b. First English edition, second printing.
- PS3511.I9 B4 1922c C.2

109. *The Beautiful and Damned.*
- London: Collins, [1925?].
NOTES: Bruccoli A8.2.c. Cheap edition.
- PS3511.I9 B4 1925

110. *The Beautiful and Damned.*
- Garden City, N.Y.: Permabooks, [1951], #P123.
- Wrappers.
NOTES: Bruccoli A8.3. Second American edition.
- PS3511.I9 B4 1951

111. *The Beautiful and Damned.*
- [Harmondsworth, England]: Penguin Books, [1966], #2414.
- Wrappers.
NOTES: Bruccoli A8.5. Third English edition, first printing.
- PS3511.I9 B4 1966b

112. *The Beautiful and Damned.*
- [Harmondsworth, England]: Penguin Books, [1966], #2414.
- Wrappers: "80c" label for Australian sale.
NOTES: Bruccoli A8.5. Third English edition, first printing.
- PS3511.I9 B4 1966b

113. *The Beautiful and Damned.*
- [Harmondsworth, England]: Penguin Books, [1968], #2414.
- Wrappers.
NOTES: Bruccoli A8.5. Third English edition, second printing.
- PS3511.I9 B4 1968b

114. *The Beautiful and Damned.*
- [Harmondsworth, England]: Penguin, [1974], #2414.
- Wrappers.
NOTES: Bruccoli A8.5. Third English edition, sixth printing.
- PS3511.I9 B4 1974

115. *The Beautiful and Damned.*
- [Harmondsworth, England]: Penguin Books, [1985].
- Wrappers.
NOTES: Bruccoli A8.5. Third English edition, sixteenth printing.
- PS3511.I9 B4 1985

116. *The Beautiful and Damned.*
- New York: Collier Books, [1986].
- Wrappers.
NOTES: First Scribner Classic/Collier Edition 1986.
- PS3511.I9 B4 1986

117. *The Beautiful and Damned.*
- Retold by Margaret Tarner; Illustrated by Laura Potter.
- [Oxford; Portsmouth, N.H.]: Heinemann, [1992].
- Wrappers.
NOTES: Heinemann Guided Readers.
- PS3511.I9 B4 1992

118. *The Beautiful and Damned.*
- New York: Washington Square Press, 1995.
NOTES: First printing.
- PS3511.I9 B4 1996

119. *The Beautiful and Damned.*
- With an Introduction by Jay Parini.
- [New York]: Signet Classic, [1998], CE 2664.
- Wrappers.
NOTES: First Scribner Classic Printing, January, 1998.
- PS3511.I9 B4 1998

120. *The Beautiful and Damned.*
- New York: Bantam Books, [1998].
- Wrappers.
NOTES: A Bantam Classic Book; "April 1998".
- PS3511.I9 B4 1998b

121. *The Beautiful and Damned.*
- With an Introduction by Kermit Vanderbilt.
- [New York]: Penguin Books, [1998].
- Wrappers.
NOTES: Penguin Twentieth-Century Classics.
- PS3511.I9 B4 1998c

122. *The Beautiful and Damned.*
- Edited with an Introduction and Notes by Alan Margolies.
- Oxford & New York: Oxford University Press, 1998.
- Wrappers.
NOTES: Oxford World's Classics.
- PS3511.I9 B4 1998d

Tales of the Jazz Age (1922)

123. *Tales of the Jazz Age.*
     - New York: Charles Scribner's Sons, 1922.
     - Sample dust jacket.
     NOTES: Bruccoli Supplement A9.1.
        Salesmen's dummy of the first edition, consisting of half title, title page, table of contents, and the first 16 pages of the story "The Jelly-Bean," repeated three times, as sample text. Table of contents and titles of two stories vary from the published book. Table of contents lists 10 stories; the published volume includes 11.
        Binding varies from that of the published version. The title and author's name are blind-stamped on the upper cover with a John Held, Jr. saxophone player from the dust jacket.
     - PS3511.I9 T25 1922

124. *Tales of the Jazz Age.*
     - New York: Charles Scribner's Sons, 1922.
     - Dust jacket.
     NOTES: Bruccoli A9.1.a$_a$. First edition, first printing.
        Laid in: Printed review slip.
     - PS3511.I9 T3

125. *Tales of the Jazz Age.*
     - New York: Charles Scribner's Sons, 1922.
     NOTES: Bruccoli A9.1.a$_a$. First edition, first printing.
        Tipped in front: ALS, undated, from FSF to Charles C. Baldwin. See Item 1155.
     - PS3511.I9 T3 C.2

126. *Tales of the Jazz Age.*
     - New York: Charles Scribner's Sons, 1922.
     NOTES: Bruccoli A9.1.a$_a$. First edition, first printing.
     Ober Agency office file copy. Label: "HAROLD OBER" on free front endpaper. "HAROLD OBER ASSOCIATES" stamped in red on rear pastedown endpaper.
     - PS3511.I9 T3 C.3

127. *Tales of the Jazz Age.*
     - New York: Charles Scribner's Sons, 1922.
     - Dust jacket: "F•E•L". Slipcase.
     NOTES: Bruccoli Supplement A9.1.a, Note seven.
        Facsimile of the first edition produced by First Edition Library (Shelton, Conn., 1994?).
        Laid in: Publisher's note.
     - PS3511.I9 T3 1994

128. *Tales of the Jazz Age.*
- New York: Charles Scribner's Sons, 1922.
  NOTES: Bruccoli A9.1.b. First edition, second or third printing. Removed: FSF letter to Rosalind Smith.
- PS3511.I9 T3 1922b C.1

129. *Tales of the Jazz Age.*
- New York: Charles Scribner's Sons, 1922.
  NOTES: Bruccoli A9.1.b. First edition, second or third printing. Inscribed by FSF to Dorothy Williamson.
- PS3511.I9 T3 1922b C.2

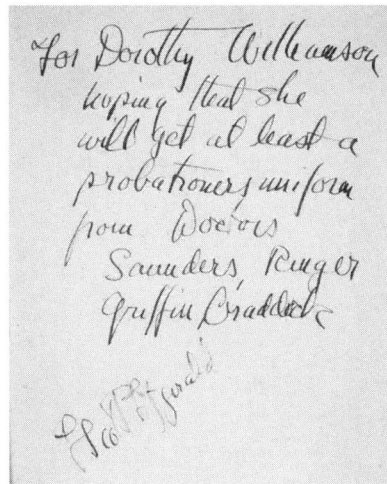

130. *Tales of the Jazz Age.*
- New York: Charles Scribner's Sons, 1922.
  NOTES: Bruccoli A9.1.b. First edition, second or third printing. Signed and dated 9 April 1923, by FSF.
- PS3511.I9 T3 1922b C.3

131. *Tales of the Jazz Age.*
- New York: Charles Scribner's Sons, 1922.
  NOTES: Bruccoli A9.1.c. First edition, second or third printing. Scribners office copy with label on front pastedown endpaper.
- PS3511.I9 T3 1922b C.4

132. *Tales of the Jazz Age.*
- Toronto: Copp Clark Co., 1922.
- Dust jacket: Blank rear and flaps.
  NOTES: Bruccoli Supplement A9.1.a$_b$. Canadian issue of Scribner sheets.
- PS3511.I9 T3 1922c
- Another copy.

133. *Tales of the Jazz Age.*
- London: W. Collins Sons, [1923].
  NOTES: Bruccoli A9.2.a$_1$. First English edition, first printing, first state.
- PS3511.I9 T3 1923

134. *Tales of the Jazz Age.*
- London: W. Collins Sons, [1923].
NOTES: Bruccoli A9.2.a$_2$. First English edition, first printing, second state.
- PS3511.I9 T3 1923b C.1

135. *Tales of the Jazz Age.*
- London: W. Collins Sons, [1923].
NOTES: Bruccoli A9.2.a$_2$. First English edition, first printing, second state. Library binding; Times Book Club label on rear pastedown endpaper.
- PS3511.I9 T3 1923b C.2

136. *Tales of the Jazz Age.*
- London: W. Collins Sons, [1927?].
- Dust jacket: "COLLINS' 2' - NOVELS".
NOTES: Bruccoli Supplement A9.2.b. Second edition, second printing.
- PS3511.I9 T3 1927
- Two additional copies (one in dust jacket).

137. *Six Tales of The Jazz Age and Other Stories.*
- With an Introduction by Frances Fitzgerald Lanahan.
- New York: Charles Scribner's Sons, [1960].
- Dust jacket.
NOTES. Bruccoli A9.3.a. Second American edition (revised contents). "A-1.60[H]".
- PS3511.I9 S5 1960

138. *Six Tales of The Jazz Age and Other Stories.*
- With an Introduction by Frances Fitzgerald Lanahan.
- New York: Charles Scribner's Sons, [1960].
- Dust jacket.
NOTES: Bruccoli A9.3.a. Reprint of second American edition (revised contents). "B-4.60[H]".
- PS3511.I9 S5 1960b

139. *Six Tales of The Jazz Age and Other Stories.*
- With an Introduction by Frances Fitzgerald Lanahan.
- New York: Charles Scribner's Sons, [1969], #SL157.
- Wrappers.
NOTES: Bruccoli A9.3.b. Reprint of second American edition (revised contents). "B-1.69[Col]".
- PS3511.I9 T3 1969

140. *Six Tales of The Jazz Age and Other Stories.*
- With an Introduction by Frances Fitzgerald Lanahan.
- New York: Charles Scribner's Sons, [1970], #SL157.
- Wrappers.

NOTES: Bruccoli A9.3.b. Reprint of second American edition (revised contents). "C-11.70(c)".
- PS3511.I9 T4 1968

141. *Six Tales of The Jazz Age and Other Stories.*
- With an Introduction by Frances Fitzgerald Lanahan.
- New York: Charles Scribner's Sons, [n.d.]
- Wrappers.
NOTES: Bruccoli A9.3.b. The Scribner Library of Contemporary Classics. Fifteenth printing.
- PS3511.I9 T3 1970

The Vegetable (1923)

142. *The Vegetable or from President to Postman.*
- New York: Charles Scribner's Sons, 1923.
- Dust jacket.
NOTES: Bruccoli A10.1.a. First edition, first printing. Review copy with publisher's slip laid in.
- PS3511.I9 V4 1923 C.1

143. *The Vegetable or from President to Postman.*
- New York: Charles Scribner's Sons, 1923.
NOTES: Bruccoli A10.1.a. First edition, first printing. Review copy with publisher's slip pasted on front pastedown endpaper.
- PS3511.I9 V4 1923 C.4

144. *The Vegetable or from President to Postman.*
- New York: Charles Scribner's Sons, 1923.
NOTES: Bruccoli A10.1.a. First edition, first printing. Inscribed by FSF to Ernest Truex, who played the lead role of Jerry Frost in the Atlantic City try-out.
- PS3511.I9 V4 1923 C.2

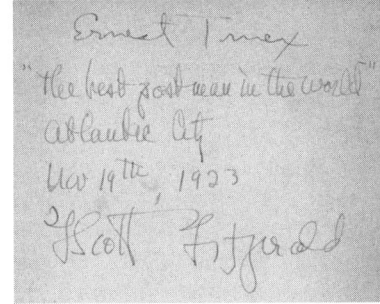

145. *The Vegetable or from President to Postman.*
- New York: Charles Scribner's Sons, 1923.
NOTES: Bruccoli A10.1.a. First edition, first printing. Presentation copy from Charles Fenton to Kay and Stan.
- PS3511.I9 V4 1923 C.6

146. *The Vegetable or from President to Postman.*
- New York: Charles Scribner's Sons, 1923.
NOTES: Bruccoli A10.1.a. First edition, first printing. Scribner Press Bindery Office copy.
- PS3511.I9 V4 1923 C.5

147. *The Vegetable or from President to Postman.*
- New York: Charles Scribner's Sons, 1923.
NOTES: Bruccoli A10.1.a. First edition, first printing. Inscribed by FSF to Harold and Anne Ober.
- PS3511.I9 V4 1923 C.3

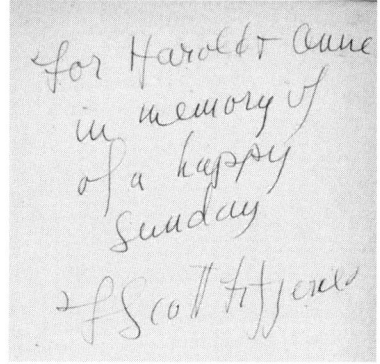

148. *The Vegetable or from President to Postman.*
- New York: Charles Scribner's Sons, 1923.
NOTES: Bruccoli A10.1.a. First edition, first printing. Inscribed by FSF to Siegfried Weisberger, proprietor of Peabody Bookshop in Baltimore.
Note by MJB: "This book was given to me by John Cook Wyllie".
Laid in: Obituary of Weisberger. With: ALS (1 p.) from Wyllie to "Mr. Bruccoli".
- PS3511.I9 V4 1923 C.7

149. *The Vegetable or from President to Postman.*
- New York: Charles Scribner's Sons, 1923.
NOTES: Bruccoli A10.1.a. First edition, first printing. Inscribed by FSF to Scribners editor John W. Rogers, Jr.
- PS3511.I9 V4 1923 C.8

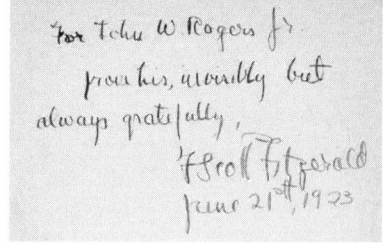

150. *The Vegetable or from President to Postman.*
   - New York: Charles Scribner's Sons, 1923.
   - Dust jacket.
   NOTES: Bruccoli A10.1.a. First edition, first printing. Inscribed by FSF to songwriter Gene Buck.
   - PS3511.I9 V4 1923 C.9

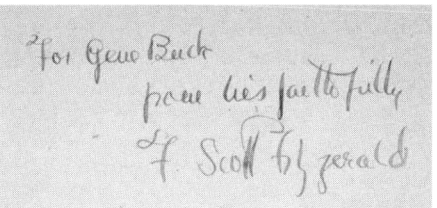

151. *The Vegetable or from President to Postman.*
   - [Folcroft, Penn.: Folcroft Press, 1971].
   NOTES: Bruccoli A10.1.b. Unauthorized reprint. Laid in: Prospectus.
   - PS3511.I9 V4 1971

152. *The Vegetable or from President to Postman.*
   - Clifton, N.J.: A. M. Kelley, 1972.
   NOTES: Bruccoli A10.1.c. Scribner Reprint Editions, third printing.
   - PS3511.I9 V4 1972

153. *The Vegetable or from President to Postman.*
   - A New Edition, with Unpublished Scenes and Corrections and an Introduction by Charles Scribner III.
   - New York: Charles Scribner's Sons, [1976].
   - Dust jacket.
   NOTES: Bruccoli A10.1.d. Fourth printing (augmented). Laid in: ALS, 4 May 1976, from Charles Scribner III to MJB.
   - PS3511.I9 V4 1976 C.1

154. *The Vegetable or from President to Postman.*
   - A New Edition, with Unpublished Scenes and Corrections and an Introduction by Charles Scribner III.
   - New York: Charles Scribner's Sons, [1976], #SL644.
   - Wrappers.
   NOTES: Bruccoli A10.1.d. Contemporary Classics. First printing.
   - PS3511.I9 V4 1976 C.2

155. *The Vegetable or from President to Postman.*
   - A New Edition, with Unpublished Scenes and Corrections and an Introduction by Charles Scribner III.
   - New York: Collier Books/Macmillan, [1987].
   - Wrappers.
   NOTES: First Scribner Classic/Collier Edition.
   - PS3511.I9 V4 1987

156. *The Vegetable.*
   - Edited with Notes by Susumu Kawanishii.
   - Tokyo: Tsurumi Shoten, 1978.
   - Wrappers; dust jacket.
   NOTES: Bruccoli A10.2. English-language Japanese edition with introduction and notes in Japanese.
   - PS3511.I9 V4 1987

The Great Gatsby (1925)

157. *The Great Gatsby.*
   - [New York: Charles Scribner's Sons, 1925].
   NOTES: Galley proofs. Running title: "Fitzgerald's Trimalchio".
       At head of first galley: "Gal 1—Fitzgerald's Trimalchio—46725—12-12-31".
       On first galley "Trimalchio" is crossed out and "The Great Gadsby" substituted in pencil by unknown hand.
       With: Sotheby-Parke-Bernet invoice and MJB check to Seven Gables laid in.
   - PS3511.I9 G7 1924

158. *Trimalchio by F. Scott Fitzgerald.*
   - A facsimile edition of the original galley proofs for *The Great Gatsby.*
   - Afterword by Matthew J. Bruccoli.
   - [Columbia]: University of South Carolina Press in cooperation with the Thomas Cooper Library, 2000.
   - Unbound sheets, boxed.
   NOTES: Bruccoli Supplement A49.
       "This facsimile publication of the galley proofs for 'Trimalchio' is limited to five hundred copies on laid paper, of which this is copy 1."
       Includes facsimile of FSF's May 1924 letter to Charles C. Baldwin.
       Laid in: Publisher's promotional cards, reproducing page 1 of the galleys.
   - PS3511.I9 T74 2000

159. [Jacket art for *The Great Gatsby*], c. 1924.
   - Francis Cugat.
   - 9 items.
   NOTES: First item: Preliminary sketch of railroad scene (charcoal with pen-and-ink, watercolor, and gouache on paper).
       Second item: Enlarged version of railroad scene (charcoal with pen-and-ink, watercolor, and gouache on paper).
       Third item: Sketch of face over house (pencil and crayon on paper).

Second item

Fourth item: Sketch of face over Long Island Sound (pencil and crayon on paper).

Fifth item: Sketch of face over New York skyline (pencil, crayon, charcoal, and gouache on paper).

Sixth item: Study of face over carnival lights (pencil and watercolor on paper).

Seventh item: Study of face and geometric patterns (pencil on paper).

Eighth item: Sketch of nocturnal carnival (crayon over oil on board).

Fifth item

Ninth item: Painting of final jacket (gouache on paper)—Cugat's copy.
- Arlyn Bruccoli Collection: on deposit.

160. *The Great Gatsby.*
   - New York: Charles Scribner's Sons, 1925.
   NOTES: Bruccoli A11.1.a. First edition, first printing.
   "Marked by MJB at Princeton, Nov. 1969. All F notes in his copy transferred."
   - PS3511.I9 G7 1925 C.1

161. *The Great Gatsby.*
   - New York: Charles Scribner's Sons, 1925.
   NOTES: Bruccoli A11.1.a. First edition, first printing.
   Pasted-in presentation inscription from FSF to Van Wyck Brooks on free front endpaper. Embossed ownership stamp of Van Wyck Brooks.
   Laid in: TLS to MJB from Mrs. Van Wyck Brooks, 26 October 1964, and xerox of letter [13 June 1925] from FSF to Van Wyck Brooks.
   - PS3511.I9 G7 1925 C.2

162. *The Great Gatsby.*
   - New York: Charles Scribner's Sons, 1925.
   - Dust jacket: With lower-case "j" in Jay Gatsby on the back at line 14, hand corrected in ink.
   NOTES: Bruccoli A11.1.a. First edition, first printing.
   - PS3511.I9 G7 1925 C.3

163. *The Great Gatsby.*
- New York: Charles Scribner's Sons, 1925.
- Dust jacket: With capital "J" on back.

NOTES: Bruccoli A11.1.a. First edition, first printing.
- PS3511.I9 G7 1925 C.4

164. *The Great Gatsby.*
- New York: Charles Scribner's Sons, 1925.

NOTES: Bruccoli A11.1.a. First edition, first printing.
Signature of Lionel Trilling on free front endpaper with his markings throughout.
- PS3511.I9 G7 1925 C.5

165. *The Great Gatsby.*
- New York: Charles Scribner's Sons, 1925.

NOTES: Bruccoli A11.1.a. First edition, first printing.
Scribner bindery copy, annotated on front pastedown endpaper with production details, 1925–41. Label on front cover.
- PS3511.I9 G7 1925 C.6
- Another copy.

166. *The Great Gatsby.*
- With introduction by Charles Scribner III.
- New York: Charles Scribner's Sons, [1989].
- Dust jacket.

NOTES: Facsimile of first edition.
"In celebration of the grand opening of Scribner's Bookstore".
Signed presentation copy from Charles Scribner III to MJB.
- PS3511.I9 G7 1989

167. *The Great Gatsby.*
- New York: Charles Scribner's Sons, 1925.
- Dust jacket. Slipcase.

NOTES: Bruccoli Supplement A11.1.a. Note nine.
Facsimile of first printing produced by Collectors Reprints, Inc. (New York, 1991?).
- PS3511.I9 G7 1991e

168. *The Great Gatsby.*
- New York: Charles Scribner's Sons, 1925.

NOTES: Bruccoli A11.1.b. First edition, second printing.
Rubber stamp of Shakespeare & Co. bookshop. MJB highlights throughout.
- PS3511.I9 G7 1925b

169. *The Great Gatsby.*
- New York: Charles Scribner's Sons, 1925.

NOTES: Bruccoli A11.1.b. First edition, second printing.

Note in the hand of FSF's nurse at Grove Park Inn, on half title: "Endpapers torn out by F. Scott Fitzgerald. Dorothy Williamson Ritz". Explanatory note by MJB on front pastedown endpaper.
- PS3511.I9 G7 1925b C.2

170. *The Great Gatsby.*
- New York: Charles Scribner's Sons, 1925.
- Dust jacket with excerpts from reviews.
NOTES: Bruccoli A11.1.b. First edition, second printing.
- PS3511.I9 G7 1925b C.3

171. *The Great Gatsby.*
- New York: Charles Scribner's Sons, 1925.
NOTES: Bruccoli A11.1.b. First edition, second printing. Ober Agency office file copy. Label: "HAROLD OBER" on free front endpaper.
- PS3511.I9 G7 1925b C.4

172. *The Great Gatsby.*
- London: Chatto & Windus, [1926].
- Dust jacket: "7S.NET".
NOTES: Bruccoli A11.1.c. First English printing, from American plates.
- PS3511.I9 G7 1926 C.1

173. *The Great Gatsby.*
- London: Chatto & Windus, [1926].
- Dust jacket: "2/6 NET" label.
NOTES: Bruccoli Supplement A11.1.c. Inscribed by FSF to Edwin Barret.
- PS3511.I9 G7 1926 C.3

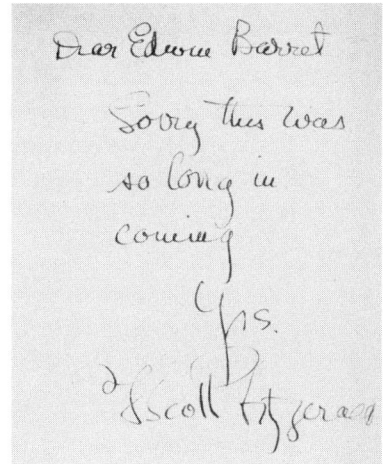

174. *The Great Gatsby.*
- London: Chatto & Windus, [1926].
- Dust jacket: "2/-" label.
NOTES: Bruccoli Supplement A11.1.c.
- PS3511.I9 G7 1926 C.2

175. *The Great Gatsby.*
- London: Chatto & Windus, [1926].
NOTES: Bruccoli A11.1.d.
- PS3511.I9 G7 1927

176. *The Great Gatsby.*
- With a New Introduction by F. Scott Fitzgerald.
- New York: Modern Library, [1934].
- Dust jacket.
NOTES: Bruccoli A11.1.e.
  Inscribed by FSF to Michael Balcon, producer of *A Yank at Oxford.*
- PS3511.I9 G7 1934 C.1
- Another copy (without inscription).

177. *The Great Gatsby.*
- With a New Introduction by F. Scott Fitzgerald.
- New York: Modern Library, [1934].
- Dust jacket: Rubber-stamped "DISCONTINUED TITLE".
NOTES: Bruccoli A11.1.e.
- PS3511.I9 G7 1934 C.2
- Another copy in "DISCONTINUED" dust jacket; two additional copies in variant cloths without dust jacket.

178. *The Great Gatsby.*
- "The Sunday Novel Supplement," *Chicago Herald and Examiner* (23 May 1937), pp. [1]–16; Illustrated by Harold E. Snyder.
NOTES: At head of title: "The Sunday Novel . . . Complete In This Issue".
- PS3511.I9 G7 1937b

179. *The Great Gatsby.*
- "The Sunday Novel Supplement," *Philadelphia Inquirer* (23 May 1937), pp. [1]–16; Illustrated by Harold E. Snyder.
NOTES: At head of title: "The Sunday Novel . . . Complete In This Issue."
- PS3511.I9 G7 1937c

180. *The Great Gatsby.*
- New York: Charles Scribner's Sons, 1942.
NOTES: Bruccoli A11.1.f. First edition, fifth printing.
- PS3511.I9 G7 1942

181. *The Great Gatsby.*
- Introduction by Lionel Trilling.
- New York: New Directions, [1945].
- Dust jacket.

NOTES: Bruccoli A11.1.g. The New Classics Series. First edition, sixth printing. Signature of Diana Trilling.
- PS3511.I9 G7 1945
- Another copy (without signature).

182. *The Great Gatsby*.
- New York: Grosset & Dunlap, [1949].
- Light blue boards.
NOTES: Bruccoli A11.1.h. First edition, seventh printing. Sylvia Plath's copy with her bookplate; marked by her on pages 21, 60, 74, 80, 136, 137, 140, 141, 165, 174, 175, 181, and 215.
- PS3511.I9 G7 1949 C.1

183. *The Great Gatsby*.
- New York: Grosset & Dunlap, 1949.
- Gray cloth. Dust jacket with wrap-around band advertising 1949 Paramount movie.
NOTES: Bruccoli A11.1.h. First edition, seventh printing. Stamped on bottom edge: "OFFICE FILE COPY".
- PS3511.I9 G7 1949 C.2

184. *The Great Gatsby*.
- New York: Grosset & Dunlap, 1949.
- Light blue boards. Dust jacket.
NOTES: Bruccoli A11.1.h. First edition, seventh printing.
- PS3511.I9 G7 1949 C.3
- Another copy in light blue boards in dust jacket; another copy in gray cloth without dust jacket.

185. *The Great Gatsby*.
- New York: Editions for the Armed Services, [1945?], #862.
- Wrappers.
NOTES: Bruccoli A11.3. Third edition.
- PS3511.I9 G7 1945b

186. *The Great Gatsby*.
- New York: Bantam Books, [1945], #8.
- Wrappers; in 1949 dust jacket showing Alan Ladd in a scene from the Paramount movie.
NOTES: Bruccoli A11.5. Fifth edition, first printing.
- PS3511.I9 G7 1945c

187. *The Great Gatsby*.
- New York: Bantam Books, [1945], #8.
- Wrappers.
NOTES: Bruccoli A11.5. Fifth edition, first printing.
- PS3511.I9 G7 1946b C.1

188. *The Great Gatsby.*
- New York: Bantam Books, [1946], #8.
- Wrappers.

NOTES: Bruccoli A11.5. Fifth edition, third printing.
- PS3511.I9 G7 1946b C.2

189. *The Great Gatsby.*
- New York: Bantam Books, [1951], #8.
- Wrappers.

NOTES: Bruccoli A11.5. Fifth edition, fourth printing.
- PS3511.I9 G7 1951

190. *The Great Gatsby.*
- New York: Bantam Books, [1954], #8.
- Wrappers.

NOTES: Bruccoli A11.5. "6th Printing (new edition) March, 1954". Not new edition.
- PS3511.I9 G7 1954b

191. *Great American Short Novels.*
- Edited by William Phillips.
- New York: Dial Press, [1946].
- Dust jacket.

NOTES: Bruccoli A11.6. Sixth edition. Fifth printing. Includes *The Great Gatsby.*
- PS3511.I9 G7 1946

192. *Great American Short Novels.*
- Edited by William Phillips.
- New York: Dial Press, [1950].
- Dust jacket.

NOTES: Bruccoli A11.6. Sixth edition. Sixth printing. Includes *The Great Gatsby.*
- PS3511.I9 G7 1950b

193. *The Great Gatsby.*
- [London]: Grey Walls, [1948].
- Dust jacket.

NOTES: Bruccoli A11.7. First English edition.
- PS3511.I9 G7 1948
- Another copy with wrap-around band advertising movie.

194. *The Great Gatsby.*
- [London]: Grey Walls, [1949].
- Dust jacket.

NOTES: Bruccoli A11.7. First English edition. "Second impression, 1949".
- PS3511.I9 G7 1949b

195. *The Great Gatsby.*
- Harmondsworth, England: Penguin Books, [1950], #746.
- Wrappers.

NOTES: Bruccoli A11.8. Second English edition. First Penguin edition.
- PS3511.I9 G7 1950

196. *The Great Gatsby.*
- [Harmondsworth, England]: Penguin Books, [1954], #746.
- Wrappers.

NOTES: Bruccoli A11.8. Second English edition.
- PS3511.I9 G7 1954

197. *The Great Gatsby.*
- [Harmondsworth, England]: Penguin, [1958], #746.
- Wrappers.

NOTES: Bruccoli A11.8. Second English edition.
- PS3511.I9 G7 1958b

198. *The Great Gatsby.*
- [Harmondsworth, England]: Penguin Books, [1961], #746.
- Wrappers.

NOTES: Bruccoli A11.8. Penguin Modern Classics. Second English edition, fourth printing.
- PS3511.I9 G7 1961b

199. *The Great Gatsby.*
- [Harmondsworth, England]: Penguin Books, [1967], #746.
- Wrappers.

NOTES: Bruccoli A11.8. Penguin Modern Classics. Second English edition, reprinted, ninth printing.
- PS3511.I9 G7 1967c

200. *The Great Gatsby.*
- [Harmondsworth, England]: Penguin Books, [1969], #746.
- Wrappers.

NOTES: Bruccoli A11.8. Penguin Modern Classics. Second English edition, reprinted, thirteenth printing.
- PS3511.I9 G7 1969b

201. *The Great Gatsby.*
- [Harmondsworth, England]: Penguin Books, [1974].
- Wrappers.

NOTES: Bruccoli A.11.8. Reprint of second English edition, twentieth printing.
- PS3511.I9 G7 1974c

202. *The Great Gatsby.*
- Stockholm: The Polyglot Club, 1950.
- Wrappers.

NOTES: Bruccoli A11.9. The Polyglot's Choice Series. English-language Swedish edition with Swedish gloss.
- PS3511.I9 G7 1950b

203. *The Great Gatsby.*
- New York: Charles Scribner's Sons, [1957].
- Wrappers.
NOTES: Bruccoli A11.10.a. Student's Edition. "A-8.57 [C]".
- PS3511.I9 G7 1957

204. *The Great Gatsby.*
- New York: Charles Scribner's Sons, [1958].
- Wrappers.
NOTES: Bruccoli A11.10.a. Student's Edition. "B-1.58[C]".
- PS3511.I9 G7 1958

205. *The Great Gatsby.*
- New York: Charles Scribner's Sons, [1959].
- Dust jacket.
NOTES: Bruccoli A11.10.b. "C-7.59 [H]".
- PS3511.I9 G7 1953

206. *The Great Gatsby.*
- New York: Charles Scribner's Sons, [1960], #SL1.
- Wrappers.
NOTES: Bruccoli A11.10.b. Scribner Library. "A-1.60[C]".
- PS3511.I9 G7 1960

207. *The Great Gatsby.*
- New York: Charles Scribner's Sons, [1961], #SL1.
- Wrappers.
NOTES: Bruccoli A11.10.b. Scribner Library. "D-3.61[C]".
- PS3511.I9 G7 1961c

208. *The Great Gatsby.*
- New York: Charles Scribner's Sons, [1962], #SL1.
- Wrappers.
NOTES: Bruccoli A11.10.b. Scribner Library. "F-8.62[Col]".
- PS3511.I9 G7 1962

209. *The Great Gatsby.*
- New York: Charles Scribner's Sons, [1963], #SL1.
- Wrappers.
NOTES: Bruccoli A11.10.b. Reprint. "G-4.63[Col]".
   Notes and corrections by MJB in ink and pencil.
- PS3511.I9 G7 1963 C.2
- Another copy (without notes and corrections).

210. *The Great Gatsby.*
- New York: Charles Scribner's Sons, [1963], #SL1.
- Wrappers.
NOTES: Bruccoli A11.10.b. "H-10.63[Col]".
- PS3511.I9 G7 1963b

211. *The Great Gatsby.*
- New York: Charles Scribner's Sons, [1965], #SL1.
- Wrappers.
NOTES: Bruccoli A11.10.b. "J-2.65[Col]".
- PS3511.I9 G7 1965

212. *The Great Gatsby.*
- New York: Charles Scribner's Sons, [1968], #SL1.
- Wrappers.
NOTES: Bruccoli A11.10.b. "N-8.68[Col]".
- PS3511.I9 G7 1968e

213. *The Great Gatsby.*
- New York: Charles Scribner's Sons, [1969], #SL1.
- Wrappers.
NOTES: Bruccoli A11.10.b. "P-9.69[C]".
- PS3511.I9 G7 1969

214. *The Great Gatsby.*
- New York: Charles Scribner's Sons, [1970], #SL1.
- Wrappers.
NOTES: Bruccoli A11.10.b. "R-10.70[C]".
- PS3511.I9 G7 1970

215. *The Great Gatsby.*
- New York: Charles Scribner's Sons, [1971], #SL1.
- Wrappers.
NOTES: Bruccoli A11.10.b. "S-3.71[C]".
- PS3511.I9 G7 1971

216. *The Great Gatsby.*
- New York: Charles Scribner's Sons, [1975?], #SL1.
- Wrappers.
NOTES: Bruccoli A11.10.b. Contemporary Classics/Scribner Library. Thirty-first printing.
- PS3511.I9 G7 1975b

217. *The Great Gatsby.*
- New York: Charles Scribner's Sons, [1975?], #SL1.
- Wrappers.
NOTES: Bruccoli A11.10.b. Contemporary Classics/Scribner Library. Thirty-second printing.
- PS3511.I9 G7 1975b

218. *The Great Gatsby.*
- New York: Charles Scribner's Sons, [1980?].
- Wrappers. Rack size.

NOTES: Bruccoli A11.10.c. Contemporary Classics/Scribner Library. Fourteenth printing.
- PS3511.I9 G7 1980c

219. *The Great Gatsby.*
- New York: Charles Scribner's Sons, [1981].
- Dust jacket.

NOTES: Bruccoli A11.10.d. Hudson River Editions.
- PS3511.I9 G7 1981b

220. *The Great Gatsby.*
- Edited and Annotated by Naotaro Tatsuno Kuchi and Nobuyuki Kiuchi.
- Tokyo: Kairyudo, [1960], #11.
- Wrappers. Dust jacket.

NOTES: Bruccoli A11.12. Kairyudo's Mentor Library. English-language Japanese edition.
- PS3511.I9 G7 1960b

221. *The Great Gatsby.*
- Foreword and Study Guide by Albert K. Ridout.
- New York: Charles Scribner's Sons, [1961].

NOTES: Bruccoli A11.13. "A-9.61[V]".
- PS3511.I9 G7 1961

222. *The Great Gatsby.*
- Foreword by Albert K. Ridout.
- New York: Charles Scribner's Sons, [1968].

NOTES: Reprint of Bruccoli A11.13. Scribner School Edition. "A-1.68[MCOL]".
- PS3511.I9 G7 1968b

223. *The Great Gatsby.*
- Foreword by Albert K. Ridout.
- New York: Charles Scribner's Sons, [1968], #SSP2.
- Wrappers.

NOTES: Reprint of Bruccoli A11.13. Scribner School Paperbacks. "A-1.68[M]".
- PS3511.I9 G7 1968c

224. *The Great Gatsby.*
- Foreword by Albert K. Ridout.
- New York: Charles Scribner's Sons, [1973?].

NOTES: Bruccoli A11.13. Scribner School Edition. Fourth printing.
- PS3511.I9 G7 1973

225. *The Great Gatsby.*
- Foreword by Albert K. Ridout.
- New York: Charles Scribner's Sons, [1976?].
- Taipei: Caves Books, [1976].
- Wrappers.
NOTES: Bruccoli A11.13. Pirated facsimile of Scribner edition. Second printing.
- PS3511.I9 G7 1976

226. *The Great Gatsby.*
- Foreword by Albert K. Ridout.
- New York: Charles Scribner's Sons, [1990?].
- Wrappers.
NOTES: Bruccoli A11.13. Twenty-second printing.
- PS3511.I9 G7 1990

227. *A Quarto of Modern Literature . . . Fifth Edition.*
- Edited by Leonard Brown.
- New York: Charles Scribner's Sons, [1964].
- Dust jacket.
NOTES: Bruccoli A11.15. "A-3.64[V]". Includes *The Great Gatsby.*
- PR1149.B7 1964

228. *Three Great American Novels.*
- Includes *The Great Gatsby* with an Introduction by Malcolm Cowley.
- New York: Charles Scribner's Sons, [1967].
- Dust jacket.
NOTES: Bruccoli A11.16. Modern Standard Authors. "A-9.67[c]".
- PS3511.I9 G7 1967

229. *The Great Gatsby.*
- With Commentary and Notes by J. F. Wyatt.
- London: The Bodley Head, [1967].
NOTES: The Bodley Head Series.
- PS3511.I9 G7 1967

230. *The Great Gatsby.*
- Illustrations by Charles Raymond.
- London: Folio Society, 1968.
- Slipcase.
NOTES: Bruccoli A11.18.
- PS3511.I9 G7 1968d

231. *The Great Gatsby.*
- New York: Charles Scribner's Sons, 1968.
NOTES: Bruccoli A11.19. Scribners Large Type Edition. "A-5.68[C]".
  Laid in: press release. "This was last note JCW sent for FN. MJB".
- PS3511.I9 G7 1968

232. *Fitzgerald's The Great Gatsby: The Novel, The Critics, The Background.*
- Compiled by Henry Dan Piper.
- New York: Charles Scribner's Sons, [1970].
- Wrappers.

NOTES: Bruccoli A11.20. Scribner Research Anthologies. "A-3.70[H]".
- PS3511.I9 G87 1970

233. *The Great Gatsby.*
- New York: Bantam, [1974], #T7448.
- Wrappers.

NOTES: Bruccoli A11.22. Tie-in edition for the 1974 movie.
- PS3511.I9 G7 1974b

234. *The Great Gatsby.*
- New York: Bantam, [1974], #T7448.
- Wrappers.

NOTES: Bruccoli A11.22. Second printing. "Published in Canada."
- PS3511.I9 G7 1974d

235. *The Great Gatsby.*
- New York: Bantam, [1974], #T7448.
- Wrappers.

NOTES: Bruccoli A11.22. Twelfth printing. July? 1974.
- PS3511.I9 G7 1974o

236. *The Great Gatsby.*
- Franklin Center, Penn.: Franklin Library, 1974.

NOTES: Bruccoli A11.23.
- PS3511.I9 G7 1974

237. *The Great Gatsby.*
- [Ringwood, Victoria]: Penguin Books, [1974].
- Wrappers.
- PS3511.I9 G7 1974f

238. *The Great Gatsby.*
- With an Introduction by J. B. Priestley.
- [London]: John Player Special Collection, [1975].
- Dust jacket.
- PS3511.I9 G7 1975b C.1

239. *The Great Gatsby.*
- New York: Charles Scribner's Sons, [1975], #SL1.
- Wrappers.

NOTES: Bruccoli A11.24. Scribner Library/Contemporary Classics.
- PS3511.I9 G7 1975b C.2

240. *The Great Gatsby.*
- New York: Charles Scribner's Sons, [1985].
- Wrappers.
NOTES: Scribner Library/Contemporary Classics. Thirty-eighth printing.
- PS3511.I9 G7 1985

241. *The Great Gatsby.*
- Bath, England: Lythway Press, 1975.
- Label: "Sample Complete Copy".
NOTES: Bruccoli A11.25. Large-print edition.
- PS3511.I9 G7 1975

242. *The Great Gatsby.*
- Bath, England: Lythway Press, 1977.
- Wrappers.
NOTES: Bruccoli A11.25. Reprint of large-print edition. Sample copy.
- PS3511.I9 G7 1977

243. *The Great Gatsby and The Last Tycoon.*
- With an Introduction by J. B. Priestley.
- London: Book Club Associates, [1977].
- Dust jacket.
NOTES: Bruccoli A11.26. Book Club Edition. Sample Complete Copy.
- PS3511.I9 G7 1977

244. *The Great Gatsby.*
- Edited with an Introduction and Notes by Luigi Castigliano.
- Monadori: Edizioni Scholastiche, [1977].
- Wrappers.
NOTES: Bruccoli A11.27. English-language Italian edition; annotated.
- PS3511.I9 G7 1977c

245. *The Scribner Quarto of Modern Literature.*
- Edited by A. Walton Litz.
- New York: Charles Scribner's Sons, [1978].
NOTES: Bruccoli A11.28. Includes *The Great Gatsby.* Complimentary copy.
- PS3511.I9 G7 1978

246. *The Great Gatsby.*
- Illustrated by Chuck Wilkinson.
- Franklin Center, Penn.: Franklin Library, 1980.
NOTES: Bruccoli A11.29. The 100 Greatest Masterpieces of American Literature.
- PS3511.I9 G7 1980

247. *The Great Gatsby.*
- With an Introduction by Charles Scribner III and Illustrations by Fred Meyer.
- [New York]: Limited Editions Club, [1980].
- Slipcase.

NOTES: Bruccoli A11.30.
> Laid in: prospectuses.
> Signed by Scribner and Meyer.
- PS3511.I9 G7 1980b

248. *The Great Gatsby.*
    - With an Introduction, Notes, and Bibliography by M. Sivaramkrishna.
    - Delhi: Oxford University Press, 1981.
    - Wrappers.
    NOTES: Bruccoli A11.31. Sample copy.
    - PS3511.I9 G7 1981

249. *The Great Gatsby.*
    - Illustrated by Bruce Dean.
    - Franklin Center, Penn.: Franklin Library, [1982].
    NOTES: Bruccoli A11.32.
    > Laid in: TLS, 1 November 1982, from Charles Scribner III to Frances Scott Fitzgerald Smith.
    - PS3511.I9 G7 1982

250. *The Great Gatsby.*
    - Illustrated by Bruce Dean.
    - Franklin Center, Penn.: Franklin Library, 1982.
    NOTES: Bruccoli A11.32.
    > "This special edition of THE GREAT GATSBY was prepared for subscribers to the Oxford Library of the World's Great Books".
    - PS3511.I9 G7 1982b

251. *The Great Gatsby.*
    - Illustrated by Bruce Dean.
    - [New York]: Oxford University Press, [1982].
    NOTES: Bruccoli A11.32. Reprint of Franklin Library Edition with new title page.
    - PS3511.I9 G7 1982b

252. *The Great Gatsby.*
    - [London: Viaduct Publications, Ltd., 1982].
    - Wrappers. Comic-book format.
    NOTES: Bruccoli A11.33. *Complete Bestsellers,* Volume 2, Number 6. Cover Painting by T. Chantrell; Text Illustrations by C. L. Doughty.
    - PN6120.2.C656

253. *The Great Gatsby.*
    - Edited and Annotated by Dagmar Pohlenz and Richard Matin.
    - [Paderborn]: Ferdinand Schöningh, [1984].
    - Wrappers.
    NOTES: Bruccoli A11.34. English-language German edition.
    - PS3511.I9 G7 1984c

254. *The Great Gatsby.*
   - Illustrated by Michael Graves.
   - San Francisco: Arion Press, 1984.
   - Slipcase.
   NOTES: Bruccoli A11.35. One of 400 copies signed by Graves.
   Laid in: Prospectus, etc. relating to the production of the book, with TLS, 11 January 1985, from Andrew Hoyem to MJB.
   - PS3511.I9 G7 1984

255. *The Great Gatsby.*
   - [London: Marshall Cavendish, 1988].
   - Wrappers.
   NOTES: With: *The Great Writers: Their Lives, Works and Inspiration,* Part 37, Volume 3.
   - PS3511.I9 G7 1988

256. *The Great Gatsby.*
   - Herausgegeben von Susanne Lenz.
   - Stuttgart: Philipp Reclam, [1989].
   - Wrappers.
   NOTES: English-language German edition. Notes and bibliography in German.
   - PS3511.I9 G7 1989b

257. *The Great Gatsby.*
   - Introduction and Notes by Tony Tanner.
   - [London]: Penguin Books, [1990].
   - Wrappers.
   NOTES: Penguin Twentieth-Century Classics.
   - PS3511.I9 G7 1990c

258. *The Great Gatsby.*
   Edited by Stephanie Colomb.
   - [Harlow, England]: Longman, [1991].
   - Wrappers.
   - PS3511.I9 G7 1991f

259. *The Great Gatsby.*
   - Edited by Matthew J. Bruccoli; Textual Consultant, Fredson Bowers.
   - Cambridge; New York: Cambridge University Press, [1991].
   - Dust jacket.
   NOTES: On blank preliminary page: "Andrew Brown of CUP objected to my emendations for <u>retinas</u> and <u>Astoria</u> . . . the Lanahans—in their capacity as Trustees—blocked publication of <u>GG</u> with these emendations. I capitulated. My subsequent shame for my cowardice and bad scholarship compelled me to resign as editor of the CUP Fitz Edition, Matthew J. Bruccoli".
   - PS3511.I9 G7 1991

260. *The Great Gatsby.*
- Edited and with an Introduction by Matthew J. Bruccoli.
- [London]: Scribners, [1991].
- Dust jacket.

NOTES: The Cambridge Text.
> Note on half title: "24, 64, 117: Limey tamperings. MJB This text was supposed to be an <u>exact</u> reprint of the CUP edition; but corruptions were introduced when the tape or disc was re-run. See pp. 34, 56, 74, 126." There are corrections in MJB's hand on these pages.
- PS3511.I9 G7 1991b

261. "James Dickey on the Cambridge/Bruccoli Edition of *The Great Gatsby*," 15 January 1992.
- James Dickey.
- 1 page.

NOTES: Signed typed blurb.
- PS3554.I32 D63 1992

261a. "Statement on CUP Gatsby," 15 January 1992.
- James Dickey.
- 4 pages (TS, 1 p.; MS, 1 p.; RTS, 1 p.; TS signed, 1 p.).
- On deposit

262. *The Great Gatsby.*
- With an Introduction by Matthew J. Bruccoli.
- London: Charles Scribner's Sons, 1991.

NOTES: The Cambridge Text. Includes "Winter Dreams."
> On front endpaper and half title: "17 Oct 91 London MJB ... See 34, 56, 74, 126, 155". Additional MJB annotations throughout.
- PS3511.I9 G7 1991d

263. *The Great Gatsby.*
- With an Introduction by Charles Scribner III and Illustrations by Fred Meyer.
- Norwalk, Conn.: The Easton Press, [1991].
- PS3511.I9 G7 1991c

264. *The Great Gatsby.*
- With an Introduction by Matthew J. Bruccoli.
- [London]: Abacus, [1992].
- Wrappers.

NOTES: The Cambridge Text. Corrected by MJB.
- PS3511.I9 G7 1992

265. *The Great Gatsby.*
- New York: Collier Books, [1992].
- Wrappers: The Authorized Text. Rack size.

NOTES: A Scribner Classic. First Collier Books Edition 1992.
>Inscribed by Charles Scribner III to MJB. Annotated by MJB with note on rear blank page: "... Jack told me that he and Bobbie have the authority to outvote my editorial decisions. 27.17 retinas [irises 72.24 Astoria [Long Island City 132.3 Long Island City [stet M J Bruccoli 12 May 92".
- PS3511.I9 G7 1992b

266. *The Great Gatsby.*
- Preface and Notes by Matthew J. Bruccoli.
- New York: Collier Books; Toronto: Maxwell Macmillan Canada, [1992].
- Wrappers.

NOTES: A Scribner Classic. First Collier Books Edition 1992.
>Inscribed by Charles Scribner III to MJB.
- PS3511.I9 G7 1992b

267. *The Great Gatsby.*
- Preface and Notes by Matthew J. Bruccoli.
- New York: Collier Books, [1992].
- Wrappers.

NOTES: A Scribner Classic. First Collier Books Edition 1992.
>Note on half title: "S. J. Lanahan tampered with this text. 10 June 92 MJB".
- PS3511.I9 G7 1992c C.2

268. *The Great Gatsby.*
- Preface and Notes by Matthew J. Bruccoli.
- New York: Collier Books, [1992].
- Wrappers.

NOTES: A Scribner Classic. First Collier Books Edition 1992.
>Annotations on half title: "25 May 92 132 72 27 The Long Island City/Astoria contradiction resulted from Jack Lanahan's arrogant interference. He informed me that he and Bobbie were outvoting and overruling me. MJB".
- PS3511.I9 G7 1992c C.3

269. *The Great Gatsby.*
- Preface and Notes by Matthew J. Bruccoli.
- New York: Collier Books, [1992].
- Page proofs.

NOTES: Corrected and signed by MJB.
- PS3511.I9 G7 1992d C.1

270. *The Great Gatsby.*
- Preface and Notes by Matthew J. Bruccoli.
- New York: Collier Books, [1992].
- Wrappers.

NOTES: A Scribner Classic. First Collier Books Edition 1992. Third printing. Annotations on half title: "Corrections were supposed to be made in my back matter. But that dope . . . did not do his job, even though my corrections were set in type and proofed. MJB 28 April 93".
- PS3511.I9 G7 1992d C. 2

271. *The Great Gatsby.*
- Edited by David Crystal and Derek Strange with an Introduction by Anthony Burgess.
- [London]: Penguin English, [1992].
- Wrappers.

NOTES: Penguin Authentic Texts.
- PS3511.I9 G7 1992e

272. *The Great Gatsby.*
- Retold by Margaret Tarner.
- [Oxford; Portsmouth, N.H.]: Heinemann ELT, [1992].

NOTES: Heinemann ELT Guided Readers.
- PE1127.L6 F582 1992

273. *The Great Gatsby.*
- Ware, England: Wordsworth Editions Limited, 1993.
- Wrappers.

NOTES: Wordsworth Classics.
- PS3511.I9 G7 1993

274. *The Great Gatsby.*
- Edited by Jeffrey Myers.
- London: J. M. Dent, [1993].
- Wrappers.

NOTES: Everyman Library.
- PS3511.I9 G7 1993c

275. *The Great Gatsby.*
- [Berlin]: Cornelsen, [1993].
- Wrappers.

NOTES: English-language German edition. Senior English Library. "Bestellnummer 68013."
- PS3511.I9 G7 1993b

276. *The Great Gatsby.*
- Notes by Rudolph F. Rau.
- Stuttgart: Ernst Klett Schulbuchverlag, [1994].

NOTES: Proof copy with manuscript corrections of edition prepared for the use of German students of English by Ernst Klett Schulbuchverlag. Sent to MJB for his corrections.
Laid in: Letter from the publisher to MJB and Xerox of reply.
- PS3511.I9 G7 1994 C.1

277. *The Great Gatsby.*
   - [London]: Bloomsbury Classics, [1994].
   - Wrappers.
   - PS3511.I9 G7 1994

278. *The Great Gatsby.*
   - [London]: Compact Books, [1994].
   - Dust jacket.
   - PS3511.I9 G7 1994c

279. *The Great Gatsby.*
   - Retold by Katherine Mattock; Illustrated by Choy Man Yung.
   - [Oxford]: Oxford University Press, [1994].
   - Wrappers.
   NOTES: Oxford Progressive English Readers. Fifth printing.
   - PS3511.I9 G7 1994d

280. *The Great Gatsby.*
   - Edited by Ken Bush.
   - [Cambridge]: Cambridge University Press, [1995].
   - Wrappers.
   NOTES: Annotated on title page by MJB: "This text purports to be the Bruccoli CUP Critical Edition. But it alters Fitz's long dashes and suppresses one space break. CUP violated agreement to submit text to Trustees for approval. Trustees did not see this text until it was in book form. At first Trustees voted to have books destroyed. Andrew Brown protested. Trustees then voted to accept. I refused to accept this text. At Henry Dunow's earnest pleading I gave him my proxy. . . . MJB 23 July 95".
   - PS3511.I9 G7 1995 C.2

281. *The Great Gatsby.*
   - Edited by Ken Bush.
   - [Cambridge]: Cambridge University Press, [1995].
   - Wrappers.
   NOTES: Annotated on title page by MJB: "This is the foul text that CUP published without letting me proof. Fitz Trust has demanded that all copies be destroyed. MJB 18 April 95 Then the other Trustees and Dunow yielded to pressure from Andrew Brown. 25 July 95".
   - PS3511.I9 G7 1995 C.1

282. *The Great Gatsby.*
   - Preface and Notes by Matthew J. Bruccoli.
   - New York: Simon & Schuster, [1995].
   - Wrappers.
   NOTES: Scribner Paperback Fiction. Ninth printing.
   - PS3511.I9 G7 1995b

283. *The Great Gatsby.*
- Thorndike, Maine: G. K. Hall; Bath, Avon: Chivers Press, [1995].
- Dust jacket.

NOTES: Large Type Books.
- PS3511.I9 G7 1995c

284. *The Great Gatsby.*
- Preface by Matthew J. Bruccoli.
- [New York: Charles Scribner's Sons, 1996].
- Dust jacket.

NOTES: Scribner Classics. First printing.
- PS3511.I9 G7 1996 C.1

285. *The Great Gatsby.*
- Preface by Matthew J. Bruccoli.
- [New York: Charles Scribner's Sons, 1996].
- Dust jacket.

NOTES: Scribner Classics. Seventh printing.
- PS3511.I9 G7 1996 C.3

286. *The Great Gatsby.*
- Edited by Matthew J. Bruccoli; Textual Consultant Fredson Bowers.
- [Cambridge; New York]: Cambridge University Press, [1998].
- Dust jacket.

NOTES: Note on free front endpaper: "7th printing — with proper emendations. MJB 21 Aug 98 Seventh Printing The hell with the Lanahans."
- PS3511.I9 G7 1996b

287. *The Great Gatsby.*
- [Cambridge]: Cambridge University Press, [1998].
- Wrappers.

NOTES: South Asian Edition. On back wrapper: "Special Edition for sale in south Asia only. Not for export elsewhere."
- PS3511.I9 G7 1998

288. *The Great Gatsby.*
- [London]: Penguin, [1998?].
- Wrappers.

NOTES: Sixty-seventh printing.
- PS3511.I9 G7 1998b

289. *The Great Gatsby.*
- Eden Prairie, Minn.: Department 56 Literary Classics, [1999].

NOTES: Inscribed by Charles Scribner III to MJB. ALS, 20 December 1999, from Scribner to MJB.
- PS3511.I9 G7 1999b

290. *The Great Gatsby.*
- Retold by Celia Turvey.
- [Harlow: Pearson Education, 2000].
- Wrappers.
NOTES: Penguin Readers Level 5.
- PS3511.I9 G7 2000

291. *The Great Gatsby.*
- With an Introduction and Notes by Tony Tanner.
- [London]: Penguin, [2000].
- Wrappers.
NOTES: Penguin Classics. Second printing.
- PS3511.I9 G7 2000b

The Great Gatsby / A Facsimile of the Manuscript (1973).

292. *The Great Gatsby.*
- A Facsimile of the Manuscript.
- Edited with an Introduction by Matthew J. Bruccoli.
- Washington: Microcard Editions Books, 1973.
- Slipcase.
NOTES: Bruccoli A12. Numbered 1103 out of first printing of 2000 copies. "A Bruccoli Clark Book".
- PS3511.I9 G7 1973
- Another copy (un-numbered).

All the Sad Young Men (1926)

293. *All the Sad Young Men.*
- New York: Charles Scribner's Sons, 1926.
- Dust jacket.
NOTES: Bruccoli A13.1.a. First edition, early printing on basis of type batter.
- PS3511.I9 A72 1926 C.5
- Another copy.

294. *All the Sad Young Men.*
- New York: Charles Scribner's Sons, 1926.
NOTES: Bruccoli A13.1.a. First edition, early printing.
Inscribed by FSF to Dorothy Williamson.
- PS3511.I9 A72 1926 C.1

295. *All the Sad Young Men.*
- New York: Charles Scribner's Sons, 1926.
NOTES: Bruccoli A13.1.a. First edition, early printing.
Inscribed by FSF to his secretary Alice Wootton. Contents page annotated by FSF, with dates of the stories.
- PS3511.I9 A72 1926 C.2

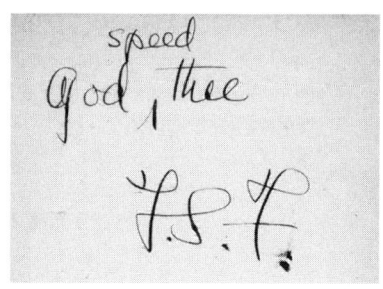

296. *All the Sad Young Men.*
- New York: Charles Scribner's Sons, 1926.
NOTES: Bruccoli A13.1.a. First edition, early printing.
Ownership inscription and annotations (pp. 4–5) of Elizabeth P. Van Peet?, a childhood friend of FSF.
- PS3511.I9 A72 1926 C.6

297. *All the Sad Young Men.*
- New York: Charles Scribner's Sons, 1926.
NOTES: Bruccoli A13.1.a. First edition, early printing.
Signed by Charles Scribner, Jr.
- PS3511.I9 A72 1926 C.8

298. *All the Sad Young Men.*
- New York: Charles Scribner's Sons, 1926.
- Dust jacket.
NOTES: Bruccoli A13.1.a. First edition, early printing.
Inscribed by FSF to H. Walton Quigley.
- PS3511.I9 A72 1926 C.9

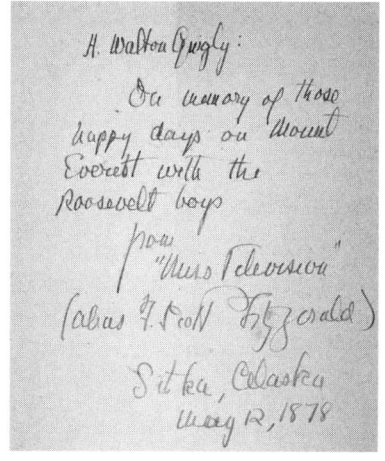

299. *All the Sad Young Men.*
- New York: Charles Scribner's Sons, 1926.
NOTES: Bruccoli A13.1.a. First edition, late printing.
Inscribed by James Dickey to MJB, February 1979.
- PS3511.I9 A72 1926 C.2

300. *All the Sad Young Men.*
- New York: Charles Scribner's Sons, 1926.
- Dust jacket.
NOTES: Bruccoli A13.1.a. First edition, early printing.
   Ober Agency office file copy. Red stamp of "HAROLD OBER ASSOCIATES" on front pastedown. Label: "HAROLD OBER" on free front endpaper.
- PS3511.I9 A72 1926 C.10

301. [Dust jacket proof for *All The Sad Young Men*, 1926?].
- [Cleonike Damianakes].
- 1 sheet.
- Proof of dust jacket for FSF's third collection of short stories.
NOTES: Illustration of female figure holding a globe, signed "CLEON." Does not include text from flaps or back.
- PS3511.I9 A722 1926

302. *All the Sad Young Men.*
- New York: Charles Scribner's Sons, 1926. [i.e., Philadelphia: Quality Books, 1969].
NOTES: Bruccoli A13.1.d. Unauthorized reprint.
- PS3511.I9 A72 1968

303. *All the Sad Young Men.*
- [Folcroft, Penn.]: Folcroft Press, [1970].
NOTES: Bruccoli A13.1.d. Later printing of 1969 unauthorized reprint.
- PS3511.I9 A72 1970

John Jackson's Arcady (1928)

304. *John Jackson's Arcady.*
- A Contest Selection; Arranged by Lilian Holmes Strack.
- Boston: Walter H. Baker Co., [1928].
- Wrappers.
NOTES: Bruccoli A14. Baker's Manuscript Readings.
- PS3511.I9 J6 1928

Tender Is the Night (1934)

305. *Tender Is the Night: A Romance.*
- Galley proofs of the first 33 pages of *Tender Is the Night*, here titled "Richard Diver," as serialized in the January 1934 issue of *Scribner's Magazine*.
NOTES: Corrections, including title, in the hand of Alfred Dashiell, editor of *Scribner's Magazine*.
   First page reproduced in the *F. Scott Fitzgerald Collection Notes*, no. 1 (September 1995).
- PS3511.I9 T4 1933

50 Books and Collections

306. *Tender Is the Night: A Romance.*
- Decorations by Edward Shenton.
- New York: Charles Scribner's Sons, 1934.
- Wrappers.
NOTES: Bruccoli A15.1.a. Review copy.
- PS3511.I9 T39

307. *Tender Is the Night: A Romance.*
- Decorations by Edward Shenton.
- New York: Charles Scribner's Sons, 1934.
- Dust jacket: Blurbs by T. S. Eliot, H. L. Mencken, and Paul Rosenfeld.
NOTES: Bruccoli A15.1.a. First edition, first printing. Review copy with publisher's slip laid in.
- PS3511.I9 T4 C.1

308. *Tender Is the Night: A Romance.*
- Decorations by Edward Shenton.
- New York: Charles Scribner's Sons, 1934.
NOTES: Bruccoli A15.1.a. First edition, first printing.
- PS3511.I9 T4 C.2
- Another copy.

309. *Tender Is the Night: A Romance.*
- Decorations by Edward Shenton.
- New York: Charles Scribner's Sons, 1934.
NOTES: Bruccoli A15.1.a. First edition, first printing.
- PS3511.I9 T4 C.3
- Another copy.

310. *Tender Is the Night: A Romance.*
- Decorations by Edward Shenton.
- New York: Charles Scribner's Sons, 1934.
NOTES: Bruccoli A15.1.a. First edition, first printing. Inscribed by FSF to Paula Post.
- PS3511.I9 T4 C.4

311. *Tender Is the Night: A Romance.*
- Decorations by Edward Shenton.
- New York: Charles Scribner's Sons, 1934.
- Dust jacket.
NOTES: Bruccoli A15.1.a. First edition, first printing.
Inscribed by FSF to Lady Florence Willert.
Laid in: xerox of ALS, 6 August 1938, from Lady Willert to FSF, and transcription.
- PS3511.I9 T4 C.5

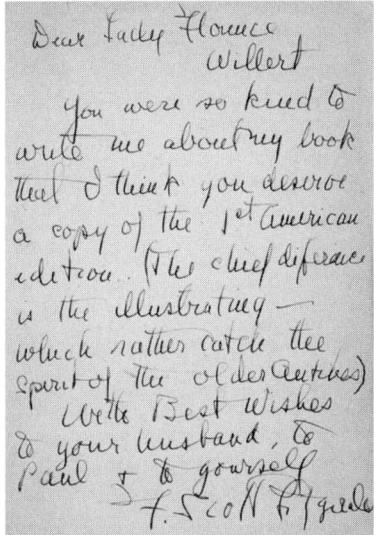

312. *Tender Is the Night: A Romance.*
- Decorations by Edward Shenton.
- New York: Charles Scribner's Sons, 1934.
- Dust jacket: Blurbs by Mary Colum, Gilbert Seldes, and Marjorie Kinnan Rawlings.
NOTES: Bruccoli A15.1.a. First edition, first printing.
- PS3511.I9 T4 C.6

313. *Tender Is the Night: A Romance.*
- Decorations by Edward Shenton.
- New York: Charles Scribner's Sons, 1934.
NOTES: Bruccoli A15.1.a. First edition, first printing.
Signature of Sheilah Graham on preliminary blank page.
- PS3511.I9 T4 C.7

314. *Tender Is the Night: A Romance.*
- New York: Charles Scribner's Sons, 1934.
NOTES: Preliminary leaf excised from a copy of *Tender Is the Night* with FSF inscription to Laura Guthrie.
- PS3511.I9 Z4835

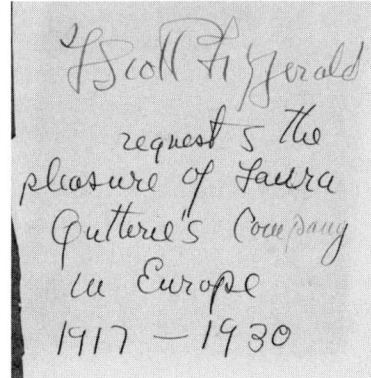

315. *Tender Is the Night: A Romance.*
- New York: Charles Scribner's Sons, 1934.

NOTES: Preliminary leaf excised from a copy of *Tender Is the Night* with FSF inscription to writer Cameron Rogers.
- PS3511.I9 Z4888 1934

316. [Illustrations for Tender Is the Night].
- Edward Shenton.
- 17 pen-and-ink drawings.
- On deposit.

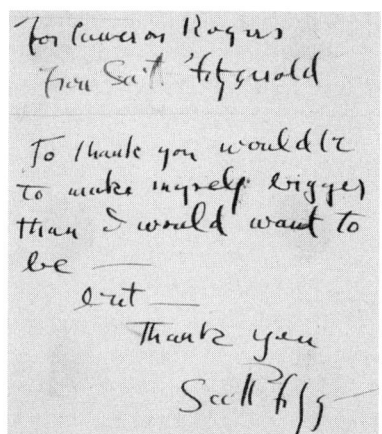

315.

316.

317. *Tender Is the Night: A Romance.*
- Decorations by Edward Shenton.
- New York: Charles Scribner's Sons, 1934.
- Dust jacket: "F.E.L." [First Edition Library]. Slipcase.

NOTES: Bruccoli Supplement A15.1.a, Note one.
Facsimile of the first printing produced by Collectors Reprints, Inc. (New York, 1992).
Laid in: Introductory insert.
Annotations by MJB: "Yellow stickers and highlighting flag variants between book and revised book galleys. NB: Revised book galleys are highlighted. 9 April 92".
- PS3511.I9 T4 1992

318. *Tender Is the Night: A Romance.*
- Decorations by Edward Shenton.
- New York: Charles Scribner's Sons, 1934.

NOTES: Bruccoli A15.1.b. First edition, second printing.
Inscribed by FSF to Theodora Gager.
- PS3511.I9 T4 1934b C.1
- Two additional copies (without inscription).

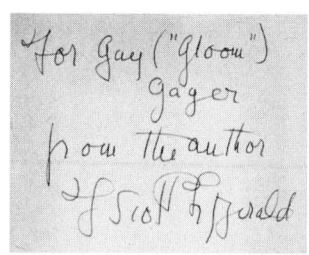

319. *Tender Is the Night: A Romance.*
 - Decorations by Edward Shenton.
 - New York: Charles Scribner's Sons, 1934.
 NOTES: Bruccoli A15.1.b. First edition, second printing.
   Ober Agency office file copy. Holograph pencil note in unidentified hand loosely inserted: "Since the 1st installment of Tender Is the Night was copyrighted Jan 34 in 1933 (Dec) - this copyright notice in the book is technically not accurate, in my opinion." Label: "HAROLD OBER" on free front endpaper.
 - PS3511.I9 T4 1934b C.4

320. *Tender Is the Night: A Romance.*
 - Decorations by Edward Shenton.
 - New York: Charles Scribner's Sons, 1934.
 NOTES: Bruccoli A15.1.c. First edition, third printing.
   Inscribed by FSF to Alice Wootton.
 - PS3511.I9 T4 1934c C.1

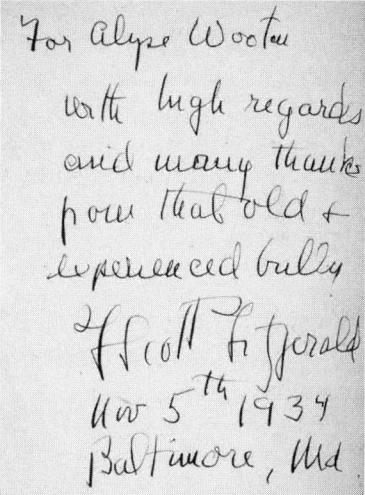

321. *Tender Is the Night: A Romance.*
 - Decorations by Edward Shenton.
 - New York: Charles Scribner's Sons, 1934.
 NOTES: Bruccoli A15.1.c. First edition, third printing.
   Inscribed by FSF to Harry Nardini.
 - PS3511.I9 T4 1934c C.2

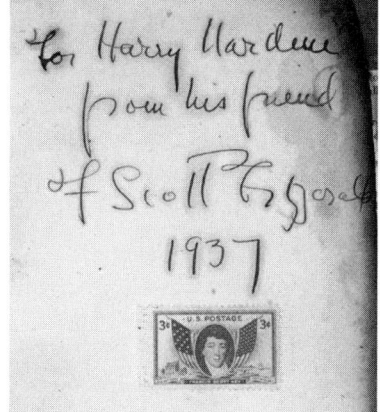

322. *Tender Is the Night: A Romance.*
- Decorations by Edward Shenton.
- New York: Charles Scribner's Sons, 1934.

NOTES: Bruccoli A15.1.c. First edition, third printing.
Inscribed by FSF to director Edward H. Griffith. Copy later owned by Irving Wallace.
- PS3511.I9 T4 1934b C.3

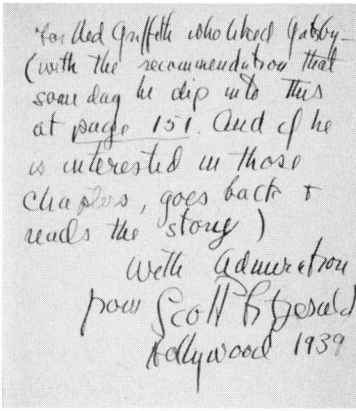

323. *Tender Is the Night: A Romance.*
- Decorations by Edward Shenton.
- New York: Charles Scribner's Sons, 1951.
- Dust jacket.

NOTES: Bruccoli A15.1.d. First edition, fourth printing.
- PS3511.I9 T2 1951

324. *Tender Is the Night: A Romance.*
- London: Chatto & Windus, 1934.
- Wrappers.

NOTES: Bruccoli A15.2.a. First English edition, proof copy.
- PS3511.I9 T4 1934e

325. *Tender Is the Night: A Romance.*
- London: Chatto & Windus, 1934.
- Dust jacket.

NOTES: First English edition, first printing. Bruccoli, A15.2.a.
Laid in: TLS, 21 April 1966, from Ian Parsons of Chatto and Windus to MJB concerning cheap editions of *The Great Gatsby* and *Tender Is the Night*.
- PS3511.I9 T4 1934f

326. *Tender Is the Night: A Romance.*
- London: Chatto & Windus, 1934.
- Dust jacket: "2/6" label.

NOTES: Bruccoli A15.2.a. 1936 remainder copy from first English edition, first printing.
- PS3511.I9 T4 1936

327. *Tender Is the Night.*
- London: Grey Walls, [1948].
- Dust jacket.

NOTES: Bruccoli A15.4. Second English edition.
- PS3511.I9 T4 1948

328. *Tender Is the Night.*
- New York: Bantam Books, [1951], #A867.
- Wrappers.
NOTES: Bruccoli A15.5. A Bantam Giant. Third American edition, first printing.
- PS3511.I9 T4 1951 C.1

329. *Tender Is the Night.*
- New York: Bantam Books, [1951], #A867.
- Wrappers.
NOTES: Bruccoli A15.5. A Bantam Giant. Third American edition, third printing.
- PS3511.I9 T4 1951 C.2

330. *Tender Is the Night.*
- New York: Charles Scribner's Sons, [1960], #SL2.
- Rebound (possible library binding).
NOTES: Bruccoli A15.6.a. Scribner Library. "A-1.60[C]".
- PS3511.I9 T4 1960

331. *Tender Is the Night.*
- New York: Charles Scribner's Sons, [1961], #SL2.
- Wrappers.
NOTES: Bruccoli A15.6.a. Scribner Library. "E-8.61[C]".
- PS3511.I9 T4 1961

332. *Tender Is the Night.*
- New York: Charles Scribner's Sons, [1963], #SL2.
- Wrappers.
NOTES: Bruccoli A15.6.a. Scribner Library. "H-10.63[Col]".
- PS3511.I9 T4 1963

333. *Tender Is the Night.*
- New York: Charles Scribner's Sons, [1964], #SL2.
- Wrappers.
NOTES: Bruccoli A15.6.a. Scribner Library. "I-9.64[Col]".
- PS3511.I9 T4 1964

334. *Tender Is the Night.*
- New York: Charles Scribner's Sons, 1977.
- Dust jacket.
NOTES: Bruccoli A15.6.b. Hudson River Editions. First printing.
- PS3511.I9 T4 1977

335. *Tender Is the Night.*
- New York: Bantam Books, [1962], #S2385/5.
- Wrappers.
NOTES: Bruccoli A15.7. Fifth American edition, first printing.
"PRINTED IN CANADA".
- PS3511.I9 T4 1962b

336. *Tender Is the Night.*
- New York: Bantam Books, [1962], #S2385/5.
- Wrappers.

NOTES: Bruccoli A15.7. Fifth American edition, second printing.
- PS3511.I9 T4 1962c

337. *Tender Is the Night.*
- New York: Bantam Books, [1962], #S2385/5.
- Wrappers.

NOTES: Bruccoli A15.7. Fifth American edition, third printing.
- PS3511.I9 T4 1962

338. *Tender Is the Night.*
- New York: Bantam Books, [1962], #S2385/5.
- Wrappers.

NOTES: Bruccoli A15.7. Fifth American edition, fifth printing.
- PS3511.I9 T4 1962f

339. *Tender Is the Night.*
- Garden City, N.Y.: International Collectors Library, [1980?].

NOTES: Bruccoli A15.8.b.
- PS3511.I9 T4 1980

340. *Tender Is the Night.*
- New York: Charles Scribner's Sons, [1982].
- Wrappers.

NOTES: Bruccoli A15.9.a. Scribner Classics. Fifth printing.
- PS3511.I9 T4 1982

341. *Tender Is the Night.*
- Introduction by Charles Scribner III.
- New York: Charles Scribner's Sons, [1985].
- Wrappers.

NOTES: Bruccoli A15.9.b. Showtime Television tie-in edition. First printing.
- PS3511.I9 T4 1985

342. *Tender Is the Night.*
- New York: Collier Books, [1986].
- Wrappers.

NOTES: Bruccoli A15.9.a. First Scribner Classic/Collier Edition 1986.
- PS3511.I9 T4 1986

343. *Tender Is the Night.*
- With an Introduction by Charles Scribner III and Illustrations by Fred Meyer.
- New York: Limited Editions Club, [1982].
- Slipcase.

NOTES: Bruccoli A15.10. Number 1494 of 2000 Copies. Signed by Meyer and Scribner.

Books and Collections 57

Laid in: *The Monthly Letters of the Limited Editions Club,* #524.
- PS3511.I9 T4 1982

344. *Tender Is the Night: A Romance.*
- Editorial Note and List of Variants by Arnold Goldman.
- [Harmondsworth, England]: Penguin, [1982].
- Wrappers.

NOTES: Bruccoli A15.11. Inscribed by Goldman to MJB.
- PS3511.I9 T4 1982b

345. *Tender Is the Night.*
- Moscow: Raduga Publishers, 1983.
- Dust jacket.

NOTES: Bruccoli A15.12. English-language Russian edition. With Russian introduction, explanatory notes, and bibliography.
- PS3511.I9 T4 1983

346. *Tender Is the Night: A Romance.*
- [Ringwood, Victoria]: Penguin Books, [1985].
- Wrappers.

NOTES: Sixth printing of 1982 Penguin edition. Tie-in for BBC movie.
- PS3511.I9 T4 1985b

347. *Tender Is the Night: A Romance.*
- [London]: Penguin Books, [1986].
- Wrappers.

NOTES: Annotated on p. i by Ray Bradbury: "PARIS AGAIN! MAY 24, 1993". Inscribed on inside cover: "READ WHILE CROSSING PARIS MAY, 1993— AND NOW GIVEN TO MATTHEW BRUCCOLI WITH ADMIRATION RAY BRADBURY MAY, 2002."
Laid in: TLS from Bradbury to MJB, 8 May 2002.
- PS3511.I9 T4 1986b

348. *Tender Is the Night: A Romance.*
- Introduction by Charles Scribner III.
- New York: Collier Books/Macmillan, [1986].
- Wrappers.

NOTES: First printing. First Scribner Classic/Collier Edition 1986.
- PS3511.I9 T4 1986

349. *Tender Is the Night: A Romance.*
- Introduction by Dennis Potter; Lithographs by Glynn Boyd Harte.
- London: Folio Society, 1987.
- Slipcase.

NOTES: Bruccoli A15.13.a.
- PS3511.I9 T4 1987

350. *Tender Is the Night.*
- [Ware, England]: Wordsworth Classics, [1995].

- Wrappers.
- PS3511.I9 T4 1995

351. *Tender Is the Night.*
- New York: Simon & Schuster, [1995].
- Wrappers.
NOTES: First printing. First Scribner Paperback Fiction Edition 1995.
- PS3511.I9 T4 1995

352. *Tender Is the Night: A Romance.*
- Text Established by Matthew J. Bruccoli.
- London: Samuel Johnson, 1995.
- Wrappers, spiral-bound.
NOTES: "This volume reproduces the editor's marked copy of the first printing of *Tender Is the Night,* providing the emendations required for a critical edition."
    Laid in: Keepsake distributed at The Englisches Seminar, Westfäliche Wilhelms-Universität, Münster, 1994.
- PS3511.I9 T4 1995

353. *Tender Is the Night.*
- New York: Charles Scribner's Sons, 1996.
- Dust jacket.
NOTES: First printing.
- PS3511.I9 T4 1996

354. *Tender Is the Night: A Romance.*
- Text Established by Matthew J. Bruccoli.
- London: J. M. Dent, 1996.
- Wrappers.
NOTES: Everyman Library; Centennial Edition.
    Annotated on p. i: "MJB 13 Aug 96 Published in U.K. because <u>TITN</u> is in public domain there. Not for sale in USA. This edition is right because the Lanahans and Brown could not tamper with it. Everyman people were splendid."
- PS3511.I9 T4 1996

355. *Tender Is the Night.*
- London: Penguin Books, 1997.
- Wrappers.
NOTES: Second printing. Revised edition, unidentified as such.
- PS3511.I9 T4 1997

356. *Tender Is the Night: A Romance.*
- Edited by Arnold Goldman; With an Introduction and Notes by Richard Godden.
- [London]: Penguin Books, [1998].
- Wrappers.

NOTES: Penguin Twentieth-Century Classics.
Annotated on p. 1 by MJB: "This is a travesty."
- PS3511.I9 T4 1998

Tender Is the Night / Revised Edition (1951)

357. *Tender Is the Night: A Romance.*
- "With the Author's Final Revisions"; Preface by Malcolm Cowley.
- New York: Charles Scribner's Sons, 1951.
- Dust jacket.
NOTES: Bruccoli A16.1.a$_1$. First revised edition, first printing, first state.
Laid in: Review slip and errata sheet.
- PS3511.I9 T4 1951c

358. *Tender Is the Night: A Romance.*
- "With the Author's Final Revisions"; Preface by Malcolm Cowley.
- New York: Charles Scribner's Sons, 1951.
- Dust jacket.
NOTES: Bruccoli A16.1.a$_2$. First revised edition, first printing, second state. Three leaves were canceled in Cowley's introduction to correct four errors.
- PS3511.I9 T4 1951d

359. *Tender Is the Night: A Romance.*
- "With the Author's Final Revisions"; Preface by Malcolm Cowley.
- New York: Charles Scribner's Sons, 1956.
- Dust jacket.
NOTES: Bruccoli A16.1.d.
- PS3511.I9 T4 1956

360. *Tender Is the Night: A Romance.*
- "With the Author's Final Revisions"; Preface by Malcolm Cowley.
- New York: Charles Scribner's Sons, [1959].
- Dust jacket.
NOTES: Bruccoli A16.1.e. "J-9.59[MH]".
- PS3511.I9 T4 1959

361. *Tender Is the Night: A Romance.*
- "With the Author's Final Revisions"; Preface by Malcolm Cowley.
- New York: Charles Scribner's Sons, [1970], #SL2.
- Wrappers.
NOTES: Bruccoli A16.1.f. "O-5.70[MC]".
This printing in the Scribner Library Series inadvertently used the plates of the Cowley edition, as did the two subsequent printings.
Laid in: TLS, 30 March 1973, from Philip C. Coleman of Scribners to MJB concerning printings of *Tender Is the Night*.
- PS3511.I9 T4 1970

362. *Tender Is the Night.*
- "With the Author's Final Revisions"; Preface by Malcolm Cowley.
- London: Grey Walls Press, [1953].
- Dust jacket.

NOTES: Bruccoli A16.2.a. First revised English edition, first printing.
- PS3511.I9 T4 1953 C.1
- Two additional copies.

363. *Tender Is the Night: A Romance.*
- "With the Author's Final Revision"; Preface by Malcolm Cowley.
- [Harmondsworth, England]: Penguin Books, [1955], #906.
- Wrappers.

NOTES: Bruccoli A16.3. Second English edition.
- PS3511.I9 T4 1955

364. *Tender Is the Night: A Romance.*
- "With the Author's Final Revision"; Preface by Malcolm Cowley.
- [Harmondsworth, England]: Penguin Books, [1958], #906.
- Wrappers.

NOTES: Bruccoli A16.3. Second English edition, second printing.
- PS3511.I9 T4 1958

365. *Tender Is the Night: A Romance.*
- "With the Author's Final Revision"; Preface by Malcolm Cowley.
- [Harmondsworth, England]: Penguin Books, [1961], #906.
- Wrappers.

NOTES: Bruccoli A16.3. Penguin Modern Classics. Second English edition, third printing.
- PS3511.I9 T4 1961

366. *Tender Is the Night: A Romance.*
- "With the Author's Final Revision"; Preface by Malcolm Cowley.
- [Harmondsworth, England]: Penguin Books, [1966], #906.
- Wrappers: "80¢" label.

NOTES: Bruccoli A16.3. Penguin Modern Classics. Second English edition, sixth printing.
- PS3511.I9 T4 1966

367. *Tender Is the Night: A Romance.*
- "With the Author's Final Revision"; Preface by Malcolm Cowley.
- [Harmondsworth, England]: Penguin Books, [1970], #906.
- Wrappers.

NOTES: Bruccoli A16.3. Second English edition, eighth printing.
- PS3511.I9 T4 1970b

368. *Tender Is the Night: A Romance.*
- "With the Author's Final Revision"; Preface by Malcolm Cowley.
- [Harmondsworth, England]: Penguin Books, [1974], #906.

- Wrappers.

NOTES: Bruccoli A16.3. Second English edition, twelfth printing.
- PS3511.I9 T4 1974

369. *Tender Is the Night.*
- "With the Author's Final Revision"; Preface by Malcolm Cowley.
- [Harmondsworth, England]: Penguin Books, [1978], #906.
- Wrappers.

NOTES: Bruccoli A16.3. Fifteenth printing.
From the library of David Garnett, with his library label.
Annotated by Garnett on title page transcribing an original inscription by FSF in the copy of *Tender Is the Night* intended for Garnett.
- PS3511.I9 T4 1978

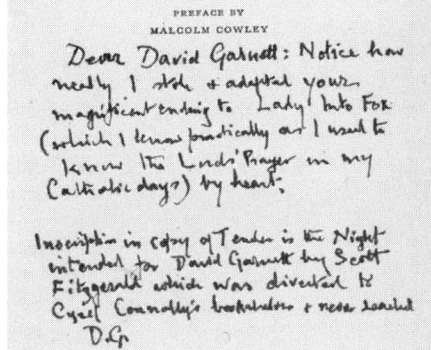

370. *Tender Is the Night.*
- [London]: Penguin, [1999].
- Wrappers.

NOTES: Revised edition. First printing.
"This is the 'author's final version' — but not identified. MJB".
- PS3511.I9 T4 1999 C.1

371. *Tender Is the Night.*
- [London]: Penguin, [1999?].
- Wrappers.

NOTES: Revised edition. Sixth printing.
- PS3511.I9 T4 1999 C.2

Taps at Reveille (1935)

372. *Taps at Reveille.*
- New York: Charles Scribner's Sons, 1935.
- Dust jacket.

NOTES: Bruccoli A18.1.a₁. First edition, only printing, first state.
Review copy with publisher's slip laid in.
- PS3511.I9 T34 1935 C.2

373. *Taps at Reveille.*
- New York: Charles Scribner's Sons, 1935.

373.

NOTES: Bruccoli A18.1.a₁. First edition, only printing, first state.
Inscribed by FSF to Anthony Buttitta.
Revised in pencil by FSF on pp. 350, 351, 384.
- PS3511.I9 T34 1935

374. *Taps at Reveille.*
    - New York: Charles Scribner's Sons, 1935.
    NOTES: Bruccoli A18.1.a₁. First edition, only printing, first state.
    Inscribed by FSF to Louise Cooder.
    - PS3511.I9 T34 1935 C.2

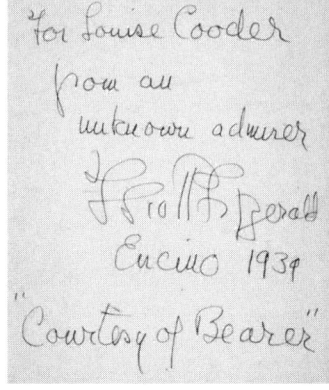

375. *Taps at Reveille.*
    - New York: Charles Scribner's Sons, 1935.
    - Dust jacket.
    NOTES: Bruccoli A18.1.a₁. First edition, only printing, first state.
    Inscribed by FSF to Harry Nardini.
    - PS3511.I9 T34 1935 C.4

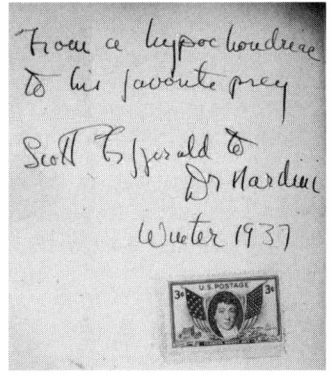

376. *Taps at Reveille.*
    - New York: Charles Scribner's Sons, 1935.
    NOTES: Bruccoli A18.1.a₂. First edition, only printing, second state.
    Pages 349–52 cancelled, making 3 revisions in the text of "One Interne."
    Inscribed by FSF to Annah Williamson.
    - PS3511.I9 T34 1935b C.1

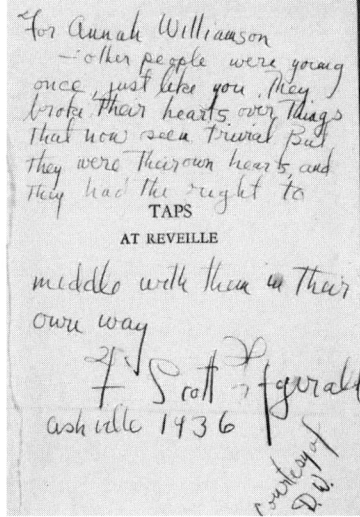

377. *Taps at Reveille.*
- New York: Charles Scribner's Sons, 1935.
  NOTES: Bruccoli A18.1.a$_2$. First edition, only printing, second state. Inscribed to Carroll Davis on free front endpaper; re-inscribed on front flyleaf by Scottie Fitzgerald to MJB.
- On deposit.

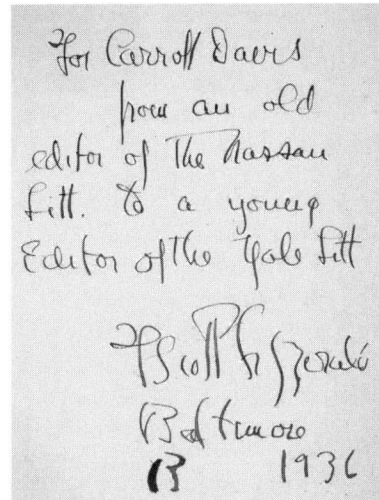

378. *Taps at Reveille.*
- New York: Charles Scribner's Sons, 1935.
- Dust jacket.
  NOTES: Bruccoli A18.1.a$_2$. First edition, only printing, second state.
- PS3511.I9 T34 1935b C.2

379. *Taps at Reveille.*
- New York: Charles Scribner's Sons, 1935.
  NOTES: Bruccoli A18.1.a$_2$. First edition, only printing, second state. Cancel at pp. 351–52 incorrectly tipped in: pp. 352–351.
- PS3511.I9 T34 1935b C.3

380. *Taps at Reveille.*
- New York: Charles Scribner's Sons, 1935.
  NOTES: Bruccoli A18.1.a$_2$. First edition, only printing, second state. Inscribed by FSF to Paula Post.
- PS3511.I9 T34 1935b C.4

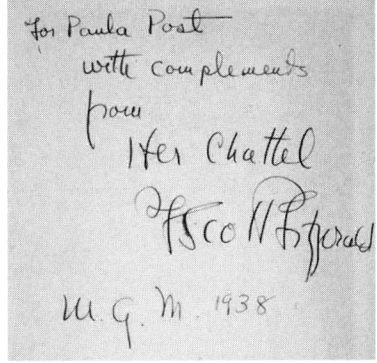

381. *Taps at Reveille.*
- New York: Charles Scribner's Sons, [1960].
- Dust jacket.
  NOTES: Bruccoli A18.2.a. Second edition. Review copy with publisher's slip laid in.
- PS3511.I9 T34 1960

382. *Taps at Reveille.*
- New York: Charles Scribner's Sons, 1971, #SL274.
- Wrappers.

NOTES: Bruccoli A18.2.b. Contemporary Classics/Scribner Library. "A-9.71[M]."
- PS3511.I9 T3 1971

383. *Taps at Reveille.*
- New York: Charles Scribner's Sons, [1971?], #SL274.
- Wrappers.

NOTES: Bruccoli A18.2.b. Contemporary Classics/Scribner Library. "3 . . . 19 C/P 20 . . . 4".
- PS3511.I9 T3 1963

384. *Taps at Reveille.*
- New York: Charles Scribner's Sons, [1976].

NOTES: Bruccoli A18.2.c. Hudson River Edition.
- PS3511.I9 T3 1976

The Last Tycoon (1941); The Love of the Last Tycoon (1993)

385. *The Last Tycoon: An Unfinished Novel.*
- Edited with a Foreword by Edmund Wilson; with *The Great Gatsby* and Selected Stories.
- New York: Charles Scribner's Sons, 1941.
- Dust jacket.

NOTES: Bruccoli A19.1.a. First edition, first printing.
Review copy with publisher's slip laid in. Also "With Compliments of Publishers" card.
- PS3511.I9 L3 1941

386. *The Last Tycoon: An Unfinished Novel.*
- Edited with a Foreword by Edmund Wilson; with *The Great Gatsby* and Selected Stories.
- New York: Charles Scribner's Sons, 1941.
- Dust jacket.

NOTES: Bruccoli A19.1.a. First edition, first printing.
Ober Agency office file copy. Label: "HAROLD OBER" on free front endpaper.
- PS3511.I9 L3 1941 C.2

387. *The Last Tycoon: An Unfinished Novel.*
- Edited with a Foreword by Edmund Wilson; with *The Great Gatsby* and Selected Stories.
- New York: Charles Scribner's Sons, 1945.

- Dust jacket.
NOTES: Bruccoli A19.1.c. First edition, third printing.
- PS3511.I9 L3 1945

388. *The Last Tycoon: An Unfinished Novel.*
- Edited with a Foreword by Edmund Wilson; with *The Great Gatsby* and Selected Stories.
- New York: Charles Scribner's Sons, 1948.
NOTES: Bruccoli A19.1.e. First edition, fifth printing.
- PS3511.I9 L3 1948

389. *The Last Tycoon: An Unfinished Novel.*
- Edited with a Foreword by Edmund Wilson; with *The Great Gatsby.*
- New York: Charles Scribner's Sons, 1951.
- Dust jacket.
NOTES: Bruccoli A19.1.f.
- PS3511.I9 L3 1951

390. *The Last Tycoon: An Unfinished Novel.*
- Edited with a Foreword by Edmund Wilson.
- New York: Charles Scribner's Sons, [1959].
- Dust jacket.
NOTES: Bruccoli A19.1.i. "B-4.59 [MH]".
- PS3511.I9 L3 1959

391. *The Last Tycoon: An Unfinished Novel.*
- Edited with a Foreword by Edmund Wilson.
- New York: Charles Scribner's Sons, n.d.
- Taipei: Big Wave, [1975?].
- Wrappers.
NOTES: Bruccoli A19.1.n. Pirated reprint.
- PS3511.I9 L3 1975

392. *The Last Tycoon: An Unfinished Novel.*
- Edited with a Foreword by Edmund Wilson.
- New York: Charles Scribner's Sons, [1977].
- Dust jacket.
NOTES: Bruccoli A19.1.o. Hudson River Editions.
- PS3511.I9 L3 1977

393. *The Last Tycoon: An Unfinished Novel.*
- Edited with a Foreword by Edmund Wilson.
- New York: Charles Scribner's Sons, [1983?].
- Wrappers.
NOTES: Bruccoli A19.1.p. Scribner Classics.
- PS3511.I9 L3 1983

394. *The Last Tycoon: An Unfinished Novel.*
- Edited with a Foreword by Edmund Wilson.
- New York: Collier Books/Macmillan, [1986].
- Wrappers.
NOTES: First Scribner Classic/Collier Edition 1986.
- PS3511.I9 L3 1986

395. *The Last Tycoon: An Unfinished Novel.*
- Edited with a Foreword by Edmund Wilson.
- London: Grey Walls, [1949].
- Dust jacket.
NOTES: Bruccoli A19.2.a. First English edition, first printing.
- PS3511.I9 L3 1949

396. *The Last Tycoon: An Unfinished Novel.*
- Edited with a Foreword by Edmund Wilson.
- London: Grey Walls, [1949].
- Dust jacket.
NOTES: Bruccoli A19.2.b. First English edition, second printing.
- PS3511.I9 L3 1949b

397. *The Last Tycoon.*
- Edited with a Foreword by Edmund Wilson.
- [Harmondsworth, England]: Penguin Books, [1960], #1495.
- Wrappers.
NOTES: Bruccoli A19.4. First printing.
- PS3511.I9 L3 1960

398. *The Last Tycoon.*
- Edited with a Foreword by Edmund Wilson.
- [Harmondsworth, England]: Penguin Books, [1965], #1495.
- Wrappers.
NOTES: Bruccoli A19.4. Fourth printing.
- PS3511.I9 L3 1965 C.1

399. *The Last Tycoon.*
- Edited with a Foreword by Edmund Wilson.
- [Harmondsworth, England]: Penguin Books, [1965], #1495.
- Wrappers: 65c price label over original price on upper cover.
NOTES: Bruccoli A19.4. Fourth printing. Distributed in Australia.
- PS3511.I9 L3 1965 C.2

400. *The Last Tycoon.*
- Edited with a Foreword by Edmund Wilson.
- [Harmondsworth, England]: Penguin Books, [1968], #1495.
- Wrappers.

NOTES: Bruccoli A19.4. Fifth printing.
- PS3511.I9 L3 1968

401. *The Last Tycoon.*
- Edited with a Foreword by Edmund Wilson.
- [Harmondsworth, England]: Penguin, [1974].
- Wrappers.
NOTES: Bruccoli A19.4. "Sample Complete Copy"; "Proof Copy". Eighth printing.
- PS3511.I9 L3 1974

402. *The Last Tycoon.*
- Edited with a Foreword by Edmund Wilson.
- [Harmondsworth, England]: Penguin Books, [1977].
- Wrappers.
NOTES: Bruccoli A19.4. Tenth printing.
- PS3511.I9 L3 1977

403. *The Last Tycoon.*
- Edited with a Foreword by Edmund Wilson.
- [Harmondsworth, England]: Penguin Books, [1977].
- Wrappers.
NOTES: Bruccoli A19.4. Tenth printing. "Made and printed in Australia".
- PS3511.I9 L3 1977 C.2

404. *The Last Tycoon.*
- Edited with a Foreword by Edmund Wilson.
- New York: Bantam, [1976], #10419–5.
- Wrappers.
NOTES: Bruccoli A19.7. First printing.
- PS3511.I9 L3 1976

405. *The Last Tycoon: An Unfinished Novel.*
- Edited by Edmund Wilson.
- New York: Charles Scribner's Sons, 1990.
NOTES: Book-of-the-Month Club Edition.
- PS3511.I9 L3 1990

406. *The Love of The Last Tycoon: A Western.*
- Edited by Matthew J. Bruccoli.
- [Cambridge]: Cambridge University Press, [1993].
- Wrappers: "Advance uncorrected proofs"; dust jacket: "PROOF".
NOTES: "27 Oct 93 MJB".
- PS3511.I9 L3

407. *The Love of The Last Tycoon: A Western.*
- Edited by Matthew J. Bruccoli.
- [Cambridge]: Cambridge University Press, [1993].

NOTES: Typescript (and partial computer printout) and typeset copy with annotations.

Editorial matter only; does not include text.
- PS3511.I9 L29

408. *The Love of The Last Tycoon: A Western.*
- Edited by Matthew J. Bruccoli.
- [Cambridge; New York]: Cambridge University Press, [1993].
- Dust jacket.

NOTES: *The Cambridge Edition of the Works of F. Scott Fitzgerald.*
Review copy with publisher's slip laid in. MJB's signature on title page. Inscribed on p. i: "The Lanahans and Brown weren't able to damage this edition—but they tried. MJB".
- PS3511.I9 L3 1993

409. *The Love of The Last Tycoon: A Western.*
- Edited with Preface and Notes by Matthew J. Bruccoli.
- New York: Scribner Paperback Fiction, [1994].
- Wrappers.

NOTES: First Scribner Edition 1994.
Denunciation of cover art by MJB on cover.
- PS3511.I9 L3 1994 C.1

410. *The Love of The Last Tycoon: A Western.*
- Edited with Preface and Notes by Matthew J. Bruccoli.
- New York: Scribner Paperback Fiction, [1994].
- Wrappers.

NOTES: First Scribner Edition 1994.
Annotated by MJB on front cover: "I denounced this cover. MJB".
- PS3511.I9 L3 1994 C.2

411. *The Love of The Last Tycoon: A Western.*
- Edited and with an Introduction by Matthew J. Bruccoli.
- [London]: Little, Brown, [1994].
- Dust jacket.

NOTES: The Cambridge Edition. Publisher's complimentary copy.
- PS3511.I9 L3 1994b

412. *The Love of The Last Tycoon: A Western.*
- Edited and with an Introduction by Matthew J. Bruccoli.
- [London]: Abacus, [1995].
- Wrappers.

NOTES: The Cambridge Edition. Reprint of Little, Brown edition.
- PS3511.I9 L3 1995

413. *The Love of The Last Tycoon: A Western.*
- Edited by Matthew J. Bruccoli.

- Cambridge: Cambridge University Press, 1994.
- Dust jacket.
NOTES: "Reprinted 1994".
- PS3511.I9 L3 1994c

414. *The Last Tycoon: An Unfinished Novel.*
- Foreword by Edmund Wilson.
- New York: Book-of-the-Month Club, [2000].
- Dust jacket.
- PS3511.I9 L3 2000

415. "The Last Tycoon."
- Irwin Shaw.
- [Culver City, Calif.]: M-G-M, March 1966.
- Mimeograph in wrappers.
NOTES: Unproduced screenplay adaptation of *The Last Tycoon*. On front cover: "FIRST DRAFT SCREENPLAY". See Item 1227.
- PN1997.L378842 1966

The Crack-Up (1945)

416. *The Crack-Up.*
- With Other Uncollected Pieces, Note-books, and Unpublished Letters edited by Edmund Wilson; Together with Letters to Fitzgerald from Gertrude Stein, Edith Wharton, T. S. Eliot, Thomas Wolfe and John Dos Passos, and Essays and Poems by Paul Rosenfeld, Glenway Wescott, John Dos Passos, John Peale Bishop and Edmund Wilson.
- [New York: New Directions, 1945].
- Dust jacket.
NOTES: Bruccoli A20.1.a. First edition, first printing.
   Laid in: Two letters, 19 and 29 July 1960, from James Laughlin to MJB concerning publishing history of *The Crack-Up*.
   Laid in: Publisher's catalogue.
- PS3511.I9 C7 1945 C.1

417. *The Crack-Up.*
- [New York]: New Directions, [1945].
NOTES: Bruccoli A20.1.a. First edition, first printing.
   Laura Z. Hobson's annotated copy.
- PS3511.I9 C7 C.2

418. *The Crack-Up.*
- [New York]: New Directions, [1945].
NOTES: Bruccoli A20.1.a. First edition, first printing.
   Margaret Case Harriman's annotated copy.
- PS3511.I9 C7 C.4

419. *The Crack-Up.*
- [New York]: New Directions, [1945].
NOTES: Bruccoli A20.1.c. First edition, reprint.
With bookplate of Charles Marquis Warren and Anne Crawford Warren.
- PS3511.I9 C7 1945b C.2
- Three additional copies of undifferentiated reprints (without bookplate).

420. *The Crack-Up.*
- [New York]: New Directions, [1945].
- Dust jacket: "17/6" label on front flap.
NOTES: Bruccoli A20.1.d . "A New Directions Book."
British Empire issue of American printing with label facing title page.
Laid in: Letter from Lawrence D. Stewart to MJB about *Tender Is the Night* and *The Crack-Up,* 19 July 1960.
- PS3511.I9 C7 1947 C.1

421. *The Crack-Up.*
- [New York: New Directions, 1945].
NOTES: Bruccoli A20.1.d.
Rebound in red cloth from Boots Lending Library. Grommet at head of spine. "Boots Booklovers Library" label on front cover.
- PS3511.I9 C7 1947 C.2

422. *The Crack-Up.*
- [New York]: New Directions Paperbook, [1956], #54.
- Wrappers.
NOTES: Bruccoli A20.1.f. First printing.
- PS3511.I9 C7 1956

423. *The Crack-Up.*
- [New York]: New Directions Paperbook, [1956?], #54.
- Wrappers.
NOTES: Bruccoli A20.1.f. Fifth printing.
- PS3511.I9 C7 1956e

424. *The Crack-Up.*
- [New York]: New Directions Paperbook, [1956?], #54.
- Wrappers.
NOTES: Bruccoli A20.1.f. Sixth printing.
- PS3511.I9 C7 1956f

425. *The Crack-Up.*
- [New York]: New Directions Paperbook, [1956?], #54.
- Wrappers.
NOTES: Bruccoli A20.1.f. Seventh printing.
- PS3511.I9 C7 1956g

426. *The Crack-Up.*
- Edited by Hitoshi Miyata.
- Tokyo: Nan'un-do, [1958].
- Wrappers.

NOTES: Bruccoli A20.2. English-language Japanese edition. Notes in Japanese.
- PS3511.I9 C7 1958

427. *The Crack-Up with other Pieces and Stories.*
- [Harmondsworth, England]: Penguin, [1965], #2326.
- Wrappers: "3'6".

NOTES: Bruccoli A20.3.a. First English edition, first printing.
- PS3511.I9 C7 1965

428. *The Crack-Up with other Pieces and Stories.*
- [Harmondsworth, England]: Penguin, [1965], #2326.
- Wrappers: "5'6".

NOTES: Bruccoli A20.3.a, Note.
- PS3511.I9 C7 1965 C.2

429. *The Crack-Up with other Pieces and Stories.*
- [Harmondsworth, England]: Penguin, [1968], #2326.
- Wrappers.

NOTES: Bruccoli A20.3.b.
- PS3511.I9 C7 1968

430. *The Crack-Up with other Pieces and Stories.*
- [Harmondsworth, England]: Penguin, [1974].
- Wrappers.

NOTES: Bruccoli A20.3.c. Fifth printing.
- PS3511.I9 C7 1974

431. *The Crack-Up with other Pieces and Stories.*
- [Harmondsworth, England]: Penguin, [1983].
- Wrappers.

NOTES: Bruccoli A20.3.c. Tenth printing.
- PS3511.I9 C7 1983

432. *The Jazz Age.*
- Introduction by E. L. Doctorow.
- [New York]: New Directions, [1996], #NDP830.
- Wrappers. Spiral-bound.

NOTES: A New Directions Bibelot. Review copy with promotional material laid in.
- PS3511.I9 J39 1996b

The Stories of F. Scott Fitzgerald (1951)

433. *The Stories of F. Scott Fitzgerald.*
     - A Selection of 28 Stories with an Introduction by Malcolm Cowley.
     - New York: Charles Scribner's Sons, 1951.
     - Dust jacket.
     NOTES: Bruccoli A21.1.a. First edition, first printing.
     > On free front endpaper: "Malcolm Cowley Contains eleven previously uncollected stories. My name is misspelled on spine. M.C."
     - PS3511.I9 A6 1951b
     - Another copy with corrected spine (without annotation).

434. *The Stories of F. Scott Fitzgerald.*
     - A Selection of 28 Stories with an Introduction by Malcolm Cowley.
     - New York: Charles Scribner's Sons, [1954].
     - Dust jacket.
     NOTES: Bruccoli A21.1.f. Book Club Edition.
     - PS3511.I9 A6 1954b

435. *The Stories of F. Scott Fitzgerald.*
     - A Selection of 28 Stories with an Introduction by Malcolm Cowley.
     - New York: Charles Scribner's Sons, [1959].
     - Dust jacket.
     NOTES: Bruccoli A21.1.g. First edition, seventh printing. "H-7.59 [H]".
     - PS3511.I9 A6 1959

436. *The Stories of F. Scott Fitzgerald.*
     - A Selection of 28 Stories with an Introduction by Malcolm Cowley.
     - New York: Charles Scribner's Sons, [1966], #SL135.
     - Wrappers.
     NOTES: Bruccoli A21.1.j. Scribner Library. "A-6.66 [Col]".
     - PS3511.I9 A6 1966

437. *The Stories of F. Scott Fitzgerald.*
     - A Selection with Notes by Malcolm Cowley; Illustrated by John Collier.
     - Franklin Center, Penn.: The Franklin Library, 1977.
     - Slipcase with *Notes from the Editors* inserted.
     - PS3511.I9 A6 1977

438. *The Stories of F. Scott Fitzgerald.*
     - A Selection of 28 Stories with an Introduction by Malcolm Cowley.
     - New York: Charles Scribner's Sons, [1983].
     - Wrappers.
     NOTES: Bruccoli 21.1.m. Scribner Classics.
     - PS3511.I9 A6 1983

439. *The Stories of F. Scott Fitzgerald.*
   - A Selection of 28 Stories with an Introduction by Malcolm Cowley.
   - New York: Collier Books, [1986].
   - Wrappers: rack size.
   NOTES: "First Scribner Classic/Collier Edition, 1986".
   - PS3511.I9 A6 1986

Afternoon of an Author (1957)

440. *Afternoon of an Author: A Selection of Uncollected Stories and Essays.*
   - With an Introduction and Notes by Arthur Mizener.
   - Princeton, N.J.: Princeton University Library, 1957.
   - Dust jacket.
   NOTES: Bruccoli A22.1.a. First edition, first printing. Laid in: Prospectuses.
   - PS3511.I9 A6 1957

441. *Afternoon of an Author: A Selection of Uncollected Stories and Essays.*
   - With an Introduction and Notes by Arthur Mizener.
   - New York: Charles Scribner's Sons, [1958].
   - Dust jacket.
   NOTES: Bruccoli A22.1.b. Second printing. "A.2–58[MH]".
   With bookplate of Charles Marquis Warren and Anne Crawford Warren.
   - PS3511.I9 A6 1958
   - Another copy in dust jacket (without bookplate).

442. *Afternoon of an Author: A Selection of Uncollected Stories and Essays.*
   - With an Introduction and Notes by Arthur Mizener.
   - New York: Charles Scribner's Sons, [1972], #SL322.
   - Wrappers.
   NOTES: Bruccoli A22.1.c. The Scribner Library. "A-1.72[M]".
   - PS3511.I9 A6 1972

443. *Afternoon of an Author: A Selection of Uncollected Stories and Essays.*
   - With an Introduction and Notes by Arthur Mizener.
   - New York: Charles Scribner's Sons, [1986].
   - Dust jacket.
   NOTES: Bruccoli A22.1.c. Reprint.
   - PS3511.I9 A6 1986c C.1

444. *Afternoon of an Author: A Selection of Uncollected Stories and Essays.*
   - With an Introduction and Notes by Arthur Mizener.
   - New York: Charles Scribner's Sons, [1986], #SL332.
   - Wrappers.
   NOTES: Bruccoli A22.1.c. Reprint.
   - PS3511.I9 A6 1986c C.2

445. *Afternoon of an Author: A Selection of Uncollected Stories and Essays.*
- With an Introduction and Notes by Arthur Mizener.
- New York: Charles Scribner's Sons, [1981].
- Dust jacket.

NOTES: Bruccoli A22.1.d. Hudson River Editions, first printing.
- PS3511.I9 A6 1981

446. *Afternoon of an Author: A Selection of Uncollected Stories and Essays.*
- With an Introduction and Notes by Arthur Mizener.
- London: Bodley Head, [1958].
- Wrappers. Printed paper label on front cover.

NOTES: Published as Bruccoli A22.2. Proof copy.
- PS3511.I9 A6 1958b

447. *Afternoon of an Author: A Selection of Uncollected Stories and Essays.*
- With an Introduction and Notes by Arthur Mizener.
- London: Bodley Head, [1958].
- Dust jacket.

NOTES: Bruccoli A22.2. First English edition, first printing.
- PS3511.I9 A6 1958c
- Another copy in dust jacket.

448. *Afternoon of an Author: A Selection of Uncollected Stories and Essays.*
- With an Introduction and Notes by Arthur Mizener.
- New York: Collier Books/Macmillan, [1987].
- Wrappers.

NOTES: "First Scribner Classic/Collier Edition 1987". Reprint.
- PS3511.I9 A6 1987

The Pat Hobby Stories (1962)

449. *The Pat Hobby Stories.*
- With an Introduction by Arnold Gingrich.
- New York: Charles Scribner's Sons, [1962].
- Dust jacket.

NOTES: Bruccoli A23.1.a. First edition, first printing. "A-6.62[V]".
  Laid in: letter from Edward White, director of Scribners publicity and promotion, to MJB.
- PS3511.I9 P3 C.1

450. *The Pat Hobby Stories.*
- With an Introduction by Arnold Gingrich.
- New York: Charles Scribner's Sons, [1962].
- Dust jacket.

NOTES: Bruccoli A23.1.a. First edition, first printing.

Inscribed by Gingrich to producer/director Fletcher Markle; with Markle's bookplate.
- PS3511.I9 P3 C.2

451. *The Pat Hobby Stories.*
    - With an Introduction by Arnold Gingrich.
    - New York: Charles Scribner's Sons, [1969].
    - Dust jacket.
    NOTES: Bruccoli A23.1.d. First edition, fourth printing. "D-11.69[V]".
    - PS3511.I9 P3 1969

452. *The Pat Hobby Stories.*
    - With an Introduction by Arnold Gingrich.
    - New York: Charles Scribner's Sons, [1970].
    - Wrappers.
    NOTES: Bruccoli A23.1.e. First edition, reprint. "A-6.70[c]".
    - PS3511.I9 P3 1970

453. *The Pat Hobby Stories.*
    - With an Introduction by Arnold Gingrich.
    - [Harmondsworth, England]: Penguin Books, [1967], #2589.
    - Wrappers.
    NOTES: Bruccoli A23.2. First English edition, first printing.
    The Stories of F. Scott Fitzgerald, Vol. 3.
    - PS3511.I9 P3 1967 C.1

454. *The Pat Hobby Stories.*
    - With an Introduction by Arnold Gingrich.
    - [Harmondsworth, England]: Penguin Books, [1967], #2589.
    - Wrappers: "80c".
    NOTES: Bruccoli A23.2, Note. First English edition, first printing.
    The Stories of F. Scott Fitzgerald; Vol. 3.
    Printed for Australian distribution.
    - PS3511.I9 P3 1967 C.2

455. *The Pat Hobby Stories.*
    - With an Introduction by Arnold Gingrich.
    - [Harmondsworth, England]: Penguin Books, [1974], #2589.
    - Wrappers.
    NOTES: Bruccoli A23.2.b. Second English printing.
    The Stories of F. Scott Fitzgerald, Vol. 3.
    - PS3511.I9 P3 1974

456. *The Pat Hobby Stories.*
    - With an Introduction by Arnold Gingrich.
    - [Harmondsworth, England]: Penguin Books, [1983].
    - Wrappers.

76 Books and Collections

   NOTES: Bruccoli A23.2.b. Fifth printing.
   The Stories of F. Scott Fitzgerald; Vol. 3.
   - PS3511.I9 P3 1983

457. *The Pat Hobby Stories.*
   - Edited with Notes by T. Koyama & K. Hosokoshi.
   - Tokyo: Sansyusya, [1974].
   - Wrappers.
   NOTES: Bruccoli A23.3. English-language Japanese edition. Notes and introduction in Japanese.
   - PS3511.I9 P3 1974b

458. *The Pat Hobby Stories.*
   - With an Introduction by Arnold Gingrich.
   - New York: Collier Books/Macmillan, [1988].
   - Wrappers.
   NOTES: "First Scribner Classic/Collier Edition 1988".
   - PS3511.I9 P3 1988

459. *Pat Hobby and Orson Welles and Other Short Stories.*
   - Choix et Annotation par Martine Skopan.
   - [Paris]: Livre de Poche, [1988].
   - Wrappers.
   NOTES: English-language French edition. Notes and glossary in French.
   - PS3511.I9 P3 1988b

The Letters of F. Scott Fitzgerald (1963)

460. *The Letters of F. Scott Fitzgerald.*
   - Edited by Andrew Turnbull.
   - New York: Charles Scribner's Sons, [1963].
   - Galley proofs.
   NOTES: Published as Bruccoli A24.1.d.
       Laid in: TLS, 16 July 1963, from Andrew Turnbull to MJB.
   - PS3511.I9 Z539

461. *The Letters of F. Scott Fitzgerald.*
   - Edited by Andrew Turnbull.
   - New York: Charles Scribner's Sons, [1963].
   - Dust jacket.
   NOTES: Bruccoli A24.1.a. First edition, first printing. "A-9.63[V]".
       Review copy with publisher's slip laid in.
   - PS3511.I9 Z54

462. *The Letters of F. Scott Fitzgerald.*
   - Edited by Andrew Turnbull.
   - New York: Charles Scribner's Sons, [1963].

- Dust jacket.
NOTES: Bruccoli A24.1.a. First edition, second printing. "B-10.63[V]".
- PS3511.I9 Z54 1963c

463. *The Letters of F. Scott Fitzgerald.*
- Edited by Andrew Turnbull.
- London: Bodley Head, 1964.
- Wrappers: "UNCORRECTED PROOF COPY".
NOTES: Published as Bruccoli A24.1.d.
- PS3511.I9 Z54 1964b

464. *The Letters of F. Scott Fitzgerald.*
- Edited by Andrew Turnbull.
- London: Bodley Head, [1964].
- Dust jacket.
NOTES: Bruccoli A24.1.d. First edition, first English printing. Laid in: TLS, 8 June 1964, from Christie's to MJB concerning the purported sale of a FSF letter included in this volume. See p. 190.
- PS3511.I9 Z54 1964

465. *The Letters of F. Scott Fitzgerald.*
- Edited and with an Introduction by Andrew Turnbull.
- [New York: Dell], 1965, #4745.
- Wrappers.
NOTES: Bruccoli A24.1.e. A Delta Book.
- PS3511.I9 Z54 1965

466. *The Letters of F. Scott Fitzgerald.*
- Edited by Andrew Turnbull.
- New York: Charles Scribner's Sons, [1981?].
- Dust jacket.
NOTES: Bruccoli A24.1.f. Hudson River Editions. First printing.
- PS3511.I9 Z54 1981

467. *The Letters of F. Scott Fitzgerald.*
- Edited and with an Introduction by Andrew Turnbull.
- [New York: Dell, 1966], #4745.
- Wrappers.
NOTES: Bruccoli A24.2. Second edition. "First Laurel Edition".
- PS3511.I9 Z54 1966

468. *The Letters of F. Scott Fitzgerald.*
- Edited by Andrew Turnbull.
- [Harmondsworth, England]: Penguin Books, [1968], #2612.
- Wrappers.
NOTES: Bruccoli A24.3. Third edition.
- PS3511.I9 Z54 1968

469. *The Letters of F. Scott Fitzgerald.*
- Edited by Andrew Turnbull.
- New York: Bantam Books, [1971].
- Wrappers.
NOTES: Bruccoli A24.4. Fourth edition.
- PS3511.I9 Z54 1971

The Apprentice Fiction of F. Scott Fitzgerald (1965)

470. *The Apprentice Fiction of F. Scott Fitzgerald: 1909–1917.*
- Edited with an Introduction by John Kuehl.
- New Brunswick, N.J.: Rutgers University Press, [1965].
- Dust jacket.
NOTES: Bruccoli A25.1.a. First edition, first printing. Inscribed by Kuehl to MJB.
- PS3511.I9 Z5

471. *The Apprentice Fiction of F. Scott Fitzgerald: 1909–1917.*
- Edited with an Introduction by John Kuehl.
- New Brunswick, N.J.: Rutgers University Press, [1974].
- Wrappers.
NOTES: Bruccoli A25.1.b. Second printing.
- PS 3511.I9 Z5 C.2

Thoughtbook of Francis Scott Key Fitzgerald (1965)

472. *Thoughtbook of Francis Scott Key Fitzgerald.*
- With an Introduction by John R. Kuehl.
- Princeton, N.J.: Princeton University Library, 1965.
NOTES: Bruccoli A26. First edition, only printing. See Item 1073. Inscribed by Kuehl to MJB, 2 April 1965.
- PS3511.I9 T5 1965

Dearly Beloved (1969)

473. *Dearly Beloved: A Short Story.*
- With Graphics by Byron Burford, and a Note by Matthew J. Bruccoli.
- Iowa City: Windhover Press of the University of Iowa, 1969.
NOTES: Bruccoli A27. Number 4 of 30 copies signed by Byron Burford. Laid in: Prospectus.
- PS3511.I9 D4 1969 C.2

474. *Dearly Beloved: A Short Story.*
- With Graphics by Byron Burford, and a Note by Matthew J. Bruccoli.
- Iowa City: Windhover Press of the University of Iowa, 1969.
NOTES: Bruccoli A27. Number 184 of 300 numbered copies.
- PS3511.I9 D4 1969 C.1
- Another copy (#80).

Three Hours Between Planes (1970)

475. *Three Hours Between Planes.*
    - [Agincourt, Canada: Book Society of Canada, 1970], #116.
    - Folio.
    NOTES: Bruccoli A28. Book Society Searchlight.
        With: "Commentary," order form, and invoice.
    - PS3511.I9 T6 1970

F. Scott Fitzgerald in His Own Time: A Miscellany (1971)

476. *F. Scott Fitzgerald In His Own Time: A Miscellany.*
    - Edited by Matthew J. Bruccoli and Jackson R. Bryer.
    - Galley proofs; extensively corrected in red ink.
    NOTES: Published as Bruccoli A29.1.a
    - PS3511.I9 Z5589

477. *F. Scott Fitzgerald In His Own Time: A Miscellany.*
    - Edited by Matthew J. Bruccoli and Jackson R. Bryer.
    - Galley proofs. In manuscript: "Keep. Office Master Set"; corrected in pencil.
    NOTES: Published as Bruccoli A29.1.a.
    - PS3511.I9 Z5589

478. *F. Scott Fitzgerald In His Own Time: A Miscellany.*
    - Edited by Matthew J. Bruccoli and Jackson R. Bryer.
    - [Kent, Ohio]: Kent State University Press, [1971].
    NOTES: Bruccoli A29.1.a. First edition, first printing.
    - PS3511.I9 Z559

479. *F. Scott Fitzgerald In His Own Time: A Miscellany.*
    - Edited by Matthew J. Bruccoli and Jackson R. Bryer.
    - New York: Popular Library, [1974].
    - Wrappers.
    NOTES: Bruccoli A29.1.b. Second printing.
    - PS3511.I9 Z559 1976

Dear Scott/Dear Max (1971)

480. *Dear Scott/Dear Max: The Fitzgerald-Perkins Correspondence.*
    - Edited by John Kuehl and Jackson R. Bryer.
    - New York: Charles Scribner's Sons, [1971].
    - Page proof with editorial queries and annotated by MJB.
    NOTES: Published as Bruccoli A30.1.a.
    - PS3511.I9 Z556 1970

481. *Dear Scott/Dear Max: The Fitzgerald-Perkins Correspondence.*
- Edited by John Kuehl and Jackson R. Bryer.
- New York: Charles Scribner's Sons, [1971].
- Wrappers.
NOTES: Bruccoli A30.1.a. Advance review copy.
- PS3511.I9 Z556

482. *Dear Scott/Dear Max: The Fitzgerald-Perkins Correspondence.*
- Edited by John Kuehl and Jackson R. Bryer.
- New York: Charles Scribner's Sons, [1971].
- Dust jacket.
NOTES: Bruccoli A30.1.a.
  Laid in: Review slip.
  Annotated by MJB.
- PS3511.I9 Z556 1971 C.2

483. *Dear Scott/Dear Max: The Fitzgerald-Perkins Correspondence.*
- Edited by John Kuehl and Jackson R. Bryer.
- New York: Charles Scribner's Sons, [1971].
- Dust jacket.
NOTES: Bruccoli A30.1.a, Note 2. Canadian review copy of Scribners printing, distributed by John Wiley & Sons, Canada.
- PS3511.I9 Z556 1971 C.1

484. *Dear Scott/Dear Max: The Fitzgerald-Perkins Correspondence.*
- Edited by John Kuehl and Jackson R. Bryer.
- London: Cassell, [1973].
- Dust jacket.
NOTES: Bruccoli A30.1.b. First edition, first English printing.
- PS3511.I9 Z556 1973

485. *Dear Scott/Dear Max: The Fitzgerald-Perkins Correspondence.*
- Edited by John Kuehl and Jackson R. Bryer.
- New York: Charles Scribner's Sons, [1973], #SL460.
- Wrappers.
NOTES: Bruccoli A30.1.c. Lyceum Editions/Scribner Library.
- PS3511.I9 Z556 1973b

As Ever, Scott Fitz— (1971)

486. *As Ever, Scott Fitz—.*
- Letters Between F. Scott Fitzgerald and His Literary Agent Harold Ober, 1919–1940.
- Edited by Matthew J. Bruccoli with the Assistance of Jennifer McCabe Atkinson.
- Xeroxed proofs. 44 pages.

NOTES: Published as Bruccoli A31.1.a.
Edited by Scottie Fitzgerald, with undated ALS to MJB.
- On deposit.

487. *As Ever, Scott Fitz—*.
- Letters Between F. Scott Fitzgerald and His Literary Agent Harold Ober, 1919–1940.
- Edited by Matthew J. Bruccoli with the Assistance of Jennifer McCabe Atkinson.
- Revised galley proofs.

NOTES: Published as Bruccoli A31.1.a.
- PS3511.I9 Z495

488. *As Ever, Scott Fitz—*.
- Letters Between F. Scott Fitzgerald and His Literary Agent Harold Ober, 1919–1940.
- Edited by Matthew J. Bruccoli with the Assistance of Jennifer McCabe Atkinson; Foreword by Scottie Fitzgerald Smith.
- Philadelphia: Lippincott, 1971.
- Wrappers.

NOTES: Published as Bruccoli A31.1.a. Proof copy.
Signed by Jennifer McCabe Atkinson and MJB; inscribed by Scottie Fitzgerald.
- PS3511.I9 Z496 1971

489. *As Ever, Scott Fitz—*.
- Letters Between F. Scott Fitzgerald and His Literary Agent Harold Ober, 1919–1940.
- Edited by Matthew J. Bruccoli with the Assistance of Jennifer McCabe Atkinson. Foreword by Scottie Fitzgerald Smith
- Philadelphia: Lippincott, [1972].
- Dust jacket.

NOTES: Bruccoli A31.1.a. First edition, first printing.
Laid in: Promotional material, blurbs, and reviews. Also dummy cover and dust jacket.
Title page inscription by Scottie Fitzgerald.
- PS3511.I9 Z554

490. *As Ever, Scott Fitz—*.
- Letters Between F. Scott Fitzgerald and His Literary Agent, Harold Ober, 1919–1940.
- Edited by Matthew J. Bruccoli with the Assistance of Jennifer McCabe Atkinson.
- London: Woburn Press, 1973.
- Wrappers.

NOTES: Published as Bruccoli A31.1.b. Proof copy.
- PS3511.I9 Z554 1973

491. *As Ever, Scott Fitz—.*
- Letters Between F. Scott Fitzgerald and His Literary Agent, Harold Ober, 1919–1940.
- Edited by Matthew J. Bruccoli with the Assistance of Jennifer McCabe Atkinson.
- London: Woburn Press, 1973.
- Dust jacket.

NOTES: Bruccoli A31.1.b. First edition, first English printing. Title page inscription by Scottie Fitzgerald, 8 January 1974.
- PS3511.I9 Z554 1973b

492. [Scrapbook], 1972.
- Scottie Fitzgerald.

NOTES: Collects reviews and clippings for *As Ever, Scott Fitz—*.
- On deposit.

The Basil and Josephine Stories (1973)

493. *The Basil and Josephine Stories.*
- Edited with an Introduction by Jackson R. Bryer and John Kuehl.
- [New York: Charles Scribner's Sons, 1973].
- Wrappers.

NOTES: Review copy. Published as Bruccoli A32.1.a. Laid in: TLS, 6 June 1973, from Susan Richman, Scribners publicity director, to MJB.
- PS3511.I9 B33 1973

494. *The Basil and Josephine Stories.*
- Edited with an Introduction by Jackson R. Bryer and John Kuehl.
- [New York: Charles Scribner's Sons, 1973].
- Dust jacket.

NOTES: Bruccoli A32.1.a. First edition, first printing. Laid in: press release.
- PS3511.I9 B33

495. *The Basil and Josephine Stories.*
- Edited with an Introduction by Jackson R. Bryer and John Kuehl.
- New York: Popular Library, [1976].
- Wrappers.

NOTES: Bruccoli A32.2. Second edition.
- PS3511.I9 B33 1976

496. *The Basil and Josephine Stories.*
- Edited with an Introduction by Jackson R. Bryer and John Kuehl.
- New York: Collier Books/Macmillan, [1987].
- Wrappers.

NOTES: "First Scribner Classic/Collier Edition 1987".
- PS3511.I9 B33 1987

497. *The Basil and Josephine Stories.*
- Edited with an Introduction by Jackson R. Bryer and John Kuehl.
- [New York]: Simon & Schuster, [1997].
- Wrappers.

NOTES: "First Scribner Paperback Fiction edition 1997".
- PS3511.I9 B37 1997

F. Scott Fitzgerald's Ledger (1972)

498. *F. Scott Fitzgerald's Ledger, A Facsimile.*
- Introduction by Matthew J. Bruccoli.
- Washington, D.C.: NCR/Microcard Editions, [1972]. A Bruccoli Clark Book.
- Slipcase.

NOTES: Bruccoli A33. Number 42 of a first printing of 1000 copies.
MJB's copy with his signature and annotations concerning discussions with publisher Albert Diaz.
Laid in: Prospectus and xeroxed letter from Diaz to MJB concerning 500 spoiled copies, 25 April 1973.
- PS3511.I9 Z558 1972

499. TLS from James Dickey, Columbia, S.C, to Matthew J. Bruccoli, 19 September 1973.
- 1 page.

NOTES: Includes blurb for *F. Scott Fitzgerald's Ledger.*
- PS3554.I32 D63 1973

Bits of Paradise (1973)

500. *Bits of Paradise: 21 Uncollected Stories by F. Scott and Zelda Fitzgerald.*
- Selected by Scottie Fitzgerald Smith and Matthew J. Bruccoli; with a Foreword by Scottie Fitzgerald Smith.
- London: Bodley Head, [1973].
- Wrappers: "UNCORRECTED PROOF COPY"; dust jacket.

NOTES: Published as Bruccoli A34.1.a.
- PS3511.I9 B57

501. *Bits of Paradise: 21 Uncollected Stories by F. Scott and Zelda Fitzgerald.*
- Selected by Scottie Fitzgerald Smith and Matthew J. Bruccoli; with a Foreword by Scottie Fitzgerald Smith.
- London: Bodley Head, [1973].
- Dust jacket.

NOTES: Bruccoli A34.1.a. First edition, first printing.
Inscribed to MJB by Scottie Fitzgerald, 8 January 1974.
- PS3511.I9 B57 1973

84   Books and Collections

502. *Bits of Paradise 21 Uncollected Stories by F. Scott and Zelda Fitzgerald.*
- Selected by Matthew J. Bruccoli with the Assistance of Scottie Fitzgerald Smith.
- New York: Charles Scribner's Sons, [1973].
- Dust jacket.

NOTES: Bruccoli A34.1.b. First edition, first American printing.
  Review copy with publisher's slip and photograph of Scott and Zelda Fitzgerald laid in.
  Inscribed to Mary Bruccoli by Scottie Fitzgerald, 8 October 1974.
- PS3511.I9 B57 1973b

503. *Bits of Paradise: 21 Uncollected Stories by F. Scott and Zelda Fitzgerald.*
- Selected by Matthew J. Bruccoli, with the Assistance of Scottie Fitzgerald Smith.
- New York: Charles Scribner's Sons, [1974].
- Dust jacket.

NOTES: Bruccoli A34.1.c. Second printing.
- PS3511.I9 B58 1974

504. *Bits of Paradise: 21 Uncollected Stories by F. Scott and Zelda Fitzgerald.*
- Selected by Matthew J. Bruccoli with the Assistance of Scottie Fitzgerald Smith.
- New York: Pocket Books, [1976], #80250.
- Wrappers.

NOTES: Bruccoli A34.2. Second edition.
  First book publication for "Dice, Brass-Knuckles & Guitar."
  Laid in: Card with note from Charles Scribner III.
- PS3511.I9 B5 1976

505. *Bits of Paradise: 21 Uncollected Stories by F. Scott and Zelda Fitzgerald.*
- Selected by Scottie Fitzgerald Smith and Matthew J. Bruccoli with a Foreword by Scottie Fitzgerald Smith.
- [Harmondsworth, England]: Penguin Books, [1976].
- Wrappers.

NOTES: Bruccoli A34.3. Third edition.
- PS3511.I9 B57 1976b

506. *Bits of Paradise: 21 Uncollected Stories by F. Scott and Zelda Fitzgerald.*
- Selected by Scottie Fitzgerald Smith and Matthew J. Bruccoli with a Foreword by Scottie Fitzgerald Smith.
- [Harmondsworth, England]: Penguin Books, [1982].
- Wrappers.

NOTES: Bruccoli A34.3. Third edition, second printing.
- PS3511.I9 B57 1982

507. *Bits of Paradise: 21 Uncollected Stories by F. Scott and Zelda Fitzgerald.*
- Selected by Scottie Fitzgerald Smith and Matthew J. Bruccoli; with a Foreword by Scottie Fitzgerald Smith.
- [Harmondsworth, England]: Penguin Books, [1984].
- Wrappers.

NOTES: Bruccoli A34.3. Third edition, third printing.
- PS3511.I9 B5 1984

508. *Bits of Paradise: 21 Uncollected Stories by F. Scott and Zelda Fitzgerald.*
- Selected by Scottie Fitzgerald Smith and Matthew J. Bruccoli; with a Foreword by Scottie Fitzgerald Smith.
- [Harmondsworth, England]: Penguin Books, [1986].
- Wrappers.

NOTES: Bruccoli A34.3. Penguin Modern Classics. Third edition, fourth printing.
- PS3511.I9 B5 1986

509. *Bits of Paradise: 21 Uncollected Stories by F. Scott and Zelda Fitzgerald.*
- Selected by Scottie Fitzgerald Smith and Matthew J. Bruccoli; with a Foreword by Scottie Fitzgerald Smith.
- [London]: Penguin Books, [1988].
- Wrappers.

NOTES: Penguin Modern Classics. Third edition, fifth printing.
- PS3511.I9 B5 1988

510. *Bits of Paradise: 21 Uncollected Stories by F. Scott and Zelda Fitzgerald.*
- Selected by Scottie Fitzgerald Smith and Matthew J. Bruccoli; with a Foreword by Scottie Fitzgerald Smith.
- [London]: Penguin Books, [1995].
- Wrappers.

NOTES: Penguin Modern Classics. Third edition, sixth printing.
- PS3511.I9 B5 1995

Preface to *This Side of Paradise* (1975)

511. *F. Scott Fitzgerald's Preface to This Side of Paradise.*
- Edited by John R. Hopkins.
- Iowa City, Iowa: Windhover Press and Bruccoli Clark, 1975.
- Binding dummy.

NOTES: Bruccoli A35.
Laid in: Prospectus, TLS, 10 January 1976, from K. K. Merker, Windhover Press, to MJB apologizing for misfortunes during production of the book, and TLS, 3 June 1975, from Constance Sayre concerning the book's binding.
- PS3511.I9 T482

512. *F. Scott Fitzgerald's Preface to This Side of Paradise.*
- Edited by John R. Hopkins.
- Iowa City, Iowa: Windhover Press and Bruccoli Clark, 1975.
NOTES: Bruccoli A35.
- PS3511.I9 T482 1975

The Cruise of the Rolling Junk (1976)

513. *The Cruise of the Rolling Junk.*
- With an Introduction by Matthew J. Bruccoli.
- Bloomfield Hills, Mich. and Columbia, S.C.: Bruccoli Clark, 1976.
- Dummy binding; dust jacket.
NOTES: Bruccoli A36.
- PS3511.I9 Z515 1976 C.3

514. *The Cruise of the Rolling Junk.*
- With an Introduction by Matthew J. Bruccoli.
- Bloomfield Hills, Mich.: Bruccoli Clark, 1976.
- Unbound sheets in dust jacket.
NOTES: Bruccoli A36. Review copy.
- PS3511.I9 Z515 1976 C.4

515. *The Cruise of the Rolling Junk.*
- With an Introduction by Matthew J. Bruccoli.
- Bloomfield Hills, Mich. and Columbia, S.C.: Bruccoli Clark, 1976.
- Dust jacket.
NOTES: Bruccoli A36.
   Inscription by MJB about C. E. Frazer Clark.
- PS3511.I9 Z515 1976 C.1
- Another copy (without inscription).

516. *The Cruise of the Rolling Junk.*
- With an Introduction by Matthew J. Bruccoli.
- Bloomfield Hills, Mich. and Columbia, S.C.: Bruccoli Clark, 1976.
- Dust jacket; second binding, using new die, so noted by MJB.
NOTES: Bruccoli A36.
   Laid in: Publisher's invoice with typed note by C. E. Frazer Clark.
- PS3511.I9 Z515 1976 C.2

Three Comrades (1978)

517. *F. Scott Fitzgerald's Screenplay for Three Comrades by Erich Maria Remarque.*
- Edited with an Afterword by Matthew J. Bruccoli.
- Carbondale: Southern Illinois University Press, [1978].
- Mechanicals.

NOTES: Published as Bruccoli A37.
- PN1997.T47 1978g

518. *F. Scott Fitzgerald's Screenplay for Three Comrades by Erich Maria Remarque.*
    - Edited with an Afterword by Matthew J. Bruccoli.
    - Carbondale: Southern Illinois University Press, [1978].
    - Galley proofs. Corrected in red and green ink and red pencil.
    NOTES: Published as Bruccoli A37.
    - PN1997.T47 1978e

519. *F. Scott Fitzgerald's Screenplay for Three Comrades by Erich Maria Remarque.*
    - Edited with an Afterword by Matthew J. Bruccoli.
    - Carbondale: Southern Illinois University Press, [1978].
    - Page proofs. Three sets.
    NOTES: Published as Bruccoli A37.
    - PN1997.T47 1978f

520. *F. Scott Fitzgerald's Screenplay for Three Comrades by Erich Maria Remarque.*
    - Edited with an Afterword by Matthew J. Bruccoli.
    - Carbondale: Southern Illinois University Press, [1978].
    - Unbound signatures.
    NOTES: Published as Bruccoli A37.
    - PN1997.T47 1978c

521. *F. Scott Fitzgerald's Screenplay for Three Comrades by Erich Maria Remarque.*
    - Edited with an Afterword by Matthew J. Bruccoli.
    - Carbondale: Southern Illinois University Press, [1978].
    - Xerox of the original typescript of the screenplay, corrected and annotated for the edition published by Southern Illinois University, 1978.
    NOTES: Published as Bruccoli A37.
    - PN1997.T47 1978h

522. *F. Scott Fitzgerald's Screenplay for Three Comrades by Erich Maria Remarque.*
    - Edited with an Afterword by Matthew J. Bruccoli.
    - Carbondale: Southern Illinois University Press, [1978].
    - Unbound signatures. Two sets.
    NOTES: Published as Bruccoli A37.
    - PN1997.T47 1978d C.2

523. *F. Scott Fitzgerald's Screenplay for Three Comrades by Erich Maria Remarque.*
    - Edited with an Afterword by Matthew J. Bruccoli.
    - Carbondale: Southern Illinois University Press, [1978].
    - Wrappers, comb binding.
    NOTES: Bruccoli A37.1.a, Note. Screenplay Library.
        Review copy with dust jacket and press release laid in.
    - PN1997.T47 1978d C.1

524. *F. Scott Fitzgerald's Screenplay for Three Comrades by Erich Maria Remarque.*
- Edited with an Afterword by Matthew J. Bruccoli.
- Carbondale: Southern Illinois University Press, [1978].
- Dust jacket.
NOTES: Bruccoli A37.1.a. Screenplay Library.
    Inscribed on p. i: "No Vern Sternberg, no Screenplay Library. He was the best publisher I ever worked with. MJB".
- PN1997.T47 1978 C.1

525. *F. Scott Fitzgerald's Screenplay for Three Comrades by Erich Maria Remarque.*
- Edited with an Afterword by Matthew J. Bruccoli.
- Carbondale: Southern Illinois University Press, [1978].
- Wrappers.
NOTES: Bruccoli A37.1.a. Screenplay Library.
- PN1997.T47 1978 C.2

526. *F. Scott Fitzgerald's Screenplay for Three Comrades by Erich Maria Remarque.*
- Edited with an Afterword by Matthew J. Bruccoli.
- Carbondale: Southern Illinois University Press, [1978].
- Wrappers; "Distributed by Frederick Ungar Publishing Co., Inc." label.
NOTES: Bruccoli A37.1.a. Screenplay Library.
- PN1997.T47 1978 C.3

527. *F. Scott Fitzgerald's Screenplay for Three Comrades by Erich Maria Remarque.*
- Edited with an Afterword by Matthew J. Bruccoli.
- Carbondale: Southern Illinois University Press, [1978].
- Wrappers; "Faber Net £5.95" label.
NOTES: Bruccoli A37.1.a. Screenplay Library. American edition distributed in England by Faber & Faber.
- PN1997.T47 1978b

528. *F. Scott Fitzgerald's Screenplay for Three Comrades by Erich Maria Remarque.*
- Edited with an Afterword by Matthew J. Bruccoli.
- New York: Popular Library, [1979].
- Wrappers.
NOTES: Bruccoli A37.2. Screenplay Library. Second edition, first printing.
- PN1997.T47 1979

The Notebooks of F. Scott Fitzgerald (1978)

529. *The Notebooks of F. Scott Fitzgerald.*
- Edited by Matthew J. Bruccoli.
- New York: Harcourt Brace Jovanovich/Bruccoli Clark, [1978].
- Wrappers; proof copy.
NOTES: Published as Bruccoli A38.1.a.
- PS3511.I9 N6

530. *The Notebooks of F. Scott Fitzgerald.*
- Edited by Matthew J. Bruccoli.
- Bloomfield Hills, Mich. & Columbia, S.C.: Bruccoli Clark, 1978.
- Wrappers, spiral bound; two volumes.

NOTES: Published as Bruccoli A38.1.a. Review copy.
"Uncorrected proof of 5 April 1978 MJB".
- PS3511.I9 N6

531. *The Notebooks of F. Scott Fitzgerald.*
- Edited by Matthew J. Bruccoli.
- New York: Harcourt Brace Jovanovich/Bruccoli Clark, [1978].
- Dust jacket.

NOTES: Bruccoli A38.1.a. First edition, first printing.
Laid in: Promotional card.
- PS3511.I9 N6 1978

532. *The Notebooks of F. Scott Fitzgerald.*
- Edited by Matthew J. Bruccoli.
- New York: Harcourt Brace Jovanovich/Bruccoli Clark, [1978].
- Dust jacket.

NOTES: Bruccoli A38.1.b. First edition, second printing.
Laid in: Promotional card and facsimile of FSF's library card from *Notebooks*.
- PS3511.I9 N6 1978b

533. *The Notebooks of F. Scott Fitzgerald.*
- Edited by Matthew J. Bruccoli.
- New York: Harcourt Brace Jovanovich/Bruccoli Clark, [1978].
- Dust jacket.

NOTES: Bruccoli A38.1.b. First edition, second printing.
Laid in: Promotional card.
- PS3511.I9 N6 1978b

F. Scott Fitzgerald's St. Paul Plays (1978)

534. *F. Scott Fitzgerald's St. Paul Plays 1911–1914.*
- Edited with an Introduction by Alan Margolies.
- Princeton, N.J.: Princeton University Library, 1978.
- Dust jacket.

NOTES: Bruccoli A39.
Laid in: Order card.
Inscribed by Margolies to MJB, 24 October 1978.
- PS3511.I9 A19 1978

The Price Was High (1979)

535. *The Price Was High: The Last Uncollected Stories of F. Scott Fitzgerald.*
- Edited by Matthew J. Bruccoli.
- New York; London: Harcourt Brace Jovanovich / Bruccoli Clark, [1979].
- Wrappers: "UNCORRECTED PROOF".
NOTES: Published as Bruccoli A40.1.a.
- PS3511.I9 P7

536. *The Price Was High: The Last Uncollected Stories of F. Scott Fitzgerald.*
- Edited by Matthew J. Bruccoli.
- New York: Harcourt Brace Jovanovich / Bruccoli Clark, [1979].
- Dust jacket.
NOTES: Bruccoli A40.1.a. First edition, first printing. "First edition/BCDE". Typos marked by MJB.
- PS3511.I9 P7 C.2
- Another copy (without markings).

537. *The Price Was High: The Last Uncollected Stories of F. Scott Fitzgerald.*
- Edited by Matthew J. Bruccoli.
- New York: Harcourt Brace Jovanovich / Bruccoli Clark, [1979].
- Dust jacket.
NOTES: Bruccoli A40.1.b. First edition, second printing.
- PS3511.I9 P7 1981b

538. *The Price Was High: The Last Uncollected Stories of F. Scott Fitzgerald.*
- Edited by Matthew J. Bruccoli.
- London; Melbourne; New York: Quartet Books, [1979].
- Dust jacket.
NOTES: Bruccoli A40.1.c_1. First edition, first English printing, first state. "EDITORIAL FILE COPY".
- PS3511.I9 P7 1979c C.1

539. *The Price Was High: The Last Uncollected Stories of F. Scott Fitzgerald.*
- Edited by Matthew J. Bruccoli.
- London; Melbourne; New York: Quartet Books, [1979].
- Dust jacket.
NOTES: Bruccoli A40.1.c_1. First edition, first English printing, first state. Laid in: Dust jacket proof.
- PS3511.I9 P7 1979c C.2

540. *The Price Was High: The Last Uncollected Stories of F. Scott Fitzgerald.*
- Edited by Matthew J. Bruccoli.
- London; Melbourne: Quartet Books, [1979].
- Dust jacket.
NOTES: Bruccoli A40.1.c_2. First edition, first English printing, second state.
- PS3511.I9 P7 1979d

541. *The Price Was High: The Last Uncollected Stories of F. Scott Fitzgerald.*
- Edited by Matthew J. Bruccoli.
- New York: Harcourt Brace Jovanovich / Bruccoli Clark, [1981].
- Wrappers.
NOTES: Bruccoli A40.1.d. First edition, fourth printing. A Harvest Book.
- PS3511.I9 P7 1981

542. *The Price Was High: The Last Uncollected Stories of F. Scott Fitzgerald.*
- Edited by Matthew J. Bruccoli.
- [London]: Pan Books, [1981].
- Wrappers; two volumes.
NOTES: Bruccoli A40.2. Second edition. Picador Edition.
- PS3511.I9 P7 1981b

543. *The Price Was High: The Last Uncollected Stories of F. Scott Fitzgerald.*
- Edited by Matthew J. Bruccoli.
- New York: MJF Books, [1995].
- Dust jacket.
NOTES: Reprint edition.
- PS3511.I9 P7 1995

Correspondence of F. Scott Fitzgerald (1980)

544. *Correspondence of F. Scott Fitzgerald.*
- Edited by Matthew J. Bruccoli.
- Setting copy, corrected in red and green pencil. In three boxes.
NOTES: Published as Bruccoli A41.1.a. Includes photocopies of letters.
- PS3511.I9 Z529

545. *Correspondence of F. Scott Fitzgerald.*
- Edited by Matthew J. Bruccoli.
- Galley proofs.
NOTES: Published as Bruccoli A41.1.a. Consists of three sets of galleys, all with corrections in pencil. Set A includes 238 pp., Set B includes 233 pp. (lacking the last part of the Appendix), and Set C includes 334 pp.
- PS3511.I9 Z5291

546. *Correspondence of F. Scott Fitzgerald.*
- Edited by Matthew J. Bruccoli and Margaret M. Duggan with the Assistance of Susan Walker.
- New York: Random House, [1980].
- Wrappers: "UNCORRECTED PROOF".
NOTES: Published as Bruccoli A41.1.a.
- PS3511.I9 Z53

547. *Correspondence of F. Scott Fitzgerald.*
- Edited by Matthew J. Bruccoli and Margaret M. Duggan with the Assistance of Susan Walker.
- New York: Random House, [1980].
- Dust jacket.
NOTES: Bruccoli A41.1.a. First edition, first printing.
- PS3511.I9 Z53 1980

548. *Correspondence of F. Scott Fitzgerald.*
- Edited by Matthew J. Bruccoli and Margaret M. Duggan, with the Assistance of Susan Walker.
- New York: Random House, [1980].
- Dust jacket.
NOTES: Bruccoli A41.1.b. First edition, reprint. "Book Club Edition" (Literary Guild).
- PS3511.I9 Z53 1980c

Poems, 1911–1940 (1981)

549. *F. Scott Fitzgerald Poems 1911–1940.*
- Edited by Matthew J. Bruccoli; Foreword by James Dickey.
- Printer's mechanicals, pasted up from proofs.
NOTES: Published as Bruccoli A42.1.
- PS3511.I9 P59

550. *F. Scott Fitzgerald Poems 1911–1940.*
- Edited by Matthew J. Bruccoli; Foreword by James Dickey.
- Bloomfield Hills, Mich. and Columbia, S.C.: Bruccoli Clark, 1981.
- Publisher's dummy, unbound signatures inserted in original binding.
NOTES: Published as Bruccoli A42.1. Initialed by MJB.
- PS3511.I9 P6 1981 C.1

551. *F. Scott Fitzgerald Poems 1911–1940.*
- Edited by Matthew J. Bruccoli; Foreword by James Dickey.
- Bloomfield Hills, Mich. and Columbia, S.C.: Bruccoli Clark, 1981.
- Unbound signatures.
NOTES: Published as Bruccoli A42.1.
- PS3511.I9 P6 1981 C.2

552. *F. Scott Fitzgerald Poems 1911–1940.*
- Edited by Matthew J. Bruccoli; Foreword by James Dickey.
- Bloomfield Hills, Mich. and Columbia, S.C.: Bruccoli Clark, 1981.
- Dust jacket.
NOTES: Bruccoli A42.1.a_a. Number 15 of 100 signed by James Dickey. Inscribed by James Dickey to MJB.
- PS3511.I9 P6 1981b C.2

553. *F. Scott Fitzgerald Poems 1911–1940.*
- Edited by Matthew J. Bruccoli; Foreword by James Dickey.
- Bloomfield Hills, Mich. and Columbia, S.C.: Bruccoli Clark, 1981.
- Dust jacket.
NOTES: Bruccoli A42.1.a$_a$.
   Inscribed by James Dickey to MJB on inserted limitation leaf of copy 24.
- PS3511.I9 P6 1981

554. *F. Scott Fitzgerald Poems 1911–1940.*
- Edited by Matthew J. Bruccoli; Foreword by James Dickey.
- Bloomfield Hills, Mich. and Columbia, S.C.: Bruccoli Clark, 1981.
- Dust jacket.
NOTES: Bruccoli A42.1.a$_a$. Number 84 of 100 signed by James Dickey.
- PS3511.I9 P6 1981 C.2

555. *F. Scott Fitzgerald Poems 1911–1940.*
- Edited by Matthew J. Bruccoli; Foreword by James Dickey.
- Bloomfield Hills, Mich. and Columbia, S.C.: Bruccoli Clark, 1981.
- Dust jacket.
NOTES: Bruccoli A42.1.a$_a$. Number 100 of 100 signed by James Dickey. Inscribed by James Dickey to MJB.
- PS3511.I9 P6 1981b C.1

556. *F. Scott Fitzgerald Poems 1911–1940.*
- Edited by Matthew J. Bruccoli; Foreword by James Dickey.
- Bloomfield Hills, Mich. and Columbia, S.C.: Bruccoli Clark, 1981.
- Dust jacket.
NOTES: Bruccoli A42.1.a$_a$. Book "out of series" signed by James Dickey. Inscribed by James Dickey to MJB.
- PS3511.I9 P6 1981b C.3

557. "The Unreflecting Shield," 1981.
- James Dickey.
- 7 items.
NOTES: Five drafts of Dickey's introduction for *Poems 1911–1940*. RTS (4 pp.), RTS (6 pp.), TS (6 pp.), RTS (6 pp.), RTS, notes (1 p.), RTS, "possible titles" (1 p.), and TS, "Idea for cover of book" (1 p.).
- PS3554.I32 D63 1981

558. "The Unreflecting Shield," 1981.
- James Dickey.
NOTES: Final text. Xerox, 6 pp.
- On deposit.

F. Scott Fitzgerald: Inscriptions (1988)

559. *F. Scott Fitzgerald: Inscriptions.*
    - Columbia, S.C.: Matthew J. Bruccoli, 1988.
    NOTES: Compiled by MJB from his collection. Items 1–31: Publications by FSF inscribed by him; Items 32–86: Books by other authors inscribed to FSF. Number 30 of 200 copies: "For the Thomas Cooper Library MJB".
    - PS3511.I9 Z6138 1988

Manuscript Facsimile Edition (1990–91)

560. *This Side of Paradise: The Manuscripts and Typescripts.*
    - Introduced and Arranged by Matthew J. Bruccoli.
    - New York: Garland, 1990.
    - 2 volumes.
    NOTES: Bruccoli Supplement A44.1.a.
    - PS3511.I9 A6 vol. 1

561. *The Beautiful and Damned: The Manuscript.*
    - Introduced and Arranged by Alan Margolies.
    - New York: Garland, 1990.
    - 2 volumes.
    NOTES: Bruccoli Supplement A44.1.a.
    - PS3511.I9 A6 vol. 2

562. *The Great Gatsby: The Revised and Rewritten Galleys.*
    - Introduced and Arranged by Matthew J. Bruccoli.
    - New York: Garland, 1990.
    NOTES: Bruccoli Supplement A44.1.a.
    - PS3511.I9 A6 vol. 3

563. *Tender Is the Night: The Melarky and Kelly Versions.*
    - Introduced and Arranged by Matthew J. Bruccoli.
    - New York: Garland, 1990.
    - 2 volumes.
    NOTES: Bruccoli Supplement A44.1.a.
    - PS3511.I9 A6 1990 vol. 4

564. *Tender Is the Night: The Diver Version.*
    - Introduced and Arranged by Matthew J. Bruccoli.
    - New York: Garland, 1991.
    - 5 volumes.
    NOTES: Bruccoli Supplement A44.1.a.
    - PS3511.I9 A6 1990 vol. 4

565. *The Last Tycoon: Manuscript and Revised Typescript for the First 17 Episodes, with the Author's Plans and Notes.*

- Introduced and Arranged by Matthew J. Bruccoli.
- New York: Garland, 1990.
- 3 volumes.

NOTES: Bruccoli Supplement A44.1.a.
- PS3511.I9 A6 vol. 5

566. *The Vegetable, Stories, and Articles.*
- Introduced and Arranged by Matthew J. Bruccoli.
- New York: Garland, 1991.
- 3 volumes.

NOTES: Bruccoli Supplement A44.1.a.
- PS3511.I9 A6 1990 vol. 6

Babylon Revisited: The Screenplay (1993)

567. *Babylon Revisited: The Screenplay.*
- With an Introduction by Budd Schulberg and Afterword by Matthew J. Bruccoli.
- New York: Carroll & Graf Publishers, 1993, #9307.
- Wrappers.

NOTES: Bruccoli Supplement A45.1.a.
    Signed by Schulberg.
- Ps3511.I9 B315 1993
- Another copy (not signed).

A Life in Letters (1994)

568. *A Life in Letters.*
- Edited by Matthew J. Bruccoli with the Assistance of Judith S. Baughman.
- New York: Charles Scribner's Sons; Toronto: Maxwell Macmillan Canada, [1994].
- Page proofs.

NOTES: Bruccoli Supplement A46.1.a.
- On deposit.

569. *A Life in Letters.*
- Edited by Matthew J. Bruccoli with the Assistance of Judith S. Baughman.
- New York: Charles Scribner's Sons; Toronto: Maxwell Macmillan Canada, [1994].
- Wrappers: "Uncorrected advance proof".

NOTES: Bruccoli Supplement A46.1.a. Signed by MJB.
- PS3511.I9 Z48

569A. [Statement on *A Life in Letters*].
- James Dickey.

NOTES: Drafts for blurb dictated to MJB by Dickey, 2 pp. revised by Dickey.
- On deposit

570. *A Life in Letters.*
- Edited by Matthew J. Bruccoli with the Assistance of Judith S. Baughman.
- New York: Charles Scribner's Sons, [1994].
- Dust jacket.
NOTES: Bruccoli Supplement A46.1.a. Signed by MJB and JSB.
- PS3511.I9 Z48 1994

571. *A Life in Letters.*
- Edited by Matthew J. Bruccoli with the Assistance of Judith S. Baughman.
- New York: Simon & Schuster, [1995].
- Wrappers.
NOTES: Bruccoli Supplement A46.1.b. "First Touchstone Edition 1995".
- PS3511.I9 Z48 1995

572. *A Life in Letters.*
- Edited by Matthew J. Bruccoli with the Assistance of Judith S. Baughman.
- [London]: Penguin, [1998].
- Wrappers.
NOTES: Bruccoli Supplement A46.1.c. First edition, first British printing.
- PS3511.I9 Z48 1998

Six Letters to an Apprentice (1994)

573. *Six Letters to an Apprentice.*
- Facsimiles letters by F. Scott Fitzgerald, Willa Cather, George Ade, Ellen Glasgow, Don Marquis, Ring Lardner; With a Foreword by Ernest Kroll.
- [Riverside]: Thaumatrope Press, University of California, Riverside, 1994.
- Portfolio.
NOTES: Bruccoli Supplement A47. Six letters written to Ernest Kroll in response to his letters asking for advice on how one learns to write.
- PN137.S53 1994

F. Scott Fitzgerald on Authorship (1996)

574. *F. Scott Fitzgerald on Authorship.*
- Edited by Matthew J. Bruccoli with Judith S. Baughman.
- Columbia: University of South Carolina Press, [1996].
- Dust jacket.
- PS3511.I9 Z464 1996

F. Scott Fitzgerald: The Princeton Years (1996)

575. *F. Scott Fitzgerald: The Princeton Years Selected Writings, 1914–1920.*
- Edited and with an Introduction by Chip Deffaa.
- [Fort Bragg, Calif.]: Cypress House Press, [1996].

- Wrappers.
NOTES: "Uncorrected Galley Proof".
- PS3511.I9 A6

576. *F. Scott Fitzgerald: The Princeton Years: Selected Writings, 1914–1920.*
- Edited and with an Introduction by Chip Deffaa.
- [Fort Bragg, Calif.]: Cypress House Press, [1996].
- Wrappers.
- PS3511.I9 A6 1996b

Collections of Fitzgerald Works

577. *The Portable F. Scott Fitzgerald.*
- Selected by Dorothy Parker; Introduction by John O'Hara.
- New York: The Viking Press, 1945.
NOTES: Bruccoli AA1. The Viking Portable Library. First edition, first printing.
- PS3511.I9 A6 1945

578. *The Portable F. Scott Fitzgerald.*
- Selected by Dorothy Parker; Introduction by John O'Hara.
- New York: The Viking Press, 1945.
NOTES: Bruccoli AA1.
    The Viking Portable Library.
    First edition, first printing.
    Kenneth Millar's annotated copy.
    Three pages of annotations
        published in *F. Scott Fitzgerald
        Centenary Exhibition Catalogue.*
- On deposit.

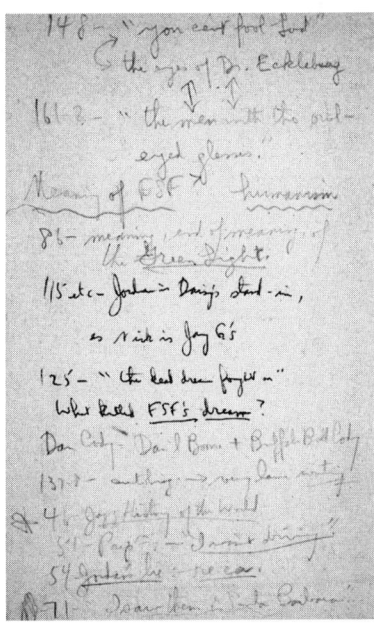

579. *The Portable F. Scott Fitzgerald.*
- Selected by Dorothy Parker;
    Introduction by John O'Hara.
- New York: The Viking Press, 1945.
NOTES: Bruccoli AA1. The Viking Portable Library. First edition, second printing.
    Laid in: TLS, undated, from Malcolm Cowley to MJB discussing the publication of *The Portable F. Scott Fitzgerald.*
- PS3511.I9 A6 1945b C.1

580. *The Portable F. Scott Fitzgerald.*
- Selected by Dorothy Parker; Introduction by John O'Hara.
- New York: The Viking Press, 1945.

NOTES: Bruccoli AA1. First edition, second printing.
The Viking Portable Library. Signature of Cleanth Brooks.
The Great Gatsby and *Tender Is the Night* underlined throughout.
- PS3511.I9 A6 1945b C.2

581. *The Portable F. Scott Fitzgerald.*
- Selected by Dorothy Parker; Introduction by John O'Hara.
- New York: The Viking Press, 1949.
- Dust jacket.

NOTES: Bruccoli AA1. First edition, third printing.
The Viking Portable Library.
- PS3511.I9 A6 1949

582. *The Indispensable F. Scott Fitzgerald.*
- Selected by Dorothy Parker; Introduction by John O'Hara.
- New York: The Book Society, 1949.
- Boxed.

NOTES: Bruccoli AA1.
On copyright page: "The text of this edition of *The Indispensable F. Scott Fitzgerald* is identical with *The Portable F. Scott Fitzgerald.*"
- PS3511.I9 A6 1949b
- Another copy.

583. *The Diamond as Big as the Ritz and Other Stories.*
- With an Introduction by Louis Untermeyer.
- New York: Editions for the Armed Services, [1946], #1043.
- Wrappers.

NOTES: Bruccoli AA2.
- PS3511.I9 D5 1946

584. *Borrowed Time.*
- Short Stories Selected by Alan and Jennifer Ross.
- [London]: The Grey Wall Press, [1951].
- Dust jacket.

NOTES: Bruccoli AA3.
- PS3511.I9 A6 1951

585. *Three Novels of F. Scott Fitzgerald.*
- New York: Charles Scribner's Sons, [1953].

NOTES: Bruccoli AA4. Modern Standard Authors. First printing.
Includes: *The Great Gatsby,* with an Introduction by Malcolm Cowley; *Tender Is the Night,* with the Author's Final Revisions, edited by Malcolm Cowley; *The Last Tycoon, An Unfinished Novel,* edited by Edmund Wilson.
- PS3511.I9 T46 1953

Books and Collections 99

586. *Babylon Revisited and Winter Dreams.*
- Introduction and Notes by Ikuo Uemura.
- Tokyo: Kenkyusha, [1955].
- Wrappers.

NOTES: Bruccoli H1. English-language edition with Introduction and Notes in Japanese.
- PS3511.I9 B3 1955

587. *Three Novels of F. Scott Fitzgerald.*
- New York: Charles Scribner's Sons, [1957].
- Dust jacket.

NOTES: Bruccoli AA4, Note. Reprint of 1953 edition. "D-7.57[H]".
- PS3511.I9 T46 1957

588. *Three Novels of F. Scott Fitzgerald.*
- New York: Charles Scribner's Sons, [1958].
- Dust jacket.

NOTES: Bruccoli AA4. Reprint of 1953 edition. "F-9.58[H]".
- PS3511.I9 T46 1958

589. *May Day.*
- Edited with Notes by Toshisaburo Koyama and Ken-ichi Haya.
- Tokyo: Nan'un-do, [1958].
- Wrappers.

NOTES: Bruccoli H2. English-language edition with Notes and Introduction in Japanese.
- PS3511.I9 M3 1958

590. *The Bodley Head Scott Fitzgerald.*
- With an Introduction by J. P. Priestley.
- London: Bodley Head, [1958–63].
- 6 volumes; All in dust jacket.

NOTES: Bruccoli AA5.

Volume I (*The Great Gatsby, The Last Tycoon, and Some Shorter Pieces*): First, third, fourth printings; fourth printing with wrap-around band advertising movie.

Volume II (*Tender Is the Night, Autobiographical Pieces, Letters to Frances Scott Fitzgerald and Four Short Stories*): First and fourth printings.

Volume III (*This Side of Paradise and Six Short Stories*): First printing and "Revised edition 1965" with different contents.

Volume IV (*The Beautiful and Damned and Two Short Stories*): First printing and "Revised edition 1967" with different contents.

Volume V and Volume VI (*The Short Stories of F. Scott Fitzgerald Selected and Introduced by Malcolm Cowley and Twelve Short Stories*): "Uncorrected Proof Copy" in wrappers and first printings of both volumes. Second printing of Volume VI.

100 Books and Collections

> Annotations on Table of Contents of Vols. V & VI by MJB.
- PS3511.I9 A6 1958b

591. *Babylon Revisited.*
- Notes by Yoshitaka Sakai.
- Tokyo: Nan'un-do, [1959].
- Wrappers.
NOTES: Bruccoli H3. English-language edition with Notes in Japanese.
- PS3511.I9 B3 1959

592. *Babylon Revisited and Other Stories.*
- New York: Charles Scribner's Sons, [1960], #SL22.
- Wrappers.
NOTES: Bruccoli AA6. The Scribner Library. "A-8.60 [C]".
> Review copy with publisher's slip laid in.
- PS3511.I9 B3

593. *Two Short Stories of F. Scott Fitzgerald.*
- Edited with Notes by Mitsuo Yoshida.
- Tokyo: Shohakusha, [1960].
- Wrappers.
NOTES: Bruccoli H4. Text in English.
- PS3511.I9 T9 1960

594. *A Night at the Fair and Forging Ahead.*
- With Introduction and Notes by Yoshihide Ueki.
- [Tokyo]: Yamaguchi Shoten, [1961].
- Wrappers; dust jacket.
NOTES: Bruccoli H5. Text in English.
- PS3511.I9 N56 1961

595. *Babylon Revisited and Other Stories.*
- New York: Charles Scribner's Sons, [1962], #SL22.
- Wrappers.
NOTES: Bruccoli AA6. The Scribner Library. "C-4.62 [C]".
> From the library of Harold Brodkey with his signature.
- PS3511.I9 B3 1962

596. *Babylon Revisited and Other Stories.*
- New York: Charles Scribner's Sons, [1964], #SL22.
- Wrappers.
NOTES: Bruccoli AA6. The Scribner Library. "F-2.64 [Col]".
- PS3511.I9 B3 1964

597. *Babylon Revisited and Other Stories.*
- New York: Charles Scribner's Sons, [1966], #SL22.
- Wrappers.

NOTES: Bruccoli AA6. The Scribner Library. "I.12.66 [Col]".
   Table of contents annotated by MJB.
- PS3511.I9 B3 1966

598. *Babylon Revisited and Other Stories.*
- New York: Charles Scribner's Sons, [1968], #SL22.
- Wrappers.
NOTES: Bruccoli AA6. Scribner Library. Later printing. "J-8.68 [Col]".
- PS3511.I9 B3 1968

599. *Babylon Revisited and Other Stories.*
- New York: Charles Scribner's Sons, [1969].
- Dust jacket.
NOTES: Bruccoli AA6. "K-12.69 [C]".
- PS3511.I9 B3 1969

600. *Babylon Revisited and Other Stories.*
- New York: Charles Scribner's Sons, [1984].
- Wrappers.
NOTES: Bruccoli AA6. Scribner Classics. First printing.
- PS3511.I9 B3 1984.

601. *Babylon Revisited and Other Stories.*
- New York: Collier Books / Macmillan, [1987].
- Wrappers.
NOTES: Bruccoli AA6. "First Scribner Classic / Collier Edition 1987". First printing.
- PS3511.I9 B3 1988.

602. *Babylon Revisited and Other Stories.*
- New York: Charles Scribner's Sons, [1988].
- Wrappers.
NOTES: The Scribner Library of Contemporary Classics.
- PS3511.I9 B3 1988

603. *Babylon Revisited and Other Stories.*
- With Afterword by Matthew J. Bruccoli.
- New York: Scribner Paperback Fiction / Simon & Schuster, [1996], #1111.
- Wrappers.
- PS3511.I9 B3 1996

604. *The Baby Party & Gretchen's Forty Winks.*
- Edited with Notes by Hiroshi Yamamoto.
- [Tokyo?]: Gakuseisha, [1962].
- Wrappers.
NOTES: Bruccoli H6. English-language edition with Notes and Introduction in Japanese.
- PS3511.I9 B23 1962

605. *The Diamond as Big as The Ritz.*
- With Introduction and Notes by Toshisaburo Koyama.
- Japan: Yamaguchi Shoten, 1962.
- Wrappers.

NOTES: Bruccoli H7. Today Library, 58. Text in English.
- PS3511.I9 D5 1962

606. *Three "Basil" Stories.*
- Annotated, with an Introduction by Akio Atsumi.
- Tokyo: Kenkyusha, [1964].
- Wrappers.

NOTES: Bruccoli H8. Kenkyusha Pocket English Series, 210. Text in English.
- PS3511.I9 A6 1964

607. *The Short Stories of F. Scott Fitzgerald.*
- Edited with Notes by Tamotsu Nishiyama and Yasutaka Awa.
- [Tokyo]: Eichōsha, [1968].
- Wrappers.

NOTES: Bruccoli H9. Eichōsha's New Current Books. Text in English.
- PS3511.I9 A6 1968c
- Another copy in variant front wrapper.

608. *The Ice Palace and Magnetism.*
- Edited with Notes by Shuichi Motoda and Akira Kataoka.
- Tokyo: Eichōsha, [1968].
- Wrappers.

NOTES: Bruccoli H10. English-language edition.
- PS3511.I9 I3 1968
- Another copy in variant front wrapper.

609. *The Diamond as Big as The Ritz and Other Stories.*
- [Harmondsworth, England]: Penguin Books, [1962], #1733.
- Wrappers.

NOTES: Bruccoli AA7. Penguin Modern Classics. First printing.
- PS3511.I9 D5 1962

610. *The Diamond as Big as The Ritz and Other Stories.*
- [Harmondsworth, England]: Penguin Books, [1963], #1733.
- Wrappers.

NOTES: Bruccoli AA7. Penguin Modern Classics. Second printing.
- PS3511.I9 D5 1963

611. *The Diamond as Big as The Ritz and Other Stories.*
- [Harmondsworth, England]: Penguin Books, [1965], #1733.
- Wrappers.

NOTES: Bruccoli AA7. Penguin Modern Classics. Third printing.
- PS3511.I9 D5 1965

612. *The Diamond as Big as The Ritz and Other Stories.*
- [Harmondsworth, England]: Penguin, [1969], #1733.
- Wrappers.
NOTES: Bruccoli AA8. *The Stories of F. Scott Fitzgerald,* Volume 1.
- PS3511.I9 D5 1969

613. *The Diamond as Big as The Ritz and Other Stories.*
- [Harmondsworth, England]: Penguin, [1974], #1733.
- Wrappers.
NOTES: Bruccoli AA8. *The Stories of F. Scott Fitzgerald,* Volume 1. Eighth printing.
Publisher's sample copy.
- PS3511.I9 D5 1974

614. *The Diamond as Big as The Ritz and Other Stories.*
- [Harmondsworth, England]: Penguin, [1990].
- Wrappers.
NOTES: Bruccoli AA8. *The Stories of F. Scott Fitzgerald,* Volume 1. Twentieth printing.
- PS3511.I9 D5 1990
See *Crack-Up* for Penguin publication of *The Crack-Up with Other Pieces and Stories (The Stories of F. Scott Fitzgerald, Volume 2).*
See *Pat Hobby Stories* for Penguin publication of *The Pat Hobby Stories (The Stories of F. Scott Fitzgerald, Volume 3).*

615. *Bernice Bobs Her Hair and Other Stories.*
- [Harmondsworth, England]: Penguin Books, [1968], #2736.
- Wrappers: "Publisher's Sample Copy" label.
NOTES: Bruccoli AA8. *The Stories of F. Scott Fitzgerald,* Volume 4. First printing.
- PS3511.I9 B35 1968

616. *Bernice Bobs Her Hair and Other Stories.*
- [Harmondsworth, England]: Penguin Books, [1968], #2736.
- Wrappers.
NOTES: Bruccoli AA8. *The Stories of F. Scott Fitzgerald,* Volume 4. First printing.
- PS3511.I9 B35 1968

617. *Bernice Bobs Her Hair and Other Stories.*
- [Harmondsworth, England]: Penguin Books, [1974], #2736.
- Wrappers.
NOTES: Bruccoli AA8. *The Stories of F. Scott Fitzgerald,* Volume 4.
- PS3511.I9 B35 1974

618. *Bernice Bobs Her Hair and Other Stories.*
- [Harmondsworth, England]: Penguin Books, [1984].
- Wrappers.
NOTES: Bruccoli AA8. *The Stories of F. Scott Fitzgerald,* Volume 4. Sixth printing.
- PS3511.I9 B35 1984

619. *Bernice Bobs Her Hair and Other Stories.*
- [Harmondsworth, England]: Penguin Books, [1990?].
- Wrappers.
NOTES: Bruccoli AA8. *The Stories of F. Scott Fitzgerald,* Volume 4. Ninth printing.
- PS3511.I9 B35 1990

620. *The Lost Decade and Other Stories.*
- [Harmondsworth, England]: Penguin, [1968], #2891.
- Wrappers.
NOTES: Bruccoli AA8. *The Stories of F. Scott Fitzgerald,* Volume 5.
- PS3511.I9 L6 1968

621. *The Lost Decade and Other Stories.*
- [Harmondsworth, England]: Penguin, [1975].
- Wrappers.
NOTES: Bruccoli AA8. *The Stories of F. Scott Fitzgerald,* Volume 5. Fourth printing.
- PS3511.I9 L6 1975

622. *The Lost Decade and Other Stories.*
- [Harmondsworth, England]: Penguin, [1987].
- Wrappers.
NOTES: Bruccoli AA8. *The Stories of F. Scott Fitzgerald,* Volume 5. Ninth printing.
- PS3511.I9 L6 1987

623. *The Fitzgerald Reader.*
- Edited by Arthur Mizener.
- New York: Charles Scribner's Sons, [1963].
- Dust jacket.
NOTES: Bruccoli AA11. "3.63 [H]". Review copy with publisher's slip. Laid in: Letter from Henry Dan Piper to MJB.
- PS3511.I9 A6 1963 C.1

624. *The Fitzgerald Reader.*
- Edited by Arthur Mizener.
- New York: Charles Scribner's Sons, [1963].
- Dust jacket.
NOTES: Bruccoli AA11. Modern Standard Authors edition.
- PS3511.I9 A6 1963 C.2

625. *The Fitzgerald Reader.*
- Edited by Arthur Mizener.
- New York: Charles Scribner's Sons, [1965], #SL118.
- Wrappers.
NOTES: Bruccoli AA11. "B-6.65[Col]".
- PS3511.I9 A6 1965

626. *The Fitzgerald Reader.*
- Edited by Arthur Mizener.
- New York: Charles Scribner's Sons, [1968].
- Wrappers.
NOTES: Bruccoli AA11. "E-12.68[Col]".
- PS3511.I9 A6 1968

627. *Letters to His Daughter.*
- Edited by Andrew Turnbull; With an Introduction by Frances Fitzgerald Lanahan.
- New York: Charles Scribner's Sons, [1965].
- Spiral binding.
NOTES: Published as Bruccoli AA12. Uncorrected proof.
- PS3511.I9 Z54

628. *Letters to His Daughter.*
- Edited by Andrew Turnbull; With an Introduction by Frances Fitzgerald Lanahan.
- New York: Charles Scribner's Sons, [1965].
- Dust jacket.
NOTES: Bruccoli AA12. Review copy with publisher's slip laid in.
- PS3511.I9 Z55

629. *The Letters of F. Scott Fitzgerald to His Daughter.*
- Edited by Andrew Turnbull; With an Introduction by Frances Fitzgerald Lanahan.
- [Tokyo]: Sansyusya, [1985?].
- Wrappers.
NOTES: Edited with Notes by Kayoko Miyauchi; with an Introduction by Haruki Murakami. Text in English.
- PS3511.I9 Z543 1985

630. *Three Novels by F. Scott Fitzgerald.*
- New York: Charles Scribner's Sons, 1968.
- Boxed set of *This Side of Paradise, The Beautiful and Damned,* and *The Great Gatsby.*
NOTES: Bruccoli AA13. *TSOP* ("H-10.68[Col]"); *B&D* ("F-12.68[MCOL]"); *GG* ("O.569[C]").
- PS3511.I9 T459

631. *The Ice Palace and Absolution.*
- Edited with Notes by M. Kasahara and T. Tasaka.
- [Tokyo?]: Kōbunsha, [1969].
- Wrappers.
NOTES: Bruccoli H11. English-language edition with Notes and Introduction in Japanese.
- PS3511.I9 I3 1969

632. *Selected Stories.*
- Edited by Biancamaria Tedeschini Lalli.
- [Milan]: U. Mursia, [1970].

NOTES: Bruccoli AA14. English-language edition with Italian Notes and Introduction.
- PS3511.I9 A6 1970

633. Book-club set issued by the Literary Guild and other book clubs beginning in 1970.
- New York: Charles Scribner's Sons, [1970–73].
- Five volumes.

NOTES: Bruccoli AA15. Set includes: *This Side of Paradise; The Great Gatsby; Tender Is the Night; The Last Tycoon: An Unfinished Novel;* and *The Stories of F. Scott Fitzgerald A Selection of 28 Stories* With an Introduction by Malcolm Cowley.
- *TSOP* (PS3511.I9 T49 1970b); *GG* (PS3511.I9 G7 1970b); *TITN* (PS3511.I9 T4 1970b); *LT* (PS3511.I9 L3 1970); *Stories* (PS3511.I9 A6 1973).

634. *Absolution May Day Babylon Revisited.*
- Edited by A. Le Vot; Translated by M.-P. Castlenau and B. Willerval.
- [Paris]: Aubier-Flammarion, [1972].

NOTES: Bruccoli AA16. Inscribed by Le Vot to MJB.
- PS3511.I9 A34 1972

635. *Crazy Sunday.*
- Edited with Notes by K. Takamura.
- Osaka: Kyioku Tosho, 1972.
- Wrappers.

NOTES: Bruccoli H12. English-language edition with Notes and Introduction in Japanese.
- PS3511.I9 C74 1972

636. *The Basil and Josephine Stories.*
- Edited with Notes by Hiroshige Yoshida and Totsuo Namba.
- Tokyo: Eihōsha, 1973.
- Wrappers.

NOTES: Bruccoli H13. English Language Textbook with Japanese annotations.
- PS3511.I9 B33 1974

637. *Selected Short Stories.*
- Edited by P. Costa and D. Caldi.
- Turin: G. B. Petrini, 1973.

NOTES: Bruccoli AA17. English-language edition with Notes in Italian.
- PS3511.I9 A16 1973

638. *The Diamond as Big as the Ritz and Other Stories.*
- Simplified and Abridged by Roland John; Illustrated by Robin Wiggins.
- [Harlow, England]: Longman, [1974].
- Wrappers.

NOTES: Bruccoli AA18. Longman Structural Readers: Fiction, Stage 5. English Language Textbooks for Foreign Speakers.
- PS3511.I9 A6 1974

639. *Babylon Revisited and Other Stories.*
- Edited with Notes by Fumi Adachi.
- [Tokyo]: Hokuseido Press, [1976].
- Wrappers.

NOTES: Bruccoli H14. English-language edition with Notes and Introduction in Japanese.
- PS3511.I9 B3 1976

640. *The Great Gatsby; Tender Is the Night; This Side of Paradise; The Beautiful and Damned; The Last Tycoon.*
- [London]: Heinemann/Octopus, [1977].
- Dust jacket with wrap-around band.

NOTES: Bruccoli AA19.
- PS3511.I9 A6 1977b

641. *F. S. Fitzgerald.*
- Edited with Notes by Katsuji Takamura.
- [Tokyo: Eichōsha, 1977].
- Wrappers.

NOTES: Bruccoli H15. Eichōsha Great American Authors Series. English-language edition with Notes and Introduction in Japanese.
- PS3511.I9 A6 1977c

642. *Last Kiss & Other Stories.*
- Edited with Notes by Takashi Tasaka and Yoshiya Chiba.
- Tokyo: Shinozaki Shorin, 1978.
- Wrappers.

NOTES: Bruccoli H16. English-language edition with Notes and Introduction in Japanese.
   Laid in: errata slip.
- PS3511.I9 L2 1978

643. *Selected Short Stories.*
- Moscow: Progress Publishers, 1979.

NOTES: Bruccoli AA20. English-language edition with Russian Introduction and Notes.
- PS3511.I9 A6 1979

644. *F. Scott Fitzgerald On Writing.*
- Edited by Larry W. Phillips.
- New York: Charles Scribner's Sons, [1985].
- Dust jacket.
NOTES: Bruccoli AA21.
- PS3511.I9 A6 1985

645. *F. Scott Fitzgerald On Writing.*
- Edited by Larry W. Phillips.
- [London]: Equation, [1988].
- Dust jacket.
NOTES: Reprint of Scribners edition.
- PS3511.I9 F2 1988

646. *The Collected Short Stories of F. Scott Fitzgerald.*
- [Harmondsworth, England]: Penguin, [1986].
- Wrappers.
- PS3511.I9 A6 1986b C.1

647. *The Collected Short Stories of F. Scott Fitzgerald.*
- [Harmondsworth, England]: Penguin, [1986].
- Wrappers: "Sample Complete Copy" label.
- PS3511.I9 A6 1986b C.2

648. *The Collected Short Stories of F. Scott Fitzgerald.*
- [Harmondsworth, England]: Penguin, n.d.
- Wrappers.
NOTES: Penguin Twentieth-Century Classics. Fourth printing.
- PS3511.I9 A6 1986d

649. *The Collected Short Stories of F. Scott Fitzgerald.*
- [London]: Penguin, [1990?]
- Wrappers.
NOTES: Third printing of 1986 edition.
- PS3511.I9 A6 1990

650. *Short Stories / Nouvelles.*
- Choix, Introduction et Notes par Dominique Lescanne.
- [Paris]: Presses Pocket, [1988].
- Wrappers.
NOTES: English-language edition with Introduction and Notes in French.
- PS3511.I9 A6 1988b

651. *The Short Stories of F. Scott Fitzgerald: A New Collection.*
- Edited and with a Preface by Matthew J. Bruccoli.
- New York: Charles Scribner's Sons, 1989.
- Xeroxed page proofs, with corrections.
- PS3511.I9 A6 1989e

652. *The Short Stories of F. Scott Fitzgerald: A New Collection.*
- Edited and with a Preface by Matthew J. Bruccoli.
- New York: Charles Scribner's Sons, 1989.
- Setting copy.
- PS3511.I9 A6 1989f

653. *The Short Stories of F. Scott Fitzgerald: A New Collection.*
- Edited and with a Preface by Matthew J. Bruccoli.
- New York: Charles Scribner's Sons, [1989].
- Two volumes in wrappers: "Uncorrected Advance Proof."
NOTES: Volume 2 in dust jacket.
- PS3511.I9 A6 1989b

654. *The Short Stories of F. Scott Fitzgerald: A New Collection.*
- Edited and with a Preface by Matthew J. Bruccoli.
- New York: Charles Scribner's Sons, [1989].
- Wrappers.
NOTES: First printing.
- PS3511.I9 A6 1989

655. *The Short Stories of F. Scott Fitzgerald: A New Collection.*
- Edited and with a Preface by Matthew J. Bruccoli.
- New York: Charles Scribner's Sons, [1989].
- Dust jacket.
NOTES: Book-of-the-Month Club Edition.
- PS3511.I9 A6 1989b C.2

656. *The Short Stories of F. Scott Fitzgerald: A New Collection.*
- Edited and with a Preface by Matthew J. Bruccoli.
- New York: Charles Scribner's Sons, [1989].
- Wrappers.
NOTES: Issued by Quality Paperback Book Club/Book-of-the-Month. Laid in: Prospectus for QPBC and BOMC.
- PS3511.I9 A6 1989b C.3

657. *The Short Stories of F. Scott Fitzgerald: A New Collection.*
- Edited and with a Preface by Matthew J. Bruccoli.
- [London]: Scribners, [1989].
- Wrappers.
NOTES: Uncorrected proof.
- PS3511.I9 A6 1991b

658. *The Short Stories of F. Scott Fitzgerald: A New Collection.*
- Edited and with a Preface by Matthew J. Bruccoli.
- [London]: Abacus, [1992].
- PS3511.I9 A6 1992

659. *The Short Stories of F. Scott Fitzgerald: A New Collection.*
- Edited and with a Preface by Matthew J. Bruccoli.
- New York: Scribner Paperback Fiction / Simon & Schuster, [1995].
- Wrappers.

NOTES: "First Scribner Paperback Fiction Edition 1995".
- PS3511.I9 A6 1995

660. [Book-of-the-Month Club set].
- New York: Charles Scribner's Sons, [1990].
- Four volumes.

NOTES: Set includes: *This Side of Paradise; The Great Gatsby; Tender Is the Night;* and *The Last Tycoon: An Unfinished Novel.*
- *TSOP* (PS3511.I9 T49 1980); *GG* (PS3511.I9 G7 1990b); *TITN* (PS3511.I9 T4 1990); *LT* (PS3511.I9 L3 1990).

661. Easton Press Collector's Edition.
- Norwalk, Conn.: Easton Press, [1991].
- Seven volumes.

NOTES: *Babylon Revisited,* with a Preface by Matthew J. Bruccoli and Illustrations by Richard Sparks; *The Beautiful and Damned,* Illustrations by Frank Mayo; *The Great Gatsby,* with an Introduction by Charles Scribner III and Illustrations by Fred Meyer; *The Last Tycoon,* with a Foreword by Edmund Wilson and Illustrations by Mario Stasollo; *Tales of the Jazz Age,* With a Foreword by Charles Scribner III and Illustrations by Richard Sparks; *Tender Is the Night,* with an Introduction by Charles Scribner III and Illustrations by Fred Meyer; *This Side of Paradise.*
- *BR* (PS3511.I9 A6 1991); *B&D* (PS3511.I9 B4 1991); *TSOP* (PS3511.I9 T49 1987); *GG* (PS3511.I9 G7 1991c); *TJA* (PS3511.I9 T3 1991); *TITN* (PS3511.I9 T4 1991); *LT* (PS3511.I9 L3 1991).

662. *The Fantasy and Mystery Stories of F. Scott Fitzgerald.*
- Selected and Introduced by Peter Hanning.
- London: Robert Hale, [1991].
- Dust jacket.

NOTES: On free front endpaper: "This is the first unauthorized collection published after FSF went into public domain in the UK. MJB".
- PS3511.I9 F3 1991

663. *The Baby Party and Other Stories.*
- Retold by Stephen Waller.
- [London]: Penguin English, [1991].
- Wrappers.

NOTES: Simply Stories: Level 4.
- PS3511.I9 B24 1991

664. *The Baby Party and Other Stories.*
- Retold by Stephen Waller.
- [London]: Penguin English, [1991].
- Wrappers.
NOTES: Simply Stories: Level 4. Fifth printing.
- PS3511.I9 B24 1991b

665. *Babylon Revisited.*
- [Tokyo]: Kodansha, [1991].
NOTES: English-language edition with Notes in Japanese.
- PS3511.I9 A6 1991c

666. *F. Scott Fitzgerald.*
- *The Great Gatsby; Tender Is the Night; This Side of Paradise; The Beautiful and Damned; The Last Tycoon.*
- London: BCA, [1991].
- Dust jacket.
- PS3511.I9 A6 1994

667. *F. Scott Fitzgerald.*
- *The Great Gatsby; Tender Is the Night; This Side of Paradise; The Beautiful and Damned; The Last Tycoon.*
- [London]: Chancellor Press, [1991].
- Dust jacket.
- PS3511.I9 A6 1994b

668. *The Diamond as Big as the Ritz and Other Stories.*
- Hong Kong: Oxford University Press, 1993.
- Wrappers.
NOTES: Abridged text.
- PS3511.I9 D5 1993

669. *The Cut Glass Bowl and Other Stories.*
- Retold by Margaret Tarner; Illustrated by Barry Rowe.
- [Oxford; Portsmouth, N.H.]: Heinemann ELT, [1995].
- Wrappers.
NOTES: Heinemann ELT Guided Readers.
- PS3511.I9 C87 1995

670. *The Selected Works of F. Scott Fitzgerald.*
- Tokyo: Hon-No-Tomosha, 1996.
- Nine volumes.
NOTES: Facsimiles of the first editions.
Volume 1: *This Side of Paradise;* Volume 2: *Flappers and Philosophers;* Volume 3: *The Beautiful and Damned;* Volume 4: *Tales of the Jazz Age;* Volume 5: *The Vegetable;* Volume 6: *The Great Gatsby;* Volume 7:

All the Sad Young Men; Volume 8: *Tender Is the Night;* Volume 9: *Taps at Reveille.*
- PS3511.I9 A6 1996c

671. *Love in the Night.*
- [London: Orion, 1996].
- Wrappers.

NOTES: A Phoenix Paperback. Includes "The Swimmers."
- PS3511.I9 L7 1996

672. *This Side of Paradise; Flappers and Philosophers.*
- New York: Gramercy Books, 1996.
- Dust jacket.

NOTES: Gramercy Modern Classics.
- PS3511.I9 A6 1996b
- Another copy.

673. *"The Diamond as Big as The Ritz" and Other Stories.*
- Mineola, N.Y.: Dover Publications, [1998].
- Wrappers.

NOTES: Dover Thrift Editions.
- PS3511.I9 A6 1998

674. *The Ice Palace and Other Stories.*
- New Brunswick, N.J.; London: Transaction Publishers, [1998].

NOTES: Large-print edition.
- PS3511.I9 A6 1998

675. *Jazz Age Stories.*
- Edited with an Introduction and Explanatory Notes by Patrick O'Donnell.
- [New York]: Penguin Books, [1998].
- Wrappers.

NOTES: First printing. Penguin Twentieth-Century Classics.
- PS3511.I9 A6 1998c

676. *The Baby Party and Other Stories.*
- Retold by Stephen Walker.
- [Harlow, England: Pearson Education Limited, in Association with Penguin Books Ltd., 1999].

NOTES: Penguin Readers: Level 5.
- PS3511.I9 B24 1999

677. *Novels and Stories, 1920–1922.*
- New York: Library of America, [2000].
- Unbound signatures.
- PS3511.I9 A6 2000 C.2

678. *Novels and Stories, 1920–1922.*
- New York: Library of America, [2000], #117.
- Dust jacket.

NOTES: First printing. Press release inserted.
- PS3511.I9 A6 2000 C.1

679. *The Collected Short Stories of F. Scott Fitzgerald.*
- [London]: Penguin, [2000].
- Wrappers.

NOTES: Penguin Classics.
- PS3511.I9 A6 2000b

680. *Before Gatsby: The First Twenty-Six Stories.*
- Edited by Matthew J. Bruccoli with the Assistance of Judith S. Baughman.
- [Columbia]: University of South Carolina Press, [2001].
- Wrappers, spiral bound.

NOTES: Uncorrected page proof. Related item: proof of dust jacket in envelope. Inscribed by MJB and Baughman on title page.
- PS3511.I9 A6 2001b

681. *Before Gatsby: The First Twenty-Six Stories.*
- Edited by Matthew J. Bruccoli with the Assistance of Judith S. Baughman.
- [Columbia]: University of South Carolina Press, [2001].
- Wrappers.

NOTES: Initialed by MJB and JSB.
- PS3511.I9 A6 2001b

II First Book Appearances by F. Scott Fitzgerald

Volumes in which work by Fitzgerald appears for the first time in a book or pamphlet written or edited by someone else (Bruccoli B and BB items).

682. *A Book of Princeton Verse II, 1919.*
    - Edited by Henry Van Dyke, Morris William Croll, Maxwell Struthers Burt, [and] James Creese, Jr.
    - Princeton, N.J.: Princeton University Press, [1919].
    - Dust jacket.
    NOTES: Bruccoli B1. Includes "Marching Streets," "The Pope at Confession," and "My First Love."
    - PN6110.C7 B6 1919

683. *The American Credo: A Contribution Toward the Interpretation of the National Mind.*
    - George Jean Nathan and H. L. Mencken.
    - New York: Knopf, 1920.
    NOTES: Bruccoli B2. FSF claimed the following items in his own marked copy: 22, 51, 193, 248, 429, 433, 442, 449, 450, 455.
    - E168.N27

684. *The New American Credo: A Contribution Toward the Interpretation of the National Mind.*
    - George Jean Nathan.
    - New York; London: Knopf, 1927.
    NOTES: Bruccoli B2. Revised edition.
    - PS3527.A72 1927

685. *O. Henry Memorial Award Prize Stories.*
    - Selected by Society of Arts and Sciences; Introduction by Blanche Colton Williams.
    - Garden City, N.Y.: Doubleday, Page, 1921.
    NOTES: Bruccoli B3. Includes "The Camel's Back."
    - PZ1.O11 1920

686. *Best Short Stories of 1922 and the Yearbook of the American Short Story.*
    - Edited by Edward J. O'Brien.
    - Boston: Small, Maynard, [1923].
    - Dust jacket.
    NOTES: Bruccoli B4. Includes "Two for a Cent."
    - PZ1.B446235 1922

687. *Aces: A Collection of Short Stories.*
- Dorothy Canfield . . . [et al]; Compiled by the Community Workers of the New York Guild for the Jewish Blind.
- New York; London: G. P. Putnam's Sons, [1924].
- Dust jacket.
NOTES: Bruccoli B5. Includes "Gretchen's Forty Winks."
- PS645.C66 1924

688. *The World's Best Short Stories of 1926.*
- Sixteen Tales Selected by the Editors of the Leading American Magazines Under the Auspices of the *New York World;* With a Foreword by William Johnston.
- New York: George H. Doran, 1926.
NOTES: Bruccoli B7. Includes "One of My Oldest Friends."
- PZ1.W69

689. *Cream of the Jug: An Anthology of Humorous Stories.*
- Edited by Grant Overton.
- New York; London: Harper & Brothers, 1927.
NOTES: Bruccoli B8.
Includes "The Pusher-in-the-Face."
- PS648.H84 C7 1927

690. *Samples; A Collection of Short Stories.*
- Community Workers of the New York Guild for the Jewish Blind.
- New York: Boni & Liveright, [1927].
- Dust jacket.
NOTES: Bruccoli B9. Includes "The Dance."
- PS645.C68 1927

691. *You — At Twenty.*
- New York: College Humor, 1927.
NOTES: Bruccoli B10. Promotional book for *College Humor* magazine.
  Includes "My Old New England Homestead on the Erie," illustrations
    by Russell Patterson.
  Includes biographical sketch of FSF.
- PS3511.I9 M9 1927

692. *Three Years, 1924–1927: The Story of a New Idea and Its Successful Adaptation.*
- With a Postscript by H. L. Mencken.
- New York: The American Mercury, 1927.
NOTES: Bruccoli B11. Six hundred copies signed by the editor and publisher of
    the *American Mercury.*
  Previously unpublished note by FSF.
- PN4900.A55 T5

693. *Ten Years of Princeton '17: A Record of the Class of 1917 of Princeton University for the Decade 1917–1927.*
- Editorial Committee: Wells Drorbaugh, Chairman.
- Princeton, N.J.: [The Class], 1929.

NOTES: Bruccoli B12. Includes "Princeton".
   Laid in: TLS, 21 October 1963, to MJB from Seland Whitney Landon, a Fitzgerald classmate, concerning the book.
- LD4604 1917 D7

694. *Frances Newman's Letters.*
- Frances D. Newman; Edited by Hansell Baugh; With a Prefatory Note by James Branch Cabell.
- New York: Liveright, 1929.
- Dust jacket.

NOTES: Bruccoli B13. Includes previously unpublished letter from FSF.
- PS3527.E883 Z5 1929

695. *Great Modern Short Stories.*
- Edited by Grant Overton.
- New York: The Modern Library, [1930].
- Dust jacket.

NOTES: Bruccoli B14. Includes "At Your Age."
- PZ1.O96 GR 823.9

696. *Best Short Stories of 1931 and the Yearbook of the American Short Story.*
- Edited by Edward J. O'Brien.
- New York: Dodd, Mead, 1931.
- Dust jacket.

NOTES: Bruccoli B15. Includes "Babylon Revisited."
- PZ1.B446235 1931

697. *Best Short Stories of 1931 II: American.*
- London: Jonathan Cape, [1932].

NOTES: Bruccoli B15, Note.
- PS648.S5 B45 1931

698. *The New Yorker Scrapbook.*
- Garden City, N. Y.: Doubleday, Doran, 1931.
- Dust jacket.

NOTES: Bruccoli B16. "First Edition".
   Includes "A Short Autobiography (with Acknowledgements to Nathan)."
- PS659.N4

699. *The Tiger's Family Album: A Compendium of Half a Century of Princeton Wit and Humor, If Any, in Prose, Picture and Poesy.*
- [Princeton, N.J.]: Princeton University Press, [1931].

NOTES: Bruccoli B17.

"Published on the Occasion of the Fiftieth Anniversary of the Founding of the Princeton Tiger . . ."
- PN6231.C6 T5 1931

700. *The Best American Love Stories of the Year.*
- Selected and with an Introduction by Margaret Widdemer.
- New York: Tudor, 1932.
NOTES: Bruccoli B18. Includes "A New Leaf."
- PS648.L6 B46 1932b

701. *Best Short Stories of 1933 and the Yearbook of the American Short Story.*
- Edited by Edward J. O'Brien.
- Boston: Houghton Mifflin, 1933.
NOTES: Bruccoli B19. Includes "Crazy Sunday."
- PZ1.B446235

702. *O. Henry Memorial Award Prize Stories.*
- Edited by Harry Hansen.
- Garden City, N.Y.: Doubleday, Doran, 1933.
- Dust jacket.
NOTES: Bruccoli B20. Includes "Family in the Wind."
- PZ1.O11 1933
  Bruccoli B21, the 1934 Modern Library reprinting of *The Great Gatsby* with a new introduction by FSF, is listed in section I.

703. *These Stories Went to Market.*
- Vernon Mckenzie.
- New York: Robert M. McBride, [1935].
NOTES: Bruccoli B22. Includes FSF's previously unpublished notes on his stories, p. xviii.
- PZ1.M199

704. *The New Republic Anthology, 1915–1935.*
- Edited by Groff Conklin; Introduction by Bruce Bliven.
- New York: Dodge, [1936].
NOTES: Bruccoli B23. Includes "Ring."
- PS536.N4

705. *Colonial and Historic Homes of Maryland in Two Volumes: One Hundred Original Etchings.*
- Don Swann; With Descriptive Text by Don Swann, Jr.; Introduction by Herbert R. O'Conor; Foreword by Francis Scott Key Fitzgerald.
- Baltimore: The Etchcrafters Art Guild, 1939.
NOTES: Bruccoli B24. Prospectus. Previously unpublished "Foreword."
- NE2012.S92 A43

706. *Colonial and Historic Homes of Maryland: One Hundred Original Etchings.*
- Don Swann; With Descriptive Text by Don Swann, Jr.; Introduction by Herbert R. O'Conor; Foreword by Francis Scott Key Fitzgerald.
- Baltimore: The Etchcrafters Art Guild, 1939.
- Slipcase.

NOTES: Bruccoli B25. "Edition Limited to Two Hundred Copies."
Reprinted by Johns Hopkins University Press (Baltimore & London), [1975].
- NE2012.S92 A43

707. *Best Short Stories of 1940 and the Yearbook of the American Short Story.*
- Edited by Edward J. O'Brien.
- Boston: Houghton Mifflin, 1940.
- Dust jacket.

NOTES: Bruccoli B26. Includes "Design in Plaster."
- PZ1.B446235 1940

708. *Innocent Merriment; An Anthology of Light Verse.*
- Selected by Franklin P. Adams.
- New York, London: Whittlesey House, McGraw-Hill, [1942].
- Dust jacket.

NOTES: Bruccoli B27. Includes "Obit on Parnassus."
- PD1195.H8 A3

709. *Modern Reading: Number Eight.*
- Edited by Reginald Moore.
- London: Wells Gardner, Darton, 1943.
- Wrappers.

NOTES: Bruccoli B28. Big Ben Books. Includes "Two Old-timers."
- PN6014.M54 1943

710. *Esquire's 2nd Sports Reader.*
- Edited, and with an Introduction, by Arnold Gingrich.
- New York: A. S. Barnes, [1946].
- Dust jacket.

NOTES: Bruccoli B29. Includes "'Send Me In, Coach.'"
- GV191.E82 796.082

711. *Of Making Many Books: A Hundred Years of Reading, Writing and Publishing.*
- Roger Burlingame.
- New York: Charles Scribner's Sons, 1946.
- Dust jacket.

NOTES: Bruccoli B30. Includes previously unpublished FSF letters.
- Z473.B9 655.4747

712. *The Lives of Eighteen from Princeton.*
- Edited by Willard Thorp.
- Princeton, N.J.: Princeton University Press, 1946.
- Dust jacket.
NOTES: Bruccoli B31. Arthur Mizener's "F. Scott Fitzgerald [1896–1940] The Poet of Borrowed Time" includes previously unpublished material from FSF letters.
- LD4598.T5

713. *We Were Interrupted.*
- Burton Rascoe.
- Garden City, N.Y.: Doubleday, [1947].
- Dust jacket.
NOTES: Bruccoli B32. First edition. Includes three previously unpublished letters to Rascoe from FSF.
- PS3535.A74 Z53

714. *The Eighth McGregor Room Seminar in Contemporary Prose and Poetry: The Work of F. Scott Fitzgerald.*
- [Charlottesville: University of Virginia, 1948].
- Single sheet, French fold.
NOTES: Bruccoli B33. Includes previously unpublished FSF material.
- PS3511.I9 Z725 1948

715. *Editor to Author: The Letters of Maxwell E. Perkins.*
- Maxwell E. Perkins; Selected and Edited with Commentary and an Introduction by John Hall Wheelock.
- New York: Charles Scribner's Sons, 1950.
- Dust jacket.
NOTES: Bruccoli B34. Includes previously unpublished FSF letter to Perkins.
- Z473.P4 A4

716. *The Far Side of Paradise: A Biography of F. Scott Fitzgerald.*
- Arthur Mizener.
- Boston: Houghton Mifflin, 1951.
- Dust jacket.
NOTES: Bruccoli B35. Includes previously unpublished FSF material letters, scrapbooks, ledger, manuscripts, and notes.
- PS3511.I9 Z7

717. *Ideas for Writing: Readings for College Composition.*
- Kenneth L. Knickerbocker.
- New York: Holt, 1951.
NOTES: Bruccoli B36. Includes "The Invasion of the Sanctuary."
- PE1417.K6

718. *Sherwood Anderson, His Life and Work.*
- James Erwin Schevill.
- [Denver]: University of Denver Press, [1951].
- Dust jacket.
NOTES: Bruccoli B37. Includes previously unpublished FSF letter to Anderson.
- PS3501.N4 Z8

719. *The Girls from Esquire.*
- Introduction by Frederic A. Birmingham.
- New York: Random House, 1952.
- Dust jacket.
NOTES: Bruccoli B38.
    Includes "The Woman from Twenty-One."
- PN6120.95.W7 E7 1952

720. *The Girls from Esquire.*
- Introduction by Frederic A. Birmingham.
- London: Arthur Barker, 1953.
NOTES: Bruccoli B38.
    Includes "The Woman from Twenty-One."
- PN6120.95.W7 E7 1953b

721. *The Fourth Round: Stories for Men, an Anthology.*
- Edited by Charles Grayson.
- New York: Holt, [1953].
- Dust jacket.
NOTES: Bruccoli B39. Includes "The Bowl."
- PN6120.95.B73 G7 1953

722. *The Flowers of Friendship: Letters Written to Gertrude Stein.*
- Edited by Donald Clifford Gallup.
- New York: Knopf, 1953.
- Dust jacket.
NOTES: Bruccoli B40. Includes three previously unpublished FSF letters.
- PS3537.T323 Z6

723. *The Esquire Treasury.*
- Edited by Arnold Gingrich.
- New York: Simon and Schuster, 1953.
- Dust jacket.
NOTES: Bruccoli B41. Includes "Pat Hobby's Christmas Wish."
- PN6014.E7

724. *The Esquire Treasury: The Best of Twenty Years of Esquire Fact, Fiction, and Laughter Including Seventy-Three Stories and Articles, Fifty-Seven Drawings, Cartoons, and Photographs by Some of the Most Distinguished American Writers, Artists and Photographers.*

- Edited by Arnold Gingrich.
- London: William Heineman, 1954.
- Dust jacket.

NOTES: Bruccoli B41. Includes "Pat Hobby's Christmas Wish."
- PN6014.E7 1954

725. *Great Tales of City Dwellers.*
- Edited by Alex Austin.
- New York: Lion Library Editions, [1955], #53.
- Wrappers.

NOTES: Bruccoli B42. Lion Library Edition. Includes "A Millionaire's Girl." Story credited to FSF but written by ZF.
- PZ1.A9 GR PS648.C5 A9 1955

726. *With Love from Gracie: Sinclair Lewis, 1912–1925.*
- Grace Hegger Lewis.
- New York: Harcourt, Brace, [1955].
- Dust jacket.

NOTES: Bruccoli B43. Previously unpublished letter to Lewis from FSF.
- PS3523.E94 Z62

727. *13 Great Stories.*
- Edited by Daniel Talbot.
- New York: Dell, [1955].
- Wrappers.

NOTES: Bruccoli B44. A Dell 1st Edition. Includes "The World's Fair."
- PS659.T3 1955

728. *Great Tales of the Far West.*
- Edited by Alex Austin.
- New York: Lion Library Editions, 1956, #88.
- Wrappers.

NOTES: Bruccoli B45. Includes "The Last Kiss."
- PS648.W4 G4 1956

729. *The Letters of Thomas Wolfe.*
- Thomas Wolfe; Collected and Edited, with an Introduction and Explanatory Text, by Elizabeth Nowell.
- New York: Charles Scribner's Sons, [1956].

NOTES: Bruccoli B46. Includes previously unpublished FSF letter to Wolfe.
- PS3545.O337 Z54

730. *The Ladies' Home Journal Treasury.*
- Selected from the Complete Files by John Mason Brown and the Editors of *The Ladies' Home Journal.*
- New York: Simon and Schuster, [1956].

NOTES: Bruccoli B47. Includes "Imagination—and a Few Mothers."
- PS536.L3

731. *Scott Fitzgerald at La Paix.*
- Andrew W. Turnbull.
- Cambridge: Massachusetts Institute of Technology, 1956.
- Wrappers.

    NOTES: Bruccoli B48. *Publications in the Humanities* / Massachusetts Institute of Technology, Department of Humanities; no. 22.
    Previously unpublished FSF inscriptions and letters.
    Laid in: Three letters from Andrew Turnbull to Mr. Johns, thanking him for information on FSF.
- PS3511.I85 Z85 1956

732. *Wives and Lovers.*
- Edited by Alex Austin.
- New York: Lion Library Editions, 1956.
- Wrappers.

    NOTES: Bruccoli B49. Includes "Flight and Pursuit."
- PN6120.95.L6 W5 1956

733. *The Papers of Christian Gauss.*
- Edited by Katherine Gauss Jackson and Hiram Haydn.
- New York: Random House, [1957].
- Dust jacket.

    NOTES: Bruccoli B50. Includes seven previously unpublished FSF letters and one wire.
- LD4606.G3 A5 923.773

734. *Authors At Work.*
- An Address Delivered by Robert H. Taylor at the Opening of an Exhibition of Literary Manuscripts at the Grolier Club; Together with a Catalogue of the Exhibition by Herman W. Liebert, and Facsimiles of Many of the Exhibits.
- New York: Grolier Club, 1957.
- Dust jacket.

    NOTES: Bruccoli B51. Previously unpublished facsimile of first page of revised typescript of "The Perfect Life."
- PN149.T3

735. *The Armchair Esquire.*
- Edited by Arnold Gingrich and L. Rust Hills. Introduction by Granville Hicks.
- New York: Putnam, [1958].
- Dust jacket.

    NOTES: Bruccoli B52. Includes "Three Acts of Music."
- PN6014.E68

736. *The Armchair Esquire.*
- Edited by Arnold Gingrich and L. Rust Hills; Introduction by Granville Hicks.
- London: William Heinemann, 1959.
- Dust jacket.

NOTES: Bruccoli B52. English edition.
   Includes "Three Acts of Music." Headnote quotes FSF.
- PN6014.E68 1959

See section XIV for entries on *Beloved Infidel* (Bruccoli B53).

737. *Joy Ride.*
- Dwight Taylor.
- New York: Putnam, [1959].

NOTES: Bruccoli B54. Review copy.
   Includes previously unpublished FSF verse and reports conversation. Laid in: TLS, 2 March 1959, to MJB concerning *Tender Is the Night*.
- PS3539.A885 Z52

738. *Stephen Leacock, Humorist and Humanist.*
- Ralph L. Curry.
- Garden City, N. Y.: Doubleday, 1959.
- Dust jacket.

NOTES: Bruccoli B55.
   Includes previously unpublished FSF letter to Leacock.
- PR6023.E15 Z7

739. *Les Années Vingt: Les Écrivains Américains a Paris et Leurs Amis, 1920–1930:* Exposition du 11 Mars Au 25 Avril 1959 / Centre Culturel Américain.
- [Paris: 1959].
- Wrappers.

NOTES: Bruccoli B56. Includes previously unpublished FSF drawing: "The Festival of St. James."
- Z1225.U47

740. *Shakespeare and Company.*
- Sylvia Beach.
- New York: Harcourt, Brace, [1959].
- Dust jacket.

NOTES: Bruccoli B56. Includes FSF drawing: "The Festival of St. James."
- Z305.B32

741. *Shakespeare and Company.*
- Sylvia Beach.
- London: Faber and Faber, [1960].
- Dust jacket.

NOTES: Bruccoli B56. Includes FSF drawing: "The Festival of St. James."
- Z305.B32 1959b

742. *Paris in the Twenties: An Exhibition of Souvenirs of British, French and American Writers from Shakespeare and Company.*
- United States Information Service (London, England).
- London: USIS, 1960.
- Wrappers.
NOTES: Bruccoli B56. Includes FSF drawing: "The Festival of St. James."
- Z1225.U61 1960

743. *Ellery Queen's Mystery Annual.*
- Edited by Ellery Queen.
- New York: Random House, [1960].
- Dust jacket.
NOTES: Bruccoli B57. Includes "The Mystery of the Raymond Mortgage."
- PZ1.A1 E4 15th

744. *Scott Fitzgerald.*
- Andrew Turnbull.
- New York: Charles Scribner's Sons, [1962].
- Dust jacket.
NOTES: Bruccoli B58. Includes previously unpublished FSF material from letters, ledger, scrapbooks, manuscripts, and notes.
- PS3511.I9 Z88

745. *Scott Fitzgerald.*
- Andrew Turnbull.
- London: Bodley Head, 1962.
- Dust jacket.
NOTES: Bruccoli B58. Includes previously unpublished FSF material from letters, ledger, scrapbooks, manuscripts, and notes.
- PS3511.I9 Z88 1962

746. *Between Friends: Letters of James Branch Cabell and Others.*
- James Branch Cabell; Edited by Padraic Colum and Margaret Freeman Cabell; With an Introduction by Carl Van Vechten.
- New York: Harcourt, Brace & World, [1962].
- Dust jacket.
NOTES: Bruccoli B59.
    Includes previously unpublished FSF letters.
- PS3505.A153 Z53

747. *That Summer in Paris: Memories of Tangled Friendships with Hemingway, Fitzgerald, and Some Others.*
- Morley Callaghan.
- New York: Coward-McCann, 1963.
- Dust jacket.
NOTES: Bruccoli B60. Includes previously unpublished FSF letter and wire. Laid in: Reviews and other promotional material.
- PS3505.A4342 Z52 1963

748. *F. Scott Fitzgerald.*
- Kenneth Eugene Eble.
- New York: Twayne Publishers, [1963].
- Dust jacket.
NOTES: Bruccoli B61. Twayne's United States Authors Series, #36.
Material from unpublished Preface to *This Side of Paradise* and galleys of *The Great Gatsby*.
- PS3511.I9 Z6

749. *The Compleat Neurotica.*
- Edited by Jay Irving Landesman and Gershon Legman.
- New York: Hacker Art Books, 1963.
- Vol. 1, no. 1 (Spring 1948)–vol. 9 (Winter 1952). Dust jacket.
NOTES: Bruccoli B62. Includes unauthorized publication of "The Boy Who Killed His Mother."
- AP2.N3676 V.1–9.

750. *The Composition of Tender Is the Night.*
- Matthew J. Bruccoli.
- [Pittsburgh]: University of Pittsburgh Press, [1963].
- Galleys with MJB holograph and manuscript corrections, dated "1–28–63."
NOTES: Published as Bruccoli B63. Includes previously unpublished FSF material from manuscripts and letters.
- PS3511.I9 T449

751. *The Composition of Tender Is the Night.*
- Matthew J. Bruccoli.
- [Pittsburgh]: University of Pittsburgh Press, [1963].
- Dust jacket.
NOTES: Bruccoli B63. Includes previously unpublished FSF material from manuscripts and letters.
- PS3511.I9 T45

752. *Love and Revolution: My Journey Through an Epoch.*
- Max Eastman.
- New York: Random House, [1964].
- Dust jacket.
NOTES: Bruccoli B64. Includes previously unpublished FSF letter to Eastman. Reports conversation with FSF.
- PS3509.A752 Z52

753. *The Art of F. Scott Fitzgerald.*
- Sergio Perosa; Translated by Charles Matz and the Author.
- Ann Arbor: University of Michigan Press, [1965].
- Dust jacket.

NOTES: Bruccoli B65. Review copy, annotated by MJB.
Includes previously unpublished material from typescripts and manuscripts of "The Romantic Egoist," *The Great Gatsby,* and *The Last Tycoon.*
- PS3511.I9 Z813

754. *F. Scott Fitzgerald: A Critical Portrait.*
- Henry Dan Piper.
- New York: Holt, Rinehart and Winston, 1965.
- Plate proofs.
NOTES: Published as Bruccoli B66. Includes previously unpublished FSF material from letters, notes, and typescripts.
With corrections by MJB and proof of dust jacket.
- PS3511.I9 Z82 1965

755. *F. Scott Fitzgerald: A Critical Portrait.*
- Henry Dan Piper.
- London: Bodley Head, 1966.
- Dust jacket.
NOTES: Bruccoli B66. Includes previously unpublished FSF material from letters, notes, and typescripts.
- PS3511.I9 Z82 1966

756. *A Gift of Joy.*
- Helen Hayes with Lewis Funke.
- New York: M. Evans; Distributed by Lippincott, Philadelphia, [1965].
NOTES: Bruccoli B67. Review copy with publisher's slip laid in. Includes two previously unpublished FSF poems.
- PN2287.H35 A3

757. *The Smart Set: A History and Anthology.*
- Carl R. Dolmetsch; With an Introductory Reminiscence by S. N. Behrman.
- New York: Dial Press, 1966.
- Dust jacket.
NOTES: Bruccoli B68. Review copy. Laid in: Prospectus.
Includes "The Debutante, a One-Act Play."
- PN4900.S65 D6

758. *The Penguin Book of Modern Verse Translation.*
- Introduced and Edited by George Steiner.
- Harmondsworth, England: Penguin, 1966.
- Wrappers.
NOTES: Bruccoli B69. The Penguin Poets.
Includes FSF translation of Rimbaud's "Voyelles."
- PN6101.S8

759. *Spellbound in Darkness: Readings in the History and Criticism of the Silent Film.*
- George C. Pratt.
- Rochester, N.Y.: University School of Liberal & Applied Studies, University of Rochester, 1966.
- Comb-bound wrappers.
NOTES: Bruccoli B70. Includes FSF interview "Has the Flapper Changed?" by Margaret Reid.
- PN1993.5.A1 P73

See section XIV for entries on *College of One* (Bruccoli B71).

760. *Creative Writing & Rewriting: Contemporary American Novelists at Work.*
- John Kuehl.
- New York: Appleton-Century-Crofts, [1967].
- Wrappers.
NOTES: Bruccoli B73. Includes draft and published versions of chapter 1 of *The Great Gatsby.*
- PS129.K8

761. *Write and Rewrite: A Study of the Creative Process.*
- John Kuehl.
- New York: Meredith Press, [1967].
- Dust jacket.
NOTES: Bruccoli B74. Includes draft and published versions of chapter 1 of *The Great Gatsby.*
- PS129.K8 1967b

762. *Connoisseur's Haven: The Pittsburgh Bibliophiles' Journey to Baltimore 27–29 October 1967.*
- Robert C. Alberts.
- [Pittsburgh, Penn.: 1967].
- Wrappers.
NOTES: Bruccoli B75. 250 copies printed.
Includes previously unpublished inscription by FSF to H. L. Mencken in Ernest Hemingway's *Men Without Women.*
- Z991.P4 A4

763. *The Moving Image: A Guide to Cinematic Literacy.*
- Robert Gessner.
- New York: Dutton, 1968.
- Dust jacket.
NOTES: Bruccoli B76.
Includes previously unpublished material from F. Scott Fitzgerald's screenplay "Cosmopolitan" ("Babylon Revisited").
- PN1994.G43 791.43

128   First Book Appearances

764. *The Moving Image: A Guide to Cinematic Literacy.*
- Robert Gessner.
- London: Cassell, 1968.
- Dust jacket.

  NOTES: Bruccoli B76. Includes unpublished material from F. Scott Fitzgerald's screenplay "Cosmopolitan" (Babylon Revisited).
- PN1994.G39 1968

765. *Ernest Hemingway: A Life Story.*
- Carlos Baker.
- New York: Charles Scribner's Sons, 1969.
- Dust jacket.

  NOTES: Bruccoli B77. Includes material from three unpublished telegrams, pp. 293, 316.
  Annotated by MJB.
- PS3515.E37 Z575 1969

766. *Fitzgerald/Hemingway Annual 1969.*
- Edited by Matthew J. Bruccoli (Managing Editor: C. E. Frazer Clark, Jr.).
- Washington, D.C.: NCR/Microcard Editions, [1969].

  NOTES: Bruccoli B78.
  Includes "Dearly Beloved" and untitled poem "Valentine was a Saint . . ."
  Signed by MJB and inscribed and signed by Clark, 29 September 1969.
- PS3511.I9 Z617 1969

767. *Fitzgerald Newsletter.*
- Editor: Matthew J. Bruccoli.
- Washington, D.C.: NCR/Microcard Editions, [1969].
- No. 1 (Spring 1958) – no. 40 (Winter 1968).

  NOTES: Bruccoli B79. Reprint. Originally published quarterly.
  Includes previously unpublished material from letters, notes, inscriptions, and typescripts.
  With: 41 issues of *Fitzgerald Newsletter* (complete run) on deposit.
- PS3511.I9 Z62 814

768. *Lillian Gish: The Movies, Mr. Griffith, and Me.*
- Lillian Gish with Ann Pinchot.
- Englewood Cliffs, N.J.: Prentice-Hall, [1969].
- Dust jacket.

  NOTES: Bruccoli B80. Signed by Gish.
  Includes previously unpublished FSF inscription.
- PN2287.G55 A3 C.2
- Another copy unsigned.

769. *Fitzgerald/Hemingway Annual 1970.*
- Edited by Matthew J. Bruccoli and C. E. Frazer Clark, Jr.
- Washington, D.C.: NCR/Microcard Editions, [1970].

NOTES: Bruccoli B81.
> Includes previously unpublished material: FSF letter to Ernest Hemingway; facsimile of manuscript for "When Vanity Kissed Vanity"; untitled poem; FSF's revisions in "Fitzgerald's Marked Copy of *The Great Gatsby;* and "Six Letters to Mencken."
- PS3511.I9 Z617 1970

770. *Zelda: A Biography.*
- Nancy Milford.
- New York: Harper & Row, 1970.
- Dust jacket.
NOTES: Bruccoli B82. Previously unpublished FSF material from letters and notes.
- PS3511.I9234 Z8 1970

771. *Zelda: A Biography.*
- Nancy Milford.
- London: Bodley Head, 1970.
- Dust jacket.
NOTES: Bruccoli B82. Previously unpublished FSF material from letters and notes.
- PS3511.I9234 Z8 1970b

See section XIV (Sheilah Graham section) for entry on *The Garden of Allah* (Bruccoli B83).

772. *Profile of F. Scott Fitzgerald.*
- Edited by Matthew J. Bruccoli.
- Columbus, Ohio: Charles E. Merrill Publishing Co., 1971.
- Wrappers.
NOTES: Bruccoli B84. Charles E. Merrill Profiles.
> Includes "My Generation." Inscribed by Vance Bourjaily, one of the contributors, to MJB.
- PS3511.I9 Z56

773. *Crazy Sundays: F. Scott Fitzgerald in Hollywood.*
- Aaron Latham.
- New York: Viking, [1971].
- Dust jacket.
NOTES: Bruccoli B85. Includes previously unpublished FSF material from letters, notes and scripts throughout.
- PS3511.I9 Z675

774. *Crazy Sundays: F. Scott Fitzgerald in Hollywood.*
- Aaron Latham.
- London: Secker & Warburg, [1972].
- Dust jacket.

NOTES: Bruccoli B85. Includes previously unpublished FSF material from letters, notes and scripts throughout.
- PS3511.I9 Z675 1972

775. *Exiles from Paradise: Zelda and Scott Fitzgerald.*
- Sara Mayfield.
- New York: Delacorte, 1971.
- Spiral-bound wrappers: "UNCORRECTED PROOF".
NOTES: Published as Bruccoli B86.
Includes previously unpublished FSF material from letters, notebooks, manuscripts, and inscriptions.
- PS3511.I9 Z685

776. *Exiles from Paradise: Zelda and Scott Fitzgerald.*
- Sara Mayfield.
- New York: Delacorte, 1971.
- Dust jacket.
NOTES: Bruccoli B86.
Includes previously unpublished FSF material from letters, notebooks, manuscripts, and inscriptions.
- PS3511.I9 Z685 1971

777. *Fitzgerald/Hemingway Annual 1971.*
- Edited by Matthew J. Bruccoli and C. E. Frazer Clark, Jr.
- Washington, D.C.: NCR/Microcard Editions, [1971].
NOTES: Bruccoli B87.
Includes previously unpublished material: Facsimiles of FSF signatures; "Preface to *This Side of Paradise*"; "Fitzgerald's Ledger"; facsimile of first page of FSF story 'The I.O.U.' in "The Lost and Unpublished Stories of F. Scott Fitzgerald"; list of FSF corrections and facsimiles notes in "Fitzgerald's Marked Copy of *This Side of Paradise*"; FSF statement on Girl Scouts; material from FSF scripts in "Fitzgerald's Film Scripts of 'Babylon Revisited'"; "Oh, Sister, Can You Spare Your Heart"; facsimile of FSF inscription in "T.S. Eliot's Copy of *Gatsby*"; FSF letter (25 September 1934) in "Fitzgerald Recommends Nathanael West for a Guggenheim"; quotes from FSF letters in "The Fitzgerald-Mencken Correspondence."
Volume also includes a recording of FSF reciting verse.
- PS3511.I9 Z617 1971

778. *America Awakes: A New Appraisal of the Twenties.*
- Jan Farrington.
- Richmond, Virginia: Westover Publishing, [1971].
- Dust jacket.
NOTES: Bruccoli B88.
Includes FSF inscription and letter to Sylvia Beach.
- E169.1.F2

779. *F. Scott Fitzgerald and Ernest M. Hemingway in Paris: An Exhibition at the Bibliothéque Benjamin Franklin, in Conjunction with a Conference at the Institut D'Études Américaines, 23–24 June 1972.*
- Bloomfield Hills, Mich.: Bruccoli-Clark, 1972.
- Wrappers.

NOTES: Bruccoli B89. no. 1 of 650 copies.
   Includes facsimile of FSF letter and previously unpublished inscription to Van Wyck Brooks.
   Inscribed to MJB by C. E. Frazer Clark, 9 June 1972.
   With RTS (6 pp.) of Scottie Fitzgerald's introduction on deposit.
- PS3511.I9 Z615
- Another copy signed by conference participant.
   Another copy: 1 of 5 in special binding inscribed by Clark to MJB, 21 July 1972.

780. *Scott Fitzgerald and His World.*
- Arthur Mizener.
- London: Thames and Hudson, 1972.
- Dust jacket.

NOTES: Bruccoli B90. Includes previously unpublished FSF inscriptions.
- PS3511.I9 Z72 1972

781. *The Left Bank Revisited: Selections from the Paris Tribune, 1917–1934.*
- Edited with an Introduction by Hugh Ford; Foreword by Matthew Josephson.
- University Park: Pennsylvania State University Press, 1972.
- Dust jacket.

NOTES: Bruccoli B91. Includes interview: "Fitzgerald Back from Riviera; Is Working On Novel" from *Chicago Daily Tribune (Paris Edition)*.
- DC715.F67

782. *Fitzgerald/Hemingway Annual 1972.*
- Edited by Matthew J. Bruccoli and C. E. Frazer Clark, Jr.
- Washington, D.C.: NCR/Microcard Editions, [1973].

NOTES: Bruccoli B92.
   Includes previously unpublished material: "Fitzgerald on *Ulysses*: A Previously Unpublished Letter to Bennet Cerf"; "Six Previously Unpublished Fitzgerald Letters to Hunt Stromberg"; "An Additional Fitzgerald Lyric for 'It Is Art'"; "A Fitzgerald Auto-bibliography"; "Fitzgerald on 'The Ice Palace': A Newly Discovered Letter"; "10 Best Books I Have Read"; and "Fitzgerald to Roger Burlingame: A New Letter."
- PS3511.I9 Z617 1972

783. *O'Hara: A Biography.*
- Finis Farr.
- Boston: Little, Brown, [1973].

- Dust jacket.

NOTES: Bruccoli B93.
> Includes FSF inscription to John O'Hara in *Tender Is the Night*.
- PS3529.H29 Z67

784. *Fitzgerald/Hemingway Annual 1973.*
- Edited by Matthew J. Bruccoli and C. E. Frazer Clark, Jr.
- Washington, D.C.: NCR/Microcard Editions, [1974].

NOTES: Bruccoli B94.
> Facsimiles FSF's inscription to John O'Hara in *Tender Is the Night*.
- PS3511.I9 Z617 1973

785. *The Romantic Egoists.*
- Edited by Matthew J. Bruccoli, Scottie Fitzgerald Smith, and Joan P. Kerr; Art Editor, Margareta F. Lyons.
- New York: Charles Scribner's Sons, [1974].
- Unbound signatures in dust jacket.

NOTES: Bruccoli B95.
> Includes "The Pampered Men." Reproduces FSF letters, inscriptions, and notes.
- PS3511.I9 Z5593 1974

786. *The Romantic Egoists.*
- Edited by Matthew J. Bruccoli, Scottie Fitzgerald Smith, and Joan P. Kerr; Art Editor, Margareta F. Lyons.
- New York: Charles Scribner's Sons, [1974].
- Dust jacket.

NOTES: Annotated by Scottie Fitzgerald.
> Laid in: Clippings and editorial material.
- PS3511.I9 Z5593

787. *The Romantic Egoists.*
- Edited by Matthew J. Bruccoli, Scottie Fitzgerald Smith, and Joan P. Kerr; Art Editor, Margareta F. Lyons.
- New York: Charles Scribner's Sons, [1974].
- In slipcase.

NOTES: Bruccoli B95. no. 438 of 500 copies signed by the editors.
- PS3511.I9 Z5593 1974

788. [Working notes for *The Romantic Egoists*].
- Scottie Fitzgerald.
- 9 pieces.
- PS3511.I9 Z55925

789. "Statement on *The Romantic Egoists*," c. 1974.
- James Dickey.
- 1 p.

NOTES: TS with holograph note to MJB: "Let's go in <u>big</u> underlined type, with just what we've got here. Long blurbs don't get read I've found—".
- PS3554.I32 D63 1974

790. *F. Scott Fitzgerald.*
- Howard Greenfeld.
- New York: Crown Publishers, [1974].
- Unbound signatures inserted in dust jacket.
NOTES: Bruccoli B96. First edition. Review copy with publisher's slip laid in. Includes facsimile of previously unpublished *Tender Is the Night* galley.
- PS3511.I9 Z644

791. *Fitzgerald/Hemingway Annual 1974.*
- Edited by Matthew J. Bruccoli and C. E. Frazer Clark, Jr.
- Washington, D.C.: NCR/Microcard Editions, [1975].
NOTES: Bruccoli B97.
Includes previously unpublished material: Facsimile of FSF's inscription to Mrs. A. D. Sayre in *The Diary of Otto Braun;* letters to Brooks Bowman; and facsimile of revised TS in "The Discarded Ending of 'The Offshore Pirate.'"
- PS3511.I9 Z617 1974

792. *The Twenties: From Notebooks and Diaries of the Period.*
- Edmund Wilson; Edited with an Introduction by Leon Edel.
- New York: Farrar, Straus and Giroux, 1975.
- Dust jacket.
NOTES: Bruccoli B98. Includes previously unpublished FSF poem "Dog! Dog! Dog!"
- PS3545.I6245 Z536 1975

793. *Fitzgerald/Hemingway Annual 1975.*
- Edited by Matthew J. Bruccoli and C. E. Frazer Clark, Jr.
- Washington, D.C.: NCR/Microcard Editions, [1975].
NOTES: Bruccoli B99.
Includes previously unpublished material: Facsimile of FSF inscription to Ernest Truex in *The Vegetable* and facsimile of revised TS in "The Coda of 'The Swimmers.'"
- PS3511.I9 Z617 1975

See section XIV (Sheilah Graham section) for entry on *The Real F. Scott Fitzgerald* (Bruccoli B100).

794. *Pages: The World of Books, Writers, and Writing.*
- Matthew J. Bruccoli, Editorial Director; C. E. Frazer Clark, Jr., Managing Editor.
- Detroit: Gale Research, [1976].
- Dust jacket.

795. *Some Time in the Sun.*
- Tom Dardis.
- New York: Scribner, [1976].
NOTES: Bruccoli B102. Review copy.
  Laid in: Promotional material and TLS, 28 May 1976, from Budd Schulberg to MJB about his fiction treatment of FSF. Also CC, 28 May 1976, of Schulberg letter to Robert Dahlin of *Publishers' Weekly*.
- PS129.D3

796. *Cleopatra's Barge: The Crowninshield Story.*
- David L. Ferguson.
- Boston: Little, Brown, [1976].
NOTES: Bruccoli B102a. First edition.
  Includes letter from FSF to Frank Crowninshield.
- CS71.C9563 F4 1976

797. *Fitzgerald/Hemingway Annual 1976.*
- Edited by Matthew J. Bruccoli; Associate editors Margaret M. Duggan and Richard Layman.
- Englewood, Colo.: Information Handling Services, [1978].
NOTES: Bruccoli B103.
  Includes previously unpublished material: Facsimile of FSF inscription to Harold Ober; "'Ballet Shoes': A Movie Synopsis"; facsimiles inscription in *The Great Gatsby* and letter to Robert Kerr in "One Not-Forgotten Summer Night"; facsimiles *The Beautiful and Damned* inscription and note to Oscar and Xandra Kalman and letter to Elizabeth Clarkson Wann in "Fitzgerald in St. Paul"; and FSF's letter to Ernest Hemingway in "F. Scott Fitzgerald's Critique of *A Farewell to Arms.*"
- PS3511.I9 Z617 1975

798. *Cast of Thousands.*
- Anita Loos.
- New York: Grosset & Dunlap, [1977].
- Dust jacket.
NOTES: Bruccoli B104. Author's inscription to Wilhelmina and Bob Wynn.
- PN2285.L633

799. *Letters On Literature and Politics, 1912–1972.*
- Edmund Wilson; Edited by Elena Wilson; Introduction by Daniel Aaron; Foreword by Leon Edel.
- New York: Farrar, Straus and Giroux, [1977].
- Dust jacket.

Previous notes for entry above page:
NOTES: Bruccoli B101. Includes facsimile of previously unpublished FSF appraisal of his library.
- PN35.P35

NOTES: Bruccoli B105. Includes quotation from previously unpublished FSF inscription.
- PS3545.I6245 Z54 1977

800. *Paris-New York, Échanges Littéraires au Vingtième Siècle: Exposition, 9 Juin–12 Septembre 1977.*
- Paris: Bibliothèque Publique d'Information, Centre National d'Art et de Culture Georges Pompidou, 1977.
- Wrappers.
NOTES: Bruccoli B106. Includes facsimiles of previously unpublished FSF letter to Nino Frank.
- PQ143.U6 P3 809

801. *The Last of the Novelists: F. Scott Fitzgerald and the Last Tycoon.*
- Matthew J. Bruccoli.
- Carbondale: Southern Illinois University Press, 1977.
- Setting copy.
NOTES: Published as Bruccoli B107.
- PS3511.I9 L3539

802. *The Last of the Novelists: F. Scott Fitzgerald and the Last Tycoon.*
- Matthew J. Bruccoli.
- Carbondale: Southern Illinois University Press, 1977.
- Proofs.
NOTES: Published as Bruccoli B107. Corrections by MJB, 3 June 1977.
- PS3511.I9 L3539

803. *"The Last of the Novelists": F. Scott Fitzgerald and the Last Tycoon.*
- Matthew J. Bruccoli.
- Carbondale: Southern Illinois University Press, [1977].
- Dust jacket.
NOTES: Bruccoli B107. With MJB's autograph annotations. Includes previously unpublished FSF material from manuscripts and notebooks.
- PS3511.I9 L354

804. [Statements on *The Last of the Novelists*], 1977.
- 4 items.
NOTES: TLS from James Dickey to Vernon Sternberg, 8 August 1977, and TLS from Wallace Markfield to Vernon Sternberg, 7 August 1977; both include blurbs for *The Last of the Novelists.*
CC of Dickey's letter with typed copy of blurb inscribed with note: "—for Matt—from James Dickey, 8 August 1977".
- PS3554.I32 D63 1977

805. *In Their Time / 1920–1940: Fiestas, Moveable Feasts, and "Many Fêtes"; An Exhibition in the University of Virginia Library, December 1977–March 1978.*
- Bloomfield Hills, Mich.: Bruccoli Clark, 1977.

- Wrappers.
- NOTES: Bruccoli B108. Includes facsimiles or quotes from previously unpublished FSF letters, manuscripts, and inscriptions.
- PS379.I5

806. *In Their Time / 1920–1940: An Exhibition in the University of Virginia Library.*
   - Charlottesville: Associates of the University of Virginia Library, 1977.
   - Wrappers.
   - NOTES: Bruccoli B108. Includes facsimiles or quotes from previously unpublished FSF letters, manuscripts, and inscriptions.
   - PS379.I52

807. *Fitzgerald/Hemingway Annual 1977.*
   - Edited by Margaret M. Duggan and Richard Layman; Consulting editor Matthew J. Bruccoli.
   - Detroit: Gale Research, [1977].
   - NOTES: Bruccoli B109.
        Includes previously unpublished material: Facsimile of FSF inscription to Victoria Schulberg in *Tender Is the Night*; outline and treatment for "The Feather Fan"; and "The Defeat of Art."
   - PS3511.I9 Z617 1976

808. *Scott and Ernest: The Authority of Failure and the Authority of Success.*
   - Matthew J. Bruccoli.
   - New York: Random House, 1978.
   - Wrappers.
   - NOTES: Bruccoli B110. Uncorrected proof.
        Includes quotes from and facsimiles of previously unpublished FSF letters.
        Inscribed by Albert Erskine: "For MJB my only copy AE 2/28/78".
        With TLS (2 pp.) vetting report from Vernon Sternberg, 18 April 1977.
   - PS3511.I9 Z565

809. *Scott and Ernest: The Authority of Failure and the Authority of Success.*
   - Matthew J. Bruccoli.
   - New York: Random House, [1978].
   - Dust jacket.
   - NOTES: Bruccoli B110. MJB's copy with annotations.
        Includes quotes from and facsimiles of previously unpublished FSF letters.
        Laid in: Prospectus and review from *Time*.
   - PS3511.I9 Z565 C.1

810. *Scott and Ernest: The Authority of Failure and the Authority of Success.*
   - Matthew J. Bruccoli.
   - Carbondale & Edwardsville: Southern Illinois University Press, [1980].

- Wrappers.
NOTES: Bruccoli B110.
- PS3511.I9 Z565 C.2

811. *Fitzgerald and Hemingway: A Dangerous Friendship.*
- Matthew J. Bruccoli.
- New York: Carroll & Graf, [1994].
- Wrappers.
- PS3511.I9 Z55932

812. *Fitzgerald and Hemingway: A Dangerous Friendship.*
- Matthew J. Bruccoli.
- [London]: André Deutsch, [1994].
- Dust jacket.
- PS3511.I9 Z5593 1995

813. *Max Perkins: Editor of Genius.*
- A. Scott Berg.
- New York: Dutton, [1978].
NOTES: Bruccoli B111. Quotes FSF letters and conversations.
- PN149.9.P4 B4

814. *Fitzgerald/Hemingway Annual 1978.*
- Edited by Matthew J. Bruccoli and Richard Layman.
- Detroit: Gale Research, [1979].
NOTES: Bruccoli B112.
   Includes previously unpublished material: Facsimile of FSF inscription to Gene Buck in Joseph Conrad's *Youth*; "Lipstick"; "The Fitzgeralds' Letters to the Hoveys"; "My Ten Favorite Plays"; and "Fitzgerald's Favorite Story."
- PS3511.I9 Z617 1978

815. *Fitzgerald/Hemingway Annual 1979.*
- Edited by Matthew J. Bruccoli and Richard Layman.
- Detroit: Gale Research, [1980].
NOTES: Bruccoli B113.
   Includes previously unpublished material: FSF letters in "Ruth Sturtevant and F. Scott Fitzgerald (1916–1921)"; facsimile drawing in "F. Scott Fitzgerald Plans a Library for Princeton"; "Fitzgerald's Revisions for 'Marching Streets'"; facsimile of FSF annotations in "Fitzgerald's Last Issue of *The Princeton Alumni Weekly*"; interview with FSF and Walter Wanger in "Fitzgerald at the Winter Carnival"; FSF letter to Adelaide Neall in "Fitzgerald and the *Post*: A New Letter"; FSF letters to John Franklin Carter in "Two New Fitzgerald Letters"; and reading list prepared by FSF in "The Education of Dorothy Richardson."
- PS3511.I9 Z617 1979

816. *GWTW; The Screenplay.*
- Sidney Howard; Based on the Novel by Margaret Mitchell; Editor, Richard Harwell.
- New York: Collier, 1980.
- Wrappers.

NOTES: Bruccoli B114. Includes previously unpublished FSF version of a scene.
- PN1997.G588 1980

817. *Some Sort of Epic Grandeur: A Biography of F. Scott Fitzgerald.*
- Matthew J. Bruccoli.
- 14 boxes (Holograph and typescripts), 1980–81.

NOTES: Published as Bruccoli B115.
Consists of holograph manuscript of biography written in pencil on lined yellow legal paper (2 boxes); typescript (first draft?) on manuscript, each interleaved with holograph notes, emendations, and additions in pencil on sheets of lined yellow legal paper (5 boxes); 2 typescripts of later drafts with corrections in ink and pencil (4 boxes); typescript with corrections in purple and blue ink by Scottie Fitzgerald (1 box); and the setting copy with corrections in ink and red pencil (2 boxes).
- PS3511.I9 Z5655

818. *Some Sort of Epic Grandeur, A Biography of F. Scott Fitzgerald.*
- Matthew J. Bruccoli.
- New York: Harcourt Brace Jovanovich, [1981].
- Galleys with MJB corrections.

NOTES: Published as Bruccoli B115.
Includes previously unpublished FSF material: Transcription of discussion among FSF, ZF, and Dr. Thomas Rennie, "Self-Expression," and summary of movie treatment for *Tender Is the Night* by FSF and Charles Marquis Warren.
- PS3511.I9 Z5656

819. *Some Sort of Epic Grandeur: The Life of F. Scott Fitzgerald.*
- Matthew J. Bruccoli; With a Genealogical Afterword by Scottie Fitzgerald Smith.
- New York & London: Harcourt Brace Jovanovich, 1981.
- Wrappers: "Uncorrected Proofs."

NOTES: Bruccoli B115. Signed and dated "2 April 81" on front cover by MJB.
- PS3511.I9 Z566 1981b

819A. [Statement on *Some Sort of Epic Grandeur: The Life of F. Scott Fitzgerald*].
- James Dickey.

NOTES: 2 typed leaves with Dickey's revisions, inscribed "Matt's, all the way—, James Dickey, Spring, 1981".
- PS3554.I32 D63 1981b

820. *Some Sort of Epic Grandeur: The Life of F. Scott Fitzgerald.*
- Matthew J. Bruccoli; With a Genealogical Afterword by Scottie Fitzgerald Smith.
- New York & London: Harcourt Brace Jovanovich, 1981.
- Dust jacket.

NOTES: Bruccoli B115.
- PS3511.I9 Z566 1981

821. *Some Sort of Epic Grandeur: The Life of F. Scott Fitzgerald.*
- Matthew J. Bruccoli; With a Genealogical Afterword by Scottie Fitzgerald Smith.
- London: Hodder and Stoughton, [1981].
- Dust jacket.

NOTES: Bruccoli B115.
- PS3511.I9 Z566 1981c

822. *Some Sort of Epic Grandeur: The Life of F. Scott Fitzgerald.*
- Matthew J. Bruccoli; With a Genealogical Afterword by Scottie Fitzgerald Smith.
- San Diego, New York, London: Harcourt Brace Jovanovich, [1983].
- Wrappers.

NOTES: Bruccoli B115. MJB's marked copy.
- PS3511.I9 Z566 1983

823. *Some Sort of Epic Grandeur: The Life of F. Scott Fitzgerald.*
- Matthew J. Bruccoli; With a Genealogical Afterword by Scottie Fitzgerald Smith.
- New York: Harcourt Brace Jovanovich, [1981].

NOTES: Bruccoli B115. Xerox of MJB's marked pages of first edition for revised edition.
- PS3511.I9 Z566

824. *Some Sort of Epic Grandeur: The Life of F. Scott Fitzgerald.*
- Matthew J. Bruccoli; With a Genealogical Afterword by Scottie Fitzgerald Smith.
- New York: Carroll & Graf, [1991].
- Wrappers: "A Revised Edition."

NOTES: Bruccoli B115.
- PS3511.I9 Z566 1993

825. *Some Sort of Epic Grandeur: The Life of F. Scott Fitzgerald.*
- Matthew J. Bruccoli; With a Genealogical Afterword by Scottie Fitzgerald Smith.
- New York: Cardinal, [1991].
- Wrappers.

NOTES: Bruccoli B115.
- PS3511.I9 Z566 1991

826. *Roaring At One Hundred: The Princeton Tiger Magazine Centennial Album.*
- Princeton, N.J.: The Princeton Tiger, [1983].
- Wrappers.

NOTES: Bruccoli B116. Errata slips inserted.
  Includes *Tiger* cover for 15 June 1917, by FSF and J. V. Newlin.
- LH1.P8 T52 1983

827. *Fool for Love: F. Scott Fitzgerald.*
- Scott Donaldson.
- New York: Congdon & Weed: Distributed by St. Martin's Press, [1983].
- Wrappers: "UNCORRECTED PROOF."

NOTES: Bruccoli B117. First edition. Review copy with publisher's slip laid in.
  Includes quotes from previously unpublished FSF notes and letters.
- PS3511.I9 Z59 1983

828. *Against the Current: As I Remember F. Scott Fitzgerald.*
- Frances Kroll Ring; Foreword by A. Scott Berg.
- San Francisco: Donald S. Ellis; Berkeley: Distributed by Creative Arts, 1985.
- Dust jacket.

NOTES: Bruccoli B118. Author's signed presentation copy to MJB, March 1990.
  Includes FSF quotations and facsimiles previously unpublished FSF letters, wires, inscriptions, and notes.
- PS3511.I9 Z85 1985

829. *The Cinematic Vision of F. Scott Fitzgerald.*
- Wheeler Winston Dixon.
- Ann Arbor, Mich.: UMI Research Press, [1986].
- Dust jacket.

NOTES: Bruccoli B119. Studies in Modern Literature, #54.
  Includes FSF quotes and facsimiles previously unpublished material from screenplays.
- PS3511.I9 Z587 1986

830. *F. Scott Fitzgerald: September 24, 1896–September 24, 1996: Centenary Exhibition: The Matthew J. and Arlyn Bruccoli Collection.*
- The Thomas Cooper Library.
- Columbia: University of South Carolina Press, [1996].
- Wrappers.

NOTES: Bruccoli Supplement B120. Includes facsimiles of FSF manuscripts, letters, and inscriptions.
- PS3511.I9 Z874 1996

831. *Reader's Companion to F. Scott Fitzgerald's Tender Is the Night.*
- Matthew J. Bruccoli with Judith S. Baughman.
- Columbia: University of South Carolina Press, 1996.
- Spiral-bound wrappers.

NOTES: Xerox. Proof copy.
- PS3511.I9 T4515

832. *Reader's Companion to F. Scott Fitzgerald's Tender Is the Night.*
- Matthew J. Bruccoli with Judith S. Baughman.
- Columbia: University of South Carolina Press, 1996.
- Dust jacket.
NOTES: Corrected copy. Signed by MJB and JSB.
Includes previously unpublished FSF material from manuscripts and correspondence.
- PS3511.I9 T4515 1996

833. *The Langhorne Sisters.*
- James Fox.
- London: Granta, 1998.
- Dust jacket.
NOTES: Prints excerpt from a previously unpublished letter from FSF to Nora Langhorne.
American edition published as *Five Sisters: The Langhornes of Virginia* (New York: Simon & Schuster, [2000]).
- CT274.L36 F69 1998

834. *F. Scott Fitzgerald's The Great Gatsby: A Documentary Volume.*
- Edited by Matthew J. Bruccoli.
- Detroit: Gale Group, 2000.
NOTES: Bruccoli Supplement B121. *Dictionary of Literary Biography,* vol. 219.
"A Bruccoli Clark Layman Book". Includes facsimiles of FSF correspondence and contract for *The Great Gatsby.*
Reprinted as *F. Scott Fitzgerald's The Great Gatsby: A Literary Reference* (New York: Carroll & Graf, [2002]).
- PS3545.O337 Z86276 2001

835. *Thomas Wolfe: A Documentary Volume.*
- Edited by Ted Mitchell.
- Detroit: Gale Group, [2001].
NOTES: Bruccoli Supplement B122. *Dictionary of Literary Biography;* vol. 229.
On title page: "A Bruccoli Clark Layman Book".
Facsimiles wire from FSF to Wolfe.
- PS3545.O337 Z86276 2001

836. *F. Scott Fitzgerald's Tender Is the Night: A Documentary Volume.*
- Edited by Matthew J. Bruccoli and George Parker Anderson.
- Detroit: Gale Group, [2003].
NOTES: *Dictionary of Literary Biography;* vol. 273.
On title page: "A Bruccoli Clark Layman Book".
Facsimiles previously unpublished FSF inscriptions.
- PS221.D48 1978 vol. 273

Putative First Book Appearances by Fitzgerald

837. *Who's Who in America.*
- Chicago: A. N. Marquis, [1922].
- Vol. 12 (1922–23).
NOTES: Bruccoli BB1. Includes FSF biographical note based on questionnaire, p. 1117.
- E663.W56 vol. 12

838. *The Men Who Make Our Novels.*
- Charles C. Baldwin.
- New York: Dodd, Mead, 1928.
NOTES: Bruccoli BB2. Revised edition. Includes "F. Scott Fitzgerald," pp. 166–73. Based on FSF letter. See Items 158 and 1155.
- CT101.B181

839. *The Low-Down.*
- Charles G. Shaw.
- New York: Holt, [1928].
NOTES: Bruccoli BB3. Includes "F. Scott Fitzgerald," pp. 163–69. Based on interview with FSF.
- CT220.S5

840. *Living Authors: A Book of Biographies.*
- Edited by Dilly Tante [pseudonym for Stanley Kunitz] and Illustrated with 371 Photographs and Drawings.
- New York: H. W. Wilson, 1931.
NOTES: Bruccoli BB4. Includes "F. Scott Fitzgerald," pp. 127–28. Probably based on FSF letter.
- PN771.K84 1931

841. *Contemporary American Authors: A Critical Survey and 219 Bio-Bibliographies.*
- Fred B. Millett.
- New York: Harcourt, 1940.
NOTES: Bruccoli BB5. Includes "F. Scott Fitzgerald," pp. 354–55. Probably based on FSF letter.
- PS221.M5

842. *Contemporary American Authors: A Critical Survey and 219 Bio-Bibliographies.*
- Fred B. Millett.
- London: Harrap, 1940.
- Dust jacket.
NOTES: Bruccoli BB5. Includes "F(rancis) Scott (Key) Fitzgerald, 1896–," pp. 354–55. Probably based on FSF letter.
- PS221.M5 1940

843. *Charlie: The Improbable Life and Times of Charles MacArthur.*
- Ben Hecht.
- New York: Harper, [1957].
- Dust jacket.
NOTES: Bruccoli BB6. Putative FSF letter, p. 161.
- PS3525.A1147 Z7

844. *This Is Where I Came In: The Impromptu Confessions of Edward Anthony.*
- Edward Anthony.
- Garden City, N.Y.: Doubleday, 1960.
NOTES: Bruccoli BB7. Reports FSF conversation, pp. 129–30.
- PS3507.N7 Z52

845. *The Sun within Us.*
- James Drawbell.
- London: Collins, 1963.
NOTES: Bruccoli BB8. Reports FSF conversation, pp. 170–79.
- PN5123.D7 A37

846. *Hemingway: An Old Friend Remembers.*
- Jed Kiley.
- New York: Hawthorn Books, [1965].
- Dust jacket.
NOTES: Bruccoli BB9. "First Edition, April, 1965". Reports FSF conversation, pp. 57–58.
- PS3515.E37 Z666 1965

847. *An Unfinished Woman: A Memoir.*
- Lillian Hellman.
- Boston: Little, Brown, [1969].
- Dust jacket.
NOTES: Bruccoli BB10. First edition. Reports apocryphal FSF conversation, pp. 68–69. Untrustworthy.
- PS3515.E343 Z5 812

848. *After the Good Gay Times: Asheville, Summer of '35, a Season with F. Scott Fitzgerald.*
- Tony Buttitta.
- New York: Viking Press, 1974.
- Dust jacket.
NOTES: Bruccoli BB11. Includes Buttitta's reconstruction of FSF conversations.
- PS3511.I9 Z572

849. *The Lost Summer: A Personal Memoir of F. Scott Fitzgerald.*
- Tony Buttitta; Foreword by Bryan Forbes.
- London: Robson, 1987.
- Dust jacket.

NOTES: Bruccoli BB11. Originally published as *After the Good Gay Times* (New York: Viking, 1974).
- PS3511.I9 Z5724 1987b

850. *The Thirties: From Notebooks and Diaries of the Period.*
- Edmund Wilson; Edited, with an Introduction by Leon Edel.
- New York: Farrar, Straus, and Giroux, [1980].
- Dust jacket.

NOTES: Bruccoli BB12. Reports conversations with FSF, pp. 301–2, 323–24.
- PS3545.I6245 Z535 1980

III Periodical Appearances by F. Scott Fitzgerald

First periodical appearances by Fitzgerald (Bruccoli C items). Magazine and newspaper serializations of novels are also listed here.

851. "The Mystery of the Raymond Mortgage."
    - *Now and Then* (Saint Paul Academy [Saint Paul, Minnesota]), vol. 2, no. 1 ([October 1909]), pp. 4–8.
    NOTES: Bruccoli C1. FSF's first appearance in print.
    - LH1.S256 N683 vol. 2, no. 1

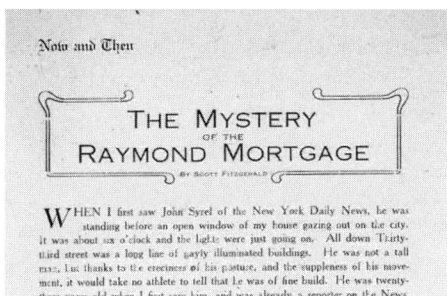

852. "Reade, Substitute Right Half."
    - *Now and Then*, vol. 2, no. 3 ([February 1910]), pp. 10–11.
    NOTES: Bruccoli C2.
    - LH1.S256 N683 vol. 2, no. 3

853. "A Debt of Honor."
    - *Now and Then* (Saint Paul Academy [Saint Paul, Minnesota]), vol. 2, no. 4 ([March 1910]), pp. 9–11.
    NOTES: Bruccoli C3.
    - LH1.S256 N683 vol. 2, no. 4

854. "S.P.A. Men in College Athletics."
    - *Now and Then* (Saint Paul Academy [Saint Paul, Minnesota]), vol. 3, no. 2 (December 1910), p. 7.
    NOTES: Bruccoli C4.
    - LH1.S256 N683 vol. 3, no. 2

855. ["Craw Bryant's a Studious Boy"] and ["There Was a Young Fellow Named Ware"].
    - *Now and Then* (Saint Paul Academy [Saint Paul, Minnesota]), vol. 2, no. 3 ([February 1910]), p. 26.
    NOTES: Bruccoli C5. Untitled limericks attributed to FSF.
    - LH1.S256 N683 vol. 2, no. 3

856. ["Paul Briggs Is a Cute Little (?) Lad"], ["There Is a Young Man Who's Not Sour"], and ["There Is an Old Lady Next Door"].
    - *Now and Then* (Saint Paul Academy [Saint Paul, Minnesota]), vol. 2, no. 5 ([June 1910]), p. 19.
    NOTES: Bruccoli C5. Untitled limerick attributed to FSF.
    - Lh1.S256 N683 vol. 2, no. 5

857. "The Room with the Green Blinds."
- *Now and Then* (Saint Paul Academy [Saint Paul, Minnesota]), vol. 3, no. 4 (June 1911), pp. 6–9.
NOTES: Bruccoli C5.
- LH1.S256 N683 vol. 3, no. 4

858. "A Luckless Santa Claus."
- *Newman News* (Hackensack, N.J.), vol. 9, no. 1 (Christmas 1912), pp. 1–7.
NOTES: Bruccoli C8.
- LH1.N4 N46 vol. 9, no. 1

859. "Pain and the Scientist."
- *Newman News* (Hackensack, N.J.), (Easter 1913), pp. 5–10.
NOTES: Bruccoli C9.
- LH1.N4 N46

860. "The Trail of the Duke."
- *Newman News* (Hackensack, N.J.), vol. 9, no. 3 (June 1913), pp. 1–7.
NOTES: Bruccoli C10.
- LH1.N4 N46 vol. 9, no. 3

861. ["There Was Once a Second Group Student"].
- *Princeton Tiger*, vol. 25, no. 6 (December 1914), p. 5.
NOTES: Bruccoli C12. Untitled limerick attributed to FSF.
- LH1.P8 T5 vol. 25, no. 6

862. "May Small Talk."
- *Princeton Tiger*, vol. 26, no. 2 (June 1915), p. 10.
NOTES: Bruccoli C14. Attributed to FSF.
- LH1.P8 T5 vol. 26, no. 2

863. "How They Head the Chapters."
- *Princeton Tiger*, vol. 26, no. 3 (September 1915), p. 10.
NOTES: Bruccoli C16. Attributed to FSF.
- LH1.P8 T5 vol. 26, no. 3

864. "The Conquest of America, as Some Writers Would Have It."
- *Princeton Tiger*, vol. 26, no. 5 (Thanksgiving 1915), p. 6.
NOTES: Bruccoli C18. Attributed to FSF.
- LH1.P8 T5 vol. 26, no. 5

865. "Three Days At Yale."
- *Princeton Tiger*, vol. 26, no. 6 (December 1915), pp. 8–10.
NOTES: Bruccoli C19. Untitled limerick attributed to FSF.
- LH1.P8 T5 vol. 26, no. 6

866. "At the Field Club."
- *Princeton Tiger*, vol. 26, no. 8 (February 1916), p. 6.
NOTES: Bruccoli C20. Attributed to FSF.
- LH1.P8 T5 vol. 26, no. 8

867. "Bohemia."
- *Princeton Tiger,* vol. 27, no. 6 (18 December 1916), p. 15.
NOTES: Bruccoli C20. Attributed to FSF.
- LH1.P8 T5 vol. 27, no. 6

868. "What Happened to Susie: A Tale of the Fifth Avenue Slums."
- *Princeton Tiger,* vol. 26, no. 8 (February 1916), p. 15.
NOTES: Bruccoli C20. Attributed to FSF.
- LH1.P8 T5 vol. 26, no. 8

869. "The Awful Optic: A Spasm in Two Fits."
- *Princeton Tiger,* vol. 26, no. 9 (March 1916), p. 7.
NOTES: Bruccoli C20. Attributed to FSF.
- LH1.P8 T5 vol. 26, no. 9

870. "The Lost Lover: The Saddest Christmas Story Ever Written."
- *Princeton Tiger,* vol. 27, no. 6 (18 December 1916), p. 8.
NOTES: Bruccoli C20. Attributed to FSF.
- LH1.P8 T5 vol. 27, no. 6

871. "To My Unused Greek Book: Acknowledgements to Keats."
- *Nassau Literary Magazine,* vol. 72, no. 3 (June 1916), p. [137].
NOTES: Bruccoli C21.
- LH1.P8 N3 vol. 72, no. 3

872. "Our Next Issue."
- *Nassau Literary Magazine,* vol. 72, no. 5 (December 1916), p. [208].
NOTES: Bruccoli C22.
- LH1.P8 N3 vol. 72, no. 5

873. "Jemina: A Story of the Blue Ridge Mountains by John Phlox, Jr."
- *Nassau Literary Magazine,* vol. 72, no. 5 (December 1916), pp. [210]–15.
NOTES: Bruccoli C23.
- LH1.P8 N3 vol. 72, no. 5

874. "The Usual Thing by Robert W. Shameless."
- *Nassau Literary Magazine,* vol. 72, no. 5 (December 1916), pp. [223]–28.
NOTES: Bruccoli C24.
- LH1.P8 N3 vol. 72, no. 5

875. "The Vampiest of the Vampires."
- *Nassau Literary Magazine,* vol. 72, no. 5 (December 1916), p. [216].
NOTES: Bruccoli C24.
- LH1.P8 N3 vol. 72, no. 5

876. "Little Minnie Mccloskey: A Story for Girls."
- *Princeton Tiger,* vol. 27, no. 5 (1 December 1916), pp. 6–7.
NOTES: Bruccoli C25. Attributed to FSF.
- LH1.P8 T5 vol. 27, no. 5

877. "One from Penn's Neck," "A Litany of Slang," "Futuristic Impressions of Editorial Boards," "'A glass of beer kills him,'" ["Oui, Le Backfield Est from Paris"], ["When You Find a Man Doing a Little More than His Duty"], "Things That Never Change!: Number 3333," and "The Old Frontiersman: A Story of the Frontier."
- *Princeton Tiger*, vol. 27, no. 6 (18 December 1916), pp. 7, 11.
NOTES: Bruccoli C26, C27, C29, C30, C31, C32, C33, and C34. Attributed to FSF.
- LH1.P8 T5 vol. 27, no. 6

878. ["The Debutante"] and ["Penrod and Sam"].
- *Nassau Literary Magazine*, vol. 72, no. 6 (January 1917), pp. [241]–52; [291]–92.
NOTES: Bruccoli C35 and C36. Review of "Penrod and Sam."
- LH1.P8 N3 vol. 72, no. 6

879. "The Spire and the Gargoyle."
- *Nassau Literary Magazine*, vol. 72, no. 7 (February 1917), pp. [297]–307.
NOTES: Bruccoli C40.
- LH1.P8 N3 vol. 72, no. 7

880. "Rain Before Dawn" and "David Blaize."
- *Nassau Literary Magazine*, vol. 72, no. 7 (February 1917), pp. 321; 343–44.
NOTES: Bruccoli C41 and C42. Review of E. F. Benson's *David Blaize* signed "F.S.F."
- LH1.P8 N3 vol. 72, no. 7

881. "Tarquin of Cheepside."
- *Nassau Literary Magazine*, vol. 73, no. 1 (April 1917), pp. [13]–18.
NOTES: Bruccoli C50.
- LH1.P8 N3 vol. 73, no. 1

882. "Babes in the Woods."
- *Nassau Literary Magazine*, vol. 73, no. 2 (May 1917), pp. [55]–64.
NOTES: Bruccoli C56.
- LH1.P8 N3 vol. 73, no. 2

883. "Princeton—The Last Day" and "The Celt and the World."
- *Nassau Literary Magazine*, vol. 73, no. 2 (May 1917), p. [95]; 104–5.
NOTES: Bruccoli C57 and C58.
Review of Shane Leslie's *The Celt and the World* signed "F.S.F."
- LH1.P8 N3 vol. 73, no. 2

884. "Sentiment—And the Use of Rouge," "On a Play Twice Seen," "Verses in Peace and War," and "God, the Invisible King."
- *Nassau Literary Magazine*, vol. 73, no. 3 (June 1917), pp. [107]–23; [149]; [152]–53.

NOTES: Bruccoli C59, C60, C61, and C62.
>Review of Shane Leslie's *Verses in Peace and War* signed "F.S.F."
>Review of H. G. Wells's *God, the Invisible King* signed "F.S.F."
- LH1.P8 N3 vol. 73, no. 3

885. "The Cameo Frame" and "The Pierian Springs and the Last Straw."
- *Nassau Literary Magazine,* vol. 73, no. 4 (October 1917), pp. [169]–72; [173]–85.
NOTES: Bruccoli C65 and C66.
- LH1.P8 N3 vol. 73, no. 4

886. "The Staying Up All Night," "Intercollegiate Petting-Cues," "Our American Poets," and "Cedric the Stoker: The True Story of the Battle of the Baltic."
- *Princeton Tiger,* vol. 28, no. 3 (10 November 1917), pp. 6, 8, 11, 12.
NOTES: Bruccoli C67, C68, C69, and C70.
>"Intercollegiate Petting-Cues" attributed to FSF.
>"Cedric the Stoker. . ." signed "F.S.F. and J.B." [John Biggs].
- LH1.P8 T5 vol. 28, no. 3

887. "City Dusk."
- *Nassau Literary Magazine,* vol. 73, no. 7 (April 1918), p. [315].
NOTES: Bruccoli C71.
- LH1.P8 N3 vol. 73, no. 7

888. "My First Love," "Marching Streets," and "The Pope at Confession."
- *Nassau Literary Magazine,* vol. 74, no. 2 (February 1919), pp. 102; 103–4; 105.
NOTES: Bruccoli C72, C73, and C74.
- LH1.P8 N3 vol. 74, no. 2

889. "Babes in the Woods."
- *The Smart Set,* vol. 60, no. 1 (September 1919), pp. 67–71.
NOTES: Bruccoli C75.
- AP2.S6 vol. 60, no. 1

890. "Porcelain and Pink: A One-Act Play."
- *The Smart Set,* vol. 61, no. 1 (January 1920), pp. 77–85.
NOTES: Bruccoli C78.
- AP2.S6 vol. 61, no. 1

891. "Dalyrimple Goes Wrong."
- *The Smart Set,* vol. 61, no. 2 (February 1920), pp. 107–16.
NOTES: Bruccoli C80.
- AP2.S6 vol. 61, no. 2

892. "Head and Shoulders."
- Illustrated by Charles D. Mitchell.

- *The Saturday Evening Post,* vol. 192, no. 10 (21 February 1920), pp. 16–17, 81–82, 85–86.
NOTES: Bruccoli C81.
- AP2.S2 vol. 192, no. 38

893. "Mr. Icky: The Quintessence of Quaintness in One Act."
- *The Smart Set,* vol. 61, no. 3 (March 1920), pp. 93–98.
NOTES: Bruccoli C82.
- AP2.S6 vol. 61, no. 3

894. "Myra Meets His Family."
- Illustrated by May Wilson Preston.
- *The Saturday Evening Post,* vol. 192, no. 38 (20 March 1920), pp. 40–53.
NOTES: Bruccoli C84.
- AP2.S2 vol. 192, no. 38

895. "The Camel's Back."
- Illustrated by Arthur William Brown.
- *The Saturday Evening Post,* vol. 192, no. 43 (24 April 1920), pp. 16–17, 157, 161, 165.
NOTES: Bruccoli C85.
- AP2.S2 vol. 192, no. 43

896. "The Cut-Glass Bowl."
- *Scribner's Magazine,* vol. 67, no. 5 (May 1920), pp. 582–592.
NOTES: Bruccoli C86.
- AP2.S4 vol. 67, no. 5

897. "Bernice Bobs Her Hair."
- Illustrated by May Wilson Preston.
- *The Saturday Evening Post,* vol. 192, no. 44 (1 May 1920), pp. 14–15, 159, 163, 167.
NOTES: Bruccoli C87.
- AP2.S2 vol. 192, no. 44–48

898. "The Ice Palace."
- Illustrated by James H. Crank.
- *The Saturday Evening Post,* vol. 192, no. 47 (22 May 1920), pp. 18–19, 163, 167, 170.
NOTES: Bruccoli C88.
- AP2.S2 vol. 192, no. 44–48

899. "The Offshore Pirate."
- Illustrated by Leslie L. Benson.
- *The Saturday Evening Post,* vol. 192, no. 48 (29 May 1920), pp. 10–11, 99–102, 106–9.
NOTES: Bruccoli C89.
- AP2.S2 vol. 192, no. 44–48

900. "The Four Fists."
- Illustrations by F. C. Yohn.
- *Scribner's Magazine,* vol. 67, no. 6 (June 1920), pp. 669–680.
NOTES: Bruccoli C90.
- AP2.S4 vol. 67, no. 6

901. "The Smilers."
- *The Smart Set,* vol. 62, no. 2 (June 1920), pp. 107–11.
NOTES: Bruccoli C91.
- AP2.S6 vol. 62, no. 2

902. "May Day: A Complete Novelette."
- *The Smart Set,* vol. 62, no. 3 (July 1920), pp. 3–32.
NOTES: Bruccoli C92.
- AP2.S6 vol. 62, no. 3

903. "Who's Who and Why: Serious and Frivolous Facts about the Great and Near Great."
- *The Saturday Evening Post,* vol. 193, no. 12 (18 September 1920), pp. 42, 61.
NOTES: Bruccoli C94.
- AP2.S2 vol. 193, no. 12

904. "His Russet Witch."
- Illustrations by Henry Raleigh.
- *Metropolitan,* vol. 53, no. 2 (February 1921), pp. [11]–13, 46–51.
NOTES: Bruccoli C100.
- AP2.M5 vol. 53, no. 2

905. "Tarquin of Cheapside."
- *The Smart Set,* vol. 64, no. 2 (February 1921), pp. 43–46.
NOTES: Bruccoli C101.
- AP2.S6 vol. 64, no. 2

906. *The Beautiful and Damned.*
- Illustrations by Leslie L. Benson.
- *Metropolitan,* Volume 54, Number 2 (September 1921)–Volume 55, Number 2 (March 1922).
NOTES: Bruccoli C104.
- AP2.M5 vol. 54, no. 2 - vol. 55, no. 2

907. "The Far-Seeing Skeptics."
- *The Smart Set,* vol. 67, no. 2 (February 1922), p. 48.
NOTES: Bruccoli C109.
- AP2.S6 vol. 67, no. 2

908. "The Diamond as Big as the Ritz."
- *The Smart Set,* vol. 68, no. 2 (June 1922), pp. 5–29.
NOTES: Bruccoli C118.
- AP2.S6 vol. 68, no. 2

909. "What I Think and Feel at 25."
- *American Magazine*, vol. 96, no. 3 (September 1922), pp. 16–17, 136–40.
NOTES: Bruccoli C119.
- AP2.A346 vol. 94, no. 3

910. "Dice, Brassknuckles & Guitar."
- Illustrations by Frederic Dorr Steele.
- *Hearst's International*, vol. 43, no. 5 (May 1923), pp. 8–13, 145–49.
NOTES: Bruccoli C129.
- AP2.H398 vol. 43, no. 5

911. "Hot & Cold Blood."
- Illustrations by Everett Shinn.
- *Hearst's International*, vol. 44, no. 2 (August 1923), pp. 80–84, 150–51.
NOTES: Bruccoli C135.
- AP2.H398 vol. 44, no. 2

912. "Gretchen's Forty Winks."
- Illustrated by Charles D. Mitchell.
- *The Saturday Evening Post*, vol. 196, no. 37 (15 March 1924), pp. 14–15, 128–32.
NOTES: Bruccoli C140.
- AP2.S2 vol. 196, no. 37

913. "Diamond Dick and the First Law of Woman."
- Illustrations by James Montgomery Flagg.
- *Hearst's International*, vol. 45, no. 4 (April 1924), pp. 58–63, 134, 136.
NOTES: Bruccoli C142.
- AP2.H398 vol. 45, no. 4

914. "Absolution."
- *American Mercury*, vol. 2, no. 6 (June 1924), pp. 141–49.
NOTES: Bruccoli C145.
- AP2.A37 vol. 2, no. 6

915. "Wait Till You Have Children of Your Own!"
- *Woman's Home Companion*, vol. 51, no. 7 (July 1924), pp. 13, 105.
NOTES: Bruccoli C146.
- AP2.W653 vol. 51, no. 7

916. "Rags Martin-Jones and The Pr-nce of W-les."
- Illustrated by C. E. Chambers.
- *McCall's*, vol. 51, no. 10 (July 1924), pp. 6–7, 32, 48, 50.
NOTES: Bruccoli C148.
- AP2.M443 vol. 51, no. 10

917. "John Jackson's Arcady."
- Illustrated by James H. Crank.
- *The Saturday Evening Post*, vol. 197, no. 4 (26 July 1924), pp. 8–9, 100, 102, 105.
NOTES: Bruccoli C151.
- AP2.S2 vol. 197, no. 4

918. "How to Live on Practically Nothing a Year."
- *The Saturday Evening Post*, vol. 197, no. 12 (20 September 1924), pp. 12, 165–66, 169–70.
NOTES: Bruccoli C152.
- AP2.S2 vol. 197, no. 12

919. "The Pusher-in-the-Face."
- Illustrated by Herbert Paus.
- *Woman's Home Companion*, vol. 52, no. 2 (February 1925), pp. 27–28, 143–144.
NOTES: Bruccoli C154.
- AP2.W653 vol. 52, no. 2

920. "Love in the Night."
- Illustrated by H. J. Mowat.
- *The Saturday Evening Post*, vol. 197, no. 37 (14 March 1925), pp. 18–19, 68–70.
NOTES: Bruccoli C155.
- AP2.S2 vol. 197, no. 37

921. "My Old New England Homestead on the Erie."
- Illustrated by Russell Patterson.
- *College Humor*, vol. 6, no. 1 (August 1925), pp. 18–19.
NOTES: Bruccoli C157.
- PN6231.C6 vol. 6, no. 1

922. "One of My Oldest Friends."
- *Woman's Home Companion*, vol. 52, no. 9 (September 1925), pp. 7–8, 120–22.
NOTES: Bruccoli C158.
- AP2.W653 vol. 52, no. 9

923. "The Adjuster."
- Illustrated by C. D. Williams.
- *The Red Book Magazine*, vol. 45, no. 5 (September 1925), pp. 47–51, 144–48.
NOTES: Bruccoli C159.
- AP2.R2829 vol. 45, no. 5

924. "What Becomes of Our Flappers and Sheiks?"
- Illustrated by John Held, Jr.
- *McCall's,* vol. 53, no. 1 (October 1925), pp. 12, 30, 42, 66, 69.
NOTES: Bruccoli C160. FSF's "Our Young Rich Boys" (pp. 12, 42, 69) and ZF's "What Became of the Flappers?" (pp. 12, 30, 66) issued with joint title.
- AP2.M443 vol. 53, no. 1

925. "A Penny Spent."
- Illustrated by Arthur William Brown.
- *The Saturday Evening Post,* vol. 198, no. 15 (10 October 1925), pp. 8–9, 160, 164, 166.
NOTES: Bruccoli C161.
- AP2.S2 vol. 198, no. 15

926. "Not in The Guidebook."
- Illustrated by James Preston.
- *Woman's Home Companion,* vol. 52, no. 11 (November 1925), pp. 9–11, 135–36.
NOTES: Bruccoli C162.
- AP2.W653 vol. 52, no. 11

927. "The Rich Boy."
- Illustrated by Frederic R. Gruger.
- *The Red Book Magazine,* vol. 46, no. 3 (January 1926)–v. 46, no. 4 (February 1926).
- [2] parts; (pp. 27–32, 144–46; 75–79, 122–26).
NOTES: Bruccoli C163.
- AP2.R2829 vol. 46, Nos. 3–4

928. "The Adolescent Marriage."
- Illustrated by Harley Ennis Stivers.
- *The Saturday Evening Post,* vol. 198, no. 36 (6 March 1926) pp. 6–7, 229–34.
NOTES: Bruccoli C165.
- AP2.S2 vol. 198, no. 36

929. "How to Waste Material: A Note on My Generation."
- *The Bookman,* vol. 63, no. 3 (May 1926), pp. 262–65.
NOTES: Bruccoli C167.
- AP2.B78 vol. 63, no. 3

930. "The Dance."
- Illustrated by Lester Ralph.
- *The Redbook Magazine,* vol. 47, no. 2 (June 1926), pp. 39–43, 134–38.
NOTES: Bruccoli C168.
- AP2.R2829 vol. 47, no. 2

931. *The Great Gatsby*
- *Famous Story Magazine,* vol. 3, no. 1 (April 1926)–vol. 4, no. 2 (August 1926).
- 5 parts.

NOTES: Bruccoli A11.1.b, Note 2.
- AP2.F275 vol. 3–4, no. 2

932. "Your Way & Mine."
- Illustrated by Frederick Chapman.
- *Woman's Home Companion,* vol. 54, no. 5 (May 1927), pp. 7–8, 61–68.

NOTES: Bruccoli C169.
- AP2.W653 vol. 54, no. 5

933. "Jacob's Ladder."
- Illustrated by Henry Raleigh.
- *The Saturday Evening Post,* vol. 200, no. 8 (20 August 1927), pp. 3–5, 57–58, 63–64.

NOTES: Bruccoli C170.
- AP2.S2 vol. 200, no. 8

934. "The Love Boat."
- Illustrated by James H. Crank.
- *The Saturday Evening Post,* vol. 200, no. 15 (8 October 1927), pp. 8–9, 134, 139–41.

NOTES: Bruccoli C171. Issue cover incorrectly dated "October 15, 1927".
- AP2.S2 vol. 200, no. 15

935. "A Short Trip Home."
- Illustrated by Grant Reynard.
- *The Saturday Evening Post,* vol. 200, no. 25 (17 December 1927), pp. 6–7, 55–58.

NOTES: Bruccoli C173.
- AP2.S2 vol. 200, no. 25

936. "The Changing Beauty of Park Avenue."
- *Harper's Bazaar,* no. 2583 (January 1928), pp. [60]–63.

NOTES: Bruccoli C174, ZF-C8. Byline: "Zelda and F. Scott Fitzgerald".
- AP2.H376 62nd Year, no. 2583

937. "Magnetism."
- Illustrated by H. Weston Taylor.
- *The Saturday Evening Post,* vol. 200, no. 36 (3 March 1928), pp. 5–7, 74, 76, 78.

NOTES: Bruccoli C176.
- AP2.S2 vol. 200, no. 36

938. "The Scandal Detectives."
- Illustrated by Henrietta McCaig Starrett.
- *The Saturday Evening Post*, vol. 200, no. 44 (28 April 1928), pp. 3–4, 178, 181–82, 185.
NOTES: Bruccoli C178.
- AP2.S2 vol. 200, no. 44

939. "He Thinks He's Wonderful."
- Illustrated by Henrietta McCaig Starrett.
- *The Saturday Evening Post*, vol. 201, no. 13 (29 September 1928), pp. 6–7, 117–18, 121.
NOTES: Bruccoli C182.
- AP2.S2 vol. 201, no. 13

940. "Outside the Cabinet-Maker's: There Was a Princess, So There Had to Be a Prince."
- *The Century Magazine*, vol. 117, no. 2 (December 1928), pp. 241–44.
NOTES: Bruccoli C184.
- AP2.C4 vol. 117, no. 2

941. "The Captured Shadow."
- Illustrated by Henrietta McCaig Starrett.
- *The Saturday Evening Post*, vol. 210, no. 26 (29 December 1928), pp. 12–13, 48, 51.
NOTES: Bruccoli C185.
- AP2.S2 vol. 201, no. 26

942. "The Perfect Life."
- Illustrations by Henrietta McCaig Starrett.
- *The Saturday Evening Post*, vol. 201, no. 27 (5 January 1929), pp. 8–9, 113, 115, 118.
NOTES: Bruccoli C186.
- AP2.S2 vol. 201, no. 27

943. "The Last of the Belles."
- Illustrations by John La Gatta.
- *The Saturday Evening Post*, vol. 201, no. 35 (2 March 1929), pp. 18–19, 75, 78.
NOTES: Bruccoli C188.
- AP2.S2 vol. 201, no. 35

944. "Basil and Cleopatra."
- Illustrated by Henrietta McCaig Starrett.
- *The Saturday Evening Post*, vol. 201, no. 43 (27 April 1929), pp. 14 15, 166, 170, 173.
NOTES: Bruccoli C190.
- AP2.S2 vol. 201, no. 43

945. "The Rough Crossing."
- Illustrated by Anton Otto Fischer.
- *The Saturday Evening Post,* vol. 201, no. 49 (8 June 1929), pp. 12–13, 66, 70, 75.
NOTES: Bruccoli C193.
- AP2.S2 vol. 201, no. 49

946. "The Original Follies Girl."
- Illustrated by Chris Marie Meeker.
- *College Humor,* vol. 17, no. 4 (July 1929), pp. 40–41, 110.
NOTES: Bruccoli C195; ZF-C12. Byline: "F. Scott and Zelda Fitzgerald". Attributed to ZF in FSF's Ledger.
- PN6231.C6 C6

947. "Southern Girl."
- Illustrated by John La Gatta.
- *College Humor,* vol. 18, no. 3 (October 1929), pp. 27–28, 94, 96.
NOTES: Bruccoli C198; ZF-C13. Byline: "F. Scott and Zelda Fitzgerald". Attributed to ZF in FSF's Ledger.
- PN6231.C6 C6

948. "The Swimmers."
- Illustrated by C. D. Williams.
- *The Saturday Evening Post,* vol. 202, no. 16 (19 October 1929), pp. 12–13, 150, 152, 154.
NOTES: Bruccoli C199.
- AP2.S2 vol. 202, no. 16

949. "Two Wrongs."
- Illustrated by H. Weston Taylor.
- *The Saturday Evening Post,* vol. 202, no. 29 (18 January 1930), pp. 8–9, 107, 109, 113.
NOTES: Bruccoli C200.
- AP2.S2 vol. 202, no. 29

950. "First Blood."
- Illustrated by H. R. Ballinger.
- *The Saturday Evening Post,* vol. 202, no. 40 (5 April 1930), pp. 8–9, 81, 84.
NOTES: Bruccoli C207.
- AP2.S2 vol. 202, no. 40

951. "A Nice Quiet Place."
- Illustrated by Harley Ennis Stivers.
- *The Saturday Evening Post,* vol. 202, no. 48 (31 May 1930), pp. 8–9, 96, 101, 103.
NOTES: Bruccoli C209.
- AP2.S2 vol. 202, no. 48

952. "A Woman with a Past."
- Illustrated by Harley Ennis Stivers.
- *The Saturday Evening Post,* vol. 203, no. 10 (6 September 1930), pp. 8–9, 133–34, 137.

NOTES: Bruccoli C211.
- AP2.S2 vol. 203, no. 10

953. "One Trip Abroad."
- Illustrated by Harley Ennis Stivers.
- *The Saturday Evening Post,* vol. 203, no. 15 (11 October 1930), pp. 6–7, 48, 51, 53–54, 56.

NOTES: Bruccoli C212.
- AP2.S2 vol. 203, no. 15

954. "The Hotel Child."
- Illustrated by Henry Raleigh.
- *The Saturday Evening Post,* vol. 203, no. 31 (31 January 1931), pp. 8–9, 69, 72, 75.

NOTES: Bruccoli C215.
- AP2.S2 vol. 203, no. 31

955. "Babylon Revisited."
- Illustrated by Henrietta McCaig Starrett.
- *The Saturday Evening Post,* vol. 203, no. 34 (21 February 1931), pp. 3–5, 82–84.

NOTES: Bruccoli C216.
- AP2.S2 vol. 203, no. 34

956. "Indecision."
- Illustrated by Henry Raleigh.
- *The Saturday Evening Post,* vol. 203, no. 46 (16 May 1931), pp. 12–13, 56, 59, 62.

NOTES: Bruccoli C217.
- AP2.S2 vol. 203, no. 46

957. "A New Leaf."
- Illustrated by H. J. Mowat.
- *The Saturday Evening Post,* vol. 204, no. 1 (4 July 1931), pp. 12–13, 90–91.

NOTES: Bruccoli C218.
- AP2.S2 vol. 204, no. 1

958. "Emotional Bankruptcy."
- Illustrated by Harley Ennis Stivers.
- *The Saturday Evening Post,* vol. 204, no. 7 (15 August 1931), pp. 8–9, 60, 65.

NOTES: Bruccoli C219.
- AP2.S2 vol. 204, no. 7

959. "Between Three and Four."
- Illustrated by George Wright.
- *The Saturday Evening Post,* vol. 204, no. 10 (5 September 1931), pp. 8–9, 69, 72.
NOTES: Bruccoli C220.
- AP2.S2 vol. 204, no. 10

960. "A Change of Class."
- Illustrated by Orison Macpherson.
- *The Saturday Evening Post,* vol. 204, no. 13 (26 September 1931), pp. 6–7, 37–38, 41.
NOTES: Bruccoli C221.
- AP2.S2 vol. 204, no. 13

961. "Echoes of the Jazz Age."
- *Scribner's Magazine,* vol. 90, no. 5 (November 1931), pp. 459–65.
NOTES: Bruccoli C222.
- AP2.S4 vol. 90, no. 5

962. "A Freeze-Out."
- Illustrated by Henry Raleigh.
- *The Saturday Evening Post,* vol. 204, no. 25 (19 December 1931), pp. 6–7, 84–85, 88–89.
NOTES: Bruccoli C223.
- AP2.S2 vol. 204, no. 25

963. "Six of One: A Story of Youth."
- Illustrated by Jack Sheridan.
- *The Redbook Magazine,* vol. 58, no. 4 (February 1932), pp. 22–25, 84.
NOTES: Bruccoli C224.
- AP2.R2829 vol. 58, no. 4

964. "Diagnosis."
- Illustrated by Henry Raleigh.
- *The Saturday Evening Post,* vol. 202, no. 34 (20 February 1932), pp. 18–19, 90, 92.
NOTES: Bruccoli C225.
- AP2.S2 vol. 204, no. 34

965. "Flight and Pursuit."
- Illustrated by Henrietta McCaig Starrett.
- *The Saturday Evening Post,* vol. 204, no. 46 (14 May 1932), pp. 16–17, 53, 57.
NOTES: Bruccoli C227.
- AP2.S2 vol. 204, no. 46

966. "Family in the Wind."
- Illustrated by Ralph Pallen Coleman.
- *The Saturday Evening Post,* vol. 204, no. 49 (4 June 1932), pp. 3–5, 71–73.
NOTES: Bruccoli C228.
- AP2.S2 vol. 204, no. 49

967. "The Rubber Check."
- Illustrated by Thomas Webb.
- *The Saturday Evening Post,* vol. 205, no. 6 (6 August 1932), pp. 6–7, 41–42, 44–45.
NOTES: Bruccoli C229.
- AP2.S2 vol. 205, no. 6

968. "What A Handsome Pair!"
- Illustrated by Henry Raleigh.
- *The Saturday Evening Post,* vol. 205, no. 9 (27 August 1932), pp. 16–17, 61–64.
NOTES: Bruccoli C230.
- AP2.S2 vol. 205, no. 9

969. "Crazy Sunday."
- *American Mercury,* vol. 27, no. 106 (October 1932), pp. 209–20.
NOTES: Bruccoli C231.
- AP2.A37 vol. 27, no. 106

970. "One Interne."
- Illustrated by H. R. Ballinger.
- *The Saturday Evening Post,* vol. 205, no. 19 (5 November 1932), pp. 6–7, 86–90.
NOTES: Bruccoli C232.
- AP2.S2 vol. 205, no. 19

971. "One Hundred False Starts."
- *The Saturday Evening Post,* vol. 205, no. 36 (4 March 1933), pp. 12, 65–66.
NOTES: Bruccoli C233.
- AP2.S2 vol. 205, no. 36

972. "On Schedule."
- Illustrated by May Wilson Preston.
- *The Saturday Evening Post,* vol. 205, no. 38 (18 March 1933), pp. 16–17, 71, 74, 77, 79.
NOTES: Bruccoli C234.
- AP2.S2 vol. 205, no. 38

973. "I Got Shoes."
- Illustrated by Henry Raleigh.
- *The Saturday Evening Post,* vol. 206, no. 13 (23 September 1933), pp. 14–15, 56–58.

NOTES: Bruccoli C236.
- AP2.S2 vol. 206, no. 13

974. "The Family Bus."
- *The Saturday Evening Post,* vol. 206, no. 19 (4 November 1933), pp. 8–9, 57, 61–62, 65–66.
NOTES: Bruccoli C238.
- AP2.S2 vol. 206, no. 19

975. *Tender Is the Night: A Romance.*
- Illustrated by Edward Shenton.
- *Scribner's Magazine,* vol. 95, no. 1 (January 1934)– vol. 95, no. 4 (April 1934).
NOTES: Bruccoli C239.
- AP2.S4 vol. 95, Nos. 1–4

976. "No Flowers."
- Illustrated by Henry Raleigh.
- *The Saturday Evening Post,* vol. 207, no. 3 (21 July 1934), pp. 10–11, 57, 58, 60.
NOTES: Bruccoli C244.
- AP2.S2 vol. 207, no. 3

977. "New Types."
- Illustrated by Gerald Leake.
- *The Saturday Evening Post,* vol. 207, no. 12 (22 September 1934), pp. 16–17, 74, 76, 78–79, 81.
NOTES: Bruccoli C246.
- AP2.S2 vol. 207, no. 12

978. "In the Darkest Hour: A Poignant Romance of Chaos and Leadership."
- Illustrated by Saul Tepper.
- *The Redbook Magazine,* vol. 63, no. 6 (October 1934), pp. 15–19, 94–98.
NOTES: Bruccoli C247.
- AP2.R2829 vol. 63, no. 6

979. "Her Last Case."
- Illustrated by Henry Raleigh.
- *The Saturday Evening Post,* vol. 207, no. 18 (3 November 1934), pp. 10–11, 59, 61–62, 64.
NOTES: Bruccoli C249.
- AP2.S2 vol. 207, no. 18

980. "Sleeping and Waking."
- *Esquire,* vol. 2, no. 7 (December 1934), pp. 34, 159–60.
NOTES: Bruccoli C250.
- AP2.E845 vol. 2, no. 7

981. "The Fiend."
- *Esquire,* vol. 3, no. 1 (January 1935), pp. 23, 173–74.
NOTES: Bruccoli C251.
- AP2.E845 vol. 3, no. 1

982. "The Count of Darkness."
- Illustrated by Alfred Simpkin.
- *The Redbook Magazine,* vol. 65, no. 2 (June 1935), pp. 20–23, 68–72.
NOTES: Bruccoli C255.
- AP2.R2829 vol. 65, no. 2

983. "The Intimate Strangers."
- Illustrated by William C. Hoople.
- *McCall's,* vol. 62, no. 9 (June 1935), pp. 12–14, 36, 38, 40, 42, 44.
NOTES: Bruccoli C256.
- AP2.M443 vol. 62, no. 9

984. "The Passionate Eskimo."
- Illustration by Dan Content and Stephen Grout.
- *Liberty,* vol. 12, no. 23 (8 June 1935), pp. 10–14, 17–18.
NOTES: Bruccoli C257.
- AP2.L541 vol. 12, no. 23

985. "Zone of Accident."
- Illustrated by Ritchie Cooper.
- *The Saturday Evening Post,* vol. 208, no. 2 (13 July 1935), pp. 8–9, 47, 49, 51–52.
NOTES: Bruccoli C258.
- AP2.S2 vol. 208, no. 2

986. "The Kingdom in the Dark."
- Illustrated by A. N. Simpkin.
- *Redbook,* vol. 65, no. 4 (August 1935), pp. 58–68.
NOTES: Bruccoli C259.
- AP2.R2829 vol. 65, no. 4

987. [Front cover].
- *The Redbook Magazine,* vol. 65, no. 5 (September 1935).
- [1] p.
NOTES: Front cover of this issue lists FSF as a contributor, but contains nothing written by him.
- AP2.R2829 vol. 65, no. 5

988. "The Crack-Up."
- *Esquire,* vol. 5, no. 2 (February 1936), pp. 41, 164.
NOTES: Bruccoli C260.
- AP2.E845 vol. 5, no. 2

989. "Pasting It Together."
- *Esquire*, vol. 5, no. 3 (March 1936), pp. 35, 182–83.
NOTES: Bruccoli C261.
- AP2.E845 vol. 5, no. 3

990. "Handle With Care."
- *Esquire*, vol. 5, no. 4 (April 1936), pp. 39, 202.
NOTES: Bruccoli C262.
- AP2.E845 vol. 5, no. 4

991. "Fate in Her Hands."
- Illustrated by Mario Cooper.
- *American Magazine*, vol. 121, no. 4 (April 1936), pp. 56–59, 168–72.
NOTES: Bruccoli C263.
- AP2.A346 vol. 121, no. 4

992. "Too Cute for Words."
- Illustrated by Henrietta McCaig Starrett.
- *The Saturday Evening Post*, vol. 208, no. 42 (18 April 1936), pp. 16–17, 87, 90, 93.
NOTES: Bruccoli C265.
- AP2.S2 vol. 208, no. 42

993. "Three Acts of Music."
- *Esquire*, vol. 5, no. 5 (May 1936), pp. 39, 210.
NOTES: Bruccoli C266.
- AP2.E845 vol. 5, no. 5

994. "The Ants At Princeton."
- *Esquire*, vol. 5, no. 6 (June 1936), pp. 35, 201.
NOTES: Bruccoli C267.
- AP2.E845 vol. 5, no. 6

995. "Inside the House."
- Illustrated by Henrietta McCaig Starrett.
- *The Saturday Evening Post*, vol. 208, no. 50 (13 June 1936), pp. 18–19, 32, 34, 36.
NOTES: Bruccoli C268.
- AP2.S2 vol. 208, no. 50

996. "Author's House."
- *Esquire*, vol. 6, no. 1 (July 1936), pp. 40, 108.
NOTES: Bruccoli C269.
- AP2.E845 vol. 6, no. 1

997. "Afternoon of an Author."
- *Esquire,* vol. 6, no. 2 (August 1936), pp. 35, 170.
NOTES: Bruccoli C270.
- AP2.E845 vol. 6, no. 2

998. "An Author's Mother."
- *Esquire,* vol. 6, no. 3 (September 1936), p. 36.
NOTES: Bruccoli C271.
- AP2.E845 vol. 6, no. 3

999. "'I Didn't Get Over.'"
- *Esquire,* vol. 6, no. 4 (October 1936), pp. 45, 194–95.
NOTES: Bruccoli C272.
- AP2.E845 vol. 6, no. 4

1000. "'Send Me in, Coach.'"
- *Esquire,* vol. 6, no. 5 (November 1936), pp. 55, 218–21.
NOTES: Bruccoli C273.
- AP2.E845 vol. 6, no. 5

1001. "An Alcoholic Case."
- *Esquire,* vol. 6, no. 8 (February 1937), pp. 32, 109.
NOTES: Bruccoli C274.
- AP2.E845 vol. 6, no. 8

1002. "'Trouble.'"
- Illustrated by Henrietta McCaig Starrett.
- *The Saturday Evening Post,* vol. 209, no. 36 (6 March 1937), pp. 14–15, 81, 84, 86, 88–89.
NOTES: Bruccoli C275.
- AP2.S2 vol. 209, no. 36

1003. *The Great Gatsby.*
- *Argosy,* vol. 22, no. 135, pp. 54–93.
NOTES: Bruccoli A11.1.a, Note 2.
- PZ1.A1 A7 vol. 22, no. 135

1004. *The Great Gatsby.*
- *Chicago Herald and Examiner* (23 May 1937), pp. [1]–15.
NOTES: At head of title: "The Sunday Novel ... Complete in This Issue". Published as a supplement.
- PS3511.I9 G7 1937b

1005. *The Great Gatsby.*
- *Philadelphia Inquirer/Public Ledger* (23 May 1937), pp. [1]–15.
NOTES: Bruccoli A11.1.b, Note 2.
At head of title: "The Sunday Novel ... Complete in This Issue". Published as a supplement.
- PS3511.I9 G7 1937c

1006. "The Honor of the Goon."
- *Esquire*, vol. 7, no. 6 (June 1937), pp. 53, 216.
NOTES: Bruccoli C276.
- AP2.E845 vol. 7, no. 6

1007. "Obit on Parnassus."
- *The New Yorker*, vol. 13, no. 16 (5 June 1937), p. 27.
NOTES: Bruccoli C277.
- AP2.N6768 vol. 13, no. 16

1008. "A Book of One's Own."
- *The New Yorker*, vol. 13, no. 27 (21 August 1937), p. 19.
NOTES: Bruccoli C278.
- AP2.N6768 vol. 13, no. 27

1009. "The Long Way Out."
- *Esquire*, vol. 8, no. 3 (September 1937), pp. 45, 193.
NOTES: Bruccoli C279.
- AP2.E845 vol. 8, no. 3

1010. "Early Success: What Happens When a Man Strikes Pay Dirt."
- *American Cavalcade*, vol. 1, no. 6 (October 1937), pp. 74–79.
NOTES: Bruccoli C280.
- AP2.A3326

1011. "The Guest in Room Nineteen."
- *Esquire*, vol. 8, no. 4 (October 1937), pp. 56, 209.
NOTES: Bruccoli C281.
- AP2.E845 vol. 8, no. 4

1012. "In the Holidays."
- *Esquire*, vol. 8, no. 6 (December 1937), pp. 82, 184, 186.
NOTES: Bruccoli C282.
- AP2.E845 vol. 8, no. 6

1013. "Financing Finnegan."
- *Esquire*, vol. 9, no. 1 (January 1938), pp. 41, 180, 182, 184.
NOTES: Bruccoli C283.
- AP2.E845 vol. 9, no. 1

1014. *This Side of Paradise.*
- *Philadelphia Record* (11 December 1938), pp. [1]–15.
NOTES: Abridged.
- PS3511.I9 T49 1938

1015. "Design in Plaster."
- *Esquire*, vol. 12, no. 5 (November 1939), pp. 51, 169.
NOTES: Bruccoli C286.
- AP2.E845 vol. 12, no. 5

1016. "The Lost Decade."
- *Esquire,* vol. 12, no. 6 (December 1939), pp. 113, 228.
NOTES: Bruccoli C287.
- AP2.E845 vol. 12, no. 6

1017. "Strange Sanctuary."
- Illustrated by Martha Moore.
- *Liberty,* vol. 16, no. 49 (9 December 1939), pp. 15–20.
NOTES: Bruccoli C288.
- AP2.L541 vol. 16, no. 49

1018. "Pat Hobby's Christmas Wish."
- *Esquire,* vol. 13, no. 1 (January 1940), pp. 45, 170–72.
NOTES: Bruccoli C289.
- AP2.E845 vol. 13, no. 1

1019. "A Man in the Way."
- *Esquire,* vol. 13, no. 2 (February 1940), pp. 40, 109.
NOTES: Bruccoli C290.
- AP2.E845 vol. 13, no. 2

1020. "'Boil Some Water—Lots of It.'"
- *Esquire,* vol. 13, no. 3 (March 1940), pp. 30, 145, 147.
NOTES: Bruccoli, C291.
- AP2.E485 vol. 13, no. 3

1021. "Pat Hobby's Secret."
- *Esquire,* vol. 8, no. 6 (June 1940), pp. 30, 107.
NOTES: Bruccoli C294.
- AP2.E845 vol. 8, no. 6

1022. "The End of Hate."
- Illustrated by Mario Cooper.
- *Collier's,* vol. 105, no. 25 (22 June 1940), pp. 9–10, 63–64.
NOTES: Bruccoli C295.
- AP2.C65 vol. 105, no. 25

1023. "Pat Hobby's Preview."
- *Esquire,* vol. 14, no. 4 (October 1940), pp. 30, 118, 120.
NOTES: Bruccoli C299
- AP2.E845 vol. 14, no. 4

1024. "Gods of Darkness."
- Illustrated by Jules Gotlieb.
- *The Redbook Magazine,* vol. 78, no. 1 (November 1941), pp. 30–33, 88–91.
NOTES: Bruccoli C310.
- AP2.A2829 vol. 78, no. 1

1025. "The Broadcast We Almost Heard Last September."
- *Furioso*, vol. 3, no. 1 (Fall 1947), pp. 8–10.
NOTES: Bruccoli C311.
- PS301.F85 vol. 3, no. 1

1026. "News of Paris—Fifteen Years Ago."
- *Furioso*, vol. 3, no. 2 (Winter 1947), pp. 5–10.
NOTES: Bruccoli C312
- PS301.F85 vol. 3, no. 2

1027. "The World's Fair."
- *Kenyon Review*, vol. 10, no. 4 (Autumn 1948), pp. [567]–578.
NOTES: Bruccoli C314.
- AP2.K426 vol. 10, no. 4

1028. "Last Kiss."
- Illustrated by Ward Brackett.
- *Collier's*, vol. 123, no. 16 (16 April 1949), pp. 16–17, 34–44.
NOTES: Bruccoli C315.
- AP2.C65 vol. 123, no. 16

1029. "The Death of My Father."
- *Princeton University Library Chronicle*, vol. 12, no. 3 (Summer 1951), pp. 187–89.
NOTES: Bruccoli 317.
- Z733.P93 C5 vol. 12, no. 4

1030. "The Boy Who Killed His Mother."
- *Neurotica*, no. 9 (Winter 1952), pp. 38–39.
NOTES: Bruccoli C318. Unauthorized publication of poem.
- AP2.N3676 no. 9

1031. "The High Cost of Macaroni."
- A Note by Henry Dan Piper.
- *Interim*, vol. 4, Nos. 1 & 2 (1954), pp. 3–15.
NOTES: Bruccoli C319
- PS1.I583 vol. 4, no. 1/2

1032. "Advice to a Young Writer: Insights for Writers and a Glimpse of One of the Best."
- *Esquire*, vol. 50, no. 4 (October 1958), pp. [158–59].
NOTES: Bruccoli F84. Includes three FSF letters. Introduction by Andrew Turnbull.
- AP2.E845 vol. 50, no. 4

1033. "Love to All of You, of All Generations."
- *Esquire,* vol. 60, no. 1 (July 1963), pp. [86]–90, 111–12.
NOTES: Bruccoli 321. Includes nine previously unpublished letters: three to Maxwell Perkins and one each to Edmund Wilson, H. L. Mencken, Richard Knight, Beatrice Dance, Roger Garis, and Zelda Fitzgerald.
- AP2.E845 vol. 60, no. 1

1034. "My Generation."
- *Esquire,* vol. 70, no. 4 (October 1968), pp. 119–21.
NOTES: Bruccoli C324.
- AP2.E845 vol. 70, no. 4

1035. "The Fitzgerald-Perkins Papers."
- Illustrated by Robert Maplethorpe.
- *Esquire,* vol. 75, no. 6 (June 1971), pp. [106]–11, 171–83.
NOTES: Bruccoli C325.
- AP2.E845 vol. 75, no. 6

1036. "Infidelity: A Screenplay."
- Illustrated by Barry Zaid.
- *Esquire,* vol. 80, no. 6 (December 1973), pp. 193–200, 290–304.
NOTES: Bruccoli C327.
- AP2.E845 vol. 80, no. 6

1037. "On Your Own."
- Photographs by Dan Weaks.
- *Esquire,* vol. 91, no. 2 (30 January 1979), pp. [56]–67.
NOTES: Bruccoli C328. Includes "Epilogue: A Woman, a Gift, and a Still Unanswered Question" by Matthew J. Bruccoli.
- AP2.E845 vol. 91, no. 2

1038. "Frances Scott Fitzgerald '38: A Remembrance."
- *Walker's* [Alumnae Bulletin of the Ethel Walker School] (Fall 1986), pp. 2–3.
NOTES: Bruccoli C331. Includes two FSF letters and facsimiles end of holograph letter to Ethel Walker School.
- LH1.E833 W3

1039. "A Full Life."
- *Princeton University Library Chronicle,* vol. 49, no. 2 (Winter 1988), pp. 167–72.
NOTES: Previously unpublished short story.
- Z733.P93 C5 vol. 49, no. 2

IV Keepsakes and Exhibition Catalogues

Keepsakes with material by Fitzgerald (Bruccoli D items) and exhibition catalogues.

1040. *Turkey Remains and How to Inter Them with Numerous Scarce Recipes from The Note-Books of F. Scott Fitzgerald.*
- [Toronto: Cooper & Beatty, 1956].
- Wrappers with wrap-around cover, 16 pp.
NOTES: Bruccoli D1.
- PS3511.I9 T87 1956

1041. *F. Scott Fitzgerald: An Exhibition Commemorating Tender Is the Night 1934–1959.*
- [Charlottesville, Virginia: n.p., 1959].
- Single-fold leaf printed on 2 pages.
NOTES: Catalogue for exhibit at Alderman Library, University of Virginia, May 1959.
- PS3511.I9 T87 1956

1042. *The Mystery of the Raymond Mortgage.*
- New York: Random House, 1960.
- Wrappers, 12 pp.
NOTES: Bruccoli D2. First edition. Reprint of author's first published work. "This first edition of F. Scott Fitzgerald's *The Mystery of Raymond Mortgage* was privately printed and limited to 750 copies".
- PS3511.I9 M95 1960

1043. *Martin's Thoughts.*
- [Charlottesville, Virginia: The Tauser Head Press, 1962].
- Single leaf, French fold.
NOTES: Bruccoli D3. "Four Copies Printed . . ."
- PS3511.I9 M2 1962

1044. [Memorial Day keepsake].
- [Pound Ridge, N.Y.]: Cycling Frog Press, [1963].
- Single leaf folded once.
NOTES: Bruccoli D4. Cycling Frog Keepsakes.
Printed by Samuel N. Antupit. Reprints passage from *Tender Is the Night* describing the visit to the trenches.
With letter from Antupit to MJB.
- PS3511.I9 K41

1045. ["Crazy Sunday" keepsake].
- [Pound Ridge, N.Y.]: Cycling Frog Press, 1963.
- Single leaf folded once.
NOTES: Bruccoli D5. Cycling Frog Keepsakes.

Printed by Samuel N. Antupit. Reprints opening line of Part V of "Crazy Sunday".
- PS3511.I9 K41 C75 1963

1046. [Letter to Perkins].
- [New York: Scribner, 1963].
- 4 leaves.

NOTES: Bruccoli D6.
Distributed by Charles Scribner's Sons in 1963 as promotional piece for Andrew Turnbull's *The Letters of F. Scott Fitzgerald,* in which this letter is published on pp. 139–40.
Facsimile of letter from FSF to Maxwell Perkins, 18 September 1919.
- PS3511.I9 L395 1963

1047. *F. Scott Fitzgerald: An Exhibition Marking the 25th Anniversary of His Death, 21 December 1965.*
- Columbus, Ohio: Printed by the F. J. Heer Printing Company for the Tauser Head Press, 1965.
- Single sheet, folded twice.

NOTES: Bruccoli D7.
"Two hundred and fifty copies—of which twenty-five are numbered and signed."
This is copy #5, initialed "M.J.B."
- PS3511.I9 Z76 1965

1048. [Letter to Maxwell Perkins]
- [n.p.] 1967.
- Broadside.

NOTES: Bruccoli D8. "Distributed June 1967 on the occasion of the fiftieth reunion of Scott Fitzgerald's class . . ."
- PS3511.I9 L4 1967

1049. *This Side of Paradise 26 March 1920 26 March 1970.*
- [Columbia, S.C.]: Fitzgerald/Hemingway Annual, [1970].
- Single leaf, folded once.

NOTES: Bruccoli D9. no. 42. Initialed by MJB.
Facsimile of "The Author's Apology."
"Fifty Copies Privately Printed for Friends of the *Fitzgerald/Hemingway Annual.*"
- PS3511.I9 A9 1970

1050. *"—and a few missing words would destroy so much".*
- Bloomfield Hills, Mich.: M. S. Clark, 1970.
- Single leaf, folded twice.

NOTES: Bruccoli D10.
Facsimile of first page of revised typescript for "My Generation" with FSF's holograph note.

Number 3 of "200 Copies Privately Printed for Distribution at the Conference on Editing and American Literature, Embassy of the United States of America, London, 1 July 1970." Initialed by MJB.
- PS3511.I9 A5 1970

1051. *The Author's Apology.*
- [Kent, Ohio: Kent State University Press, 1971].
- Single leaf printed on recto and verso.
NOTES: Bruccoli D11. One of 200 copies.
Facsimile of FSF's 1920 MS draft of a promotion piece for *This Side of Paradise.*
- PS3511.I9 A9 1971

1052. [Telegram keepsake].
- Columbia, S.C.: Matthew J. Bruccoli, 1972.
- Broadside.
NOTES: Bruccoli D12. "100 copies printed for distribution at the C.E.A.A. Symposium on the Text and the Study of American Literature, the University of Manchester 30 June 1972."
Facsimile of telegram from F. Scott Fitzgerald to Maxwell Perkins, 15 March 1934, about *Tender Is the Night.*
- PS3511.I9 T385 1972

1053. *Proposed exhibit of Fitzgeraldiania for Chas. Scribner's Sons (Borrowed from J. P. B.).* Facsimile.
- [n.p.: n.d.], 1972.
- Single leaf. Unnumbered copy.
NOTES: Prepared by John Peale Bishop and Edmund Wilson. "Twenty-Nine Copies Printed To Mark The Presentation Of *F. Scott Fitzgerald: A Descriptive Bibliography* To The Library of Congress By Frances Scott Fitzgerald Smith, 17 November 1972."
- PS3511.I9 P85 1972

1054. *F. Scott Fitzgerald's Projected Collected Works.*
- Pittsburgh: University of Pittsburgh Press, 1972.
- Broadside.
NOTES: Bruccoli D13. Date of original not known. One of 300 copies.
Facsimile of MS, published to mark the publication of Matthew J. Bruccoli's *F. Scott Fitzgerald: A Descriptive Bibliography* (Pittsburgh: University of Pittsburgh Press, 1972).
- PS3511.I9 F7 1972

1055. *The Great Gatsby 10 April 1925–10 April 1975: An Exhibition from the Collection of Matthew J. Bruccoli at the Grolier Club, 1975.*
- Columbia, S.C.: Vogue Press, 1975.
- Single galley printed on recto and verso.

172 *Keepsakes and Exhibition Catalogues*

NOTES: Bruccoli D15. "300 Copies Printed For The Grolier Club Exhibition". Includes facsimile of one uncorrected galley for "Trimalchio."
- PS3511.I9 Z6445 1975

1056. [Ring W. Lardner keepsake].
- [Columbia, S.C.: Matthew J. Bruccoli, 1976].
- Single leaf printed on verso and recto.

NOTES: Bruccoli D16.
"300 copies printed to mark publication of *Ring Lardner: A Descriptive Bibliography* by Matthew J. Bruccoli and Richard Layman . . ."
Facsimiles restaurant menu with FSF's suggested titles for Lardner's *How to Write Short Stories.*
- PS3511.I9 L15 1976

1057. [Letter to Maxwell Perkins].
- [Columbia, S.C.: MJB, 1978].
- Single leaf printed on verso and recto.

NOTES: Bruccoli D17.
"Five Hundred Copies Printed To Mark Publication Of SCOTT AND ERNEST By Matthew J. Bruccoli."
- PS3511.I9 L396 1978

1058. [Facsimile of FSF's library card].
- [New York]: Harcourt Brace Jovanovich/Bruccoli Clark, [1978].
- Card printed on verso and recto.

NOTES: Bruccoli D18. 2,000 copies distributed to mark publication of *The Notebooks of F. Scott Fitzgerald.*
Verso: Facsimile of FSF's Louisville library card when a soldier at Camp Taylor in 1918; Recto: Nine excerpts from *The Notebooks of F. Scott Fitzgerald.*
- PS3511.I9 N61 1978

1059. [John O'Hara letter to FSF regarding *Tender Is the Night*].
- [n.p.]: 1978.
- Broadside.

NOTES: "Five Hundred Copies Printed To Mark Publication Of SELECTED LETTERS OF JOHN O'HARA, Edited by Matthew J. Bruccoli (New York: Random House, July 13, 1978)."
- PS3511.I9 T4565 1978

1060. [*Some Sort of Epic Grandeur* keepsake].
- [n.p]: 1981.
- Single leaf printed on recto and verso.

NOTES: Recto: photograph of FSF; verso: statement by James Dickey. Published to mark the publication of *Some Sort of Epic Grandeur.* First printing without photo credit second printing with photo credit.
- PS3511.I9 Z5654 1981

1061. *Celestial Eyes—from Metamorphosis to Masterpiece.*
- Charles Scribner III.
- [Columbia, S.C.]: M.J.B., C.S. III, and P.S., 24 October 1991.
- Wrappers, 6 pp.
NOTES: "Published to celebrate the Critical Edition of *The Great Gatsby.*" Facsimiles 9 drafts by Francis Cugat for the dust jacket of *The Great Gatsby.*
- PS3511.I9 G779 1991

1062. *F. Scott Fitzgerald 21 December 1940–21 December 1990: An Exhibition at the Thomas Cooper Library, The University of South Carolina.*
- Matthew J. Bruccoli.
- [Columbia: University of South Carolina, 1991].
- Wrappers, 12 pp.
NOTES: Catalogue facsimiles cover of FSF's pocket notebook.
- PS3511.I9 L3 1990

1063. [*The Last Tycoon* keepsake].
- [Columbia, S.C.: MJB, 1991].
- Single leaf printed on verso and recto.
NOTES: Distributed to mark the opening of an exhibition at the Thomas Cooper Library, University of South Carolina on 21 December 1990. Verso facsimiles cover of FSF's pocket notebook; verso facsimiles notebook's first page.
- PS3511.I9 L3 1990

1064. [*The Love of the Last Tycoon* keepsake].
- [n.p.: 1993].
- Card printed on verso and recto.
NOTES: Verso facsimiles FSF's M-G-M studio Identification Card from 1931. Distributed to mark the publication of *The Love of the Last Tycoon* (1993).
- PS3511.I9 L3 1993c

1065. [Corrected proof of p. 271 of *Tender Is the Night* keepsake].
- Münster, Germany: Westfälische Wilhelms-Universität, 1994.
- Broadside.
NOTES: "Fifty copies for distribution at the Englisches Seminar, Westfällche Wilhelms-Universität, Munster, 28 November 1994." At foot of page "Westfalliche" has been corrected in ink to "Westfälische".
- PS3511.I9 T4 1994

1066. *F. Scott Fitzgerald Centenary Exhibition Catalogue, September 24, 1896–September 24, 1996: The Matthew J. and Arlyn Bruccoli Collection, the Thomas Cooper Library.*
- Columbia: University of South Carolina Press, [1996].
- Wrappers.
- PS3511.I9 Z874 1996

1067. *F. Scott Fitzgerald, 24 September 1896 to 21 December 1940: 24 September 1996 Centenary Celebration.*
- [Columbia, S.C.: University of South Carolina], 1996.
- Wrappers.
- NOTES: On page [46]: "Seven hundred and fifty copies printed for the F. Scott Fitzgerald Centenary Celebration at the University of South Carolina, 24 September 1996." This is copy no. 194.

  Tributes to FSF by Jeffrey Archer, Margaret Atwood, Paul Auster, Richard Bausch, Robert Bausch, Thomas Berger, Sydney Blair, Vance Bourjaily, Frederick Busch, Nicholas Delbanco, Don DeLillo, James Dickey, Annie Dillard, Irvin Faust, Leslie A. Fiedler, George Garrett, George V. Higgins, John Iggulden, John Jakes, John le Carré, Norman Mailer, William Maxwell, Budd Schulberg, Charles M. Schulz, Mary Lee Settle, Tony Tanner, and Arnold Wesker.

  Copy 1: Binding sample in blue wrappers.
  Copy 2: White wrappers, signed by Joseph Heller on front wrapper. Laid in: F. Scott Fitzgerald Centenary Banquet Program, also signed by Heller.
- PS3511.I9 Z6166 1996
- NOTES: James Dickey's "The Slow Surprise and The Deepening of Art": MS, 2 pp.; RTS, 1 p.; RTS, 1 p; RTS, 1 p.; RTS, 2 pp.; RTS, 2 pp.; TS, 2 pp. On deposit.

1068. *F. Scott Fitzgerald at 100: Centenary Tributes by American Writers.*
- Rockville, Maryland: Quill & Brush, 1996.
- Wrappers.
- NOTES: Statements on FSF by Alice Adams, Frederick Busch, Hortense Calisher, Thomas Caplan, Alan Cheuse, Nicholas Delblanco, Don DeLillo, Thomas Flanaghan, George Garrett, Herbert Gold, Allan Gurganus, A. R. Gurney, Joe Haldemann, Alfred Kazin, Edmund Keeley, John McPhee, James Alan McPherson, Arthur Miller, Hugh Nissenson, Reynolds Price, E. Annie Proulx, Budd Schulberg, Carolyn See, Anne Rivers Siddons, Elizabeth Spencer, Christopher Tilghman, John Updike, Richard Wilbur, and Larry Woiwode.
- PS3511.I9 Z6155 1996

1069. *Remarks at the Opening of the F. Scott Fitzgerald Centenary Exhibition and in Recognition of the Matthew J. and Arlyn Bruccoli Collection, 29 September 1996.*
- [Columbia, S.C.: Thomas Cooper Library, 1997].
- Wrappers.
- NOTES: Transcribes remarks made by Donald J. Greiner, Frederick Busch, and MJB.
- PS3511.I9 Z87425 1997

1070. [Contract for *This Side of Paradise* facsimile].
- [Columbia, S.C.: Bruccoli Clark Layman, 1998].
- Single leaf, folded once.

NOTES: "Five hundred copies produced by Bruccoli Clark Layman to mark Volume 200 of the Dictionary of Literary Biography, 13 November 1998."
- PS3511.I9 T4994 1998

1071. *Before The Great Gatsby There Was Trimalchio: F. Scott Fitzgerald's Original Version in His Galley Proofs.*
- [Columbia: University of South Carolina Press, 2000].
- Single sheet, folded twice.

NOTES: Facsimile of "The first of 57 galley sheets for 'Trimalchio.'" Promotional mailer for the University of South Carolina Press publication of *Trimalchio* published in an edition of 500 copies on 10 April 2000.
- PS3511.I9 T74

1072. *Honoring the Researchers of Carolina.*
- [Columbia, S.C.: MJB, 2002].
- Broadside.

NOTES: Facsimile of final page of RTS for "The Swimmers" from the Matthew J. and Arlyn Bruccoli Collection, Thomas Cooper Library. Printed for distribution at a dinner honoring the researchers of Carolina, 6 November 2002.

Limited to 100 copies.
- PS3511.I9 H6 2002

V F. Scott Fitzgerald Manuscripts

Fitzgerald manuscripts (MS), typescripts (TS), and revised typescripts (RTS).

1073. "Thoughtbook of Francis Scott Key Fitzgerald of St. Paul, Minn., U.S.A." [August 1910–24 February 1911.]
- MS: 14 leaves; title, 8–17, 20–23, 29–40.
  NOTES: FSF's diary, kept at age 14. Chiefly descriptions of friends and classmates with accounts of infatuations and social activities. Disbound. Entries appear complete but irregular pagination may reflect lost pages.
- PS3511.I9 T5

1074. "Martin's Thoughts," [1913?].
- MS: 1 p. in frame.
  NOTES: Two four-line stanzas both pasted on sheet headed "Verses by Scott Fitzgerald Newman School 1911-12-13" not in FSF's hand.
- PS3511.I9 M2 1913

1075. Untitled verses, [1914].
- MS: 1 p.
  NOTES: Three-stanza poem or song lyric written in pencil on lined paper.
- PS3511.I9.I8 1914

1076. "This Side of Paradise," [1919?].
- Carbon TS: 48 pp.
  NOTES: Carbon copy of the first 48 pages, plus contents and title page of *This Side of Paradise*. Pencil correction on p. 1.
- PS3511.I9 T49 1919

1077. "The Couple," [1920?].
- RTS and MS: 37 pp.; [1] 2–37.
  NOTES: Revised typescript of unpublished short story probably written in 1920 or 1921.
  First and last page facsimiled in: *F. Scott Fitzgerald Centenary Exhibition Catalogue*.
- PS3511.I9 C68 1920

1078. ["The Offshore Pirate"], [1920].
- RTS: 1 p.
  NOTES: Last page (numbered 38) of typescript of short story published: *The Saturday Evening Post*, 29 October 1920, with variant ending. Facsimiled in: *F. Scott Fitzgerald Centenary Exhibition Catalogue*.
- PS3511.I9 O5 1920

1079. [The Swimmers], [1929].
- TS: 45 pp.
- NOTES: Extensively corrected and revised in pencil by FSF. Incomplete: Page 1 wanting.
  Pages 2–46 of the revised typescript of short story published in: *The Saturday Evening Post,* 19 October 1929.
  Last page facsimiled in: *F. Scott Fitzgerald Centenary Exhibition Catalogue.*
- PS3511.I9 S9 1929

1080. "Babylon Revisited," [ca. 1931].
- Carbon TS: 35 pp.
- NOTES: Published in: *The Saturday Evening Post,* 21 February 1931.
  Envelope postmarked 7 February 1931, addressed to Mrs. Newman Smith (Rosalind Sayre Smith, FSF's sister-in-law) accompanies typescript.
- PS3511.I9 B245

1081. "Home to Maryland," [1931].
- RTS: 53 pp.; 1–20, 20 ½, 21–53.
- NOTES: Typescript, with holograph revisions on every page. Page "20 ½" (holograph) inserted following p. 20.
  Retitled "On Your Own." Published in *Esquire* (30 January 1979).
  First page published in: *F. Scott Fitzgerald Centenary Exhibition Catalogue.*
- PS3511.I9 O7 1931

1082. "The Count of Darkness," [1934].
- RTS: 39 pp.; [A] [1]-39.
- NOTES: Draft of the second story in the "Count of Darkness" or "Philippe" series.
  Typed, with holograph corrections on cover page: "A sequel to 'In the Darkest Hour' which appeared in the October Red Book. But it is also a story in itself." Revisions in pencil on each page.
  Published in: *Redbook,* June 1935.
- PS3511.I9 C65 1934

1083. "A Kingdom in the Dark," [1934].
- RTS: 39 pp.; [1]–51.
- NOTES: Draft of the third story in the "Count of Darkness" or "Philippe" series. Revisions in pencil on each page.
  Published in: *Redbook,* August 1935.
  First page facsimiled in: *F. Scott Fitzgerald Centenary Exhibition Catalogue.*
- PS3511.I9 K56 1934

1084. [Huckleberry Finn Took the First Journey Back], 1934.
- TS: 1 p.
NOTES: One paragraph. Also known as "Tribute to Mark Twain." Published in: *Mark Twain Journal* (Summer 1965).
- PS3511.I9 H9 1935

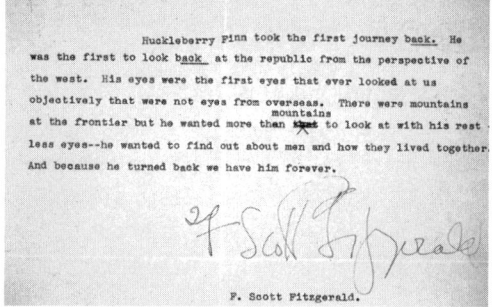

1085. "The Paroxide Blonde: A Poetic Narrative by F. Scott Fitzgerald," [c.1935].
- CC: 5 pp. with magazine illustration of Jean Harlow. Unpublished.
NOTES: Pages 1–4 each annotated "Scottie Fitzgerald fecit" [by Scottie Fitzgerald] and "Veribus est F. Scott Fitzgerald" [by FSF].
Also 2 ALSS from Scottie Fitzgerald Lanahan to Odell S. Hathaway, the purchaser of this poem, 16 January [1949] and 2 March 1949. With correspondence between Hathaway and Ben Abramson of Argus Books.
In box designed and made by Jeanne Bennett.
- PS3511.I91 P3

1086. [Debts], 17 August 1936.
- TS: 2 pp. with pencil corrections.
NOTES: Typescript typed by Isabel Owens, FSF's secretary. At foot of itemized sheet: "Sent to F.S.F. August 17."
The death of FSF's mother within a month helped pay off these debts.
No overall total, but debts amount to over $7800, excluding the $8000 FSF owed Harold Ober and $9618.09 owed Scribner, covered by assignments on FSF's life insurance policy.
- PS3511.I9 Z4801 1936

1087. Autobiographical notes, [1936?].
- MS: 4 pp.
NOTES: Holograph notes on rectos dating and judging the quality of his published short stories and brief autobiographical remarks covering the years 1934–36.
- PS3511.I9 Z4634 1936

1088. Reporter's Note Book, [1937].
- 6 pp.; 15.8 × 12 cm.
NOTES: FSF notes for *The Love of the Last Tycoon* on rectos of first 6 leaves.
- PS3511.I9 L3 1939

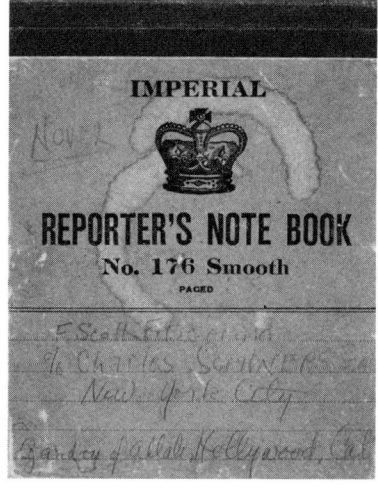

1088.

1089. "Lo, The Poor Peacock!" [c.1935–36].
- TS: 24 pp.; [1]–24.
NOTES: Published in *The Price Was High*.
- PS3511.I9 L5

1090. [Autograph note], n.d.
- MS: 1 p.
NOTES: Humorous note; probably response to autograph request.
- On deposit.

1091. [Notes on *Tender Is the Night*], n.d.
- MS: 1 p.
- On deposit.

Metro-Goldwyn-Mayer Screenplays: Working Drafts

The Warner Bros/Turner Entertainment Collection of F. Scott Fitzgerald Screenplays archive was acquired by the Thomas Cooper Library as part of the Bruccoli Collection while this catalogue was in production; therefore, the compiler was unable to provide a full and detailed description. This is an inventory of the material. The collection includes more than 2,000 pages of FSF manuscripts, revised typescripts, and working notes for four screenplays FSF worked on at Metro-Goldwyn-Mayer from July 1937 to the end of 1938: A Yank at Oxford *(produced 1938; FSF polished the dialogue),* Three Comrades *(produced 1938 from the screenplay by FSF and Edward E. Paramore),* "Infidelity" *(unproduced), and* The Women *(the FSF/Donald Ogden Stewart screenplay was rejected; produced 1939 with a screenplay by Jane Murfin and Anita Loos).*

A Yank at Oxford

1092. ["Note" on *A Yank at Oxford*], 12 July 1937.
- CC: 2 pp.

1093. [Second Half of *A Yank at Oxford*], 17 July 1937.
- CC: 18 pp.
NOTES: Subtitled: "Outline with Dialogue (Corrected Version)."

1094. Memo to Frank Wead, 20 July 1937.
- CC, 1 p.
NOTES: Wead provided dialogue for *A Yank at Oxford*.

1095. "Solution III," undated.
- TS: 2 pp.
NOTES: Plot notes for *A Yank at Oxford*.

1096. "Notes on: 'The Bombshell,'" undated.
- CC: 1 p.
NOTES: Critique of 1933 movie *Bombshell* starring Jean Harlow.

Three Comrades

1097. [Notes, schedules] "Chapter Outline" [for *Three Comrades*], 28 July 1937.
    - MS, 1 p.; CC: 21 pp.

1098. [Incomplete screenplay for *Three Comrades*], 4 August 1937.
    - MS: 11 pp.; RTS: 104 pp.

1099. [Drafts of screenplay for *Three Comrades*], 9–11 August; 18, 20, 22, 25, 27, and 29 September 1937.
    - MS: 318 pp.

1100. "Three Comrades"; "From F. S. Fitzgerald and E. E. Paramore Nov. 5, 1937."
    - MS, RTS, and mimeograph: 121 pp.

1101. [Revisions and inserts for *Three Comrades*], 3 and 9 December 1937.
    - MS: 84 pp.; RTS: 5 pp.

1102. [Inserts and revisions for *Three Comrades*], 7 June; 30 September; 7 and 20 December 1937.
    - Wire: 1 p.; MS: 33 pp.; RTS: 7 pp.; CC: 20 pp.
    NOTES: Includes "Conference Notes," 30 December 1937.
    - CC: 9.pp.

1103. [Inserts and revisions for *Three Comrades*], 15 and 28 July; 2 and 4–6 August; 22 and 23 September; 2, 5, 13, 22, 25, and 28–30 October; 3 and 5 November 1937.
    - MS: 125 pp.; RTS: 97 pp.; RCC: 43 pp.

1104. "Three Comrades Fitzgerald-Paramore First Revise Dec. 13, 1937."
    - Revised mimeograph, RTS, RCC: 172 pp.; MS: 31 pp.

1105. [Inserts and revisions for *Three Comrades*], 12, 13, 15, 18–20, and 29 November; 7 and 15 December 1937.
    - MS: 140 pp.; RTS: 30 pp.; RCC: 33 pp.; revised mimeograph: 4 pp.

1106. "Three Comrades"; "From F. S. Fitzgerald E. E. Paramore," 2 February 1938.
    - Mimeograph in binder: 124 pp.; includes 15 replacement pages dated 4 February 1938.

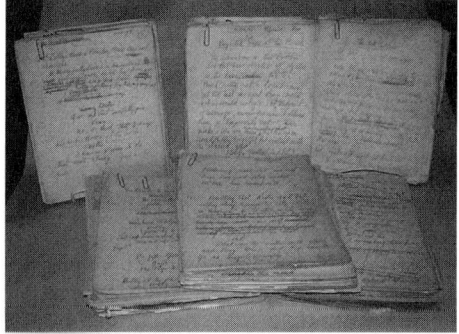

Infidelity

1107. [Early drafts for "Infidelity"], 25 February; 3, 4, 7, 17, and 22 March; 13 and 27 April 1938.
    - MS and RTS: 257 pp.

1108. [Revisions for "Infidelity"], 15, 18, 23, and 26 April 1938.
    - ALS: 2 pp.; MS: 25 pp.; RTS: 7 pp.; revised mimeograph: 71 pp.; CC: 16 pp.

1109. "Argument for Stromberg," 21 April 1938.
    - MS: 5 pp.
    NOTES: Hunt Stromberg headed the production unit making "Infidelity."

1110. "Idea Number Three," "Outline" [for "Infidelity"], 27 April 1938.
    - MS and RTS: 8 pp.

1111. "New Schedule," "Notes" [for "Infidelity"], undated.
    - MS and CC: 20 pp.

1112. [Revisions and Inserts for "Infidelity"], 3 and 25 May 1938.
    - MS, RTS, RCC, and revised mimeograph: 45 pp.

1113. "New Treatment for End of Infidelity," 8 and 10 May 1938.
    - MS and CC: 19 pp.

1114. [Memo to Hunt Stromberg about "Infidelity"], 27 June 1938.
    - MS draft: 11 pp; CC: 5 pp.

1115. [Reviews of "The Woman" and "World's Fair"], 8 February 1938.
    - RTS: 4 pp.
    NOTES: Parody reviews of nonexistent Joan Crawford movies.

The Women

1116. [Early draft of *The Women*], 31 May 1938.
    - MS: 40 pp.

1117. [Early draft of *The Women*], 31 May 1938.
    - RTS and MS: 36 pp.

1118. [Treatment for *The Women*], 3 June 1938.
    - RTS: 39 pp.; RTS: 3 pp.

182 F. Scott Fitzgerald Manuscripts

1119. [Scene breakdown for *The Women*], 6 June 1938.
- CC: 28 pp.

1120. "Addenda to Outline," 9 June 1938.
- MS: 28 pp.; TS: 5 pp.

NOTES: Plot notes for *The Women*.

1121. [Plot notes for *The Women*], 13 June 1938.
- MS: 7 pp.

1122. [Opening sequence for *The Women*], 28 and 30 June 1938.
- MS and RTS: 18 pp.
- [Scenes for *The Women*], 1 July 1938.
- RT and MS: 34 pp.

1123. [Working draft of *The Women*], 9 July 1938.
- MS and RTS: 200+ pp. Wrappers.

NOTES: On front wrapper: "From: F. S. Fitzgerald". With CC in wrappers (119 pp.).

1124. [Scene revisions for *The Women*], 8 and 9 August 1938.
- MS: 34 pp.; MS: 8 pp.; CC: 4 pp.; RTS and MS: 4 pp.

1125. ["FIRST REVISE" of *The Women*], 15 August 1938.
- RTS: 84 pp. Wrappers.

NOTES: On front wrapper: "From: F.S. Fitzgerald".

1126. [Revised opening for *The Women*], 23 August 1938.
- RTS: 12 pp.; MS: 11 pp.

NOTES: Includes MS inserts.

1127. "From the End of Episode 4." 23 September 1938.
- CC: 5 pp.

1128. [Scene revisions for *The Women*], 26 September 1837.
- Mimeo, RTS and MS: 25 pp; with MS: 11 pp.

NOTES: Includes MS inserts. Headed "Stewart-Fitzgerald" in an unidentified hand.

1129. "From the End of Episode 4."
- MS, 13 pp.

1130. "Idle Thoughts of an Idle Fellow," undated.
- MS: 5 pp.

Notes: Revised scene for *The Women*.

1131. [Miscellaneous office memos and doodles), undated.
- MS: 8 pp.

1132. [Plot and scene notes for *The Women*], undated.
- MS and RTS: 20 pp.

1133. *The Women*, 1938–1939.
- Jane Murfin.
- Four screenplays (24 October 1938, 13 March 1939, 22 March 1939, and 1 April 1939). Wrappers.

1134. Three letters from Joseph Breen to Louis B. Mayer, 21 April 1939, 25 April and 18 June 1939.
- CC: 6 pages
NOTES: Letters describe objections and suggest revisions to screenplay for *The Women*.

VI Correspondence

A. From F. Scott Fitzgerald

1135. ALS to Shane Leslie, 22 December 1917; Fort Leavenworth, Kansas.
- 3 pp.
NOTES: FSF discusses plan for novel "The Romantic Egoist."
>Published in: *F. Scott Fitzgerald: A Life in Letters.*
>With TLS from Charles Scribner II to Leslie, 29 December 1920.
>With MJB to Leslie, 27 June 1963; MS "memoranda" on FSF by Leslie on verso.
- PS3511.I9 Z485 1917b

1136. ALS to Shane Leslie, February 1918; Fort Leavenworth, Kansas.
- 1 p.
NOTES: FSF states he is sending two chapters of "The Romantic Egoist."
>Published in: *F. Scott Fitzgerald: A Life in Letters.*
- PS3511.I9 Z4851 1918

1137. TLS to Shane Leslie, 8 May 1918; 45th Infantry, Camp Gordon, Georgia.
- 1 p.
NOTES: FSF thanks Leslie for reading and commenting on two chapters of his novel and writing to Scribners about it.
>Published in: *F. Scott Fitzgerald: A Life in Letters.*
- PS3511.I9 Z4852 1918

1138. ALS to Shane Leslie, 13 January 1919; 17th Infantry Brigade Headquarters, Camp Sheridan, Alabama.
- 1 p.
NOTES: FSF expresses sorrow over the death of Monsignor Cyril Sigourney Fay.
>Published in: *F. Scott Fitzgerald: A Life in Letters.*
- PS3511.I9 Z4853 1919

1139. ALS to Shane Leslie, January–February 1919; 17th Infantry Brigade Headquarters, Camp Sheridan, Alabama.
- 3 pp.; American Red Cross Base Hospital stationery.
NOTES: FSF mentions his desire to become a priest because of Fay's influence.
>Published in: *F. Scott Fitzgerald: A Life in Letters.*
- PS3511.I9 Z4854 1919

1140. [Postcards of Kings, Queens, and prominent personages from European history].
- Paris: Levy et Neurdein Reunis, [1920–30].
- 14 postcards.

NOTES: Group of postcards featuring portraits of European Kings, Queens, and "Noble Personages" with brief biographical information. Holograph notes in upper right hand corners categorizing the cards (e.g., "Ancient Kings") in FSF's hand.
- D107.P6

1141. ALS to Isabelle Amorous, 26 February 1920; Cottage Club, Princeton, New Jersey.
   - 2 pp.
   NOTES: FSF reports his publication in *The Saturday Evening Post*, *Smart Set* and *Scribner's Magazine*. States that he and ZF have had a reconciliation. Published in: *Correspondence of F. Scott Fitzgerald*.
   - PS3511.I9 Z481 1920

1142. ALS to Martin Amorous, Rye, New York, Spring 1920; University Cottage Club, Princeton, New Jersey.
   - 2 pp. with envelope.
   NOTES: FSF reports engagement to ZF and selling the movie rights to the short story "Head and Shoulders" for $2,500.
   - PS3511.I9 Z48105 1920

1143. ALS to Martin Amorous, Rye, New York, postmarked 10 June 1920; Westport, Connecticut.
   - 1 p. with envelope; Biltmore Hotel stationery.
   NOTES: FSF invites Amorous to visit Westport.
   - PS3511.I9 Z48104 1920

1144. ALS to John Biggs, Fall 1920; 38 W. 59th St., New York City.
   - 1 p.
   NOTES: FSF reports on Scribners decision not to publish Biggs's novel.
   - PS3511.I9 Z48155 1920

1145. ALS to John Biggs, Fall 1920; 38 W. 59th St., New York City.
   - 1 p.
   NOTES: FSF praises Maxwell Perkins as "one hell of a good fellow" and reports "P.S. Am writing a movie for Dorothy Gish by request of Griffith."
   - PS3511.I9 Z48157 1920

1146. ALS to Lorena and Phil McQuillan, 28 December 1920; 38 W. 59th St., New York City.
- 3 pp.
NOTES: FSF reports to his aunt and uncle putting "finishing touches" on novel "The Beautiful Lady without Mercy"; "I really am in this game seriously and for something besides money . . . I'd rather live on less and preserve the one duty of a sincere writer—to set down life as he sees it as gracefully as he knows how."
- On deposit.

1147. ALS to "Drake," c. 1920.
- 1 p.
NOTES: FSF mentions John Peale Bishop and Frank Crowinshield.
- On deposit.

1148. ALS to Robert D. Clark, 9 February 1920 [1921]; 38 W. 59th St., New York City.
- 4 pp. with envelope.
NOTES: Includes parody letter from Shakespeare to his mother.
Published in: *F. Scott Fitzgerald: A Life in Letters.*
- PS3511.I9 Z482 1920

1149. ALS to John Biggs, 11 April 1921; 38 W. 59th St., New York City.
- 2 pp.
NOTES: FSF hopes Knopf will accept Biggs's novel. Criticizes one of Biggs's short stories, but offers to take the novel to another publisher before he leaves for Europe, should Knopf turn it down.
- PS3511.I9 Z48158 1921

1150. TLS to Dr. Frank H. Vizetelly, New York, 1922; St. Paul, Minnesota.
- 1 p.
NOTES: FSF explains the term "Bilphism," coined by Fitzgerald in *The Beautiful and Damned:* "I wanted to take a crack at Theossophy without hurting the feelings of a relative of mine. Several people have enquired about it. So I guess it will enter no dictionary." See OED.
- PS3511.I9 Z51 1922

1151. ALS to Shane Leslie, 12 March 1922; 626 Goodrich Avenue, St. Paul, Minnesota.
- 2 pp.
NOTES: FSF mentions Leslie's new book which he intends to review. States that his second novel has just been published by Scribners and generally favorably reviewed.
Published in: *Correspondence of F. Scott Fitzgerald.*
- PS3511.I9 Z4855 1922

1152. ALS to Oliver Jenkins, [June–August 1922?]; White Bear Lake, North Dakota.
- 1 p. in frame; "Hack Writer and Plagiarist" letterhead.

NOTES: "I put all my best verses into This Side of Paradise + closed the chapter. I've even dismantled the other old fragments to adorn passages of fine writing. I'll be very interested in seeing your novel but I don't feel you've hit on a good title. It's strained like The Beautiful + Damned."
- PS3511.I9 Z4851 1922

1153. ALS to the Society of Midland Authors, [July 1922]; The Yacht Club, White Bear Lake, Minnesota.
- 1 p.

NOTES: FSF declines the society's invitation.
- PS3511.I9 Z4876 1922

1154. ALS to Dorothy Connor, Philadelphia, Pennsylvania, postmarked 17 March 1924; Great Neck, Long Island, New York.
- 1 p. with envelope.

NOTES: FSF thanks Connor for compliment on *This Side of Paradise* and recommends that she read the diaries of Otto Braun.
- PS3511.I9 Z4826 1924

1155. ALS to Charles C. Baldwin, [April 1924]; Great Neck, Long Island, New York.
- 1 p.

NOTES: FSF provides brief biographical data and comments on interests and the literary scene. Regrets that "I can't write you a very full letter at present as I'm sailing for Europe in two days . . ." and remarks that "my third novel (unpublished) is just finished + quite different from my other two. . . ."

Baldwin excerpted and paraphrased some of FSF's comments for *The Men Who Make Our Novels* (New York: Dodd, Mead, 1924).

Pasted in: *Tales of the Jazz Age*. (See Item 125).

Facsimiled in: *Trimalchio* (Columbia: University of South Carolina, 2000).
- PS3511.I9 T3

1156. Postcards of Hotel du Cap d'Antibes, France, c. 1924–25.
- 2 cards.

NOTES: 1 annotated by FSF; 1 annotated by ZF.
- On deposit.

1157. Postcard to Mrs. A. D. Sayre, Montgomery, Alabama, [January–March 1925].
- 1 p. Picture of Tiberio Palace Hotel, Capri. Postmark and stamp removed.

NOTES: Holograph annotations on front of card: "All our rooms" and "Sunniest balcony in Italy."
- PS3511.I9 Z4889 1929

1158. ALS to Van Wyck Brooks, undated; 14 Rue de Tilsitt, Paris, France.
- 1 p. with envelope postmarked 13 June 1925.
NOTES: FSF comments on Brooks's recent book, *The Pilgrimage of Henry James*, James's emotional problems, and the need of novelists like James and Fitzgerald to have love as a main concern.
Published in: *F. Scott Fitzgerald: A Life in Letters.*
- PS3511.I9 Z4815 1925

1159. ALS to Carl W. Winston, postmarked 21 December 1925; 14 Rue de Tilsitt, Paris, France.
- 1 p. with envelope.
NOTES: FSF mentions Oxford in connection with *The Great Gatsby*.
- On deposit.

1160. Postcards to Frances Scott Fitzgerald, 1928–32.
- 8 postcards.
NOTES: Postcards addressed "Dear Pie" or some variation of "Dear Pie"; one addressed "Dear Diana" signed "Sincerely yours, Jupiter," sent to Scottie Fitzgerald by her father between 1928 and 1932.
Four are postmarked January 1928, Quebec. The fifth card is postmarked January 1928, Montreal. The sixth is postmarked February 1929, New York. The seventh is postmarked April 1932, Baltimore. The top third of the eighth card is removed.
Most have humorous comments, including jokes, riddles, and limericks, as well as drawings by FSF.
Published in: *F. Scott Fitzgerald Centenary Exhibition Catalogue.*
- PS3511.I9 Z48292

1161. ALS to Harold Ober, July 1929.
- 1 p. memo for cable.
NOTES: FSF acknowledges raise from *The Saturday Evening Post.*
- On deposit.

1162. Telegram to Cecilia Taylor, Norfolk, Virginia, 15 February 1932; Charlotte, North Carolina.
- 1 p.
NOTES: FSF thanks Taylor for her "courtesies" and apologizes for leaving "in such a messy condition".
- PS3511.I9 Z4879 1932

1163. TLS to Francis Swann, 19 July 1933; La Paix, Towson, Maryland.
- 4 pp.
NOTES: Brief letter to accompany RTS plan of a musical revue about gangsters

Fitzgerald planned with Swann. With three pages blocking out the scenes and offering suggestions for plot and characterization.
Published in: *Correspondence of F. Scott Fitzgerald.*
- PS3511.I9 Z48779 1933

1164. TLS to Gilbert Seldes, New York City, 2 February 1934; 1307 Park Avenue, Baltimore, Maryland.
- 2 pp.
NOTES: FSF suggests several alternate titles for a collection of Ring Lardner material.
- PS3511.I9 Z487 1934

1165. TLS to Cyril Clemens, International Mark Twain Society, Webster Groves, Missouri, 11 May 1934; 1307 Park Avenue, Baltimore, Maryland.
- 1 p.
NOTES: Author accepts his nomination to honorary membership in the Mark Twain Society. See Item 1537.
- PS3511.I9 Z482 1934

1166. Typed carbon copy to Rosalind Sayre Smith, New York City, 8 August 1934; 1307 Park Avenue, Baltimore, Maryland.
- 8 pp.
NOTES: FSF discusses Scottie Fitzgerald's current welfare, her talents, and her prospects for the future.
Published in: *Correspondence of F. Scott Fitzgerald.*
- PS3511.I9 Z4875 1934

1167. Telegram to Mrs. Randolph Wootton, c/o Carl Calmer, New York City, 28 November 1934; Baltimore, Maryland.
- 1 p.
NOTES: FSF writes that the letters of introduction have been postponed due to sickness and work on the Philippe stories but promises to send them on Saturday and Monday.
- PS3511.I9 Z4895 1934

1168. TLS to Hubert Spake, Kansas City, Missouri, 26 December 1934; 1307 Park Avenue, Baltimore, Maryland.
- 1 p.
NOTES: FSF suggests "send your best stuff on to me and I shall try to get it a hearing through my agent who is absolutely reliable."
- PS3511.I9 Z48756 1934

1169. TLS to Don Swann, 28 February 1935; 1307 Park Avenue, Baltimore, Maryland.
- 1 p.
NOTES: FSF returns Swann's poems, and comments about the difficulty in getting poems accepted by editors.
- PS3511.I9 Z48778 1935

190 Correspondence

1170. TLS to Maxwell Perkins, 2 March 1935; 1307 Park Avenue, Baltimore, Maryland.
- 1 p.
- NOTES: Letter of recommendation for Alice Wootton who had served as FSF's secretary.
- PS3511.I9 Z4864 1935

1171. ALS to Adelaide W. Neall, 1935; The Cambridge Arms, Charles St., Baltimore.
- 1 p.
- NOTES: FSF writes that he is rushing a story to her in the hope of receiving a decision to publish before Christmas. Should she accept the story, he would appreciate payment before Christmas.
  Neall was a fiction editor at *The Saturday Evening Post*.
- PS3511.I9 Z4883 1936

1172. ALS to Elizabeth Lemmon, postmarked 6 and 10 January 1936; Baltimore, Maryland.
- 2 pp. with two envelopes.
- NOTES: FSF explains that, owing to his illness, he will be unable to pay for books until February.
- PS3511.I9 Z4849 1936

1173. TLS to Ben Abramson, Argus Book Shop, Chicago, 17 March 1936; 1 East 34th Street, Baltimore, Maryland.
- 1 p.
- NOTES: Author incorrectly provides point for identifying first printing of *This Side of Paradise*.
- PS3511.I9 Z4813 1936

1174. TLS to Ben Abramson, Argus Book Shop, Chicago, 7 April 1936; 1 East 34th Street, Baltimore, Maryland.
- 1 p.
- NOTES: FSF corrects statement made in letter of 17 March about identification of the first printing of *This Side of Paradise*.
- PS3511.I9 Z4814 1936

1175. TLS to Rita Swann, Baltimore, Maryland, 21 July 1936; Grove Park Inn, Asheville, North Carolina.
- 1 p.
- NOTES: FSF discusses legal matters pertaining to his mother's estate.
  Published in: *Correspondence of F. Scott Fitzgerald*.
- PS3511.I9 Z4878 1936

1176. TL to Isabel Owens, 4 and 14 August 1936; Grove Park Inn, Asheville, North Carolina.
- 2 letters, 1 p. both.

NOTES: FSF discusses his injured shoulder, broken in a diving accident and further damaged in a fall, and alludes to financial difficulties.
- PS3511.I9 Z4885

1177. Telegram to Isabel Owens, 3 September 1936.
- 1 p. with envelope.
NOTES: FSF reports the death of his mother, 3 September 1936.
- PS3511.I9 Z4885

1178. TLS to Mrs. Clifton Sprague, Norfolk, Virginia, 16 September 1936; Asheville, North Carolina.
- 1 p.
NOTES: FSF discusses with his sister the division of personal items from their late mother's estate, the administration of her estate; corrected in his hand.
   Published in: *Correspondence of F. Scott Fitzgerald*.
- PS3511.I9 Z48757 1936

1179. TLS to Isabel Owens, Baltimore, 28 October 1936; Grove Park Inn, Asheville, North Carolina.
- 1 p.; mounted in double mat with photograph (10.4 × 7.5 cm.) of the Fitzgerald family, [Paris, 1925?].
NOTES: FSF sends Owen two checks; asks that she calculate how much he owes her for any bills she may have paid for him.
- PS3511.I9 Z497 1936

1180. Telegram to Harold Ober, New York City, 17 December 1936; Asheville, North Carolina.
- 1 p.
NOTES: FSF notifies Ober of Scottie Fitzgerald's holiday plans and of her wish to visit the Obers before the holidays end. Promises to see Ober on the 23rd, if possible.
   Published in *"As Ever, Scott Fitz—."*
- PS3511.I9 Z4862 1936

1181. ALS to Dr. Sinclair, c.1936–37; Tryon, N.C.
- 1 p.
NOTES: FSF discusses payment of ZF's dental bills. With 1-page CC to Dr. R. Burke Suitt, 28 November 1936.
- On deposit.

1182. TL to Rosalind Sayre Smith, between 1937 and 1940.
- 1 p.
NOTES: FSF responds caustically to Smith's "sanctimonious advice" reminding her of money he once loaned to her husband; corrected in his hand.
- PS3511.I9 Z4876

1183. ALS to Anne Ober, [June 1937]; [Tryon, N.C.].
- 2 pp.
NOTES: FSF discusses plans for New York trip and for Scottie Fitzgerald's summer.
- On deposit.

1184. Telegram to Anne Ober, Scarsdale, New York, 23 July [1937]; Hollywood, California.
- 1 p.
NOTES: FSF informs Ober that Helen MacArthur (Helen Hayes) will leave for Hollywood on 2 August. Suggests Scottie Fitzgerald call her on Wednesday [28 July]. Scottie Fitzgerald traveled to Hollywood with Helen Hayes in August 1937.
- PS3511.I9 Z48595 1937

1185. ALS to Anne Ober, Scarsdale, N.Y., 26 July 1937; Garden of Allah Hotel, Hollywood, California.
- 2 pp.; signed: "Scott".
NOTES: Written after FSF's first week at the M-G-M studios, his third venture in Hollywood. FSF reports on the celebrities he has seen but vows that he intends to concentrate on his work and see no one.
Published in: *F. Scott Fitzgerald Centenary Exhibition Catalogue.*
- PS3511.I9 Z488 1937

1186. Telegram to Anne Ober, New York City, 18 September 1937; Beverly Hills, California.
- 1 p.
NOTES: FSF asks if Scottie Fitzgerald is with her. In response to inquiry, states his opposition to Scottie's unchaperoned attendance at nighttime parties.
- PS3511.I9 Z48594 1937

1187. TLS to Anne Ober, 18 September 1937; Culver City, California.
- 1 p. on M-G-M stationery.
NOTES: FSF discusses Scottie Fitzgerald's conduct.
- On deposit.

1188. ALS to Anne Ober, September 1937; Hotel Paso Del Norte, El Paso, Texas.
- 1 p. on hotel stationery.
NOTES: FSF notifies Anne Ober of Scottie Fitzgerald's plans to visit, expresses his disapproval of her smoking, and writes that he is working hard but profitably in Hollywood.
- PS3511.I9 Z48594 1937

1189. Telegram to Harold and Anne Ober, 25 December 1937; Hollywood, California.
- 1 p.

NOTES: "MERRY CHRISTMAS TO TWO PEOPLE WHO MADE AN OLD YEAR POSSIBLE AND A NEW YEAR HAPPY. SCOTT FITZGERALD".
- PS3511.I9 Z48849 1937

1190. ALS to John Biggs, late 1937; The Garden of Allah, 8152 Sunset Blvd., Hollywood, California.
- 1 p. on The Garden of Allah Hotel and Villas stationery.
NOTES: FSF reports that he has just finished script of *Three Comrades* and mentions collaborator E. E. Paramore.
With file copy of Biggs's reply to FSF, typed carbon, unsigned.
Published in: *F. Scott Fitzgerald Centenary Exhibition Catalogue.*
- PS3511.I9 Z48159 1938

1191. ALS to Lorena McQuillan, n.d.; Culver City, California.
- 1 p.
NOTES: FSF offers condolence on death of his uncle Phil McQuillan.
- On deposit.

1192. Telegram to Anne Ober, 7 January [1938–40]; Hollywood, California.
- 1 p.
NOTES: "WILL PHONE SCOTTIE".
- On deposit.

1193. Miscellaneous letters to Hunt Stromberg, 22 February to 6 June 1938; [Culver City, California.
- 12 leaves.
NOTES: Last letter (6 June 1938) includes plot outline of a new screenplay with different actors and actresses which, FSF hopes, will be a great movie acceptable to the censors.
With copy of "Infidelity" typescript.
- PN1997.I6342 1938G

1194. TLS to Anne Ober, 4 March 1938; Hollywood, California.
- 3 pp.
NOTES: FSF discusses Scottie Fitzgerald and his movie work.
- On deposit.

1195. TLS to Rosalind Smith, 4 March 1938; Hollywood, California.
- 1 p.
NOTES: FSF provides correct and incorrect publication data on *The Great Gatsby.*
Removed from *Tales of the Jazz Age.* See Item 128.
- PS3511.I9 T3 1922b

1196. TLS to Harold and Anne Ober, 11 March 1938; The Garden of Allah, 8152 Sunset Blvd., Hollywood, California.
- 1 p.

NOTES: FSF discusses Scottie Fitzgerald's school play and his work on "Infidelity."
- On deposit.

1197. ALS to Zelda Fitzgerald, April 1938; The Garden of Allah, 8152 Sunset Blvd., Hollywood, California.
- 2 pp.
NOTES: FSF mentions a disastrous recent trip he made with his wife and daughter to Virginia. Discusses the importance of achieving another screen credit after *Three Comrades*. Concludes with "once we were one person and always it will be a little that way."
This letter may not have been sent.
Published in: *F. Scott Fitzgerald: A Life in Letters*.
- PS3511.I9 Z48295

1198. ALS to Anne Ober, [June 1938]; The Garden of Allah, 8152 Sunset Blvd., Hollywood, California.
- 3 pp.
NOTES: FSF discusses Scottie Fitzgerald's school conduct.
- On deposit.

1199. Telegram to Anne Ober, 8 June [1938]; Los Angeles, California.
- 1 p.
NOTES: FSF directs daughter to bring textbooks to California.
- PS3511.I9 Z4882 1938

1200. Telegram to Harold and Anne Ober, 14 June 1938; Culver City, California.
- 1 p.
NOTES: FSF reports daughter's arrival time.
- PS3511.I9 Z48822 1938

1201. Telegram to Scottie Fitzgerald, 20 June 1938; Culver City, California.
- 1 p.
NOTES: FSF urges her to study.
- On deposit.

1202. Telegram to Harold Ober, 26 June 1938; Malibu, California.
- 1 p.
NOTES: "SCOTTIE HAS DISAPPEARED".
- On deposit.

1203. Telegram to Harold Ober, 30 June [1938]; Los Angeles.
- 1 p.
NOTES: FSF will phone Scottie Fitzgerald.
- On deposit.

1204. Telegram to Anne Ober, 18 July [1938]; Los Angeles.
- 1 p.
NOTES: "SCOTTIE GOT INTO VASSAR".
- On deposit.

1205. [Leaf from Scottie Fitzgerald's scrapbook], n.d.
- 2 telegrams and 1 postcard from FSF pasted on.
NOTES: One telegram congratulates her on acceptance at Vassar.
- On deposit.

1206. TLS to Anne Ober, 25 August 1938; Culver City, California.
- 1 p. on M-G-M stationery.
NOTES: FSF discusses Scottie Fitzgerald's allowance.
- On deposit.

1207. TLS to Anne and Harold Ober, 7 September 1938; Culver City, California.
- 1 p. on M-G-M stationery.
NOTES: FSF discusses Scottie Fitzgerald.
- On deposit.

1208. Telegram to Anne Ober, 9 September [1938]; Malibu, California.
- 1 p.
NOTES: FSF discusses Scottie Fitzgerald.
- On deposit.

1209. Telegram to Harold Ober, 22 September 1938; Malibu, California.
- 1 p.
NOTES: FSF discusses Scottie Fitzgerald's allowance.
- On deposit.

1210. Telegram to Anne Ober, 28 September [1938]; Malibu, California.
- 1 p.
NOTES: FSF discusses Scottie Fitzgerald.
- On deposit.

1211. Telegram to Scottie Fitzgerald, n.d.; Malibu, California.
- 1 p.
NOTES: FSF advises her against Baltimore trip.
- On deposit.

1212. TLS to Anne Ober, 16 December 1938; Culver City, California.
- 1 p. on M-G-M stationery.
NOTES: FSF notifies Anne Ober of his daughter's holiday plans at the end of her first semester at Vassar, including "two or three nights at the beginning or end with you".
- PS3511.I9 Z48593 1938

1213. ALS to Zelda Fitzgerald, [1938]; [California].
- 2 pp.; signed "Scott".
- NOTES: FSF discusses the realities of his financial state.
- PS3511.I9 Z48295 1938

1214. TLS half-page cut from full page, c.1938.
- 1 p.
- On deposit.

1215. ALS to Zelda Fitzgerald, [1939?].
- 9 pp.
- NOTES: This letter was never sent.
    FSF explains his position in regard to ZF's furlough or discharge from Highland. He alludes to previous mention of divorce, ZF's painting, Scottie Fitzgerald, drinking, and their marriage.
- PS3511.I9 Z4 8295 1939

1216. Telegram to Anne Ober, 19 September [c.1939–40]; Hollywood, California.
- 1 p.
- NOTES: "WHERE IS SCOTTIE?"
- On deposit.

1217. TC to Charles Marquis (Bill) Warren, 15 May 1939; 5521 Amestoy Avenue, Encino, California.
- 1 p.; "File" in pencil in upper right hand corner.
- NOTES: FSF's humorous reply to Warren's letter of 13 May, which relayed gossip about FSF, ZF, and Sheilah Graham.
- PS3511.I9 Z492 1939

1218. Telegram to Scottie Fitzgerald, 21 September [1939]; Encino, California.
- 1 p.
- NOTES: FSF tells his daughter to register at Vassar. He has arranged for her tuition by borrowing from *Esquire* magazine against future stories. Published in: *F. Scott Fitzgerald Centenary Exhibition Catalogue*.
- PS3511.I9 Z4829 1939

1219. TL to Margery Sayre Brinson, 24 October 1939; Encino, California.
- 1 p.
- NOTES: FSF discusses ZF's condition. With: Attached holograph note by Scottie Fitzgerald.
- On deposit.

1220. TLS to Robert Bennett, Holmes Book Co. Los Angeles, 21 February 1940; 5521 Amestoy Avenue, Encino, California.
- 1 p. with envelope.
- NOTES: FSF comments on books sent him by Bennett, including editions of Plato and Shaw ("excellent") and *Crime and Punishment* ("type is too fine").

Published in: *Correspondence of F. Scott Fitzgerald.*
- PS3511.I9 Z4811 1940

1221. CC to State of California Franchise Tax Commissioner, Sacramento, 27 March 1940; 5521 Amestoy Avenue, Encino, California.
- 1 p.
- NOTES: FSF encloses his 1939 income tax form (not present) explaining that unemployment due to illness prevents him from meeting his federal or state tax obligations. Requests additional time to make his payments. Holograph note penciled at top: "Mr. Young . . . has given me to 'about' June 30 . . ."
- PS3511.I9 Z4819 1940

1222. TL to Isabel Owens, 13 May 1940; Hollywood, California.
- 1 p.; first page of letter.
- NOTES: FSF expresses concern over charges for furniture and personal items in storage and suggests selling or otherwise disposing of some articles to reduce the fees. FSF mentions that ZF is in Alabama and better, but he foresees no prospect of ever living with her again. Requests that Owens send his files of letters and one remaining scrapbook to California.
- PS3511.I9 Z4885

1223. TLS to Alice [Wootton] Richardson, 29 July 1940; Santa Barbara, California.
- 1 p.; signed "Scott".
- NOTES: FSF reports that he is working on a story for "little Miss Temple"; describes Hollywood as "a dump—in the human sense of the word".
- PS3511.I9 Z4865 1940

1224. TLS to Robert Bennett, Holmes Book Co. Los Angeles, 25 September 1940; 1403 N. Laurel Avenue, Hollywood, California.
- 1 p. with envelope.
- NOTES: FSF discusses Chapman's *Homer*: "For years I've wanted to read Chapman—probably on account of Keat's sonnet."
- PS3511.I9 Z4812 1940

1225. TLS to Robert Bennett, Holmes Book Co. Los Angeles, 28 November 1940; 1403 N. Laurel Avenue, Hollywood, California.
- 1 p. with envelope.
- NOTES: FSF states he has read the volume of Elizabethan poems sent by Bennett.
  Published in: *Correspondence of F. Scott Fitzgerald.*
- PS3511.I9 Z4813 1940

1226. ALS to Zelda Fitzgerald, [1940]; California.
- 9 pp.
- NOTES: FSF discusses ZF's release from Highland Hospital.
- On deposit.

1227. Collection of Papers on the F. Scott Fitzgerald—Lester Cowan Relationship, 1940–93 (bulk 1940–73).
- 120 items.

NOTES: FSF agreed to prepare a screenplay based on the short story "Babylon Revisited" for Lester Cowan. Includes Cowan's copy of the contract, agreeing to pay Fitzgerald $5,000 in stages.

Also includes copies of correspondence and legal documents on the purchase by Paramount pictures of the "Babylon Revisited" property for a total of $15,000.

Includes notes and correspondence concerning Cowan's projected production of *The Last Tycoon,* including a Xerox of the contract with Irwin Shaw to write the screenplay and memo about Scottie Fitzgerald. See Item 415.

Includes a heavily annotated setting copy of *Babylon Revisited, the Screenplay* (New York: Carroll & Graf, 1993).
- PS3511.I9 Z49

1228. [Reproduction of portrait of FSF], n.d.
- Gordon Bryant.

NOTES: Inscribed by FSF to Mrs. A. D. Sayre.
- On deposit.

1229. [Reproduction of portrait of FSF], n.d.
- Gordon Bryant.

NOTES: Inscribed by FSF to "Stephen Parrot from his brother".
- On deposit.

1230. Card to Chester Trowe, California, n.d.
- 1 p.

NOTES: Holograph inscription: "For Chester Trowe remembering another man who was sick on a Pacific Island. F. Scott Fitzgerald."

Profile portrait of FSF, mounted next to inscription.
- PS3511.I9 Z483 1928

B. To F. Scott Fitzgerald

Items arranged alphabetically by sender.

1231. Postcard, 1906.
- 1 picture postcard of St. Patrick's Cathedral, New York.

NOTES: Unsigned; addressed to FSF.
- On deposit.

1232. Postcards, 1908.
- 6 picture postcards.

NOTES: Sent to FSF from Europe by "Auntie Clara."
- On deposit.

1233. Postcard from Cecilia Fitzgerald, 8 September 1908.
- 1 p.
NOTES: Picture postcard of Francis Scott Key's home sent to FSF by his grandmother.
- On deposit.

1234. ALS from Scottie Fitzgerald, n.d.
- 4 pp.
NOTES: Scottie Fitzgerald reports news from prep school.
- On deposit.

1235. ALS from Scottie Fitzgerald, Brackney, Pennsylvania, n.d.
- 4 pp.
NOTES: Scottie Fitzgerald reports news from Camp Redwing.
- On deposit.

1236. ALS from Scottie Fitzgerald, 7 October 1939.
- 1 p.
NOTES: Scottie Fitzgerald reports on her schoolwork at Vassar.
- PS3569.M33797 Z482 1939

1237. Telegram from Helen Hayes, Albany, N.Y., 7 July 1937.
- 1 p.
NOTES: Hayes agrees to chaparone Scottie Fitzgerald to California.
- On deposit.

1238. Correspondence from Internal Revenue Service, 1934–36.
- 3 letters.
NOTES: With CC of FSF letter to IRS, 4 December 1936.
- On deposit.

1239. TL from Ring Lardner, [Great Neck?], to FSF and ZF, New York, 25 September 1927.
- 1 p. incomplete; torn lengthwise.
NOTES: Lardner writes of his work on a new baseball play (produced as *Elmer the Great*) and three other new stories.
   ZF's holograph note on verso asking her daughter to wake her for breakfast.
- PS3523.A7 Z4844 1927

1240. TS from Ring Lardner, December 1927 or 1928.
- 1 p.
NOTES: Humorous poem, 3 stanzas, 4 lines each, sent as a Christmas greeting. Annotated by FSF: "Xmas 1927 or 1928 I forget which FSF".
   Published in: *F. Scott Fitzgerald Centenary Exhibition Catalogue*.
- PS3523.A7 C67

1241. CC from Anne Ober, 4 September 1938.
- 2 pp.
NOTES: Ober gives advice about Scottie Fitzgerald at Vassar.
- On deposit.

1242. TLS from Maxwell E. Perkins, Charles Scribners Sons, 5th Avenue at 48th St., New York City, to FSF [Paris], 17 December 1929.
- 4 pp. with holograph corrections.
NOTES: Perkins discusses the story of the boxing match between Canadian author Morley Callaghan and Ernest Hemingway for which FSF served as timekeeper.
Perkins also reports on author Thomas Boyd and his divorce. Comments on good sales of *A Farewell to Arms,* but predicts a period of Depression which will hurt book sales.
Published in: *F. Scott Fitzgerald Centenary Exhibition Catalogue.*
- Z473.P4 A465 1929

1243. TLS from Maxwell E. Perkins, 597 Fifth Avenue, New York City, to FSF [California?], 8 April 1938.
- 4 pp.
NOTES: Perkins reports on Hemingway's play [*The Fifth Column*].
Annotated in pencil by FSF: "If you think you have the only troubles contemplate Ernest as revealed".
Published in: *F. Scott Fitzgerald Centenary Exhibition Catalogue.*
- Z473.P4 A466 1938

1244. Postcard from Cary Ross, Soviet Union, to FSF, Grove Park Inn, Asheville, North Carolina, 24 May 1935.
- 1 p.
NOTES: Ross sends greetings from Siberia.
- PS3535.O747 Z484 1935

1245. TLS from H. N. Swanson, 8523 Sunset Blvd., West Hollywood, California, to FSF, Selznick International, Culver City, California, 21 January 1939.
- 1 p.; signed "Swanie".
NOTES: Swanson clarifies FSF's employment status at Metro-Goldwyn-Mayer, the date of his contract's expiration, and the terms of his current employment with the Selznick studio.
FSF worked the last three weeks of his MGM contract—which expired on 27 January 1939—for David O. Selznick on the screenplay of *Gone with the Wind.*
- PN149.9.S9 A44 1939

1246. Telegram from Cecilia Taylor to FSF, Asheville, North Carolina, 4 August 1936.
- 1 p.

NOTES: Taylor telegraphs that she and Annabel [Sprague] are at a hearing in Rockville, Maryland, and have settled his mother's estate.
- PS3539.A878 Z484 1936

1247. TLS from Charles Hanson Towne, G. P. Putnam's Sons, New York City, to FSF, 1 February 1921.
- 1 p. on Putnam stationery.
NOTES: Towne returns John Biggs's manuscript along with his confidential opinion in the hopes that Biggs will understand the reasons for refusal.
- PN4874.T64 A43 1921

1248. TLSS from Charles Marquis Warren to FSF, 1934–39.
- 3 letters signed "Bill".
NOTES: First letter (6 December 1934, 1 p.): Warren addresses "Dearest Mrs. Typewriter" (Isabel Owens, FSF's secretary).
Second letter (25 February 1939, 1 p.): Warren apologizes for whatever problems he has caused, and promises to send money owed.
Third letter (13 May 1939, 2 pp.): Warren reports current gossip about FSF's relationship with Sheilah Graham and ZF's supposed death. Describes himself as a loyal friend, angered by slurs against FSF.
- PS3545.A47 Z485

C. Concerning F. Scott Fitzgerald

Items arranged alphabetically by sender.

1249. TLS from John Biggs, Wilmington, Delaware, to Scottie Fitzgerald, 3 October 1949.
- 1 p.
NOTES: Biggs reports income from FSF estate.
- On deposit.

1250. TLS from John Biggs to "Es," n.d.
- 3 pp.
NOTES: Character sketch of ZF.
- On deposit.

1251. TLS from Barry Brannen, Los Angeles, to John Biggs, 25 April 1945.
- 3 pp.
NOTES: Lawyer Brannen writes about FSF estate matters.
- On deposit.

1252. TLS from Malcolm Cowley, Sherman, Connecticut, to Scottie Fitzgerald, 18 October 1982.
- 1 p.
NOTES: Cowley writes about upcoming St. Paul event.
- On deposit.

1253. Telegram from Scottie Fitzgerald, Boston, to Anne Ober, undated.
- 1 p.
- On deposit.

1254. Telegram from Scottie Fitzgerald, Simsbury, Connecticut, to Anne Ober, 25 January, n.d.
- 1 p.
- On deposit.

1255. Telegram from Scottie Fitzgerald, Simsbury, Connecticut, to Anne Ober, 18 October, n.d.
- 1 p.
- On deposit.

1256. Telegram from Scottie Fitzgerald, Towson, Maryland, to Anne Ober, 19 September [1939?].
- 1 p.
- On deposit.

1257. TLS from Scottie Fitzgerald, to Mr. [Kenneth Charles] Kaleta, 11 November 1985.
- 1 p.
- NOTES: Scottie Fitzgerald reports that she is impressed with Kaleta's dissertation on filming FSF's works.
- PS3569.M53797 Z48 1985

1258. TLS from Scottie Fitzgerald to Matthew J. Bruccoli, n.d.
- 2 pp.
- NOTES: Scottie Fitzgerald asks MJB to help her manage FSF literary properties.
- On deposit.

1259. TLS from Scottie Fitzgerald to Matthew J. Bruccoli, 31 August, n.d.
- 2 pp.
- NOTES: Scottie Fitzgerald writes about FSF business matters.
- On deposit.

1260. ALS from Helen Hayes, Quernavaca, Mexico, to Matthew J. Bruccoli, undated.
- 2 pp.
- NOTES: Hayes discusses FSF and Charles MacArthur.
- On deposit.

1261. ALSS from Laura Hearne, Asheville, North Carolina, to Matthew J. Bruccoli, 1967; 1972.
- Six letters: dated 18 January 1967 (2 pp.); 25 January 1967 (2 pp.); 24 February 1967 (2 pp.); 3 March 1967 (1 p.); 27 March 1967 (2 pp.); and 20 February 1972 (2 pp.).
- NOTES: Hearne was FSF's secretary in Asheville. Letters discuss FSF.
- On deposit.

1262. ALS from Ernest Hemingway, Paris, France, to Grace Hall Hemingway, Oak Park, Illinois, 19 October 1925.
- 1 p.; folded, with stamp and address on outside.

NOTES: "I am giving boxing lessons 3 times a week and have Scott Fitzgerald, Ivan Opfer the caricaturist, Nathan Asch the writer and a couple of painters as pupils."
Published in: *F. Scott Fitzgerald Centenary Exhibition Catalogue*.
- PS3515.E37 Z485 1925

1263. TLS from Ernest Hemingway, [Finca Vigia], to Charles Fenton, 12 June 1952.
- 1 p.

NOTES: Hemingway discusses his opposition to biographies of living authors: "Of course since the Mizener book on Scott FitzGerald there is plenty of money to be made on biography."
- PS3515.E37 Z484 1952

1264. ALS from Monseigneur William Hemmick, Rome, to Matthew J. Bruccoli, 30 July 1963.
- 1 p.

NOTES: Hemmick writes about FSF at the Newman School.
- On deposit.

1265. ALS from Shane Leslie, London, to Matthew J. Bruccoli, 26 November 1958.
- 2 pp.

NOTES: Leslie writes about FSF.
- On deposit.

1266. ALS from Shane Leslie, London, to Matthew J. Bruccoli, 28 February 1963.
- 2 pp.

NOTES: Leslie writes about FSF. With Leslie's MS (1 p.) notes on FSF.
- On deposit.

1267. TLS from Zack MacCubin-Waters, New York City, to Scottie Fitzgerald, 13 January 1964.
- 1 p.

NOTES: MacCubin-Waters writes about ZF and *Scandalabra*.
- On deposit.

1268. ALS from Kenneth Millar, 4420 Via Esperanza, Santa Barbara, California, to Donald Davie, 989 Cottrell Way, Stanford, California, 28 October 1968.
- 2 pp.; signed "Ken".

NOTES: Millar [Ross Macdonald] discusses the work of FSF, especially *The Great Gatsby*.
- PS3525.I486 Z482 1968

1269. TLS from Archibald MacLeish, Uphill Farm, Conway, Massachusetts, to Matthew J. Bruccoli, 6 August 1969.
- 1 p. on MacLeish's stationery.
- NOTES: MacLeish mentions that he will send the proofs "along to you and the book under separate cover." MacLeish agrees with MJB about Zelda Fitzgerald: ". . . nothing written about her or by her gives any sense of what she was. . . ."
- PS3525.A27 Z483 1969

1270. TLS from Fletcher Markle to Matthew J. Bruccoli, 11 May 1987.
- 1 p.
- NOTES: Markle describes his 1955 television production of *Tender Is the Night*. With: Revised script (90 pp.), c. 1955.
- On deposit.

1271. TLS from H. L. Mencken, *The Smart Set*, New York City, to John B. Biggs, 31 March 1921.
- 1 p. on *The Smart Set* stationery.
- NOTES: Mencken reports: "I hear from Fitz that he is in the south ruining his health with the moonshine liqueurs of those parts."
- PS3525.E43 Z482 1921

1272. TLSS from Nancy Milford to Scottie Fitzgerald, 22 September and 3 October 1969.
- 9 pp.
- NOTES: With ALS from Scottie Fitzgerald to MJB asking him to read Milford's letters for her and advise her.
- On deposit.

1273. ALS from Lois Moran, Sedona, Arizona to Matthew J. Bruccoli, 20 January 1971.
- 2 pp.
- NOTES: Moran writes about FSF. With: Picture postcard of Coffee Pot Rock.
- On deposit.

1274. ALS from Gerald Murphy, New York City, to Scottie Fitzgerald, 6 January 1945.
- 2 pp.
- NOTES: Murphy acknowledges Scottie Fitzgerald's repayment of tuition loan.
- On deposit.

1275. ALS from Gerald Murphy, New York City, to Matthew J. Bruccoli, 15 February 1960.
- 2 pp.
- NOTES: Murphy writes about FSF and Walker Ellis.
- On deposit.

1276. ALS from Honoria Murphy Donnelly, McLean, Virginia, to Matthew J. Bruccoli, 8 January 1976.
- 4 pp.
NOTES: Donnelly writes about possible memoir.
- On deposit.

1277. ALS from Honoria Murphy Donnelly, McLean, Virginia, to Matthew J. Bruccoli, 8 August 1978.
- 2 pp.
NOTES: Donnelly writes about Riviera.
- On deposit.

1278. TLS from John O'Hara to Matthew J. Bruccoli, 1 November 1961.
- 1 p. on *The New Yorker* stationery.
NOTES: O'Hara writes about FSF. With: Photo of FSF annotated on verso by Belle O'Hara.
- On deposit.

1279. TLS from Laurence Olivier, New Theatre, W.C. 2, [London], to J. W. Weatherby, 29 April 1949.
- 1 p.
NOTES: Olivier acknowledges advice about *Tender Is the Night*.
- PN2598.O55 A45 1949

1280. TLS from Maxwell E. Perkins, to John Biggs, 12 April 1921.
- 2 pp. with holograph corrections.
NOTES: Perkins rejects short story "A River Idyll" and reports that he had shown the story to FSF who would be writing to him about it.
- Z473.P4 A41 1921

1281. TLS from Maxwell E. Perkins, New York City, to Gilbert Seldes, 22 November 1933.
- 2 pp. on Scribners stationery.
NOTES: Perkins discusses business arrangements for a Ring Lardner collection. Mentions that he had a "Scott Fitzgerald Night last night, but came through it pretty well."
- Z473.P4 A47 1933

1282. TLS from Maxwell E. Perkins, to John Biggs, 4 March 1941.
- 2 pp.
NOTES: Perkins writes about publication of *The Last Tycoon*.
- On deposit.

1283. TLS from Anthony Powell, Somerset, England, to Matthew J. Bruccoli, 15 June 1971.
- 1 p.
NOTES: Powell writes about "Hollywood Canteen" article.
- On deposit.

1284. ALS from Ginevra King Pirie, Lake Forest, Illinois, to Scottie Fitzgerald, postmarked 11 September 1950.
- 5 pp.
NOTES: Notes by Pirie on FSF.
- On deposit.

1285. Telegram from Tennessee Williams, Key West, Florida, to Scottie Fitzgerald, 4 October 1979.
- 1 p.
NOTES: Williams praises *The Romantic Egoists*.
- On deposit.

1286. ALS from Edmund Wilson, Wellfleet, Massachusetts, to Matthew J. Bruccoli, Charlottesville, Virginia, 16 March 1959.
- 1 p. with envelope.
NOTES: Wilson discusses *Tender Is the Night*.
- PS3545.I6245 Z4943 1959

1287. TLS from Edmund Wilson, Middletown, Connecticut, to Matthew J. Bruccoli, Columbus, Ohio, [28?] October 1964.
- 1 p. with envelope.
NOTES: Holograph note, signed, at the foot of page from MJB, who wrote Wilson asking for clarification on a claim by *Newsweek* magazine that Wilson had confirmed FSF as the author of a humorous verse in an article on the *Princeton Tiger*. Wilson states that he told *Newsweek* he knew nothing about FSF's contributions.
- PS3545.I6245 Z4945 1964

1288. ALS from Edmund Wilson, Middletown, Connecticut, to Matthew J. Bruccoli, Columbus, Ohio, 25 November 1964.
- 1 p. with envelope.
NOTES: Wilson answers a query for information on the authorship of pieces in the *Nassau Literary Magazine* and *Princeton Tiger* thought to be by FSF.
- PS3545.I6245 Z495 1964

1289. ALS from Edmund Wilson to Mrs. Ralph W. Wescott, Haddonfield, New Jersey, 11 January 1966.
- 2 pp. with envelope.
NOTES: Wilson discusses an incident in which FSF told Van Wyck Brooks that a passage in *The Ordeal of Mark Twain* sounded like a "Methodist preacher," causing Brooks to suppress it in the revised edition.
- PS3545.I6245 Z5 1966

1290. TLS from Edmund Wilson, Wellfleet, Massachusetts, to Matthew J. Bruccoli, Columbus, Ohio, 19 April 1968.
- 1 p. with envelope.

NOTES: Wilson clarifies information on FSF's literary activity at Princeton and comments that MJB and others are overdoing FSF.
- PS3545.I6245 Z49451 1968

1291. ALS from Edmund Wilson, Middletown, Connecticut, to Howard Allen, Kent, Ohio October? 1971.
- 1 p.

NOTES: Note at the end of a TLS from Howard Allen, Director of Kent State University Press, requesting that Wilson review *F. Scott Fitzgerald: In His Own Time.*
Wilson replies: "I am tired to the point of nausea of books on Scott Fitzgerald. Do tell Bruccoli to get interested in some other writer." With: Note from Allen to MJB.
- PS3545.I6245 Z494 1971

VII Selected F. Scott Fitzgerald Documents and Other Literary Documents

Fitzgerald documents (certificates, contracts, royalty reports, etc.) and other literary documents related to Fitzgerald's career.

1292. [Membership certificate of F. Scott Fitzgerald], 1 September 1903.
- National Society, Children of the American Revolution.
- 1 p. Holograph on engraved document.
  NOTES: "Be it known that Francis Scott Key Fitzgerald has been duly admitted a member of this society, by right of descent from Honorable Philip Key. . . ."
- PS3511.I9 Z72 1903

1293. [Report card], January 1912.
- Newman School.
  NOTES: FSF's "Fifth Form" report card.
- On deposit.

1294. [Dance card, Christmas 1914].
- 1 p.
  NOTES: Dance card of Ginevra King, signed "Scot Fitz" in the space for the fifth dance.
  With: Calling card of Ginevra King.
- PS3511.I9 Z484 1914

1295. Passport, 1917.
- 1 sheet. Engraved document, signed by FSF.
  NOTES: Issued to FSF. Cancelled passport intended to be used by FSF on a 1917 trip to Russia as Father Cyril Sigourney Fay's secretary.
- PS3511.I9 Z4645 1917

1296. [Commission as Second Lieutenant of Infantry], 26 October 1917.
- United States Army.
- 1 sheet.
- PS3511.I9 Z895 1917

1297. [Library card], 1918.
- Louisville Free Public Library.
  NOTES: In frame, with note "This card was the property of Miss Preston Suttle, the Louisville librarian at the time the files were brought up to date. FSFS [Frances Scott Fitzgerald Smith]".
  Library card no. 13026 issued to FSF, Camp Taylor, 45th Infantry, shows three books were charged to him during the time he was stationed at Camp Zachary Taylor.
- Z715.L6 1918

1298. [Contract for *This Side of Paradise*], 23 September 1919.
- Charles Scribner's Sons.
- 4 pp. Signed by FSF and Charles Scribner II.
- PS3511.I9 T4994 1919

1299. [Contract for "Myra Meets His Family" movie rights], 28 April 1920.
- Fox Film Corporation.
- 5 pp. Signed by FSF.
NOTES: Produced as *The Husband Hunter*.
- On deposit.

1300. [Contract for movie rights to FSF stories], 27 May 1920.
- Metro Pictures.
- 5 pp. Not signed by FSF.
- On deposit.

1301. [Contract for *The Beautiful and Damned*], 2 May 1921.
- Charles Scribner's Sons.
- 4 pp. Signed by FSF and Maxwell E. Perkins.
- On deposit.

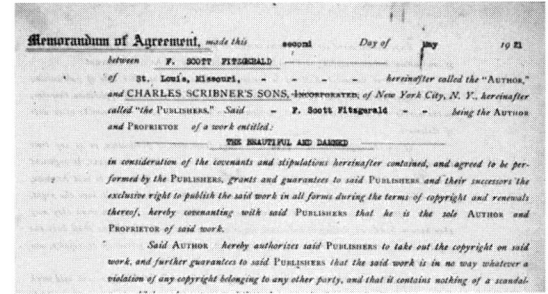

1302. [Contract for *Tales of the Jazz Age*], 12 April 1922.
- Charles Scribner's Sons.
- 4 pp. Not signed by FSF.
- On deposit.

1303. [Contract for *The Beautiful and Damned* movie rights], 24 April 1922.
- H.M and A. Warner.
- 3 pp. Not signed by FSF.
- On deposit.

1304. [Contract for *This Side of Paradise* movie rights], 12 December 1922.
- Outlook Photoplays.
- 2 pp. Signed by FSF.
NOTES: Movie not produced.
- On deposit.

1305. [Contract for *This Side of Paradise* movie rights], 12 March 1923.
- Famous Players-Lasky
- 5 pp. Signed by FSF and Jesse Lasky.
NOTES: Movie not produced.
- On deposit.

1306. [Contract for *The Vegetable*], 21 March 1923.
- Charles Scribner's Sons.
- 4 pp. Signed by FSF and Charles Scribner II.
- On deposit.

1307. [Contract for play production of *The Vegetable*], 6 July 1923.
- Sam H. Harris.
- 10 pp. Signed by FSF and Harris.
- On deposit.

1308. "Monthly Expenditure 1923".
- 1 p.
NOTES: FSF's holograph list of monthly expenditures, totalling $2,396.00. Published in: *F. Scott Fitzgerald Centenary Exhibition Catalogue*.
- PS3511.I9 M67 1923

1309. Passport, 29 April 1924.
- United States Department of State.
- 2 items (4 pp.). Stamped for Great Britain, France and Italy.
NOTES: Issued in Washington, D.C., to FSF for his family's second trip abroad. Zelda and Scottie Fitzgerald were included on FSF's passport. Photograph of FSF is signed.
With: Passport of Scottie Fitzgerald, issued Paris, France, 23 October 1924; Photograph of Scottie Fitzgerald signed: "Zelda Fitzgerald for Frances Scott Fitzgerald".
First and last pages published in: *F. Scott Fitzgerald Centenary Exhibition Catalogue*.
- PS3511.I9 Z485 1924

1310. [Contract for *The Great Gatsby*], 22 December 1924.
- Charles Scribner's Sons.
- 4 pp. Not signed by FSF.
NOTES: Pages 1 and 3 published in: *F. Scott Fitzgerald Centenary Exhibition Catalogue*.
- PS3511.I9 G7647 1924

1311. [Contract for *All the Sad Young Men*], 27 July 1925.
- Charles Scribner's Sons.
- 4 pp. Signed by FSF, ZF, and Charles Scribner II.
- On deposit.

1312. Check to Collector of Internal Revenue for $227.28, 15 March 1929.
- Guaranty Trust of New York, 5th Ave.
- 1 check.
NOTES: Signed by FSF. Stamped "PAID 14–4–29."
- PS3511.I9 Z512 1929

1313. Check to Collector of Internal Revenue for $317.69, 12 March 1930.
- Guaranty Trust of New York, 5th Ave.
- 1 check.
NOTES: Signed by FSF.
- On deposit.

1314. [Photograph portrait of Ernest Hemingway], 1931.
- 1 item.
NOTES: Inscribed to FSF by Hemingway: "To Scott from his old bedfellow Richard Halliburton. Princeton 1931."
Published in: *F. Scott Fitzgerald Centenary Exhibition Catalogue.*
- PS3515.E37 Z5256 1931

1315. [Contract for *Taps at Reveille*], 12 June 1934.
- Charles Scribner's Sons.
- 3 pp. Signed by FSF.
NOTES: Contract for "A NEW COLLECTION OF SHORT STORIES." Signed by FSF.
- PS3511.I9 T345 1934

1316. [Expenses], 1934.
- MS: 1 p.
NOTES: Summary of FSF's expenditures during the time he was living in Baltimore.
- PS3511.I9 Z4801 1934

1317. [Reading List for Dorothy Richardson, 1936].
- 1 p.
NOTES: Copy (in the hand of Dorothy Richardson) of list of "Required Books" recommended by FSF. Richardson (later Mrs. Fred Ritz) was FSF's nurse in Asheville.
Published in: *F. Scott Fitzgerald Centenary Exhibition Catalogue.*
- PS3511.I9 R43 1936

1318. [Report card], 1937.
- Ethel Walker School, Simsbury, Connecticut.

NOTES: Report card for Scottie Fitzgerald from 1 October to 17 December 1937; annotated by FSF.
- On deposit.

1319. "Last Will and Testament," Polk County, N.C., 17 June 1937.
- CC: 7 pp. Not signed.

NOTES: Revised by FSF, 10 November 1940.
- On deposit.

1320. [Map of France], 1938.
- 1 sheet.

NOTES: Map drawn by FSF for Scottie Fitzgerald.
- DC16.F47 1938

1321. Check to F. Scott Fitzgerald, 18 August 1939.
- H.N. Swanson, Inc.
- 1 check.

NOTES: Single cancelled check for 500 dollars loaned to FSF by Harold N. Swanson, drawn on a Bank of America account, Sunset-Clark branch, Hollywood, California.

On verso, in manuscript: "Pay to the account of F. Scott Fitzgerald."

H.N. Swanson was FSF's Hollywood agent. The check was an advance on FSF's salary for work at Universal Studios on "Open that Door" (unproduced).
- PN149.9.S9 C44 1939

1322. [Contract], 22 February 1940.
Phil Berg-Bert Allenberg, Inc.
- 1 p.

NOTES: Contracts with FSF to act as his agent in the entertainment industry and to assist him in negotiating for the sale of literary or dramatic material. Signed by both parties.

The Berg-Allenberg Agency represented FSF's screenwriting career following his departure from the H. N. Swanson and Leland Hayward Agencies.
- PS3511.I9 Z8143 1940

1323. [Contract for *The Last Tycoon*], 9 June 1941.
- Charles Scribner's Sons.
- 4 pp. Signed by John Biggs and Maxwell E. Perkins.
- On deposit.

1324. [Blank checks for The Estate of F. Scott Fitzgerald], c. 1940s.
- Farmers Bank of the State of Delaware
- 1 p.

NOTES: Single sheet of three checks, nos. 361–63, from Farmers Bank of the State of Delaware, Wilmington, for the account of the Estate of F. Scott Fitzgerald.

John Biggs, then a federal judge in Wilmington, was executor of FSF's estate.
- PS3511.I9 Z513

1325. TS, [Income from the Estate of F. Scott Fitzgerald], 9 December 1949.
- 3 pp.
- On deposit.

1326. TLS, H. L. Mencken to unidentified bookseller, 17 June 1946.
- 1 p. Framed with photograph of Mencken.
NOTES: Mencken orders copy of *The Crack-Up*.
Published in: *F. Scott Fitzgerald Centenary Exhibition Catalogue*.
- On deposit.

1327. [Contract for collection of stories], 21 December 1949.
- Charles Scribner's Sons.
- 4 pp. Signed by Scottie Fitzgerald and Charles Scribner III.
NOTES: Volume to be edited by Malcolm Cowley. Published as *The Stories of F. Scott Fitzgerald* (1951).
- On deposit.

1328. Royalty Reports to Mrs. Frances S. F. Lanahan [Scottie Fitzgerald], 1949–57.
- Charles Scribner's Sons and Harold Ober Associates.
- 274 pp. Holograph and TS, on printed forms.
NOTES: Reports of royalties for foreign and domestic sales of FSF's books.
- Z473.S399 1952

1329. Income tax records, 1921–40.
- 61 items.
NOTES: Retained copies of U.S. tax returns; 1937–38 California; returns for FSF and ZF filing separately; ZF's U.S. returns for 1939 and 1940; notes.
- PS3511.I9 Z4802

1330. "Daddy's Ideas about Organizing Novel into Episodes and Scenes," n.d.
- TS: 3 pp.
NOTES: FSF's literary advice to Scottie Fitzgerald.
- On deposit.

1331. [Recollection of Thomas Wolfe], n.d.
- Maxwell E. Perkins.
- RTS: 6 pp.

NOTES: Published in *To Loot My Life Clean: The Thomas Wolfe–Maxwell Perkins Correspondence,* eds. Matthew J. Bruccoli and Park Bucker (Columbia: University of South Carolina Press, 2000).
- On deposit.

1332. "Entering Scott's Night," 1996.
- James Dickey.
- MSS and TSS: 20 pp.

NOTES: Holograph and typescript copies of 13 versions of the poem written for the centenary of FSF's birth. The drafts have Dickey's revisions and annotations. The poem was published in *The New Yorker,* vol. 72, no. 45 (3 February 1997), p. 47.
- PS3554.I32 E57 1996

1333. "Literature of Despair."
- Joseph Heller.
- TS: 6 pp.

NOTES: Holograph corrections. Signed by Heller, 24 September 1996. Outline of speech given at the Fall banquet of The Thomas Cooper Society as part of the F. Scott Fitzgerald Centenary Celebration, 24 September 1996.
- PS3558.E476 L5 1996

VIII Inscriptions

Books inscribed to the Fitzgeralds, or books by other authors inscribed or annotated by Fitzgerald. The section also lists books known to have been in Fitzgerald's library.

A. Books Inscribed to the Fitzgeralds

1334. *Flaming Youth.*
- Warner Fabian [Samuel Hopkins Adams].
- New York: Boni and Liveright, [1923].
NOTES: Fifth printing, March 1923.
> Inscribed on free front endpaper: "To Scott Fitzgerald—whose 'This Side of Paradise' struck sparks from the anvil of genius—with sincere admiration of Warner Fabian".
- PS3501.D27 F53 1923

1335. *The Fair Rewards.*
- Thomas Beer.
- New York: Knopf, 1922.
NOTES: Inscribed on title page: "For F. Scott Fitzgerald from Thomas Beer τοῖς ἔμπροσθεν ἐπεκτεινόμενος".
- PS3503.E267 F3

1336. *Roll River.*
- James Boyd.
- New York: Charles Scribner's Sons, 1935.
NOTES: First printing.
> Inscribed to FSF on free front endpaper: "Dear Scott—here it is, not right I know, but first any how as an act of gratitude. I hope I see you soon. Jim Boyd".
> Presented to MJB by Scottie Fitzgerald, with a small Christmas note in her hand, inserted: "For Matt from FSF".
- PS3503.O885 R6 1935

1337. *Through the Wheat.*
- Thomas Boyd.
- New York: Charles Scribner's Sons, 1923.
NOTES: Inscribed to FSF on free front endpaper.
- PS3503.O9 T5 1923

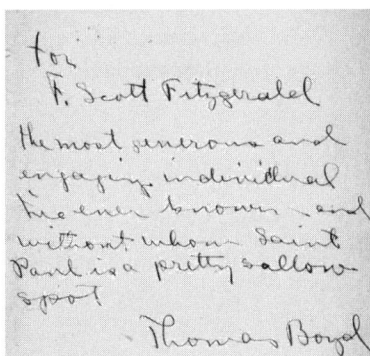

216   Inscriptions

1338. *The Pilgrimage of Henry James.*
- Van Wyck Brooks.
- New York: E. P. Dutton, [1925].
NOTES: Inscribed on free front endpaper: "For F. Scott Fitzgerald with friendly greetings Van Wyck Brooks April 22nd 1925". See Item 1158.
- PS2123.B7

1339. *Jurgen: A Comedy of Justice.*
- James Branch Cabell.
- New York: Robert M. McBride, 1919.
NOTES: Second printing.
Inscribed on free front endpaper: "For F. Scott Fitzgerald with cordial and admiring regard James Branch Cabell 20 December 1920".
- PS3505.A153 J8 1919 C.3

1340. *Figures of Earth: A Comedy of Appearances.*
- James Branch Cabell.
- New York: R. M. McBride, 1921.
NOTES: First printing.
Inscribed on free front endpaper: "For F. Scott Fitzgerald any thing hereinafter that he may like James Branch Cabell 18 February 1921"
- PS3505.A153 F5 1921

1341. *Ladies and Gentlemen: A Parcel of Reconsiderations.*
- James Branch Cabell.
- New York: McBride, 1934.
- Dust jacket.
NOTES: First printing, trade issue.
Inscribed on free front endpaper: "For F. Scott Fitzgerald anything hereinafter which he may happen to like, with the best wishes of Branch Cabell 29 September 1934".
- PS3505.A153 L3 1934

1342. *A Pushcart at the Curb.*
- John Dos Passos.
- New York: Doran, [1922].
NOTES: Inscribed to FSF and ZF on free front endpaper.
- PS3507.O743 P8 1922

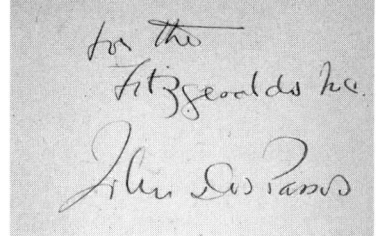

Books Inscribed to the Fitzgeralds 217

1343. *Ash-Wednesday.*
- T. S. Eliot.
- London: Faber & Faber, 1930.
- Dust jacket.

NOTES: Inscribed to FSF on title page.
- PS3509.L43 A7 1930a

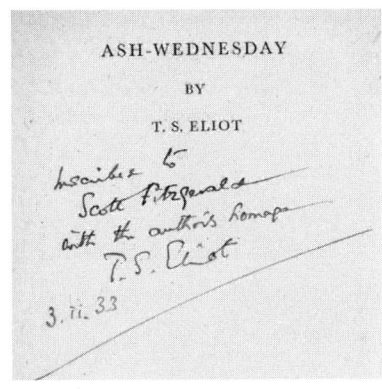

1344. *A Primer for Tomorrow: Being an Introduction to Contemporary Civilization.*
- Christian Frederick Gauss.
- New York; London: Charles Scribner's Sons, 1934.

NOTES: First printing.
   Inscribed on free front endpaper: "To F. Scott Fitzgerald whose writing has given me ever increasing satisfaction from the happy times when we met daily in the classroom. In pride and recognition Christian Gauss".
- CB425.G3 1934

1345. *The Second Empire: Bonapartism, the Prince, the President, the Emperor.*
- Philip Guedalla.
- New York, London: G. P. Putnam's Sons, 1922.

NOTES: Inscribed on free front endpaper: "Merry Xmas to Father from Scott".
- DC276.5.G8 1922

1346. *For Whom the Bell Tolls.*
- Ernest Hemingway.
- New York: Scribner, [1940].
- Dust jacket.

NOTES: Inscribed to FSF on free front endpaper.
- PS3515.E37 F6 1940

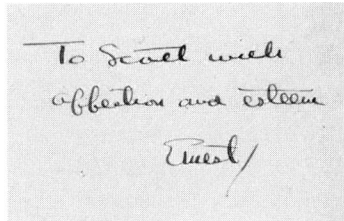

1347. *A Portrait of the Artist as a Young Man.*
- James Joyce.
- London: Jonathan Cape, [1926].
- Dust jacket.

NOTES: Fifth impression.
   Inscribed to FSF on free front endpaper.
- PR6019.O9 P63 1926

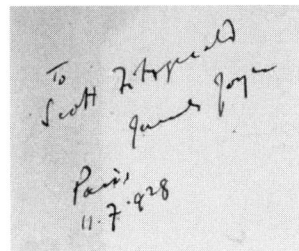

1348. *Ulysses.*
- James Joyce.
- Paris: Shakespeare and Company, 1922.

NOTES: First edition. Number 890 of 1000 copies on handmade paper. Annotated by FSF on pp. 366, 367, 374, 376, 378, 379, 384, 386, 389, 390, 392, 393, 394, 397, 399, 400, 403, and 404. ALS from Joyce to FSF pasted on free front endpaper.
- PR6019.O9 U4 1922

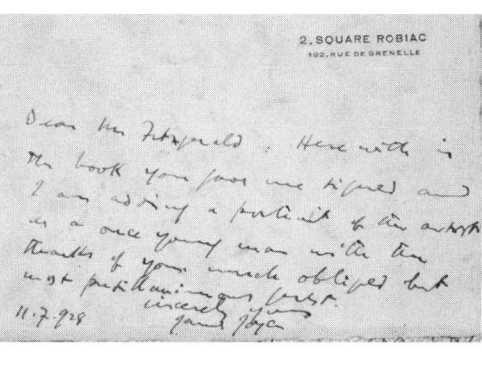

1349. *The National Anthem: A Drama.*
- J. Hartley Manners.
- New York: Doran, [1922].

NOTES: Inscribed on free front endpaper: "To Mrs. F. Scott Fitzgerald With the kindest wishes of J Hartley Manners June 1923".
- PR4974.M15 N3 1922

1350. *The Fall of the City: A Verse Play for Radio.*
- Archibald MacLeish.
- New York; Toronto: Farrar & Rinehart, [1937].

NOTES: Inscribed to FSF by MacLeish on free front endpaper.
- PS3525.A27 F3 1937

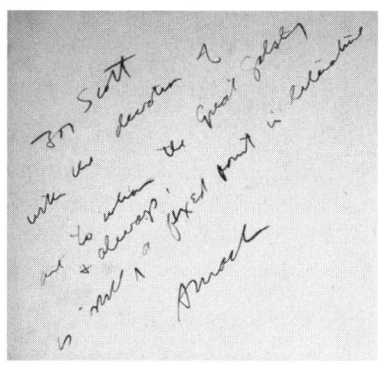

1351. *Prejudices: Second Series.*
- H. L. Mencken.
- New York: Alfred A. Knopf, 1920.

NOTES: Inscribed to FSF by Mencken on free front endpaper. In "The National Letters" chapter FSF marked the margins beside the paragraphs on the bottoms of pp. 66 and 67; he underlined pp. 69, 70, 72, 73; and he annotated pp. 69, 70, 73, 74.
- PS3525.E43 P82 1920

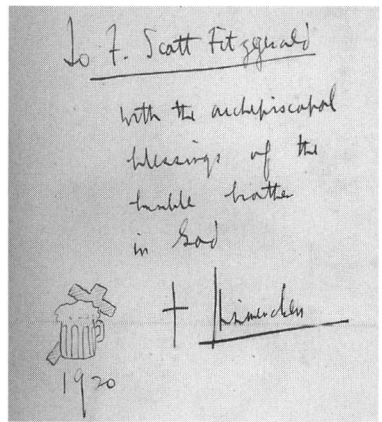

1352. *Learning To Write: Suggestions and Counsel from Robert Louis Stevenson.*
- Robert Louis Stevenson.
- Edited by John William Rogers.
- New York: Charles Scribner's Sons, 1920.
NOTES: Inscribed to FSF on free front endpaper: "To a man who can become a worthy writer and a great artist, if he will reach up high enough to pluck his birthright. Here is the word of another artist's struggle—if these gleanings can in some way help to give you the courage and determination to travel this difficult road ahead of you—the solitary, silent, unrelenting road of your own ideals, my dear Fitzgerald, my labor should have already been worth the pains Sincerely John W Rogers 30 March 1920".
- PN145.S7

1353. *How To Write.*
- Gertrude Stein.
- Paris: Plain Edition, [1931].
NOTES: Wilson A17a. 1,000 copies printed. Inscribed to FSF on free front endpaper.
Page 30 has "That is the cruelest. ... he has heard." Marked by FSF.
- PS3537.T323 H6 1931 C. 2

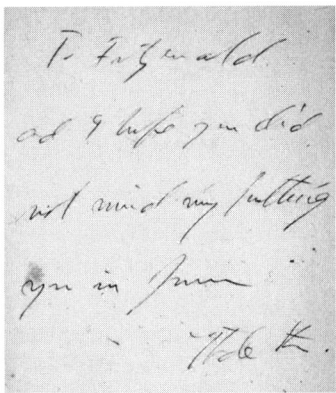

1354. *Perfect Behavior.*
- Donald Ogden Stewart.
- New York: Doran, [1922].
NOTES: Inscribed to FSF by Stewart pasted on free front endpaper: "In memory of that happy never-to-be forgotten summer in the Mammoth Cave, Ky.—with much love from The Author".
- PN6161.S714 1922

1355. *Peter Whiffle: His Life and Works.*
- Carl Van Vechten.
- New York: Alfred A. Knopf, 1922.
NOTES: "Published, April, 1922". ZF's copy.
Inscription by Van Vechten on free front endpaper: "To the gentle Zelda, with her unexplored depths, With my lowest bow, Carlo May 21–1927 Brandywine Hundred".
- PS3543.A653 P49 1922

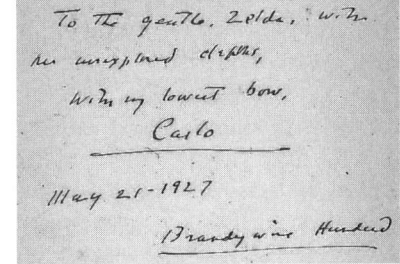

1356. *The Tattooed Countess: A Romantic Novel with a Happy Ending.*
- Carl Van Vechten.
- New York: Alfred A. Knopf, 1924.

NOTES: First edition. "First printing, July, 1924".
Inscribed on free front endpaper: "For F. Scott Fitzgerald, These scenes from American provincial life in 1897. With my deepest bow Carl Van Vechten July 24, 1924 New York".
- PS3543.A653 T3

1357. *Parties: Scenes from Contemporary New York Life.*
- Carl Van Vechten.
- New York: Knopf, 1930.

NOTES: First edition. no. 101 of 250 copies signed by author.
Inscribed on free front endpaper: "David and Rilda are not portraits of living persons but they were certainly suggested by Scott and Zelda Fitzgerald. The book as a whole fairly represents the Twenties & Speakeasy Days. Inscribed for Ingle Barr by Carl Van Vechten March 5–1959 New York".
- PS3543.A653 P3

1358. *Poets, Farewell!*
- Edmund Wilson.
- New York: Charles Scribner's Sons, 1929.

NOTES: Inscribed to FSF and ZF on free front endpaper.
Penciled annotations by FSF on pp. 1, 3, 5, and rear paste-down endpaper.
- PS3545.I6245 P6 1929

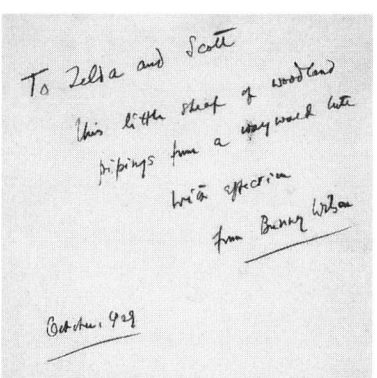

B. Books by Other Authors Inscribed or Annotated by F. Scott Fitzgerald

1359. *The Bell Haven Eight.*
- George Barton.
- Illustrated by Charles Paxson Gray.
- Philadelphia: The John C. Winston Company, [1914].
- Dust jacket.

NOTES: The Bell Haven Series. Inscribed by FSF to Harold Ober on free front end-paper. Frontispiece also annotated by FSF. Presented to MJB by Anne Ober, 1969.
- PS3508.A835 B43 1914

1360. *Act of Darkness.*
- John Peale Bishop.
- New York: Charles Scribner's Sons, 1935.
- Dust jacket.

NOTES: First printing. FSF's copy, with his signature on free front endpaper.
- PS3503.I79 A23 1935

1361. *Through the Wheat.*
- Thomas Boyd.
- New York: Charles Scribner's Sons, 1923.

NOTES: Inscribed by FSF to Newman Smith, Paris, 1 August 1925, on free front endpaper.
- PS3503.O8 T5 C.1

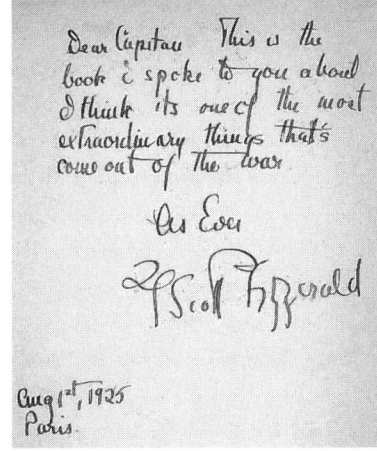

1362. *Portraits: Real and Imaginary.*
- Ernest Boyd.
- New York: George H. Doran Company, [c. 1924].

NOTES: Note by FSF on free front endpaper: "Don't bother about first stuff. Read definate portraits".

Blind impression of message by Ernest Hemingway on verso of last page: "MADAME FITZGERALD 14 RUE DE TILSITT PARIS SCOTT MISSED TRAIN PLEASE WIRE HIM CARE GARAGE I WILL BE AT HOTEL BRISTOL LYON WIRE ME ADDRESS OF GARAGE THERE HEMINGWAY".

Refers to episode in Hemingway's *A Moveable Feast.* See *Fitzgerald and Hemingway.*
- PS3503.O87 P6 1924

1363. *The Diary of Otto Braun: with Selections from his Letters and Poems.*
- Otto Braun.
- Translated from the German by Ella Winter; poetry translated by F. W. Stella Browne.
- New York: Alfred A. Knopf, 1924.

NOTES: FSF's copy with a penciled presentation inscription on front endpaper to his mother-in-law.
- PT2603.R362 1924

1364. *The Ordeal of Mark Twain.*
- Van Wyck Brooks.
- New York: E. P. Dutton & Company, [1920].
NOTES: Signature of FSF on front flyleaf.
- PS1331.B7

1365. *Pieces of Hate and Other Enthusiasms.*
- Heywood Broun.
- New York: George H. Doran, 1922.
NOTES: FSF's copy, with his penciled note on free front endpaper: "See P127." On that page Broun comments on pessimism in *This Side of Paradise.*
Presented to MJB by Scottie Fitzgerald, with her note on a card taped to free front endpaper: "For Matt from FSF."
- PS3503.R76 P5 1922

1366. *The Note-Books of Samuel Butler.*
- Samuel Butler.
- Selections Arranged and Edited by Henry Festing Jones; With an Introduction by Francis Hackett.
- New York: E. P. Dutton, [1917].
NOTES: With FSF signatures, notes on free front endpaper, and markings throughout.
- PR4349.B7 N6 1917

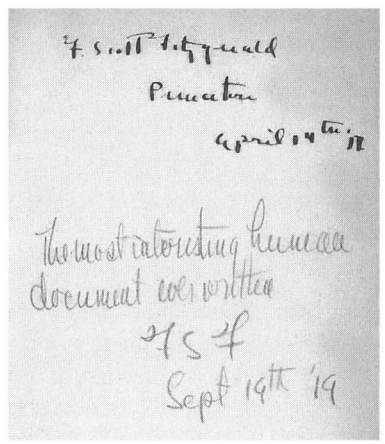

1367. *Some Letters of Monsignor Louis E. Caillet and August N. Chemidlin, 1868–1899.*
- Louis E. Caillet and August N. Chemidlin.
- Edited by Clara Hill Lindley.
- St. Paul: [Printed for private circulation], 1922.
NOTES: Signature of FSF and "See pps 9, 11, 13, 24, 95, 99" on free front endpaper with his annotations on these pages.
- CT275.C352 A3

1368. *The Mirror of the Sea.*
- Joseph Conrad.
- Garden City, N.Y.: Doubleday, Page, [1921].
NOTES: FSF's copy with his annotations on card page.
- G540.C8 1921

1369. *The Secret Agent: A Simple Tale.*
- Joseph Conrad.
- Garden City, N.Y.: Doubleday, Page, 1921.
NOTES: FSF's copy with his annotations on card page.
- PR6005.O4 S4 1921

1370. *Victory.*
- Joseph Conrad.
- Garden City, N.Y.; Toronto: Doubleday, Page, 1921.
NOTES: FSF's copy, with his notes on card page.
- PR6005.O4 V53 1921

1371. *The Sound and the Fury.*
- William Faulkner.
- New York: Jonathan Cape and Harrison Smith, 1929.
NOTES: FSF's copy, with his note on title page: "See P.286"; and his marks on that page.
- PS3511.A86 S65 1929 C.2

1372. *The Damnation of Theron Ware; Or, Illumination.*
- Harold Frederic.
- Chicago; New York: H. S. Stone & Company, 1900.
NOTES: On copyright page: "Forty-eighth thousand."
  FSF's copy, with his signature on front endpaper, and signature dated "October 1st 1920" on a preliminary page.
- PS3507.D3 1900

1373. *The Mind and Face of Bolshevism: An Examination of Cultural Life in Soviet Russia.*
- René Fülöp-Miller.
- Translated from the German by F. S. Flint and D. F. Tait.
- New York: A. A. Knopf, 1929.
NOTES: Inscribed by FSF and ZF to Thomas Rennie, ZF's psychiatrist.
- DK265.F785 1929

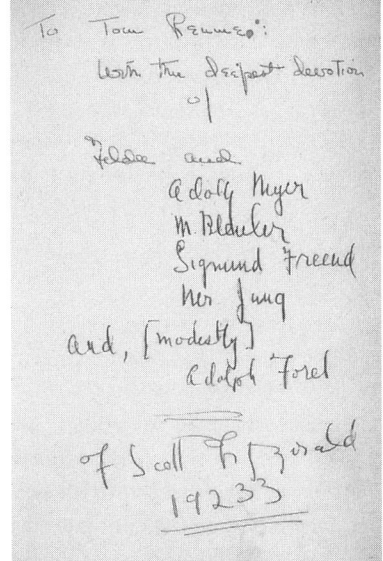

1374. *Goodbye to All That.*
- Robert Graves.
- London: Cape, [1929].
- Dust jacket.
NOTES: Fifth printing. Inscribed by FSF to Padraic and Mary Colum on free front endpaper.
- PR6013.R35 Z5 1929

1375. *Cruel Fellowship.*
- Cyril Hume.
- New York: Doran, [c. 1925].
NOTES: FSF's copy. Inscription on free front endpaper from John Farrar ("May 23rd, Majestic") to an unidentified recipient (the Vivians?) and re-inscribed in turn to FSF, 28 July 1925.
- PS3515.U42 C7 1925

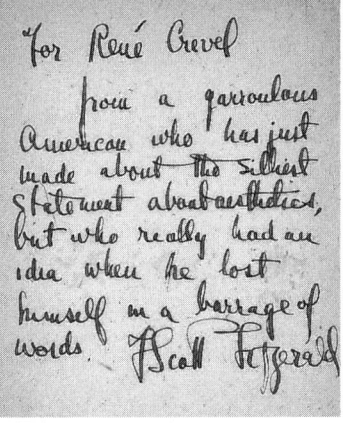

1376. *Gens De Dublin.*
- James Joyce.
- Traduit de l'Anglais par Yva Fernandez, Hélène du Pasquier, Jacques-Paul Reynaud; Préface de Valery Larbaud.
- Paris: Plon-nourrit et Cie, 1926.
- Glassine dust jacket.
NOTES: "COLLECTION D'AUTEURS ÉTRANGERS" translation of: *Dubliners.*
Inscribed by FSF to René Crevel on free front endpaper.
- PR6019.O9 D814 1926

1377. *How To Write Short Stories (With Samples).*
- Ring W. Lardner.
- New York; London: Charles Scribner's Sons, 1924.
NOTES: Bruccoli & Layman, A16.1.a. First edition, first printing.
FSF's copy, with his penciled notes. Table of contents annotated. Front endpapers signed "Fitzg—" and "<u>Read</u> Golden Honeymoon".
- PS3523.A675 A16 1924

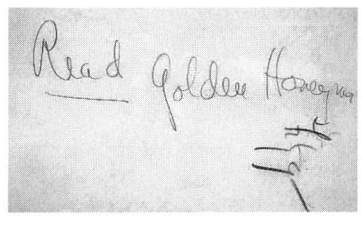

1378. *Nonsense Novels.*
- Stephen Leacock.
- London, New York: J. Lane, 1916.
NOTES: Ninth edition. FSF signature on free front endpaper. Envelope postmarked Montreal, 1917 and addressed to FSF at Princeton pasted on free front endpaper. Signed by FSF on free front endpaper.
- PR6023.E15 N7 1916

1379. "An Autopsy and a Prescription," *Hound and Horn,* vol. 5, no. 4 (July–September 1932).
- Lawrence Leighton.
NOTES: Tearsheets.
Condemns the work of FSF and certain other American writers as "repulsive, sterile, and dead."
Extensively annotated by FSF.
Pages 524, 526, 532, and 539 facsimiled in: *F. Scott Fitzgerald Centenary Exhibition Catalogue.*
- AP2.H794 vol. 5, no. 4

1380. *The End of a Chapter.*
- Shane Leslie.
- New York: Charles Scribner's Sons, 1917.
NOTES: FSF's mother's copy. On front free endpaper: "M. Fitzgerald Washington The Cairo March 1917".
- DA560.L4 1917b

1381. *Verses in Peace and War.*
- Shane Leslie.
- New York: Charles Scribner's Sons, [1917].
NOTES: FSF signature on free front endpaper and dated "May, 1917".
- PR6023.E83 V47 1917

1382. *The Passing Chapter.*
- Shane Leslie.
- New York: Charles Scribner's Sons, 1934.
NOTES: FSF signature on free front endpaper.
- DA578.L4 1934

1383. *Prejudices: Second Series.*
- H. L. Mencken.
- New York: Alfred A. Knopf, 1920.
NOTES: Inscribed to Donald Ogden Stewart by FSF.
- PS3525.E43 P82 1920 C.2

1384. *Prejudices: Fourth Series.*
- H. L. Mencken.
- New York: Alfred A. Knopf, 1924.

NOTES: First edition. Second printing before publication.
FSF's copy, with his penciled signature on half title.
Presented to MJB by Scottie Fitzgerald, with her note inserted.
- PS3525.E43 P84 1924

1385. *The Intimate Notebooks of George Jean Nathan.*
- George Jean Nathan.
- New York: A. A. Knopf, 1932.

NOTES: First edition. FSF's copy with his note on free front endpaper: "Pps. 57, 105, 107"; references to FSF on those pages underlined.
- PS3527.A72 I6 1932

1386. *A Book of Princeton Verse 1916.*
- Edited by Alfred Noyes.
- Princeton, N.J.: Princeton University Press; [etc.], 1916.

NOTES: First printing, June 1916. Edmund Wilson's first book appearance.
FSF's copy, with his signature, dated "Oct 1916" on free front endpaper, and check-marks on contents page.
- PN6110.C7 N7 1916
- Another copy with note from H. A. Rappaport to Wilson and Wilson's reply on free front endpaper.

1387. *Appointment in Samarra.*
- John O'Hara.
- New York: Harcourt, Brace, [1934].

NOTES: FSF's copy with his note on free front endpaper: "P. 133"; refers to mention of FSF.
- PS3529.H29 A68 1934

1388. *The Technique of the Drama: A Statement of the Principles Involved in the Value of Dramatic Material, in the Construction of Plays, and in Dramatic Criticism.*
- W. T. Price.
- New York: Brentano's, 1911.

NOTES: Signed twice by FSF on front free endpaper.
- PN1661.P85 1911

1389. *Wild Animals I Have Known.*
- Ernest Seton-Thompson.
- New York: Charles Scribner's Sons, 1901.

NOTES: Endpaper excised from a copy of *Wild Animals I Have Known* with inscription to FSF from "McIlvaine Christmas 1902" and re-inscribed by FSF to Scottie Fitzgerald "Easter 1927".
- On deposit.

1390. *Modern American Prose.*
- Edited by Carl Van Doren.
- New York: Harcourt, Brace, 1934.
- NOTES: Includes "The Diamond as Big as the Ritz."
  Inscribed by FSF to Newman and Rosalind Smith: "For Newman + Rosalind <u>Mes Homages</u> and love F Scott Fitzgerald Autumn 1934".
- PS659.V27

1391. *The Night Club Era.*
- Stanley Walker.
- New York: Frederick A. Stokes, 1933.
- NOTES: FSF's note on free front endpaper: "P. 56"; with reference to FSF on pp. 56–57.
- F128.627.W26

1392. *Behaviorism.*
- John B. Watson.
- New York: W. W. Norton, [1925].
- NOTES: Inscribed by FSF to A. D. Sayre, his father-in-law.
- BF199.W3 1925   1392.

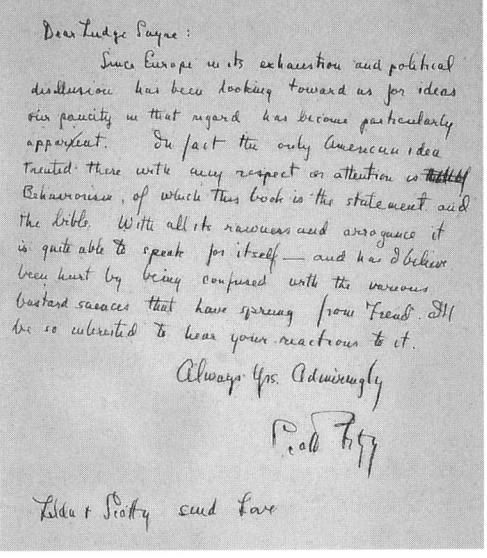

1393. *The Portrait of Mr. W.H.*
- Oscar Wilde.
- New York: Mitchell Kennerley, 1921.
- NOTES: Colophon: "One thousand copies printed May 1921". no. 517 of 1000 copies.
  FSF's copy, with his penciled note on front free endpaper: "I should skip parts III + IV which are highly tedious."
- PR2935.W4 1921

1394. *This Room and This Gin and These Sandwiches, Three Plays.*
- Edmund Wilson.
- New York: The New Republic, 1937.
- Wrappers.
- NOTES: "The Crime in the Whistler Room" annotated by FSF on p. 75.
- PS3545.I6245 T5 1937

C. Books from F. Scott Fitzgerald's Library

All were given to MJB by Scottie Fitzgerald

1395. *The Pilgrimage of Festus.*
- Conrad Aiken.
- New York: Alfred A. Knopf, 1923.
- PS3501.I5 P5 1923

1396. *Tulips and Chimneys.*
- E.E. Cummings.
- New York: Thomas Seltzer, 1923.
- PS3505 .U334 T8 1923

1397. *1914 & other Poems.*
- Rupert Brooke.
- London: Sidgwick & Jackson, 1931.
- NOTES: "Thirty-seventh Impression, May 1931."
- PR6003.R4 N5 1931

1398. *The Collected Poems of Rupert Brooke.*
- Rupert Brooke.
- New York: Dodd, Mead, [1938].
- NOTES: Bookplate of Frances Scott Fitzgerald on front endpaper.
- PR6003.R4 1938

1399. *Notes on Life & Letters.*
- Joseph Conrad.
- London; Toronto: J. M. Dent & Sons Ltd., 1921.
- NOTES: First trade edition, contents page in the third cancelled state ("sea" corrected).
- PR6005.O4 N6 1921b

1400. *Notes on My Books.*
- Joseph Conrad.
- Garden City, N.Y.; Toronto: Doubleday, Page, 1921.
- NOTES: No. 108 of 250 autographed copies. Conrad's signature on limitation page. Published also as prefatory matter in the collected edition of the author's works.
- PR6005.O4 A145 1921

1401. *The Man without a Country.*
- Edward Everett Hale.
- Boston: Little, Brown, [1904].
- NOTES: Gift inscription on front free endpaper from FSF's Aunt Lorena, Christmas, 1903, Buffalo, N.Y.
- PS1772.M3 1905

1402. *The Sun Also Rises.*
- Ernest Hemingway.
- New York: Charles Scribner's Sons, 1926.

NOTES: Hanneman, A6a. First edition, first printing, with "stoppped" on p. 181. With: Scottie Fitzgerald's autograph note inserted.
- PS3515.E37 S8 1926

1403. *The End of a Chapter.*
- Shane Leslie.
- London: William Heinemann, [1929].

NOTES: Travellers' Library.
- DA560.L4 1929

1404. *I Should Have Stayed Home.*
- Horace McCoy.
- New York: Alfred A. Knopf, 1938.
- PS3525.A1715 I2 1938

1405. *The Making of Americans.*
- Gertrude Stein.
- [Paris: Contact Editions, 1925]
- Wrappers.
- PS3537.T323 M3 1925

IX Screenplays and Movie Work by F. Scott Fitzgerald: Mimeographs and Xeroxes

Printed material related to Fitzgerald's movie work (Bruccoli J items).

1406. "A Yank at Oxford, Notes," 13 July 1937.
- [Culver City, California]: Metro-Goldwyn-Mayer, 1937.
- 15 leaves. Xerox of mimeograph. Wrappers.

NOTES: Bruccoli J8.
- PN1997.Y31 1937

1407. "A Yank at Oxford, Outline with Dialogue (Corrected Version)," 19 July 1937.
- [Culver City, California]: Metro-Goldwyn-Mayer, 1937.
- 66 leaves. Xerox of mimeograph. Wrappers.

NOTES: Bruccoli J8.
- PN1997.Y31 1937b

1408. "A Yank at Oxford," 26 July 1937.
- [Culver City, California]: Metro-Goldwyn-Mayer, 1937.
- 144 leaves. Xerox of mimeograph. Wrappers.

NOTES: Bruccoli J8. With Commander Frank Wead
- PN1997.Y31 1937c

1409. "Three Comrades," 1 September 1937.
- [Culver City, California]: M-G-M, 1938.
- 169 leaves. Xerox of mimeograph. Wrappers.

NOTES: Bruccoli J9. FSF's name alone on cover.
  Edited by MJB. Setting copy used for published version of screenplay, *F. Scott Fitzgerald's Screenplay for Three Comrades by Erich Maria Remarque* (Carbondale: Southern Illinois University, 1978).
- PN1997.T47 1937

1410. "Three Comrades by Erich Maria Remarque," 5 November 1937.
- [Culver City, California]: M-G-M, 1937.
- 157 leaves. Xerox of mimeograph. Wrappers.

NOTES: Bruccoli J9. First version with revisions of E. E. Paramore.
- PN1997.T47 1937b

1411. "Three Comrades," 7 December 1937.
- [Culver City, California]: M-G-M, 1937.
- 171 leaves. Xerox of mimeograph. Wrappers.

NOTES: Bruccoli J9. Second revision by FSF and E. E. Paramore
- PN1997.T47 1937c

1412. "Three Comrades," 13 December 1937.
- [Culver City, California]: M-G-M, 1937.
- 171 leaves. Xerox of mimeograph. Wrappers.

NOTES: Bruccoli J9. "FIRST REVISE". With E. E. Paramore.
- PN1997.T47 1937d

1413. "Three Comrades by Erich Maria Remarque," 21 December 1937.
- [Culver City, California]: M-G-M, 1937.
- 155 leaves. Xerox of mimeograph. Wrappers.
NOTES: Bruccoli J9. "2nd Revised". With E. E. Paramore.
- PN1997.T47 1937e

1414. "Three Comrades by Erich Maria Remarque," 8–21 January 1938.
- [Culver City, California]: M-G-M, 1938.
- 125 leaves. Xerox of mimeograph. Wrappers.
NOTES: Bruccoli J9. "3rd Revised". With E. E. Paramore.
- PN1997.T47 1938

1415. "Three Comrades by Erich Maria Remarque," 1 February 1938.
- [Culver City, California]: M-G-M, 1938.
- 123 leaves. Xerox of mimeograph. Wrappers.
NOTES: Bruccoli J9. With E. E. Paramore.
"Script okayed by Joseph Mankiewicz".
With: Copy of TL from FSF to Joseph Mankiewicz, 4 February 1938.
- PN1997.T47 1938b

1416. "Infidelity (Theme and Characters)," 23 February 1938.
- [Culver City, California]: M-G-M, 1938.
- [10] leaves. Xerox of mimeograph. Wrappers.
NOTES: Bruccoli J10.
- PN1997.I49 1938b

1417. "Infidelity, Miscellaneous Notes".
- [Culver City, California]: M-G-M, 3 February to 3 May 1938.
- 22 leaves. Xerox of mimeograph. Wrappers.
NOTES: Bruccoli J10.
- PN1997.I49 1938e

1418. "Infidelity."
- [Culver City, California]: M-G-M, 7 and 8 March 1938.
- 104 leaves. Xerox of mimeograph. Wrappers.
NOTES: Bruccoli J10.
- PN1997.I49 1938c

1419. "Infidelity."
- [Culver City, California]: M-G-M, 7 and 8 March 1938.
- 104 leaves. Xerox of mimeograph. Wrappers.
NOTES: Bruccoli J10. Copy including the plot outline, suggested treatment for the ending (10 May 1938), and the complete screenplay, as well as "A History of the Writing of the Screenplay".
- PN1997.I49 1938c C.2

1420. "Infidelity by Ursula Parrott."
- [Culver City, California]: M-G-M, 26 April 1938.
- 104 leaves. Xerox of mimeograph. Wrappers.
NOTES: Bruccoli J10. "First Revision."
- PN1997.I49 1938d

1421. "Infidelity, New Treatment for the End."
- [Culver City, California]: M-G-M, 10 May 1938.
- 6 leaves. Xerox of mimeograph. Wrappers.
NOTES: Bruccoli J10.
- PN1997.I49 1938f

1422. "The Women, Complete Outline."
- [Culver City, California]: M-G-M, 31 May 1938.
- 33 leaves. Xerox of mimeograph. Wrappers.
NOTES: Bruccoli J12.
- PN1997.W68 1938

1423. "The Women, Complete Outline."
- [Culver City, California]: M-G-M, 3 June 1938.
- 39 leaves. Xerox of mimeograph. Wrappers.
NOTES: Bruccoli J12.
- PN1997.W68 1938b

1424. "The Women, General Outline & Breakdown."
- [Culver City, California]: M-G-M, 6 June 1938.
- 23 leaves. Xerox of mimeograph. Wrappers.
NOTES: Bruccoli J12.
- PN1997.W68 1938c

1425. "The Women, Addenda to Outline."
- [Culver City, California]: M-G-M, 9 June 1938.
- 5 leaves. Xerox of mimeograph. Wrappers.
NOTES: Bruccoli J12.
- PN1997.W68 1938d

1426. "The Women, Play by Clare Boothe."
- [Culver City, California]: M-G-M, 9 July 1938.
- 110 leaves. Xerox of mimeograph. Wrappers.
NOTES: Bruccoli J12.
- PN1997.W68 1938e

1427. "The Women".
- [Culver City, California]: M-G-M, 15 August 1938.
- 85 leaves. Xerox of mimeograph. Wrappers.
NOTES: Bruccoli J12. "Temporary Incomplete (85 pages)."
- PN1997.W68 1938f

Screenplays and Movie Work 233

1428. "The Women, Play by Clare Boothe."
- [Culver City, California]: M-G-M, 15 August 1938.
- 84 leaves. Xerox of mimeograph. Wrappers.

NOTES: Bruccoli J12. "FIRST REVISE"; "Temporary Incomplete (84 Pages)."
- PN1997.W68 1938g

1429. "The Women."
- [Culver City, California]: M-G-M, 20 September 1938.
- 123 leaves. Xerox of mimeograph. Wrappers.

NOTES: Bruccoli J12. With Donald Ogden Stewart.
- PN1997.W68 1938h

1430. "Madame Curie, Sequence Outlines."
- [Culver City, California]: M-G-M, 21 November 1938.
- [46] leaves. Xerox of mimeograph. Wrappers.

NOTES: Bruccoli J13.
- PN1997.M225 1938

1431. "Madame Curie, Incomplete Scripts - 66 pp."
- [Culver City, California]: M-G-M, 28 November 1938.
- [66] leaves. Xerox of mimeograph. Wrappers.

NOTES: Bruccoli J13.
- PN1997.M225 1938b

1432. "Madame Curie."
- [Culver City, California]: M-G-M, 17 December 1938.
- [61] leaves. Xerox of mimeograph. Wrappers.

NOTES: Bruccoli J13.
- PN1997.M225 1938c

1433. "Madame Curie."
- [Culver City, California]: M-G-M, 27 December 1938.
- [77] leaves. Xerox of mimeograph. Wrappers.

NOTES: Bruccoli J13. "FIRST REVISE".
- PN1997.M225 1938d

1434. "Madame Curie."
- [Culver City, California]: M-G-M, 3 January 1939.
- [76] leaves. Xerox of mimeograph. Wrappers.

NOTES: Bruccoli J13. "SECOND REVISE".
- PN1997.M255 1939

1435. "The Light of Heart."
- Nunnally Johnson.
- [Culver City, California]: M-G-M, 11 July 1942.
- [94] leaves. Xerox of mimeograph. Wrappers.

NOTES: "Final Script". Rewrite of rejected FSF screenplay. Retitled "Life Begins at Eight-Thirty".
With continuity and dialogue script "TAKEN FROM THE SCREEN," 9 December 1942.
- PN1997.L5442 1942

1436. "Life Begins at Eight-Thirty."
- Nunnally Johnson.
- [Culver City, California]: M-G-M, 9 December 1942.
- [126] leaves. Xerox of mimeograph. Wrappers.

NOTES: Continuity and dialogue script "TAKEN FROM THE SCREEN".
- PN1997.LS442 1942b

X. Selected Graphic Material

A. Photographs

1437. [Portraits of Scottie Fitzgerald's grandfathers], c. 1880.
- 2 photographs framed.
- NOTES: Photograph of Judge A. D. Sayre as a student at Roanoke College, and photograph of Edward Fitzgerald. Both are framed with a FSF note pasted on back.
  With undated ALS from Scottie Fitzgerald to MJB: ". . . they're about the only things I have with FSF handwriting. I feel quite sure none of my children would understand the significance of that or take special care of them—".
- On deposit.

1438. [Advertising card, 1933].
- 1 sheet (35 × 27 cm.).
- NOTES: "Don't Miss F. Scott Fitzgerald's 'More than Just a House,' in this Week's *The Saturday Evening Post*" [picture].
  FSF's short story, "More than Just a House," was first published in *The Saturday Evening Post* (24 June 1933).
- PS3511.I9 M683 1933

1439. [Portraits of Harold and Anne Ober], n.d.
- Wallet-sized black-and-white photographs in folding case.
- On deposit.

1440. [Photograph of Scottie Fitzgerald with L. Quincy Mumford and Matthew J. Bruccoli], c. 1972.
- 1 item.
- NOTES: Photograph of MJB presenting a copy of his *F. Scott Fitzgerald: A Descriptive Bibliography* to L. Quincy Mumford, Librarian of Congress.
- PS3511.I9 Z541

1441. [Photograph of Scottie Fitzgerald], c. 1976.
- 1 item.
- NOTES: Photograph taken at 6 Pleasant Avenue, Montgomery, Alabama, where her father courted her mother in 1918.
- PS3569.M53797 246 1974

1442. [*Peanuts* original art], 22 July 1990.
- Charles M. Schulz.
- 43 × 61 cm.
NOTES: Inscribed to MJB. The strip cites Gatsby.
- PS3511.I9 G687 1990

1443. [*Peanuts* original art], 7 June 1991.
- Charles M. Schulz.
- 17 × 52 cm.
NOTES: Inscribed to MJB. The strip cites Gatsby.
- PS3511.I9 G688 1991

1444. [*Peanuts* original art], 18 December 1991.
- Charles M. Schulz.
- 17 × 52 cm.
NOTES: Inscribed to MJB. The strip cites Gatsby.
- PS3511.I9 G689 1991

1445. [Photograph of Monsignor Cyril Sigourney Fay].
- 1 item.
NOTES: Fay was head of the Newman School and the dedicatee of *TSOP*.
- On deposit.

1446. [Fitzgerald family photographs].
- 84 photographs.
NOTES: 16 photographs annotated by FSF or ZF.
- On deposit.

1447. [Picture postcard of Jesse Albert Locke], n.d.
- 1 card.
NOTES: Inscribed by Locke to FSF. Locke was headmaster of Newman School.
- On deposit.

1448. [FSF photograph].
NOTES: Photograph of FSF and Vanderbilt? judging a beauty contest.
- On deposit.

1449. [FSF photograph].
NOTES: Photograph of ZF sketching FSF.
- On deposit.

1450. [Scottie Fitzgerald baby pictures].
- 5 photographs in envelope.
- On deposit.

1451. [Scottie Fitzgerald's scrapbooks].
- 2 detached leaves.
NOTES: With 2 photographs of FSF in envelope.
- On deposit.

B. Movie Posters and Promotional Material

1452. [Lobby card for *The Chorus Girl's Romance*].
- [Hollywood: Metro Pictures, 1920].
- 1 card.
NOTES: Scene from movie based on FSF's short story, "Head and Shoulders."
- PN1997.C468 1920

1453. [Glass slide and promotional card for *The Husband Hunter*].
- Produced by William Fox.
- [n.p.: c.1921].
- 1 slide in paper mount; 1 card.
NOTES: Promotional slide for Fox Entertainments production of *The Husband Hunter* based on FSF's short story, "Myra Meets His Family." Accompanying card shows days and times different movies were shown at Proctor's Strand, Ayer, Mass. *The Husband Hunter* was scheduled to be shown Friday, 21 January with the tenth episode of *The Silent Avenger*. Such slides were shown in early movie theaters to advertise coming attractions.
- PN1997.H86726 1921

1454. [Lobby card for *The Husband Hunter*].
- Produced by William Fox.
- [n.p.]: Fox Entertainments, 1920.
- 1 card.
NOTES: Scene from movie based on FSF's short story, "Myra Meets His Family."
- PS3511.I9 M975 1920

1455. [Illustration from *The Husband Hunter*].
- *Picture Show*, vol. 5, no. 107 (14 May 1921), p. 14.
NOTES: Photo of Eileen Percy in the 1920 Fox motion picture based on FSF's short story, "Myra Meets His Family."
- PN1993.P537 vol. 5, no. 107

1456. [Movie poster for *The Off-Shore Pirate*].
- [n.p.]: Metro Pictures, [c.1921].
- 1 print (63.5 × 66 cm.).
NOTES: Color poster showing Neil Hamilton and Viola Dana.
- On deposit.

238 *Selected Graphic Material*

1457. [Lobby cards for *The Off-Shore Pirate*].
- Produced by Metro Motion Pictures.
- New York: Rotograph, [c.1921].
- 12 cards with envelope.

NOTES: Set includes title card, synopsis card and 10 "gelatines" with captions from movie.
- On deposit.

1458. "The Off-Shore Pirate."
- Donald Calhoun.
- *Motion Picture Classic,* vol. 12, no. 1 (March 1921), pp. 37–41, 76, 80.

NOTES: Includes stills from the movie.
"Fictionalized by permission from the Metro production of the story by F. Scott Fitzgerald; adapted for the screen by Waldemar Young. Directed by Dallas M. Fitz Gerald and starring Viola Dana."
- PN1993.M6743 vol. 12, no. 1

1459. [Promotional card for *The Off-Shore Pirate*].
- Produced by Metro Motion Pictures.
- Chicago: Max B. Sheffer Card Co., 1922.
- 1 postcard.

NOTES: "Viola Dana as Ardita Farnam in 'The Off-Shore Pirate'".
- PN2287.D2563 V4 1922

1460. [Glass slide for *The Beautiful and Damned*].
- Produced by Warner Brothers.
- New York: Excelsior Illustrating, [1922].
- 1 slide in paper mount.

NOTES: Promotional slide for William Seiter's 1922 production of *The Beautiful and Damned.*
- PN1997.B4492 1922

1461. [Lobby cards for *The Beautiful and Damned*].
- New York: Ullman, [1922].
- 7 cards.

NOTES: Lobby cards with captions for the Warner Brothers production of *The Beautiful and Damned* starring Marie Prevost.
- On deposit.

1462. [Publicity still for *The Beautiful and Damned*].
- [n.p.: c.1922].
- 1 photograph.
- On deposit.

Movie Posters and Promotional Material 239

1463. [Glass slide for *Grit*].
- Produced by the Film Guild.
- Long Island City, N.Y.: Photo Repro Co., Inc., [1924?].
- 1 slide in cardboard mount.

NOTES: Promotional slide for Frank Tuttle's 1924 silent film of *Grit*, a Film Guild Production distributed by Hodkinson Pictures, with source story by FSF.
- PN1997.G84724 1924

1464. [Glass slide for *The Great Gatsby*].
- Produced by Herbert Brenon.
- New York: Excelsior Illustrating, [1926?].
- 1 slide in cardboard mount.

NOTES: Promotional slide for *The Great Gatsby*.
- PN1997.G8328426 1926

1465. [Lobby cards for *The Great Gatsby*].
- Produced by Herbert Brenon.
- [n.p.: 1926?].
- 2 cards.

NOTES: Lobby card for production of *The Great Gatsby*.
- On deposit.

1466. [Lobby card for *The Wedding Night*].
- Produced by Samuel Goldwyn.
- [n.p.: United Artists, 1935].
- 1 card.

NOTES: Lobby card for *The Wedding Night* starring Gary Cooper and Anna Sten. The movie story by Edwin Knopf is a thinly disguised portrait of FSF.
- On deposit.

1467. [Movie poster for *A Yank at Oxford*].
- New York: Tooker Lithography, [c.1937].
- 1 sheet (104.2 × 68.7 cm.).

NOTES: Produced by M-G-M starring Robert Taylor. FSF worked on screenplay but did not receive screen credit.
- PN1997.Y3124 1937

1468. [Poster for *Three Comrades*].
- [n.p.]: M-G-M, 1938.
- 1 sheet (55.4 × 70 cm.).

NOTES: Screenplay by FSF and Edward E. Paramore.
- PN1997.T4724 1938

1469. [Promotional piece for *Three Comrades*].
- [n.p.]: M-G-M, 1938.
- 1 sheet with advertisement for playhouse Enosburg Falls on verso.
- PN1197.T4725 1938

1470. "Marie Antoinette."
- *Film Weekly Supplement,* 4 February 1939.
- 16 pp.

NOTES: FSF worked briefly on screenplay for producer Irving Thalberg but did not receive screen credit. Cover depicts Norma Shearer.
- On deposit.

1471. [Poster for *The Great Gatsby*].
- [n.p.]: Paramount Pictures, 1949.
- 1 sheet (100 × 67.5 cm.).

NOTES: Poster features Alan Ladd as Gatsby. Paramount logo in lower right corner, "38231," "49/87".
- PN1997.G8328424 1949b

1472. [Australian poster for *The Great Gatsby*].
- Sydney: Richardson Studio, [c. 1949].
- 1 sheet (36 × 78 cm.).

NOTES: Depicts head and shoulders portraits of three main characters. "Y" stamped on portrait of Betty Field.
- PN1997.G8328424 1949

1473. [Lobby cards for *The Great Gatsby*].
- [n.p.]: Paramount Pictures, 1949.
- 3 cards.

NOTES: Limited edition poster set "49/87" contains cards 3, 5, and 6.
- On deposit.

1474. [Publicity stills for *The Great Gatsby*].
- [n.p.]: Paramount Pictures, 1949.
- 3 photographs.
- On deposit.

1475. [Press book for *The Great Gatsby*].
- [n.p.]: Paramount Pictures, 1949.
- 24 pp.
- On deposit.

1476. *The Great Gatsby by F. Scott Fitzgerald.*
- Logan, Iowa: Perfection Form Company, [n.d.].
- Wrappers, spiral bound. On cover: "LITERARY PRINTS".

NOTES: 10 publicity stills with captions from 1949 movie *The Great Gatsby.*
- On deposit.

1477. [Press book for *The Last Time I Saw Paris*].
- [n.p.]: Loew's, 1954.
- 24 pp.

NOTES: Press book for the M-G-M production of *The Last Time I Saw Paris*, based on FSF's short story "Babylon Revisited."
- On deposit.

1478. [British press book for *The Last Time I Saw Paris*].
- London: M-G-M Pictures Limited, [c.1954].
- 12 pp.

NOTES: British press book for the M-G-M production of *The Last Time I Saw Paris*, based on FSF's short story "Babylon Revisited."
- On deposit.

1479. [Lobby cards for *Beloved Infidel*].
- Produced by Jerry Wald.
- England: National Screen Service, [c.1959].
- 8 cards.

NOTES: British lobby cards for 20th Century–Fox's 1959 production of Sheilah Graham's memoir, starring Gregory Peck and Deborah Kerr.
- On deposit.

1480. [Publicity stills for *Beloved Infidel*].
- Produced by Jerry Wald.
- [n.p.: n.d., c. 1959].
- 16 photographs.

NOTES: Black-and-white stills for 20th Century–Fox's 1959 production of Sheilah Graham's memoir, starring Gregory Peck and Deborah Kerr.
- On deposit.

1481. [Lobby cards for *Tender Is the Night*].
- Produced by Henry T. Weinstein.
- [n.p.]: 20th Century-Fox, 1961.
- 6 cards.

NOTES: Lobby cards for *Tender Is the Night*, starring Jennifer Jones, Jason Robards, Jr., Joan Fontaine, and Tom Ewell.
- On deposit.

1482. [Publicity stills for *Tender Is the Night*].
- Produced by Henry T. Weinstein.
- [n.p.: c.1961].
- 32 photographs.

NOTES: Black-and-white stills for *Tender Is the Night*, featuring stars Jennifer Jones, Jason Robards, Jr., Joan Fontaine, and Tom Ewell.
- On deposit.

242 *Selected Graphic Material*

1483. [Press book *Tender Is the Night*].
- [n.p.]: 20th Century-Fox, 1961.
- 10 pp.
- On deposit.

1484. "Tender Is the Night."
- Lyric by Paul Francis Webster; music by Sammy Fain.
  New York: Miller Music Corporation, 1961.
  NOTES: Sheet music for song from the 20th Century-Fox production of *Tender Is the Night*.
- On deposit.

1485. [Promotional card for *The Great Gatsby*].
- [n.p.: c. 1974].
- Cardboard standee.
  NOTES: Promotes both Paramount movie and Bantam's tie-in paperback edition.
- On deposit.

1486. [Publicity stills for *Tender Is the Night*].
- Produced by Showtime.
- [n.p.: c. 1985].
- 2 photographs.
  NOTES: Black-and-white stills for television production of *Tender Is the Night* starring Peter Strauss, Mary Steenburgen, John Heard, and Sean Young.
- On deposit.

C. Lois Moran Items

Actress Lois Moran and her movie Stella Dallas *provided the model for Rosemary Hoyt and* Daddy's Girl *in* Tender Is the Night.

1487. *Stella Dallas.*
- Olive Higgins Prouty.
- New York: Grosset & Dunlap, [1923].
  NOTES: Illustrated with scenes from the 1925 Samuel Goldwyn movie starring Lois Moran, Belle Bennett, and Ronald Colman.
- PS3531.R863 S7 1923

1488. [Publicity still for *Stella Dallas*].
- [Hollywood, California]: United Artists Corporation, 1925.
- 1 photoprint.
  NOTES: Produced by Samuel Goldwyn, *Stella Dallas* was released by United Artists, directed by Henry King.
- PN1997.S674 S34 1925

1489. *Samuel Goldwyn presents the Henry King production "Stella Dallas."*
- [New York: Commanday-Roth], [1925]
- 18 pp. Wrappers.
- NOTES: Promotional program for the 1925 Samuel Goldwyn production of *Stella Dallas*, starring Ronald Colman, Belle Bennett, and Lois Moran, for sale "only in theatres where 'Stella Dallas' is showing."
- PN1997 S38524 1925

1490. "The Screen's New Prodigy — Lois Moran."
- Vandamm.
- *Vanity Fair*, v. 26, no. 1 (March 1926), p. 74.
- NOTES: Vandamm photograph of Lois Moran with caption celebrating her success following the release of *Stella Dallas*.
- AP2.V3 vol. 26, no. 1

1491. [Lobby card for *The Irresistible Lover*].
- [Hollywood, California?], U.S.A : Universal, [1927?]
- 1 sheet.
- NOTES: Directed by William Beaudine, *The Irresistible Lover* starred Norman Kerry and Lois Moran.
- PN1997.I774 1927

1492. [Photograph of Lois Moran].
- [n.p.: n.d.].
- 1 sheet.
- NOTES: Black-and-white photo depicts Moran, standing, with left hand on hip and right hand outstretched toward a drop-leaf table.
- PN2287.M698 P6

1493. *The River Pirate*.
- Charles Francis Coe.
- New York: Grosset & Dunlap, [1928].
- Dust jacket.
- NOTES: Illustrated with scenes from the 1928 Fox production of *The River Pirate*, directed by William K. Howard and starring Victor McLaglen and Lois Moran.
- PS3505.O183 R584

1494. *Movie Star Composition Book: Lois Moran*.
- [n.p.: n.d., 1928].
- 24 leaves. Wrappers.
- NOTES: Blank composition book. Portrait of Moran on cover. Biographical notes on reverse.
- PN2287.M698 M69 1928

244   Selected Graphic Material

1495. [Lobby card for *Sharp Shooters*].
- Produced by William Fox.
- [Hollywood, California?]: [s.n.]., [1928?].
- 1 sheet.
- NOTES: Lobby card for the 1928 Fox Film production of *Sharp Shooters*, directed by John G. Blystone, starring George O'Brien and Lois Moran.
- PN1997.S427524 1928

1496. [Lobby card for *True Heaven*].
- Produced by William Fox.
- [Hollywood, California: n.p., 1929].
- 1 sheet.
- NOTES: Produced by Fox Film, *True Heaven* was directed by James Tinling and starred George O'Brien and Lois Moran.
- PN1997.T7 W4 1929

1497. [Glass slide for *Don't Marry*].
- Produced by William Fox.
- New York: Excelsior Illustrating, [1929].
- 1 slide in cardboard mount.
- NOTES: Promotional slide for William Fox's 1924 production of *Don't Marry*, with Lois Moran and Neil Hamilton.
- PN1997.D657 1929

1498. "Sitting by the Window"
- Con Conrad.
- New York: De Sylva, Brown and Henderson Inc., [1929].
- 5 pp. Vocal score.
- NOTES: From the Fox Movietone Production *A Song of Kentucky*. "A musical movietone with Lois Moran and Joseph Wagstaff."
- M1508.C66 S67 1929

1499. [Portrait of Lois Moran].
- Marland Stone.
- *Motion Picture*, vol. 40, no. 6 (January 1931), p. [1].
- NOTES: Cover portrait by Stone.
- PN1993.M6742 vol. 40, no. 6

1500. "She'd Better Be Nice."
- Henry F. Pringle.
- *Collier's*, vol. 90, no. 26 (24 December 1932), pp. 13, 34.
- NOTES: Photograph of Moran.
- AP2.C65 vol. 90, no. 26

XI Princetoniana

1501. *Princeton Stories.*
   - Jessie Lynch Williams.
   - New York: Scribner, 1896.
   NOTES: Inscribed by Williams. "6th Edition".
   - PS3545.W724 P9 1896

1502. *Catalogue of Princeton University.*
   - Princeton, N.J.: The University.
   NOTES: Collection includes catalogues for 1913–14, 1914–15, 1915–16, 1917–18.
   - LD4587.A3

1503. *Princeton.*
   - V. L. Collins.
   - New York: Oxford University Press, 1914.
   - LD4608.C6

1504. [Princeton class of 1917: Group photograph, Fall–Winter 1913–14?].
   NOTES: Signed on verso by more than 100 members of the 1917 freshman class, Princeton University, including FSF.
   - PS3511.I9 Z8331

1505. *The Princeton Bric-a-Brac 1915, Volume XXXIX.*
   - Princeton, N.J.: Junior Class of Princeton University, [1914].
   - LD4627.P7 vol. 39

1506. *The Princeton Bric-a-Brac 1916, Volume XL.*
   - Princeton, N.J.: Junior Class of Princeton University, [1915].
   - LD4627.P7 vol. 40

1507. *Princeton 1916:* [calendar].
   - [Princeton, N.J.?: n.p., 1915?].
   NOTES: Leaf for May 1916 has a group portrait of the Triangle Club, including FSF.
   - LD4613.P65 1915

1508. "Scott Fitzgerald: Considered the Most Beautiful 'Show Girl' in the Princeton Triangle Club's New Musical Play, The Evil Eye."
   - *The New York Times,* Rotogravure Section, 2 January 1916.
   - 1 picture. Framed.
   NOTES: Reproduction of photograph of FSF in female costume. Text mentions FSF as the author of the lyrics of *The Evil Eye.*
   - PS3511.I9 Z466 1916

1509. "Triangle Club Number."
- *The Princeton Pictorial Review* (15 January 1916).
- [Princeton, N.J.]: The Students of Princeton University.
- LH1.P8 P75

1510. *The Princeton Bric-a-Brac 1917, Volume XLI.*
- Princeton, N.J.: Junior Class of Princeton University, [1916].
NOTES: Photographs and text on Triangle Club and *Fie! Fie! Fi-Fi!*, pp. 88–95.
- LD4627.P7 vol. 41

1511. *Princeton University Library: American Library Association Visit, June 29, 1916.*
- Princeton, N.J.: University Library, 1916.
- Z733.P922

1512. *The Nassau Herald Class of Nineteen Hundred and Seventeen.*
- Princeton, N.J.: Princeton University Press, 1917.
NOTES: Portrait and short biographical sketch of FSF.
- LD4604 1917.N37

1513. *The Story of Princeton.*
- Edwin Mark Mossir; illustrated from drawings by Lester G. Hornby.
- Boston: Little, Brown, 1917.
- LD4608.N7

1514. *The Princeton Bric-a-Brac 1918, Volume XLII.*
- Princeton, N.J.: Junior Class of Princeton University, [1917].
NOTES: Photographs and text on Triangle Club and *The Evil Eye* and *Safety First*, pp. 80–89.
- LD4627.P7 vol. 42

1515. *Princeton University 1917 Commencement Week.*
- [Princeton, N.J.: n.p., 1917?].
- Leather-bound commencement program.
- LD4621.C6 1917

1516. *The Princeton Bric-a-Brac 1919, Volume XLIII.*
- Princeton, N.J.: Junior Class of Princeton University, [1918].
NOTES: Photographs and text on Triangle Club and *Safety First*, pp. 130–37.
- LD4627.P7 vol. 43

1517. *In Memoriam Princeton 1917.*
- [n.p.: n.p., 1919].
NOTES: Page [53]: "1917 in service" lists "Fitzgerald, F.S. 1st Lieutenant Infantry".
- LD4604 1917 .I6

1518. "This Side of Paradise, by F. Scott Fitzgerald."
- Alfred Gottlieb Gennert.
- *The War Baby,* Arrival 1, Howl 1 (Spring 1920), pp. 23–24.
NOTES: Book review of *This Side of Paradise* "reviewed especially for The War Baby by Alfred (Red) Gottlieb Gennert."
- LH1.P8 W3 Arrival 1, Howl 1

1519. *Princeton University Photo-gravures.*
- Princeton, N.J.: Princeton University Store, [c.1920].
- Wrappers.
NOTES: 1 printed title-leaf, 36 leaves of plates (all sepia illustrations). Inscribed "To: The 'Brookers' with love Bunny" [Edmund Wilson].
- LD4613.P7 1920

1520. *Class of 1917 Directory.*
- [n.p.: 1924?].
- Wrappers.
NOTES: On title page: "Corrected to February 2, 1924." Page 16: Entry for "Fitzgerald, Francis S. K. Great Neck, L.I., N.Y."
- LD4604 1917 .C5 1924

1521. *The Nassau Herald Class of Nineteen Hundred and Eighteen.*
- Princeton, N.J.: Princeton University Press, 1918.
NOTES: Bookplate of Library of Princeton University. Presented by Charles T. White. Class of 1918.
- LD4627.N3 1918

1522. [Membership card, 1931–32].
- Princeton Alumni Club, [1931].
NOTES: Issued to FSF; not signed by FSF.
- On deposit.

1523. *Princeton in the World War.*
- Princeton, N.J.: The Office of the Secretary, Princeton University, [1932].
NOTES: FSF entry on p. 381.
- D639.E4 P68

1524. *History of the University Cottage Club of Princeton, New Jersey, 1886 to 1936.*
- Princeton, N.J.: Privately printed, 1936.
- In box, as issued.
NOTES: FSF included in Class of 1917 listings.
- LD4616.5.C63

1525. *Princeton University Alumni Directory.*
- [Princeton, N.J.]: The University, [1939].
NOTES: "For official University and Alumni Council use, and also for individual communication of a personal nature between those listed therein."
- LD4601.A3

1526. "Princeton and F. Scott Fitzgerald."
- Frances Scott Fitzgerald.
- *Nassau Literary Magazine,* vol. 100, no. 3 (1942), pp. 45–48.

NOTES: 100th Anniversary Issue.
- LH1.P8 N3 vol. 100, no. 3

1527. *The University Cottage Club of Princeton, New Jersey 1886–1954.*
- Cottage Club, Princeton University.
- [Princeton, N.J.?: n.p., 1954?]

NOTES: "Privately printed". Includes membership list and necrology.
- LD4616.5.C65 1954

1528. *1917's Fortieth: A Pictorial Record of the Class of 1917, Princeton University, from Freshman Year to Date, June 1957.*
- Edward Durrell, Harvey H. Smith, and David W. Tibbott.
- [Princeton, N.J.: Princeton University Class of 1917, 1957].
- Wrappers.

NOTES: Includes "Excerpts from 'Princeton' by F. Scott Fitzgerald," p. 89. Laid in: "Fortieth Reunion Class of 1917 Program," [6] pp.
- LD4604 1917 .D9

1529. *Fifty Years in the Wide, Wide World, 1917–1967.*
- [Princeton, N.J.: Princeton University Class of 1917, 1967].
- Wrappers.

NOTES: Biographical sketch of FSF. Signature of Landon Raymond, '17. Laid in: program for reunion activities.
- LD4604 1917.D95

1530. *The Long Kickline.*
- Donald Marsden.
- Princeton, N.J.: Princeton Triangle Club, 1968.
- Dust jacket.

NOTES: *Fie! Fie! Fi-Fi!, The Evil Eye, Safety First!,* pp. 91–105.
- ML200.8.P866 M37

XII Memorabilia

1531. [Corset], 1890.
- 1 corset: silk and whalebone.
- NOTES: Corset worn by Mary (Mollie) McQuillan Fitzgerald, mother of FSF, at her wedding to Edward Fitzgerald, 12 February 1890, Washington, D.C.
    Donated to collection by FSF's niece Courtney Sprague Vaughan.
- Item mentioned in letter from FSF to his sister Annabel Sprague, June 1936, published in *A Life in Letters*.
- GT2075.C6 1890

1532. [Shoes], 1890.
- 1 pair of women's shoes: silk and leather.
- NOTES: Shoes worn by Mary (Mollie) McQuillan Fitzgerald, mother of F. Scott Fitzgerald, at her wedding to Edward Fitzgerald, 12 February 1890, Washington, D.C.
    Donated to collection by FSF's niece Courtney Sprague Vaughan.
    Item mentioned in letter from FSF to his sister Annabel Sprague, June 1936, published in *A Life in Letters*.
- TS1020.S5 1890

1533. "My Wedding," 1890–1900.
- Mary McQuillan Fitzgerald.
- Wedding album.
- NOTES: Recollections of the marriage of FSF's parents, Edward Fitzgerald and Mary (Mollie) McQuillan, in Washington, D.C., 12 February 1890, written by Mollie Fitzgerald ten years after and dated 12 February 1900.
    Includes 8 contemporary congratulatory letters inserted loosely. Signed by Mollie Fitzgerald on front endpaper and inscribed "For Scott Fitzgerald, September 24th '1917.'"
- CS71.F54

1534. [Doll], c. 1896.
- Belonging to Louisa Fitzgerald.
- NOTES: Louisa Fitzgerald, the older sister of FSF, died in infancy.
- Item mentioned in letter from FSF to his sister Annabel Sprague, June 1936, published in *A Life in Letters*.
- On deposit.

1535. *Popular Authors.*
- New York: McLoughlin Brothers, [n.d.].
- NOTES: Card game with autograph note from Scottie Fitzgerald to MJB and Arlyn Bruccoli.
- On deposit.

250   *Memorabilia*

1536. [Silver flask], 1918.
   NOTES: Engraved: "M. Edgerton M. Sayre to 1st Lt. F. Scott Fitzgerald 65th Infantry Camp Sheridan For-get-me-not Zelda 9-13-18 Montgomery, Ala."
   • On deposit.

1537. [Silver flask].
   NOTES: Engraved: "FSF".
   • On deposit.

1538. [Scrapbook], 1920–22.
   NOTES: Scrapbook of clippings and reviews of books by FSF. Signed FSF note dated 7 November 1907 pasted on inside front cover.
   • On deposit.

1539. [Leather briefcase].
   • Owned by FSF.
   NOTES: Address of Charles Scribner's Sons stamped in gold.
   • On deposit.

1540. [Walking stick].
   • Owned by FSF.
   • On deposit.

1541. [Glass slides of World War I scenes].
   • In wooden case with viewer.
   NOTES: Presented to MJB by Scottie Fitzgerald.
   • On deposit.

1542. Orderi di Danilo, c. 1918.
   NOTES: The medal Jay Gatsby received from "little Montenegro down on the Adriatic Sea!"
   • UB430.M6 O7

1543. [Scrapbook], 1958–71.
   • Scottie Fitzgerald.
   • 1 item (20 leaves).
   NOTES: Scrapbook of clippings and photocopied articles by and about Scottie Fitzgerald Smith. Includes reviews, especially of books about FSF interviews and society notes from the *Washington Post, Palo Alto Times, Alabama Journal,* and *Montgomery Independent* from 1958 to 1971.
   • PS3569.M53797 Z8

XIII Zelda Fitzgerald Collection

Zelda Fitzgerald items including her books, manuscripts, correspondence, artwork, documents, and periodical appearances (Bruccoli ZF items).

A. Books by Zelda Fitzgerald

1544. *Save Me the Waltz.*
- New York: Charles Scribner's Sons, 1932.
- Dust jacket.
NOTES: Bruccoli ZF-A1.1.
  Matthew J. Bruccoli's editorial annotations throughout: "This is the copy I used in editing my SIU Press text. MJB Vern Sternberg backed this job."
- PS3511.I9234.S3 1932 C.1

1545. *Save Me the Waltz.*
- New York: Charles Scribner's Sons, 1932.
- Dust jacket.
NOTES: Bruccoli ZF-A1.1.
  Label on front paste-down endpapers: CHARLES SCRIBNER'S SONS OFFICE COPY no. 2462....
  Laid in: dust jacket.
- PS3511.I9234.S3 1932 C.2

1546. [Dust jacket proof for *Save Me the Waltz*, 1932?].
- [Cleonike Damianakes].
- 1 sheet.
NOTES: Proof of dust jacket for ZF's novel with illustration of dancing man and woman by signed "Cleonike" (also known as Cleon). Does not include flap copy or photograph of ZF on back.
  PS3511.I9234 S32 1932

1547. *Save Me the Waltz.*
- London: Grey Walls Press, 1953.
- Dust jacket.
NOTES: Bruccoli ZF-A1.2. Second edition, first British edition.
- PS3511.I9234 S3 1953

1548. *Save Me the Waltz.*
- Edited by Matthew J. Bruccoli; Preface by Harry T. Moore.
- Carbondale: Southern Illinois University Press, [1967].
- Dust jacket.
NOTES: Bruccoli ZF-A1.3.a. Third edition, first printing.
  Crosscurrents: Modern Fiction.

On free front endpaper: "Vern Sternberg published this on my recommendation. Charles Scribner, Jr. [IV] was incredulous when we asked him for reprint rights. He was also patronizing. MJB".
- PS3511.I9234 S3 1967

1549. *Save Me the Waltz.*
- Edited by Matthew J. Bruccoli; Preface by Harry T. Moore.
- Carbondale: Southern Illinois University Press, [1967].
- Wrappers.

NOTES: Bruccoli ZF-A1.3.a. Arcturus Books Edition.
- PS3511.I9234 S3 1967b

1550. *Save Me the Waltz.*
- Edited by Matthew J. Bruccoli; Preface by Harry T. Moore.
- Carbondale: Southern Illinois University Press, [1967].
- Dust jacket.

NOTES: Bruccoli ZF-A1.3.a. Third edition, second printing. Crosscurrents: Modern Fiction.
- PS3511.I9234 S3 1967c

1551. *Save Me the Waltz.*
- Edited by Matthew J. Bruccoli; Preface by Harry T. Moore.
- Carbondale: Southern Illinois University Press, [1967].

NOTES: Bruccoli ZF-A1.3.a. Binding dummy. Laid in: proofs of the Arcturus and Crosscurrents editions.
- PS3511.I9234 S3 1967d

1552. *Save Me the Waltz.*
- Edited by Matthew J. Bruccoli; Preface by Harry T. Moore.
- Carbondale: Southern Illinois University Press, [1972].
- Dust jacket.

NOTES: Bruccoli ZF-A1.3.a. Third Edition, Book-of-the-Month-Club printing. Crosscurrents: Modern Fiction.
- PS3511.I9234 S3 1972

1553. *Save Me the Waltz.*
- Preface by Harry T. Moore; A Note on the Text by Matthew J. Bruccoli.
- London: Cape, 1968.
- Dust jacket.

NOTES: Bruccoli ZF-A1.3.b. Third edition, English printing.
- PS3511.I9234 S3 1968

1554. *Save Me the Waltz.*
- With a Preface by Harry T. Moore; And an Afterword by Matthew J. Bruccoli.
- [New York]: New American Library, [1968].
- Wrappers.

NOTES: Bruccoli Zf-A1.4. Fourth edition, first printing. "A Signet Book".
- PS3511.I9234 S3 1968b

1555. *Save Me the Waltz.*
- With a Preface by Harry T. Moore; And an Afterword by Matthew J. Bruccoli.
- [New York]: New American Library, 1968.
- Wrappers.

NOTES: Bruccoli ZF-A1.4. Fourth edition, third printing.
- PS3511.I9234 S3 1968d

1556. *Save Me the Waltz.*
- With a Preface by Harry T. Moore; And an Afterword by Matthew J. Bruccoli.
- [New York]: New American Library, 1968.
- Wrappers.

NOTES: Bruccoli ZF-A1.4, Note. Fourth edition, sixth printing. Marked by Scottie Fitzgerald.
- PS3511.I9234 S3 1968g

1557. *Save Me the Waltz.*
- Preface by Harry T. Moore; A Note on the Text by Matthew J. Bruccoli.
- [Harmondsworth, England]: Penguin, [1971].
- Wrappers.

NOTES: Bruccoli ZF-A1.5. Fifth edition.
- PS3511.I9234 S3 1971

1558. *Save Me the Waltz.*
- With a Preface by Harry T. Moore; And an Afterword by Matthew J. Bruccoli.
- [New York]: New American Library, [1974?].
- Wrappers.

NOTES: Bruccoli ZF-A1.4. Fourth edition, eighth printing.
- PS3511.I9234 S3 1974

1559. *Save Me the Waltz.*
- Preface by Harry T. Moore; A Note on the Text by Matthew J. Bruccoli.
- [Harmondsworth, England]: Penguin, [1982].
- Wrappers.

NOTES: Bruccoli ZF-A1.5, Note. Reprint of fifth edition.
- PS3511.I9234 S3 1982

See section I for *Bits of Paradise; 21 Uncollected Stories by F. Scott and Zelda Fitzgerald.*

1560. *Scandalabra: A Farce Fantasy In A Prologue And Three Acts.*
- Foreword by Meredith Walker.
- Bloomfield Hills, Michigan & Columbia, S.C.: Bruccoli Clark, 1980.

- Issued as a wrapped booklet in a portfolio.
  NOTES: Bruccoli ZF-A3. First edition, only printing. Copy no. 428.
  "This First Edition . . . is limited to 500 numbered copies. Copies 1 to 450 are for sale; copies I to L are reserved for the publisher."
  With: Xerox of TS.
- PS3511.I9234 S27 1980

1561. *Zelda Fitzgerald: The Collected Writings.*
- Edited by Matthew J. Bruccoli; Introduction by Mary Gordon.
- New York: Scribner, 1991.
- Wrappers: "UNCORRECTED ADVANCE PROOF".
NOTES: Initialed by MJB: "22 February 1991".
- PS3511.I9234 1991b

1562. *Zelda Fitzgerald: The Collected Writings.*
- Edited by Matthew J. Bruccoli; Introduction by Mary Gordon.
- New York: Scribner; Toronto: Collier Macmillan Canada; New York: Maxwell Macmillan International, [1991].
- Dust jacket.
- PS3511.I9234 1991

1563. *Zelda Fitzgerald: The Collected Writings.*
- Edited by Matthew J. Bruccoli; Introduction by Mary Gordon.
- London: Little, Brown, [1992].
- Dust jacket.
- PS3511.I9234 1992

1564. *Zelda Fitzgerald: The Collected Writings.*
- Edited by Matthew J. Bruccoli; Introduction by Mary Gordon.
- New York: Collier Books; Toronto: Maxwell Macmillan Canada; New York: Maxwell Macmillan International, [1992].
- Wrappers.
NOTES: "First Collier Books Edition 1992".
- PS3511.I9234 1992b

1565. *Zelda Fitzgerald: The Collected Writings.*
- Edited by Matthew J. Bruccoli; Introduction by Mary Gordon.
- [London]: Abacus, [1993].
- Wrappers.
- PS3511.I9234 1993

1566. *The Collected Writings of Zelda Fitzgerald.*
- Edited by Matthew J. Bruccoli; Introduction by Mary Gordon.
- Tuscaloosa: University of Alabama Press, [1997].
- Wrappers.
- PS3511.I9234 1997

1567. *Zelda, an Illustrated Life: The Private World of Zelda Fitzgerald*
- Edited by Eleanor Anne Lanahan.
- New York: Harry N. Abrams, 1996.
- Dust jacket.
NOTES: Review copy. Laid in: Publisher's announcement.
- PS3511.I9234 Z33 1996

B. Zelda Fitzgerald Manuscripts

1568. "Scandalabra," [1932?].
- CC: 63 pp.
NOTES: Carbon of TS of the shorter and presumed final version of the "farce-fantasy." A 91-page version was deposited for copyright in October, 1932.
See the published edition of the play (Bloomfield Hill, Mich.: Bruccoli Clark, 1980).
With: Xerox of the deposit copy, [91] leaves.
- PS3511.I9234 S27 1932

1569. "My Trip Abroad," n.d.
- MS: 35 pp.
NOTES: Draft of play.
- PS3511.I9234 M9

1570. [Notes on writing], n.d.
- MS: 2 pp.
- On deposit.

C. Zelda Fitzgerald Correspondence

1571. Postcard to Mrs. A. D. Sayre, Montgomery, Alabama, c.1924; St. Rafael, France.
- 1 card.
NOTES: Picture postcard of Fitzgeralds and nanny in Renault.
- On deposit.

1572. [Christmas card, December 1924].
- Color picture card of Piazza di Spagna, Rome.
NOTES: With holograph message from ZF to her mother.
- On deposit.

1573. ALS from Scottie Fitzgerald, South Strafford, Vermont, to ZF, n.d.
- 2 pp.
NOTES: Scottie Fitzgerald reports news from Camp Ken-Jocketee.
- On deposit.

1574. Postcard from Scottie Fitzgerald, Brussels, to ZF, Autumn 1930.
- 1 p.
- On deposit.

1575. Telegram to FSF, 28 November 1931; Nyon, Switzerland.
- 1 p.
- NOTES: ZF reports she is awaiting FSF's arrival.
- On deposit.

1576. Telegram to Mrs. Harold Ober, Scarsdale, New York, 1 July 1939; Montgomery, Alabama.
- 1 p.
- NOTES: ZF requests Scottie Fitzgerald's address and any information about her. Printed draft of Anne Ober's response on verso reports that Scottie is attending Harvard College Summer School, suggests reaching her there, and apologizes for not knowing more. Penciled date on telegram.
  Published in: *"As Ever, Scott Fitz—."*
- PS3511.I9234 Z486 1939

1577. TLS from Maxwell E. Perkins, New York, to ZF, 26 December 1940.
- 2 pp.
- NOTES: Perkins writes about FSF's death.
- On deposit.

1578. TLS from Maxwell E. Perkins, New York, to ZF, 3 January 1941.
- 2 pp.
- NOTES: Perkins writes about publication of *The Last Tycoon*.
- On deposit.

1579. ALS to Cyril Clemens, 1 February 1941; Montgomery, Alabama.
- 1 p.
- NOTES: ZF thanks Clemens for letter of condolence on the death of FSF. She mentions FSF's great admiration for Mark Twain and his influence on FSF's prose style.
- PS3511.I9234 Z483

1580. [Sermons], between 1940 and 1948.
- 3 items.
- NOTES: Short pieces on religious topics, distributed by ZF in the years after FSF's death.
  First item: "The Lord said, 'Learn of me'" (mimeograph signed).
  Second item: Untitled (mimeograph signed).
  Third item: Untitled. (Photostat of signed mimeograph).
- PS3511.I92324 G6

1581. ALS to Anne Ober, 4 July 1941; Montgomery, Alabama.
- 2 pp.
NOTES: ZF discusses Scottie Fitzgerald.
- On deposit.

1582. ALS to Harold Ober, postmarked 10 March 1945.
- 2 pp.
NOTES: ZF expresses sympathy for Ober's broken leg and discusses FSF.
- On deposit.

1583. ALS to Anne Ober, postmarked 12 August 1946; Asheville, N.C.
- 3 pp. with envelope.
NOTES: ZF expresses gratitude for kindness to Scottie Fitzgerald and herself.
- On deposit.

1584. ALS to Mrs. A. D. Sayre, postmarked 4 March 1948; Asheville, N.C.
- 3 pp.
- On deposit.

1585. AL to FSF, n.d.
- 3 pp. Incomplete.
NOTES: ZF discusses her projected novel about Nijinsky.
- On deposit.

D. Zelda Fitzgerald Artwork

1586. Card: [Lilies], c.1926.
- Gouache on paper (15.7 × 14.4 cm.).
NOTES: Hand-painted Easter card of lilies in shades of blue, gray, and green, with white. Card is inscribed in ink inside: "To wish you a happy Easter Zelda & Scott Fitzgerald."
Card was sent to Gibert Seldes.
- ND237.F45 F5

1587. [Wood serving plate].
- Diameter: 13 ¾".
NOTES: Painted in oils with transportation theme (ship, train, airplane, and various vehicles); unsigned.
- Arlyn Bruccoli Collection: on deposit.

1588. [Magnolias].
- Gouache on brown paper (25" × 6").
NOTES: Unsigned.
- Arlyn Bruccoli Collection: on deposit.

1589. [Print].
- Lithograph or other transfer medium on silver or grey paper (12" × 9 ½") pasted on green paper (17 ½" × 11").
NOTES: In ZF's hand under the print: "Greetings from Scott and Zelda Fitzgerald".
Print depicts a muscular haloed male figure, probably Jesus (as adult), head and torso, arms extended forward; this "Christmas card" has been folded to form a self-envelope.
- Arlyn Bruccoli Collection: on deposit.

1590. [Roses in a bowl].
- Gouache on cream paper (15" × 13 ½").
NOTES: Signed "Zelda Fitzgerald".
- Arlyn Bruccoli Collection: on deposit.

1591. [Dahlias or chrysanthemums in vase].
- Oil on canvas (26" × 12 ½").
NOTES: Unsigned.
- Arlyn Bruccoli Collection: on deposit.

1592. [Dancers].
- Gouache on brown paper (25" × 18 ½").
NOTES: Pair of male and female standing nude figures, locked in embrace.
In lower-left corner: "God Almighty! Zelda Fitzgerald". Just at the right of above inscription "Z22" (or possible "ZZZ" or "222") has been written.
- Arlyn Bruccoli Collection: on deposit.

E. First Book and First Periodical Appearances of Zelda Fitzgerald

1593. *Favorite Recipes of Famous Women.*
- With a Foreword by Florence Stratton.
- New York: Harper, 1925.
NOTES: Bruccoli ZF-B1. "Breakfast," p. 98.
- TX715.S88 1925 641.5

1594. "What Becomes of Our Flappers and Shieks?"
- Illustrated By John Held, Jr.
- *McCall's,* vol. 53, no. 1 (October 1925), pp. 12, 30, 42, 66, 69.
NOTES: Bruccoli C160, ZF-C6. FSF's "Our Young Rich Boys" (pp. 12, 42, 69) and ZF's "What Became of the Flappers?" (pp. 12, 30, 66) issued with joint title.
- AP2.M443 vol. 53, no. 1

1595. "The Changing Beauty of Park Avenue."
- *Harper's Bazaar,* no. 2583 (January 1928), pp. [60]–63.
NOTES: Bruccoli C174, ZF-C8.
- AP2.H376 62nd Year, no. 2583

1596. "Southern Girl."
- Illustration By John La Gatta.
- *College Humor,* vol. 18, no. 3 (October, 1929), pp. 27–28, 94, 96.
NOTES: Bruccoli C198, ZF-C13.
- PN6231.C6 C6

1597. "The Girl with Talent."
- Illustrated by Chris Marie Meeker.
- *College Humor,* 9th Year, no. 76 (April 1930), pp. 50–52, 125–27.
NOTES: Bruccoli C205, ZF-C15.
- PN6231.C6 C6 9th Year, no. 76

1598. "A Millionaire's Girl."
- Illustrated by Henry Raleigh.
- *The Saturday Evening Post,* vol. 202, no. 46 (17 May 1930), pp. 8–9, 118, 121.
NOTES: Bruccoli C208, ZF-C16.
Publication under FSF's name was Harold Ober's error.
- AP2.S2 vol. 202, no. 46

1599. "Miss Ella."
- *Scribner's Magazine,* vol. 90, no. 6 (December 1931), pp. 661–665.
NOTES: Bruccoli ZF-C18.
- AP2.S4 vol. 90, no. 6

1600. "A Couple of Nuts: A Story."
- *Scribner's Magazine,* vol. 92, no. 2 (August 1932), pp. [80]–84.
NOTES: Bruccoli ZF-C20.
- AP2.S4 vol. 92, no. 2

1601. *The Society of Baltimore Independent Artists: Fourth Annual No-Jury Exhibition October 1933*
- Baltimore Museum of Art.
- Baltimore: Fosnot & Williams, 1933.
- Wrappers.
NOTES: Reproduction of "Tiger Lillies," p. 15.
- N515.S6 1933

1602. *Spring Salon 1933 May 2nd to May 20th.*
- American Art Association.
- [New York]: Salons of America, 1933.
- Wrappers.
NOTES: Catalogue of exhibition held at Anderson Galleries.
Reproduction of "Ballet Figurine" by ZF.
- N6512.S175

1603. "'Show Mr. and Mrs. F. to Number—.'"
- *Esquire,* vol. 2, no. 1 (June 1934), pp. 23, 120.
NOTES: Bruccoli C240, ZF-C21.
- AP2.E845 vol. 2, no. 1

1604. "Footnotes on Fitzgerald: Reminiscences by the Author's Secretary."
- Frances Kroll Ring.
- *Esquire,* vol. 52, no. 6 (December 1959), pp. 149–50.
NOTES: Bruccoli F75. Includes letter from ZF to the author.
- AP2.E845 vol. 52, no. 6

1605. "The Far Side of Zelda Fitzgerald."
- *Esquire*, vol. 62, no. 6 (December 1964), pp. 158–59.
NOTES: Includes six paintings by ZF: Self-portrait, accompanied by note from FSF to ZF; 5 paper dolls, accompanied by note from ZF to Ludlow Fowler.
- AP2.E845 vol. 62, no. 6

1606. "Zelda: A Worksheet."
- [Edited by Lane Yorke].
- *Paris Review*, 89 (Fall 1983), pp. [210]–63.
NOTES: Collection of ZF's letters, primarily to FSF.
  Laid in: Letter from Harold Ober Associates to MJB, stating that neither Lane Yorke nor the *Paris Review* had permission to publish the letters.
- AP4.P245 NO. 89

F. Zelda Fitzgerald Documents

1607. *Ben Hur Christmas Eve Dinner: In Honour of Mr. and Mrs. Fred Niblo.*
- Excelsior Hotel [Rome, Italy, 1924].
  [4] pp. Menu. Wrappers.
NOTES: Signed by ZF and other guests.
  In 1924, FSF was in Rome where he revised *The Great Gatsby*. The Fitzgeralds became friendly with the cast and crew of the movie *Ben-Hur*, then being filmed in Rome.
  This copy of the dinner menu belonged to actress Carmel Myers.
- TX941.E9 B3 1924

1608. White Bear Yacht Club [White Bear Lake, Minnesota], n.d.
- 1 sheet.
NOTES: Golf scorecard signed by ZF and Kathryn Ordway.
- GV979.S3 W5 1922

1609. *Paintings by Zelda Fitzgerald; Photographs by Marion Hines, March 29–April 30, 1934.*
- [New York: Cary Ross Gallery], 1934.
- 4-page catalogue.
NOTES: List of ZF's works annotated by FSF.
- ND237.F45 A4 1934

1610. "Mama-Quotes," n.d.
- Scottie Fitzgerald.
- TS (2 pp.) and MS (8 pp.)
NOTES: Notes on conversations with ZF.
- On deposit.

1611. [Reproduction of portrait of ZF], c.1920.
- Gordon Bryant.
- On deposit.

XIV Sheilah Graham Material

Fitzgerald-related Sheilah Graham items including books, correspondence, and periodical appearances.

A. Books by Sheilah Graham

1612. *Gentleman-Crook.*
- London: Rich & Cowan, 1933.
- NOTES: On free front endpaper: "I'm dubious. MJB".
- PS3513.R219 G4 1933

1613. *Beloved Infidel: The Education of a Woman.*
- Sheilah Graham and Gerold Frank.
- New York: Holt, [1958].
- Dust jacket.
- NOTES: Bruccoli B53. Stamp of Research Library, Twentieth Century-Fox. Facsimiles of FSF manuscripts on endpapers; facsimile of FSF reading list included with illustrations; also quotes from previously unpublished notes, letters, wires, and verses.
- PN4874.G67 A3

1614. *Beloved Infidel: The Education of a Woman.*
- Sheilah Graham and Gerold Frank.
- New York: Bantam Books, [1959].
- Wrappers.
- NOTES: Bruccoli B53. Published "November, 1959".
- Pn4874.G67 A3 1959d

1615. *Beloved Infidel: The Education of a Woman.*
- Sheilah Graham and Gerold Frank.
- London: Cassel, [1959].
- Wrappers: "PROOF ONLY".
- NOTES: Bruccoli B53.
- PN4874.G67 A3 1959

1616. *Beloved Infidel: The Education of a Woman.*
- Sheilah Graham and Gerold Frank.
- London: Book Club, 1959.
- Dust jacket.
- NOTES: Bruccoli B53. "Second Edition, August 1959."
- PN4874.G67 A3 1959e

1617. *Beloved Infidel: The Education of a Woman.*
- Sheilah Graham and Gerold Frank.
- London: Transworld, [1961].

- Wrappers.

NOTES: Bruccoli B53. Corgi Books, #987.
- PN4874.G67 A3 1959c

1618. *The Rest of the Story.*
- New York: Coward-McCann, [1964].
- Dust jacket.

NOTES: Review copy.
- PN4874.G67 A32

1619. *The Rest of the Story.*
- New York: Bantam, [1965].
- Wrappers.

NOTES: "Bantam edition published June 1965".
- PN4874.G67 A32 1965

1620. *College of One.*
- TS: 2 pp.

NOTES: Signed by Graham.
- On deposit.

1621. *College of One.*
- New York: Viking Press, [1967].
- Dust jacket.

NOTES: Bruccoli B71. Review copy.
  Laid in: Review slip and newspaper advertisement for the book.
- PS3511.I9 Z64

1622. *College of One.*
- London: Weidenfeld and Nicolson, 1967.
- Dust jacket.

NOTES: Bruccoli B71.
- PS3511.I9 Z64 1967b

1623. *College of One.*
- New York: Bantam, 1968.
- Wrappers.

NOTES: Bruccoli B71.
- PS3511.I9 Z64 1968

1624. *College of One.*
- Harmondsworth: Penguin, 1969.
- Wrappers.

NOTES: Bruccoli B71.
- PS3511.I9 Z64 1969

1625. *Confessions of a Hollywood Columnist.*
- Toronto; New York: Bantam, [1970], Q5331.

- Wrappers.

NOTES: A Bantam Book.
- PN4874.G67 A315 1970

1626. *The Garden of Allah.*
- Sheilah Graham.
- New York: Crown Publishers, [1970].
- Dust jacket.

NOTES: Bruccoli B83. Review copy. Includes previously unpublished FSF verse.
- TX941.G3 G7 1970

1627. *A State of Heat.*
- New York: Grosset & Dunlap, [1972].
- Dust jacket.

NOTES: Review copy.
- PN4874.G67 A33

1628. *How to Marry Super Rich: Or, Love, Money, and the Morning After.*
- New York: Grosset & Dunlap, [1974].
- CT3203.G69

1629. *The Real F. Scott Fitzgerald Thirty-Five Years Later.*
- New York: Warner Books, [1976].
- Dust jacket.

NOTES: Bruccoli B100.
- PS3511.I9 Z612 1976

1630. *The Real F. Scott Fitzgerald Thirty-Five Years Later.*
- London: W. H. Allen, 1986.
- Dust jacket.

NOTES: Bruccoli B100.
- PS3511.I9 Z642 1986

1631. *The Late Lily Shiel.*
- New York: Grosset & Dunlap, 1978.
- Dust jacket.
- PS3513.R219 L3 1978

1632. *The Late Lily Shiel.*
- London: Allen, [1979].
- Dust jacket.
- PS3513.R219 L3 1979

1633. *My Hollywood: A Celebration and a Lament.*
- London: Michael Joseph, 1984.
- Wrappers.

NOTES: "UNCORRECTED PROOF".
- PN4874.G67 A318

1634. *My Hollywood: A Celebration and a Lament.*
- London: Michael Joseph, 1984.
- Dust jacket.
- PN4874.G67 A318

1635. [Display card for *My Hollywood* by Sheilah Graham].
- [n.p., 1984].
- 1 item.
NOTES: Promotional card for book published by Michael Joseph.
- On deposit.

1636. *Hollywood Revisited: A Fiftieth Anniversary Celebration.*
- New York: St. Martin's Press, [1985].
NOTES: Originally published in a different version under the title of *My Hollywood* (1984).
- PN4874.G67 A317 1985

B. Sheilah Graham Correspondence

1637. Telegram from Sheilah Graham, Santa Monica, California, to Harold Ober, June, n.d.
- 1 p.
NOTES: Graham discusses FSF's health.
- On deposit.

1638. ALS from Sheilah Graham to F. Scott Fitzgerald, New York City, [January 1939].
- 4 pp. on Weylan Hotel stationery.
- On deposit.

1639. TLS from Sheilah Graham, Hollywood, California, to [Cecilia Delihant] Taylor, 9 January 1941.
- 2 pp.
NOTES: Graham describes the events surrounding FSF's death.
  Cecilia ("Ceci") Delihant Taylor was FSF's cousin.
  Published in: *F. Scott Fitzgerald Centenary Exhibition Catalogue.*
- PS3513.R219 Z49 1941

1640. TLSS from Matthew J. Bruccoli, Columbia, S.C., to Sheilah Graham, 1975–81.
- 8 letters: 11 September 1975 (1 p.), 4 January 1976 (1 p.), 26 March 1976 (1 p.), 4 November 1976 (2 pp.), 9 August 1977 (1 p.), 16 January 1980 (1 p.), 10 September 1980 (1 p.), and 24 March 1981 (1 p.).
NOTES: All letters have Graham's holograph replies to MJB's questions regarding FSF. 4 January 1976, letter has Graham's reply on bottom and margin refuting Charles Warren's claim that Hemingway stayed with FSF in Malibu.
- On deposit.

1641. TLS from Sheilah Graham, London, to Matthew J. Bruccoli, 8 May 1975.
- 1 p.
NOTES: Graham answers questions about *The Last Tycoon*.
- On deposit.

1642. TLS from Sheilah Graham, London, to Matthew J. Bruccoli, 13 June 1975.
- 2 pp.
NOTES: Graham writes about her book in progress.
- On deposit.

1643. TLS from Sheilah Graham, London, to Matthew J. Bruccoli, 15 August 1975.
- 1 p.
NOTES: Graham answers questions about *The Last Tycoon*.
- On deposit.

1644. TLS from Sheilah Graham, London, to Matthew J. Bruccoli, 3 September 1975.
- 1 p.
NOTES: Graham answers questions about FSF.
- On deposit.

1645. TLS from Sheilah Graham, Palm Beach, Florida, to Matthew J. Bruccoli, 28 September 1977.
- 1 p.
- On deposit.

1646. TLS from Sheilah Graham, Palm Beach, Florida, to Matthew J. Bruccoli, 17 October 1977.
- 1 p.
NOTES: Graham writes about *The New York Times* review of *The Last of the Novelists*.
- On deposit.

1647. TLS from Sheilah Graham, Palm Beach, Florida, to Matthew J. Bruccoli, 13 January 1979.
- 1 p.
NOTES: Graham writes about FSF's eating habits.
- On deposit.

C. Fitzgerald-Related Periodical Appearances of Sheilah Graham

1648. "Looking Back on Fitzgerald."
- Andrew Turnbull, Arthur Mizener and Sheilah Graham.
- *Famous Writers Magazine* 1 (Winter 1963), pp. 16–18, 44–51
- PS1.F156 no. 1

1649. "The Education of Lily Shiel."
- *[London] Sunday Times Weekly Review* (30 January 1966), pp. 41–42.
NOTES: Excerpts from *College of One*.
- AP4.S875

1650. "What 'College of One' Taught Me."
- *[London] Sunday Times Weekly Review* (6 February 1966), pp. 42–43.
NOTES: Excerpts from *College of One*.
- AP4.S875

1651. "The Room Where Scott Died."
- *The New York Times Magazine* (26 July 1987), pp. 20–21.
- AP2.N48

XV. Blurbs by F. Scott Fitzgerald

1652. *Babel.*
- John Cournos.
- New York: Boni and Liveright, c. 1922.
- Dust jacket.

    NOTES: Bruccoli G2. On lower cover of dust jacket: "'Babel' is a beautifully written story. . . . The author's graphic atmospheres in London and Paris and New York are flawless. . . . Its love affair is the love affair of hundreds of thousands of people, one of the most real and human love episodes in recent fiction."
- PS3505.O8855 B3 1922

1653. *Lazy Laughter.*
- Woodward Boyd.
- New York: Charles Scribner's Sons, 1923.
- Dust jacket.

    NOTES: On back of dust jacket: "Thoroughly alive. Put it upon a shelf along with 'Babbitt' and 'The Bright Shawl' and watch and pray for more entertainment." Excerpt from FSF's review: "A Rugged Novel," *The Literary Review of the New York Evening Post* (28 October 1922).
- On deposit.

1654. *Lily-Iron.*
- Mary Biggs.
- New York: R. M. McBride & Company, 1927.
- Dust jacket.

    NOTES: Bruccoli G3. On front of dust jacket: "I think there is an extraordinary temperament behind this novel—a new sort of Byronesian gestering in those bleak American voids to which O'Neill has been so sensitive. . . . The *pazienza* of the heroine's story is entirely feminine, and this is in fine contrast to the strong moments toward the end of the book which sound as if they had been written by a man. An exceeding interesting novel."
- PS3503.I27 L5 1927

1655. *Mad Anthony Wayne*
- Thomas Boyd.
- New York: Charles Scribner's Sons, 1929.
- Dust jacket.

    NOTES: On back of dust jacket: "The whole book is written in the light of one sharp emotion, and hence it is as a work of art rather than as a textbook for patrioteer or pacifist that the book is arresting. . . . To my mind this is not only the best combatant story of the Great War, but

also the best war book since 'The Red Badge of Courage.'" From FSF's review in the *New York Evening Post* (26 May 1923).
- E207.W35 B78

1656. *Cast Down the Laurel.*
- Arnold Gingrich.
- New York: Alfred A. Knopf, 1935.
NOTES: Bruccoli G4. On back of dust jacket: "Beautifully written, startling in form, and promising other equally good things to come. It pleases me beyond measure that Arnold Gingrich has brought off this book, which has the same scope and appeal of his editorial ventures."
- PS3513.I723 C38 1935

1657. *What Makes Sammy Run?*
- Budd Schulberg.
- New York: Random House, 1941.
NOTES: Bruccoli G6. "PROOF COPY".
Letter from FSF to Bennett Cerf dated 13 December 1940 endorsing novel printed on back of dust jacket:
"I told Budd I was going to write you a word about his novel with permission to quote if you wanted. I read it through in one night. It is a grand book, utterly fearless and with a great deal of beauty side by side with the most bitter satire. Such things *are* in Hollywood—and Budd reports them with fine detachment. Except for its freshness and the inevitable challenge of a new and strong personality it doesn't read like a first novel at all.
It is full of excellent little vignettes—the 'extra girl' or whatever she is and her attitude on love, and the diverse yet identical attitude of the two principal women on Sammy. Especially toward the end it gets the feeling of Hollywood with extraordinary vividness. Altogether I congratulate you on publishing this fine book and I hope it has all the success it deserves."
- PS3537.C7114 W45

1658. *What Makes Sammy Run?*
- Budd Schulberg.
- New York: Random House, 1941.
- Dust jacket.
NOTES: Bruccoli G6. On copyright page: "FIRST PRINTING".
- PS3537.C7114 W6 1941

1659. *What Makes Sammy Run?*
- Budd Schulberg.
- Garden City, NY: Sun Dial Press, [1943].
- Dust jacket.
NOTES: Bruccoli G6. No FSF blurb on jacket.
- PS3537.C7114 W6 1943

1660. *What Makes Sammy Run?*
- Budd Schulberg.
- New York: Penguin Books, 1978.
- Wrappers.
NOTES: Bruccoli G6. FSF blurb on back cover. Inscribed to MJB, 20 June 1978.
- PS3537.C7114 W6 1978

1661. *The Day of the Locust.*
- Nathanael West.
  New York: New Directions, 1950.
- Dust jacket.
NOTES: Bruccoli G7. The New Classics #29.
  On back of dust jacket: "The book, though it puts Gorki's 'The Lower Depths' in the class with 'The Tale of Benjamin Bunny,' certainly has scenes of extraordinary power—if that phrase is still in use. Especially I was impressed by the pathological crowd at the premiere, the character and handling of the aspirant actress and the uncanny almost medieval feeling of some of his Hollywood background set off by those vividly drawn grotesques."
- PS3545.E8334 D3 1950

Supplement

Material—mainly placed on deposit—acquired for the Bruccoli Collection after this catalogue was in production. Items arranged chronologically.

Correspondence

1662. ALS from Scottie Fitzgerald, Wilmington, Delaware, to Mrs. Anthony Sayre, 2 January 1928.
- 4 pp. with envelope.
- On deposit.

1663. ALS from FSF, Baltimore, to Leslie McFarlane, postmarked 26 February 1936.
- 2 pp. with envelope.

NOTES: FSF discusses *Tender Is the Night* and "The Crack-Up" (*Esquire*, February 1936).
   Leslie McFarlane wrote the Hardy Boys books under the pseudonym Franklin W. Dixon.
- On deposit.

1664. ALS from Scottie Fitzgerald to FSF, c. 1935.
- 4 pp.

NOTES: SF writes about school.
- On deposit.

1665. TLS from Edgar A. Poe, Baltimore, to Isabel Owens, 17 September 1936.
- 1 p.

NOTES: Lawyer Poe writes to FSF's secretary about the estate of Mollie Fitzgerald.
- On deposit.

1666. CC letter from FSF, Asheville, N.C., to the Internal Revenue Service, 4 December 1936.
- 1 p.

NOTES: With 3 TLS from IRS to FSF.
- On deposit.

1667. CC letter from Harold Ober, New York City, to ZF, 4 May 1939.
- 1 p.

NOTES: Ober writes about FSF's trip to New York in late April 1939.
- On deposit.

1668. Signed CC letter from John Biggs, Wilmington, to Paul Brooks, 21 September 1949.
- 2 pp.

NOTES: Biggs writes about a projected collection of FSF stories.
• On deposit.

1669. TL from Barry Brannen to John Biggs, 25 April 1949.
• 3 pp.
NOTES: Lawyer Brannen writes about closing FSF estate.
• On deposit.

1670. CC letter from John Biggs, Wilmington, to Charles Scribner III, 22 August 1949.
• 2 pp.
NOTES: Biggs writes about FSF estate.
• On deposit.

1671. TLS from Malcolm Cowley, Sherman, Connecticut, to Harold Ober, 28 April 1951.
• 1 p.
NOTES: Cowley discusses projected recording about FSF; mentions Cowley's edition of *Tender Is the Night:* "Roughly speaking, every proper name is misspelled."
• On deposit.

1672. TLS from Ring Lardner, Jr., New York City, to Scottie Fitzgerald, 3 May 1955.
• 1 p.
NOTES: Lardner responds to Scottie Fitzgerald's favorable review of *The Ecstacy of Owen Muir* (1954) in *The New Republic*.
• On deposit.

1673. ALS from Shane Leslie, London, to MJB, 26 November 1958.
• 2 pp.
NOTES: Leslie writes about FSF.
• On deposit.

1674. ALS from Gerald Murphy, New York City, to Scottie Fitzgerald, 1 June 1945.
• 2 pp.
NOTES: Murphy writes about FSF and ZF.
• On deposit.

1675. ALS from Gerald Murphy, Palisades, N.Y., to MJB, 15 February 1960.
• 2 pp.
NOTES: Murphy writes about FSF and Walker Ellis.
• On deposit.

1676. ALS from Shane Leslie, London, to MJB, 28 February 1963.
• 2 pp.
NOTES: Leslie writes about FSF. With: MS page of Leslie's notes on FSF.
• On deposit.

1677. ALSS from Dorothy Richardson (Mrs. Fred Ritz), Miamisburg, Ohio, to MJB, 1963–1964.
- 3 letters (8 pp.).
NOTES: Richardson, FSF's nurse in Asheville, writes about him and books he gave her.
- On deposit.

1678. Revised CC letter from Rosalind Sayre Smith to W. W. Davidson, 19 January 1966.
- 16 pp.
NOTES: Smith writes about ZF's childhood.
- On deposit.

1679. TLS from Scottie Fitzgerald, Washington, D.C., to MJB, 6 October 1969.
- 1 p.
NOTES: SF writes about ZF biographer Nancy Milford.
- On deposit.

1680. ALS from Lois Moran, Sedona, Arizona, to MJB, 20 January 1971.
- 2 pp.
NOTES: Moran writes about FSF.
- On deposit.

1681. Telegram from Donald Ogden Stewart, London, to MJB, [1974].
- 1 p.
NOTES: Stewart regrets that illness prevents him from attending Paris celebration of FSF and Hemingway.
- On deposit.

1682. TLS from Malcolm Cowley, Sherman, Connecticut, to MJB, 28 March 1978.
- 1 p.
NOTES: Cowley's statement on *The Notebooks of F. Scott Fitzgerald* (1978).
- On deposit.

1683. TLS from Malcolm Cowley, Sherman, Connecticut, to Scottie Fitzgerald, 18 October 1982.
- 1 p.
NOTES: Cowley writes about FSF and "The Romance of Money."
- On deposit.

1684. TLS from Scottie Fitzgerald to MJB, n.d.
- 2 pp.
NOTES: Fitzgerald writes about FSF revival and her responsibilities as literary executrix.
- On deposit.

Manuscripts and Documents

1685. [Handwriting analysis for FSF], c. 1939.
- Pengraph System of Advanced Graphology.
NOTES: Stamped #3603.
- On deposit.

1686. "The Turn of the Tables," c. 1940.
- Scottie Fitzgerald.
- RTS (2 pp.).
NOTES: Chapter I of unfinished novel.
- On deposit.

1687. [Introduction], 1979.
- Malcolm Cowley.
- Thermofax TS (3 pp.) with revisions in Cowley's hand.
NOTES: Introduction for *Dictionary of Literary Biography, Vol. 4: American Writers in Paris, 1920–1939* (1980).
    With: TLS (1 p.) from Malcolm Cowley, Sherman, Connecticut, to MJB (6 February 1979).
- On deposit.

1688. "Clothes for a Summer Hotel" (A Ghost Play in 4 Scenes), 1979.
- Tennessee Williams
- Xerox of TS: 96 pp.
NOTES: With: Advertising card for 1980 Broadway production, directed by José Quintero and starring Kenneth Haigh and Geraldine Page, on deposit.
    With: *Playbill* (March 1980), PN 2000.P538.
    Based on FSF and ZF.
- PS3545.I5365 C5 1979

1689. [Unsigned recollection of FSF], n.d.
- Laura Hearne.
- MS: 1 p.
- On deposit.

Books

1690. *This Side of Paradise.*
- New York: Charles Scribner's Sons, 1920.
- Dust jacket.
NOTES: Bruccoli A5.1.g. First edition, seventh printing.
    Inscribed by FSF to Shane Leslie. Re-insribed by Leslie to Margaret Turnbull.
    ALS from FSF to Leslie dated 16 November 1920 pasted in; letter published in *The Letters of F. Scott Fitzgerald.*

Laid in: ALS about FSF and
    Father Fay from Leslie to Mrs.
    Turnbull dated 21 July 1958.
• On deposit.

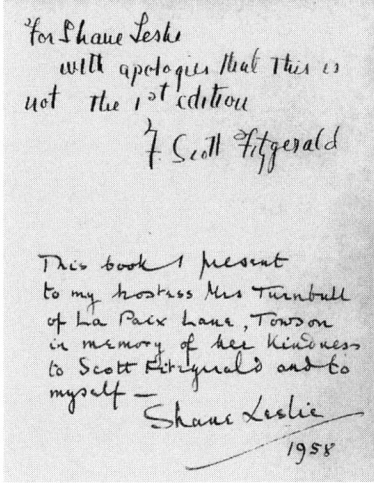

1691. *The Pat Hobby Stories.*
• With an Introduction by Arnold Gingrich.
• New York: Charles Scribner's Sons, [1962].
• Dust jacket.
NOTES: Bruccoli A23.1.b. First edition, second printing.
• On deposit.

1692. *Conversations with F. Scott Fitzgerald.*
• Edited by Matthew J. Bruccoli and Judith S. Baughman.
• Dust jacket.
• Jackson: University Press of Mississippi, 2004.
NOTES: With: Second copy in wrappers.
• PS3511.I9 Z463 2004

1693. *The Sons of Maxwell Perkins: Letters of F. Scott Fitzgerald, Ernest Hemingway, Thomas Wolfe, and their Editor.*
• Edited by Matthew J. Bruccoli and Judith S. Baughman.
• Columbia: University of South Carolina Press, 2004.
NOTES: Proof copy.
• On deposit.

Periodicals

1694. *Smart Set,* vol. 67, no. 24 (April 1922).
• Cover illustrated by "A.G.L."
NOTES: FSF wrote to Maxwell Perkins on 11 April 1922 about the cover illustration as a suggestion for the jacket art for *Tales of the Jazz Age.*
• AP2.S6

1695. "The Third Casket."
- Illustrated by Charles D. Mitchell.
- *The Saturday Evening Post,* vol. 196, no. 48 (31 May 1924), pp. 8–9, 78.

NOTES: Bruccoli C144.
- AP2 .S2 vol. 196, no. 48.

1696. "'The Sensible Thing.'"
- Illustrated by Benton Clark.
- *Liberty,* vol. 1 (5 July 1924), pp. 10–14.

NOTES: Bruccoli C149. Gift of Judith S. Baughman and Park Bucker.
- On deposit.

1697. "The Baby Party."
- Illustrated by Rose O'Neill.
- *Hearst's International,* vol. 47 (February 1925) pp. 32–37.

NOTES: Bruccoli C153.
- On deposit.

1698. [Advertising card, 1935].
- 1 sheet.

NOTES: "The Intimate Strangers by F. Scott Fitzgerald" on reproduction of magazine cover for *McCall's* (June 1935).
- On deposit.

1699. "Image on the Heart."
- Illustrated by Matt Clark.
- *McCall's,* vol. 63, no. 7 (April 1936), pp. 7–9, 52, 54, 57–58, 62.

NOTES: Bruccoli C264. Issue includes advertisement with photograph of Samuel Barlow's Eze villa, a model for the Villa America in *Tender Is the Night.*
- AP2 .M443 vol. 63, no. 7

Memorabilia

1700. [Mollie McQuillan Fitzgerald's silver tea service], c. 1900.
- 6 pieces and 1 tray.

NOTES: Monogrammed "McQ". Gift of Courtney Sprague Vaughan.
- On deposit.

1701. [School medals], 1912.
- 2 medals from Newman School.

NOTES: Won by FSF; engraved on versos: "Field Day" and "Elocution".
- On deposit.

1702. [Silver locket], c. 1918.
- Engraved "ZΣ".

NOTES: Fraternity locket from the University of Alabama given to Zelda Sayre by her collegiate admirers, in which she subsequently inserted a photograph of FSF.
- On deposit.

INDEX

This index is keyed to item numbers, not page numbers. Publishers are listed by last name: Burt, A. L.; not A. L. Burt.

Aaron, Daniel, 799
Abacus (publisher), 264, 412, 658, 1565
Abrams, Harry N. (publisher), 1567
Abramson, Ben, 1085, 1173–74
"Absolution," 914
Absolution May Day Babylon Revisited, 634
Aces: A Collection of Short Stories (Canfield et al.), 687
Act of Darkness (Bishop), 1360
Adachi, Fumi, 639
Adams, Alice, 1068
Adams, Franklin P., 708
Adams, Samuel Hopkins, 1334
"Additional Fitzgerald Lyric for 'It Is Art,' An," 782
Ade, George, 573
"Adjuster, The," 923
"Adolescent Marriage, The," 928
"Advice to a Young Writer," 1032
After the Good Gay Times (Buttitta), 848–49
"Afternoon of an Author," 997
Afternoon of an Author, 440–48
Against the Current (Ring), 828
Aiken, Conrad, 1395
Alabama Journal, 1543
Alberts, Robert C., 762
"Alcoholic Case, An," 1001
Alderman Library, University of Virginia, 1041
All the Sad Young Men, 293–303, 670, 1311
Allen, Howard, 1291
Allen, W. H. (publisher), 1630, 1632
Allenberg, Bert, 1322
America Awakes (Farrington), 778
American Art Association, 1602
American Booksellers Association, 13
American Cavalcade (magazine), 1010
American Credo, The (Nathan & Mencken), 683
American Magazine, 909, 991
American Mercury (publisher), 692
American Mercury (magazine), 692, 914, 969
Amorous, Isabelle, 1141
Amorous, Martin, 1142–43
"—and a few missing words would destroy so much," 1050

Anderson Galleries, 1602
Anderson, George Parker, 836
Anderson, Sherwood, 718
Années Vingt, Les, 739
Anthony, Edward, 844
"Ants at Princeton, The," 994
Antupit, Samuel N. (printer), 1044–45
Aoyama (publisher), 53
Appleton-Century-Crofts (publisher), 760
Appointment in Samarra (O'Hara), 1387
Apprentice Fiction of F. Scott Fitzgerald, The (ed. Kuehl), 470–71
Archer, Jeffrey, 1067
Arcturus Books Edition, 1549, 1551
Argosy (magazine), 1003
Argus Books, 1085, 1173–74
Arion Press, 254
Arlyn Bruccoli Collection, 159, 1587–92
Armchair Esquire, The (ed. Gingrich & Hills), 735–36
Art of F. Scott Fitzgerald, The (Perosa), 753
As Ever, Scott Fitz— (ed. Bruccoli), 486–92, 1576
Ash-Wednesday (Eliot), 1343
Associates of the University of Virginia Library (publisher), 806
"At the Field Club," 866
"At Your Age," 695
Atkinson, Jennifer McCabe, 486–91
Atsumi, Akio, 606
Atwood, Margaret, 1067
Aubier-Flammarion (publisher), 634
Auster, Paul, 1067
Austin, Alex, 725, 728, 732
"Author's Apology, The," 13, 1049
Author's Apology, The, 1051
"Author's House," 996
"Author's Mother, An," 998
Authors at Work (Taylor), 734
"Autopsy and a Prescription, An" (Leighton), 1379
Awa, Yasutaka, 607
"Awful Optic, The," 869

Babbit (Lewis), 1653
Babel (Cournos), 1652
"Babes in the Woods," 882, 889
"Baby Party, The," 1697
Baby Party & Gretchen's Forty Winks, The, 604

Baby Party and Other Stories, The, 663–64, 676
"Babylon Revisited," 696, 763–64, 777, 955, 1080, 1227, 1477–78
Babylon Revisited, 591, 661, 665
Babylon Revisited and Other Stories, 592, 595–603, 639
Babylon Revisited and Winter Dreams, 586
Babylon Revisited: The Screenplay, 567, 1227
Balcon, Michael, 176
Baldwin, Charles C., 125, 158, 838, 1155
"Ballet Figurine" (ZF), 1602
"'Ballet Shoes': A Movie Synopsis," 797
Ballinger, H. R., 950
Baltimore Museum of Art, 1601
Baker, Carlos, 765
Baker Co., Walter H. (publisher), 304
Baker's Manuscript Readings, 304
Bantam Books (publisher), 120, 186–90, 233–35, 328–29, 335–38, 404, 469, 1485, 1614, 1619, 1623, 1625
Bantam Classic Books, 120
Bantam Giant, 328–29
Barker, Arthur (publisher), 720
Barlow, Samuel, 1699
Barr, Ingle, 1357
Barret, Edwin, 173
Barton, George, 1359
"Basil and Cleopatra," 944
Basil and Josephine Stories, The (ed. Bryer & Kuehl), 493–97, 636
Baugh, Hansell, 694
Baughman, Judith S., 568–69, 570–72, 574, 680–81, 831–32, 1692–93, 1696
Bausch, Richard, 1067
Bausch, Robert, 1067
BCA (publisher), 666
Beach, Sylvia, 740–41, 778
Beaudine, William, 1491
Beautiful and Damned, The, 83–122, 561, 590, 630, 640, 661, 666–67, 670, 797, 906, 1150, 1152, 1301, 1303, 1460–62
Beautiful and Damned and Two Short Stories, The, 590
Beautiful and Damned: The Manuscript, The, 561
"Beautiful Lady without Mercy, The," 1146
Beer, Thomas, 1335
Before Gatsby: The First Twenty-Six Stories (ed. Bruccoli), 680–81
Before The Great Gatsby There Was Trimalchio, 1071
Behaviorism (Watson), 1392
Behrman, S. N., 757
Bell Haven Eight, The (Barton), 1359
Beloved Infidel (Graham & Frank), 1613–17
Beloved Infidel (movie), 1479–80
Ben-Hur (movie), 1607
Ben Hur Christmas Eve Dinner, 1607
Bennett, Belle, 1487, 1489

Bennett, Jeanne, 1085
Bennett, Robert, 1220, 1224–25
Benson, E. F., 880
Benson, Leslie L., 899, 906
Berg, A. Scott, 813, 828
Berg-Allenberg Agency, 1322
Berg, Phil, 1322
Berger, Thomas, 1067
"Bernice Bobs Her Hair," 897
Bernice Bobs Her Hair and Other Stories, 616–19
Best American Love Stories of the Year, The (ed. Widdemer), 700
Best Short Stories of 1922 (ed. O'Brien), 686
Best Short Stories of 1931 (ed. O'Brien), 696
Best Short Stories of 1931 II: American, 697
Best Short Stories of 1933 (ed. O'Brien), 701
Best Short Stories of 1940 (ed. O'Brien), 707
Between Friends (Cabell), 746
"Between Three and Four," 959
Bibliothéque Benjamin Franklin, 779
Bibliothèque Publique d'Information, 800
Big Ben Books, 709
Big Wave (publisher), 391
Biggs, John, 7, 27, 886, 1144–45, 1149, 1190, 1247, 1249–51, 1271, 1280, 1282, 1323, 1324, 1668–70
Biggs, Mary, 1654
Birmingham, Frederic A., 719–20
Bishop, John Peale, 416, 1053, 1147, 1360
Bits of Paradise (ed. Smith & Bruccoli), 500–510
Blair, Sydney, 1067
Bliven, Bruce, 704
Bloomsbury Classics, 277
Blystone, John G., 1495
Bodley Head (publisher), 229, 446–47, 463–64, 500–501, 590, 745, 755, 771
Bodley Head Scott Fitzgerald, The, 590
Bodley Head Series, The, 229
"Bohemia," 867
Bohmfalk, J. F., 7
"Boil Some Water—Lots of It," 1020
Bombshell, The (movie), 1096
Boni & Liveright (publisher), 690, 1334, 1652
Book Club (publisher), 1616
Book Club Associates (publisher), 243
Bookman, The (magazine), 929
"Book of One's Own, A," 1008
Book of Princeton Verse 1916, A (ed. Noyes), 1386
Book of Princeton Verse II, 1919, A (ed. Van Dyke et al.), 682
Book-of-the-Month Club (publisher), 405, 414, 655–56, 660, 1552
Book Society, The, 582
Book Society of Canada (publisher), 475
Book Society Searchlight Caption Title, 475
Booth, A. L., 3
Boots Booklovers Library, 421
Borrowed Time (ed. Ross), 584

Bourjailly, Vance, 772, 1067
Bowers, Fredson, 259, 286
"Bowl, The," 721
Bowman, Brooks, 791
"Boy Who Killed His Mother, The," 749, 1030
Boyd, Ernest, 1362
Boyd, James, 1336
Boyd, Thomas, 1242, 1337, 1361, 1655
Boyd, Woodward, 1653
Brackett, Ward, 1028
Bradbury, Ray, 347
Brannen, Barry, 1251, 1669
Braun, Otto, 791, 1154, 1363
"Breakfast" (ZF), 1593
Breen, Joseph, 1134
Brenon, Herbert, 1464–65
Brentano's (publisher), 1388
Bright Shawl, The (Hergesheimer), 1653
Brinson, Marjorie Sayre, 1219
"Broadcast We Almost Heard Last September, The," 1025
Brodkey, Harold, 595
Brooke, Rupert, 1397–98
Brooks, Cleanth, 580
Brooks, Paul, 1668
Brooks, Van Wyck, 161, 779, 1158, 1289, 1338, 1364
Brooks, Mrs. Van Wyck, 161
Broun, Heywood, 1365
Brown, Arthur William, 895, 925
Brown, John Mason, 730
Brown, Leonard, 227
Browne, F. W. Stella, 1363
Bruccoli, Arlyn, 159, 830, 1066, 1069, 1072, 1535, 1587–92
Bruccoli Clark (publisher), 498, 511–16, 529–33, 535–37, 541, 550–56, 779, 805, 1058, 1560, 1568
Bruccoli Clark Layman (publisher), 834–836, 1070
Bruccoli, Mary, 502
Bruccoli, Matthew J. (MJB), 166, 168, 750–51, 830, 1055, 1066, 1069, 1072, 1291, 1359, 1365, 1384, note preceding 1395, 1440, 1535, 1541; annotated, corrected, or initialed by, 55–56, 148, 160, 169, 209, 231, 259–60, 262, 264–65, 267–70, 280–81, 286, 317, 370, 408–10, 482, 498, 536, 590, 597, 662, 753–54, 765, 802, 803, 809, 818–19, 822–23, 832, 1047, 1049–50, 1544, 1612; correspondence, 1, 68, 104, 148, 153, 161, 254, 276, 289, 325, 347, 361, 416, 420, 449, 460, 464, 486, 493, 498–99, 511, 579, 693, 737, 795, 1044, 1135, 1258–61, 1264–66, 1269–70, 1272–73, 1275–78, 1283, 1287–88, 1290, 1437, 1640–47, 1673, 1675–76, 1677, 1679–82, 1684, 1687; edited or compiled by, 4, 259–60, 286, 292, 352, 406–13, 476–79, 486–91, 500–510, 517–28, 529–33, 535–56, 559, 560, 562–66, 568–72, 574, 651–59, 680–81, 766–67, 769, 772, 784–87, 791, 793–94, 797, 807, 814–15, 834, 836, 1331, 1409, 1548–52, 1561–66, 1692–93; inscriptions to, 92, 265, 266, 289, 299, 344, 347, 377, 472, 501, 534, 552–53, 556, 634, 772, 779, 804, 808, 1336, 1660; introductions, prefaces, afterwords, and notes by, 4, 158, 262, 264, 266–70, 282, 284–85, 292, 409–12, 473, 498, 513–28, 560, 562–67, 651–59, 661, 1554–59; written by, 751–52, 801–3, 809–12, 817–19, 820–25, 831–32, 1037, 1054, 1056–57, 1059, 1063. *See also* Fitzgerald, Scottie: Bruccoli, Matthew J. and
Bruccoli, Matthew J. (publisher), 559, 1052, 1056
Bryant, Gordon, 1228–29, 1611
Bryer, Jackson R., 476–85, 493–97
Buck, Gene, 24, 150, 814
Bucker, Park, 1331, 1696
Burford, Bryon, 473
Burgess, Anthony, 271
Burlingame, Roger, 711, 782
Burr Printing House, 8
Burt, A. L. (publisher), 26, 94–95, 710
Burt, Maxwell Struthers, 682
Busch, Frederick, 1067, 1068, 1069
Bush, Ken, 280–81
Butler, Samuel, 1366
Buttitta, Anthony, 373, 848–49

Cabell, James Branch, 694, 746, 1339–41
Cabell, Margaret Freeman, 746
Caillet, Louis E., 1367
Caldi, D., 637
Calhoun, Donald, 1458
Calisher, Hortense, 1068
Callaghan, Morley, 747
Calmer, Carl, 1167
Cambridge University Press, 259–62, 280–81, 286–87, 406–8, 411–13
"Camel's Back, The," 685, 895
"Cameo Frame, The," 885
Camp Zachary Taylor, 1058, 1297
Canfield, Dorothy, 687
Cape (publisher), 697, 1347, 1374, 1968
Cape and Smith (publisher), 1371
Caplan, Thomas, 1068
"Captured Shadow, The," 941
Cardinal (publisher), 825
Carroll & Graf Publishers, 567, 811, 824, 834, 1227
Carter, John Franklin, 815
Cary Ross Gallery, 1609
Cassell (publisher), 484, 764, 1615
Cast Down the Laurel (Gingrich), 1656
Cast of Thousands (Loos), 798
Castlenau, M.-P., 634
Castigliano, Luigi, 244

Catalogue of Princeton University, 1502
Cather, Willa, 573
Caves Books (publisher), 225
"Cedric the Stoker," 886
Celestial Eyes—from Metamorphosis to Masterpiece (Scribner), 1061
"Celt and the World, The," 883
Celt and the World, The (Leslie), 883
Centre National d'Art et de Culture Georges Pompidou, 800
Century Magazine, The, 940
Cerf, Bennett, 782, 1657
Chambers, C. E., 916
Chancellor Press, 667
"Change of Class, A," 960
"Changing Beauty of Park Avenue, The" (FSF & ZF), 936, 1595
Chantrell, T., 252
Chapman, George, 1224
Chapman, Frederick, 932
Charles E. Merrill Profiles, 772
Charles Scribner's Sons. *See* Scribners
Charlie (Hecht), 843
Chatto & Windus (publisher), 172–75, 324–26
Chemidlin, August N., 1367
Chesterton, G. K., 37
Cheuse, Alan, 1068
Chiba, Yoshiya, 642
Chicago Daily Tribune (Paris Edition), 781
Chicago Herald and Examiner, 178, 1004
Children of the American Revolution, 1292
Chivers Press, 283
Chorus Girl's Romance, The (movie), 1452
Choy Man Yung, 279
Christie's, 464
Church Co., John (publisher), 3, 5, 7
Cinematic Vision of F. Scott Fitzgerald, The (Dixon), 829
"City Dusk," 887
Clark, Benton, 1696
Clark, C. E. Frazer, Jr. 515–16, 766, 769, 779, 784, 791, 793–94
Clark, M. S. (publisher), 1050
Clark, Matt, 1699
Clark, Robert D., 1148
Class of 1917 Directory, 1520
Clemens, Cyril, 1165, 1579
CLEON, 301, 1546
Cleopatra's Barge (Ferguson), 796
"Clothes for a Summer Hotel" (Williams), 1688
"Coda of 'The Swimmers,' The," 793
Coe, Charles Francis, 1493
Coleman, Philip C., 361
Coleman, Ralph Pallen, 966
Collected Poems of Rupert Brooke, The, 1398
Collected Short Stories of F. Scott Fitzgerald, The, 646–49, 679
Collectors Reprints (publisher), 11, 167, 317

College Humor (magazine), 691, 921, 946–47, 1596–97
College of One (Graham), 1620–24, 1649–50
Collier Books (publisher), 54, 80, 116, 155, 265–70, 342, 348, 394, 439, 448, 458, 496, 601, 816, 1564
Collier, John, 437
Collier Macmillan (publisher), 1562
Collier's (magazine), 1022, 1028, 1500
Collins (publisher), 36–40, 75–77, 107–9, 133–36, 845
Collins, V. L., 1503
Colman, Ronald, 1487, 1489
Colomb, Stephanie, 258
Colonial and Historic Homes of Maryland (Swann), 705–6
Colum, Mary, 312, 1374
Colum, Padraic, 746, 1374
Commanday-Roth (publisher), 1489
Community Workers of the New York Guild for the Jewish Blind, 687, 690
Compact Books, 278
Compleat Neurotica, The (ed. Landesman & Legman), 749
Complete Bestsellers, 252
Composition of Tender Is the Night, The (Bruccoli), 751–52
Confessions of a Hollywood Columnist (Graham), 1625
Congdon & Weed (publisher), 827
Conklin, Groff, 704
Connoisseur's Haven (Alberts), 762
Connor, Dorothy, 1154
"Conquest of America, as Some Writers Would Have It, The," 864
Conrad, Con, 1498
Conrad, Joseph, 814, 1368–70, 1399–1400
Contact Editions (publisher), 1405
Contemporary American Authors (Millett), 841–42
Contemporary Classics, 154, 216–18, 239–40, 382–83
Content, Dan, 984
Conversations with F. Scott Fitzgerald (ed. Bruccoli & Baughman), 1692
Cooder, Louise, 374
Cooper & Beatty (publisher), 1040
Cooper, Gary, 1466
Cooper, Mario, 991, 1022
Cooper, Ritchie, 985
Copp Clark (publisher), 88, 132
Cornelsen (publisher), 275
correspondence. *See under* Fitzgerald, Francis Scott Key
Correspondence of F. Scott Fitzgerald (ed. Bruccoli & Duggan), 544–48, 1141, 1151, 1163, 1166, 1175, 1178, 1220, 1225
"Cosmopolitan," 763–64

Costa, P., 637
Cottage Club, Princeton, 1524, 1527
"Count of Darkness, The," 982, 1082
"Couple, The," 1077
"Couple of Nuts, A" (ZF), 1600
Cournos, John, 1652
Cowan, Lester, 1227
Coward-McCann (publisher), 747, 1618
Cowley, Malcolm, 228, 357–69, 433–39, 579, 585, 1252, 1327, 1671, 1682–83, 1687
"Crack-Up, The," 988, 1663
Crack-Up, The (ed. Wilson), 416–32, 614, 1326
Crank, James H., 898, 917, 934
"Craw Bryant's a Studious Boy," 855
Crawford, Joan, 1115
"Crazy Sunday," 701, 969, 1045
Crazy Sunday, 635
Crazy Sundays (Latham), 773–74
Cream of the Jug: An Anthology of Humorous Stories (ed. Overton), 689
Creative Arts (publisher), 828
Creative Writing & Rewriting (Kuehl), 760
Creese, Jr., James, 682
Crevel, René, 1376
Crime and Punishment (Dostoyevsky), 1220
"Crime in the Whistler Room, The" (Wilson), 1394
Croll, Morris William, 682
Crosscurrents: Modern Fiction, 1548, 1550–52
Crown Publishers, 790, 1626
Crowninshield, Frank, 796, 1147
Cruel Fellowship (Hume), 1375
Cruise of the Rolling Junk, The, 513–16
Crystal, David, 271
Cugat, Francis, 159, 1061
Cummings, E. E., 1396
Curry, Ralph L., 738
"Cut-Glass Bowl, The," 896
Cut Glass Bowl and Other Stories, The, 669
Cycling Frog Press, 1044–45
Cypress House Press, 575–76

"Daddy's Ideas about Organizing Novel into Episodes and Scenes" (Scottie Fitzgerald), 1330
Dahlin, Robert, 795
"Dalyrimple Goes Wrong," 891
Damianakes, Cleonike, 301, 1546
Damnation of Theron Ware, The (Frederic), 1372
Dana, Viola, 1456, 1458–59
Dance, Beatrice, 1033
"Dance, The," 690, 930
Dardis, Tom, 795
Dashiell, Alfred, 305
"David Blaize," 880
David Blaize (Benson), 880
Davidson, W. W., 1678
Davie, Donald, 1268

Davis, Carroll, 377
Day of the Locust, The (West), 1661
De Sylva, Brown and Henderson Inc. (publisher), 1498
Dean, Bruce, 249–51
Dear Scott/Dear Max: The Fitzgerald-Perkins Correspondence (ed. Bryer & Kuehl), 480–85
"Dearly Beloved," 766
Dearly Beloved, 473–74
"Death of My Father, The," 1029
"Debt of Honor, A," 853
"Debutante, A One-Act Play, The," 757
"Debutante, The," 878
"Defeat of Art, The," 807
Deffaa, Chip, 575–76
Delacorte (publisher), 776
Delbanco, Nicholas, 1067–68
DeLillo, Don, 1067–68
Dell (publisher), 43, 465, 467, 2727
Delta Book, 465
Dent, J. M. (publisher), 274, 354, 1399
Department 56 Literary Classics, 289
"Design in Plaster," 707, 1015
Deutsch, André (publisher), 812
"Diagnosis," 964
Dial Press, 191–92, 757
"Diamond as Big as the Ritz, The," 908, 1390
Diamond as Big as the Ritz, The, 605
Diamond as Big as the Ritz and Other Stories, The, 583, 609–14, 638, 668, 673
"Diamond Dick and the First Law of Woman," 913
Diary of Otto Braun, The, 791, 1154, 1362
Diaz, Albert, 498
"Dice, Brass-Knuckles & Guitar," 504, 910
Dickey, James, 92, 261, 261a, 299, 499, 549–58, 569A, 789, 804, 819A, 1060, 1067, 1332
Dickey, Paul B., 3, 5, 7
Dictionary of Literary Biography, 834–35, 1070, 1687
Dillard, Annie, 1067
"Discarded Ending of 'The Offshore Pirate,' The" (Atkinson), 791
Dixon, Franklin W., 1663
Dixon, Wheeler Winston, 829
Doctorow, E. L., 432
Dodd, Mead (publisher), 696, 838, 1155, 1398
Dodge (publisher), 704
"Dog! Dog! Dog!" 792
Dolmetsch, Carl R., 757
Donaldson, Scott, 827
Donnelly, Honoria Murphy, 1276
Don't Marry (movie), 1497
Doran (publisher), 688, 1342, 1349, 1354, 1362, 1365, 1375
Dos Passos, John, 416, 1342
Doubleday (publisher), 713, 738, 844
Doubleday, Doran (publisher), 698, 702

284 Index

Doubleday, Page (publisher), 685, 1369–70, 1400
Doughty, C. L., 252
Dover (publisher), 59, 673
Drawbell, James, 845
Drorbaugh, Wells, 693
Dubliners (Joyce), 1376
Duggan, Margaret M., 546–48, 797, 807
Durrell, Edward, 1528
Dutton (publisher), 763, 813, 1338, 1364, 1366

"Early Success," 1010
Eastman, Max, 752
Easton Press, The, 263,
Easton Press Collector's Edition, 661
Eble, Kenneth Eugene, 748
"Echoes of the Jazz Age," 961
Ecstasy of Owen Muir, The (Lardner), 1672
Edel, Leon, 792, 799, 850
Editions for the Armed Services, 185, 583
Editor to Author: The Letters of Maxwell E. Perkins (ed. Wheelock), 715
Edizioni Scholastiche (publisher), 244
"Education of Dorothy Richardson, The," 815
"Education of Lily Shiel, The" (Graham), 1649
"Egotist Considers, The," 53
Eichōsha (publisher), 607–8, 636, 641
Eighth McGregor Room Seminar in Contemporary Prose and Poetry (U of Virginia), 714
Eliot, T. S., 307, 416, 777, 1343
Ellery Queen's Mystery Annual, 743
Ellis, Donald S. (publisher), 828
Ellis, Walker M., 3, 1275, 1675
Elmer the Great (Lardner), 1239
Embassy of the United States of America, London, 1050
"Emotional Bankruptcy," 958
End of a Chapter, The (Leslie), 1380, 1403
"End of Hate, The," 1022
Enriched Classic, 57
"Entering Scott's Night" (Dickey), 1332
Ernst Klett Schulbuchverlag (publisher), 276
"Epilogue: A Woman, a Gift, and a Still Unanswered Question" (Bruccoli), 1037
Equation (publisher), 645
Ernest Hemingway: A Life Story (Baker), 765
Erskine, Albert, 808
Esquire (magazine), 980–81, 988–90, 993–94, 996–1001, 1006, 1009, 1011–13, 1015–16, 1018–21, 1023, 1033–37, 1081, 1218, 1603–5, 1663
Esquire's 2nd Sports Reader (ed. Gingrich), 710
Esquire Treasury, The (ed. Gingrich), 723–24
Etchcrafters Art Guild, The (publisher), 705–6
Ethel Walker School (Simsbury, Conn.), 1038, 1318
Evans, M. (publisher), 756
Everett, Joshua B., 1
Everyman Library, 274, 354

Evil Eye, The, 2, 5–6, 1508, 1514, 1530
Ewell, Tom, 1481–82
Excelsior Illustrating (publisher), 1460, 1464, 1497
Exiles from Paradise (Mayfield), 775–76

F. Scott Fitzgerald (1991 omnibus), 666–67
F. Scott Fitzgerald (Eble), 748
F. Scott Fitzgerald (Greenfeld), 790
F. Scott Fitzgerald (ed. Takamura), 641
F. Scott Fitzgerald: A Critical Portrait (Piper), 754–55
F. Scott Fitzgerald: A Descriptive Bibliography (Bruccoli), 1054, 1440
F. Scott Fitzgerald: An Exhibition Commemorating Tender Is the Night, 1041
F. Scott Fitzgerald: An Exhibition Marking the 25th Anniversary of His Death, 1047
F. Scott Fitzgerald: A Life in Letters (ed. Bruccoli), 568–72, 1135–39, 1148, 1158, 1197, 1531–32, 1534
F. Scott Fitzgerald and Ernest M. Hemingway in Paris, 779
F. Scott Fitzgerald at 100, 1068
F. Scott Fitzgerald Centenary Exhibition Catalogue, 578, 1066, 1077–79, 1081, 1083, 1160, 1185, 1190, 1218, 1240, 1242–43, 1308–10, 1314, 1317, 1326, 1379, 1639
F. Scott Fitzgerald Collection Notes, 305
"F. Scott Fitzgerald [1896–1940] The Poet of Borrowed Time" (Mizener), 712
F. Scott Fitzgerald in His Own Time: A Miscellany (ed. Bruccoli & Bryer), 476–79, 1291
F. Scott Fitzgerald Inscriptions, 559
F. Scott Fitzgerald on Authorship (ed. Bruccoli), 574
F. Scott Fitzgerald on Writing (ed. Phillips), 644
"F. Scott Fitzgerald Plans a Library for Princeton," 815
F. Scott Fitzgerald Poems 1911–1940 (ed. Bruccoli), 549–57
F. Scott Fitzgerald: September 24, 1896–September 24, 1996, 830
F. Scott Fitzgerald: The Princeton Years (ed. Deffaa), 575–76
F. Scott Fitzgerald, 24 September 1896 to 21 December 1940, 1067
F. Scott Fitzgerald 21 December 1940–21 December 1990, 1063
"F. Scott Fitzgerald's Critique of *A Farewell to Arms*" (Mann), 797
F. Scott Fitzgerald's Ledger, 498–99
F. Scott Fitzgerald's Preface to This Side of Paradise, 511–12
F. Scott Fitzgerald's Projected Collected Works, 1054
F. Scott Fitzgerald's St. Paul Plays 1911–1914 (ed. Margolies), 534

F. Scott Fitzgerald's Screenplay for Three Comrades by Erich Maria Remarque (ed. Bruccoli), 517–28, 1409
F. Scott Fitzgerald's Tender Is the Night (ed. Bruccoli & Anderson), 836
F. Scott Fitzgerald's The Great Gatsby (ed. Bruccoli), 834
Faber & Faber (publisher), 527, 741, 1343
Fabian, Warner (Samuel Hopkins Adams), 1334
Fain, Sammy, 1484
Fair Rewards, The (Beer), 1335
Fall of the City, The (MacLeish), 1350
"Family Bus, The," 974
"Family in the Wind," 702, 966
Famous Players–Lasky (studio), 1305
Famous Story Magazine, 931
Famous Writers Magazine, 1648
Fantasy and Mystery Stories of F. Scott Fitzgerald, The (ed. Hanning), 662
Far Side of Paradise, The (Mizener), 716, 1263
"Far Side of Zelda Fitzgerald, The," 1605
Farewell to Arms, A (Hemingway), 797, 1242
Farr, Finis, 783
Farrar & Rinehart (publisher), 1350
Farrar, John, 1375
Farrar, Straus and Giroux (publisher), 792, 799, 850
Farrington, Jan, 778
"Far-Seeing Skeptics, The," 907
"Fate in Her Hands," 991
Faulkner, William, 1371
Faust, Irvin, 1067
Favorite Recipes of Famous Women (Stratton), 1593
Fay, Cyril Sigourney, 1138–39, 1295, 1445, 1690
"Feather Fan, The," 807
Fenton, Charles, 145, 1263
Ferguson, David L., 796
Fernandez, Yva, 1376
Fessenden, Katherine, 68
"Festival of St. James, The," 739–42
"Fie! Fie! Fi-Fi!," 1
Fie! Fie! Fi-Fi!, 2–4, 6, 1510, 1530
Fiedler, Leslie A., 1067
Field, Betty, 1472
"Fiend, The," 981
Fifth Column, The (Hemingway), 1243
Fifty Years in the Wide, Wide World, 1529
Figures of Earth (Cabell), 1340
Film Guild, 1463
Film Weekly Supplement, 1470
"Financing Finnegan," 1013
"First Blood," 950
First Edition Library, 11, 89, 127, 317
Fischer, Anton Otto, 945
Fitz Gerald, Dallas M., 1458

Fitzgerald and Hemingway: A Dangerous Friendship (Bruccoli), 811–12, 1362
"Fitzgerald and the *Post:* A New Letter," 815
Fitzgerald, Annabelle (FSF's sister), 1178, 1246, 1531–32, 1534
"Fitzgerald at the Winter Carnival," 815
"Fitzgerald Auto-bibliography, A," 782
"Fitzgerald Back from Riviera; Is Working on Novel," 781
Fitzgerald, Cecilia, 1233
Fitzgerald, Edward (FSF's father), 1345, 1437, 1531–33
Fitzgerald, Francis Scott Key; correspondence concerning, 1249–91; correspondence from, 86, 125, 128, 158, 161, 460–69, 480–92 573, 590, 627–29, 694, 711–13, 715–16, 718, 722, 726, 729, 731, 733, 738, 744–47, 750–52, 754–55, 765, 769–71, 773–78, 779, 782, 791, 796–97, 800, 805–6, 808–9, 813–15, 827–28, 830, 832–35, 838, 843, 1032, 1038, 1046, 1048, 1052, 1057, 1135–1230, 1415, 1531, 1576, 1657, 1663, 1666, 1690, 1694; correspondence received by, 1231–48; inscriptions by FSF (in his own books), 19–20, 24, 27–30, 36, 39, 69, 73, 84, 129, 144, 147–50, 161, 173, 176, 294, 295–96, 298, 310–11, 314–15, 318, 320–22, 369, 373–77, 380, 559, 762, 768, 775–78, 779–80, 783–85, 791, 793, 797–99, 805–7, 814, 828, 830, 836, 1690; inscriptions by FSF (in other writers' books), 1359, 1361, 1363, 1373–74, 1376, 1383, 1390; photographs of, 1448–49, 1451, 1571, 1702; signed or marked by FSF, 85, 683, 1348, 1351, 1353, 1358–60, 1362, 1364–72, 1377–82, 1384–88, 1391, 1393–94, 1446. See also *Correspondence of F. Scott Fitzgerald* and *F. Scott Fitzgerald: A Life in Letters*
Fitzgerald/Hemingway Annual, 766, 769, 777, 782, 784, 791, 793, 797, 807, 814–15, 1049
"Fitzgerald in St. Paul" (Hackl), 797
Fitzgerald, Louisa (FSF's sister), 1534
Fitzgerald, Mary (Mollie) McQuillan (FSF's mother), 1086, 1177, 1246, 1380, 1531–33, 1700
"Fitzgerald-Mencken Correspondence, The" (Long), 777
Fitzgerald Newsletter, 82, 767
"Fitzgerald on 'The Ice Palace,'" 782
"Fitzgerald on *Ulysses*," 782
"Fitzgerald-Perkins Papers, The," 1035
Fitzgerald Reader, The (ed. Mizener), 623–26
"Fitzgerald Recommends Nathanael West for a Guggenheim" (Martin), 777
Fitzgerald, Scottie (Frances Scott Fitzgerald Lanahan Smith; daughter of FSF & ZF), 249, 491–92, 1053, 1085, 1219, 1239, 1241, 1249, 1252–57, 1267, 1274, 1284–85, 1297, 1309, 1318, 1320, 1327–28, 1330, 1389, 1398, 1402,

286   Index

Fitzgerald, Scottie (*continued*)
  1556, 1573–74, 1576, 1581, 1583, 1662, 1674;
  Bruccoli, Matthew J., and, 377, 486, 500–510,
  785–88, 817, 1258–59, 1272, 1336, 1365,
  1384, note preceding 1395, 1437, 1535, 1541,
  1679, 1684; correspondence with FSF, 1160,
  1180, 1201, 1205, 1211, 1218, 1234–36, 1664;
  FSF's correspondence about, 1166, 1183–84,
  1186–88, 1192, 1194, 1196–1200, 1202–4,
  1206–1210, 1212, 1215–16, 1227; photographs
  of, 1440–41, 1450, 1571; writings of, 137–41,
  488–89, 500–510, 627–29, 779, 785–88,
  819–25, 1526, 1686, 1672
"Fitzgerald to Roger Burlingame: A New Letter,"
  782
Fitzgerald, Zelda Sayre, 818, 1142, 1156, 1181,
  1217, 1222, 1239, 1248, 1250, 1267, 1269,
  1309, 1311, 1329, 1342, 1349, 1355, 1357–58,
  1373, 1446, 1436, 1607–11, 1667, 1674,
  1678–79, 1688, 1702; artwork of, 1586–92,
  1605, 1609; correspondence by ZF, 1571–85,
  1604–6; correspondence from FSF, 1033,
  1197, 1213, 1215, 1226, 1605; photographs of,
  1449, 1571; writings of, 500–510, 725, 924,
  936, 946–47, 1267, 1544–1570, 1593–1606
"Fitzgerald's Favorite Story," 814
"Fitzgerald's Film Scripts of 'Babylon Revisited'"
  (Stewart), 777
"Fitzgerald's Last Issue of *The Princeton Alumni
  Weekly*," 815
"Fitzgerald's Ledger," 777
"Fitzgeralds' Letters to the Hoveys, The"
  (Trower), 814
"Fitzgerald's Marked Copy of *The Great Gatsby*"
  (Atkinson), 769
"Fitzgerald's Marked Copy of *This Side of Paradise*" (Bruccoli), 777
"Fitzgerald's Revisions for 'Marching Streets,'"
  815
*Fitzgerald's The Great Gatsby: The Novel, The
  Critics, The Background* (comp. Piper), 232
Five Sisters (Fox), 833
Flagg, James Montgomery, 913
Flaming Youth (Fabian), 1334
Flanaghan, Thomas, 1068
Flappers and Philosophers, 64–80, 670, 672
"Flight and Pursuit," 732, 965
Flint, F. S., 1373
Flowers of Friendship, The (ed. Gallup), 722
Folcroft Press, 151, 303
Folio Society, 230, 349
Fontaine, Joan, 1481–82
Fool for Love (Donaldson), 827
"Footnote on Fitzgerald" (Ring), 1604
For Whom the Bell Tolls (Hemingway), 1346
Forbes, Bryan, 849
Ford, Hugh, 781
foreign editions (English text), 202, 244, 253,
  256, 275, 345, 459, 632, 637, 643, 650; Japanese, 53, 156, 220, 426, 457, 586, 589, 591,
  593–94, 604–8, 629, 631, 635–36, 639, 641–42,
  665
Foreword to *Colonial and Historic Homes of
  Maryland*, 705–6
Fosnot & Williams, 1601
"Four Fists, The," 900
Fourth Round, The (ed. Grayson), 721
Fowler, Ludlow, 1605
Fox (studio), 1493, 1498
Fox Entertainments, 1454
Fox Film Corporation, 1299, 1495–96
Fox, James, 833
Fox, William, 1453–54, 1495–97
Frances Newman's Letters (ed. Baugh), 694
"Frances Scott Fitzgerald '38: A Remembrance,"
  1038
Frank, Gerold, 1613–17
Frank, Nino, 800
Franklin Library, 236, 246, 249–51, 437
Frederic, Harold, 1372
"Freeze-Out, A" 962
"Full Life, A," 1039
Fülöp-Miller, René, 1373
Funke, Lewis, 756
Furioso (magazine), 1025–26
"Futuristic Impressions of Editorial Boards," 877

Gager, Theodora, 39, 318
Gakuseisha (publisher), 604
Gale (publisher), 794, 807, 814–15, 834–36
Gallup, Donald Clifford, 722
Garden of Allah, The (Graham), 1626
Garis, Roger, 1033
Garland (publisher), 560–66
Garland Manuscript Facsimile Edition, 560–66
Garnett, David, 369
Garrett, George, 1067–68
Gauss, Christian, 733, 1344
Gennert, Alfred Gottlieb, 1518
Gens De Dublin (Joyce), 1376
Gentleman-Crook (Graham), 1612
Gessner, Robert, 763–64
Gift of Joy, A (Hayes), 756
Gingrich, Arnold, 449–56, 458, 710, 723–24,
  735–36, 1656, 1691
"Girl with Talent, The" (ZF), 1597
Girls from Esquire, The (intro. Birmingham),
  719–20
Gish, Dorothy, 1145
Gish, Lillian, 768
Glasgow, Ellen, 573
"glass of beer kills him, a," 877
"God, the Invisible King," 884
God, the Invisible King (Wells), 884
Godden, Richard, 356
"Gods of Darkness," 1024

Gold, Herbert, 1068
Goldman, Arnold, 344, 356
Goldwyn, Samuel, 1466, 1487–89
Gone with the Wind (Mitchell), 816, 1245
Goodbye to All That (Graves), 1374
Gordon, Mary, 1561–66
Gorky, Maxim, 1661
Gotlieb, Jules, 1024
Graham, Sheilah, 313, 1217, 1248, 1479–80, 1612–51
Gramercy Books (publisher), 672
Granta (publisher), 833
Graves, Michael, 254
Graves, Robert, 1374
Gray, Charles Paxson, 1359
Grayson, Charles, 721
Great American Short Novels (ed. Phillips), 191–92
Great Gatsby, The, 157–292, 325, 385–89, 562, 580, 585, 590, 630, 633, 640, 660–61, 666–67, 670, 748, 753, 760–61, 769, 797, 834, 931, 1003–5, 1061, 1159, 1195, 1268, 1310, 1442–44, 1607; movie versions, 183, 186, 193, 233, 590, 1464–65, 1471–76, 1485
Great Gatsby: A Facsimile of the Manuscript, The (ed. Bruccoli), 292
Great Gatsby and the Last Tycoon, The, 243
Great Gatsby 10 April 1925–10 April 1975, The, 1055
Great Gatsby, The Last Tycoon, and Some Shorter Pieces, The, 590
Great Gatsby: The Revised and Rewritten Galleys, The, 562
Great Modern Short Stories (ed. Overton), 695
Great Tales of City Dwellers (ed. Austin), 725
Great Tales of the Far West (ed. Austin), 728
Great Writers: Their Lives, Works and Inspiration, The, 255
Greenfeld, Howard, 790
Greiner, Donald J., 1069
"Gretchen's Forty Winks," 687, 912
Grey Walls Press, 41–42, 96–97, 193–94, 327, 362, 395–96, 584, 1547
Griffin, D. D., 3
Griffith, D. W., 1145
Griffith, Edward H., 322
Grit (movie), 1463
Grolier Club (publisher), 734, 1055
Grosset & Dunlap (publisher), 31, 182–84, 798, 1487, 1493, 1627–28, 1631
Grout, Stephen, 984
Grove Park Inn, 169
Gruger, Frederic R., 927
Guedalla, Philip, 1345
"Guest in Room Nineteen, The," 1011
Guilbert, F. Warburton, 5, 7
Gurganus, Allan, 1068
Gurney, A. R., 1068

Guthrie, Laura, 314
GWTW: The Screenplay (Howard), 816

Hacker Art Books (publisher), 749
Hackett, Francis, 1366
Haigh, Kenneth, 1688
Haldemann, Joe, 1068
Hale, Edward Everett, 1401
Hale, Robert (publisher), 662
Hall, G. K. (publisher), 283
Hamilton, Neil, 1456, 1497
"Handle with Care," 990
Hanning, Peter, 662
Hansen, Harry, 702
Harcourt (publisher), 841
Harcourt, Brace (publisher), 726, 740, 1387, 1390
Harcourt, Brace & World (publisher), 746
Harcourt Brace Jovanovich (publisher), 529, 531–33, 818–19, 820, 822–23, 1058
Harlow, Jean, 1085, 1096
Harper (publisher), 843
Harper & Brothers (publisher), 689
Harper & Row (publisher), 770
Harper's Bazaar (magazine), 1595
Harrap (publisher), 842
Harriman, Margaret Case, 418
Harris, E., 7
Harris, Sam H., 1307
Harte, Glynn Boyd, 349
Harwell, Richard, 816
"Has the Flapper Changed?" (Reid), 759
Hathaway, Odell S., 1085
Hawthorn Books (publisher), 846
Haya, Ken-ichi, 589
Haydn, Hiram, 733
Hayes, Helen, 756, 1184, 1237, 1260
Hayward, Leland, 1322
"He Thinks He's Wonderful," 939
"Head and Shoulders," 892, 1142, 1452
Heard, John, 1486
Hearne, Laura, 1261, 1689
Hearst's International (magazine), 910–11, 913, 1697
Hecht, Ben, 843
Heer Printing Company, F. J., 1047
Heinemann (publisher), 117, 272, 640, 669, 724, 736, 1403
Held, John, Jr., 123, 924
Heller, Joseph, 1067, 1333
Hellman, Lillian, 847
Hemingway: An Old Friend Remembers (Kiley), 846
Hemingway, Ernest, 747, 762, 769, 779, 797, 809–12, 846, 1242–43, 1262–63, 1314, 1346, 1362, 1402, 1640
Hemingway, Grace Hall, 1262
Hemmick, William, 1264

Henderson, F. R., 36
Hennion, Marion, 69
"Her Last Case," 979
Hicks, Granville, 735–36
Higgins, George V., 1067
"High Cost of Macaroni, The," 1031
Hills, L. Rust, 735–36
Hines, Marion, 1609
"His Russet Witch," 904
History of the University Cottage Club, 1524
Hobson, Laura Z., 417
Hodder & Stoughton (publisher), 821
Hodkinson Pictures, 1463
Hokuseido Press, 639
"Hollywood Canteen" (Powell), 1283
Hollywood Revisited (Graham), 1636
Holt (publisher), 717, 721, 839, 1613
Holt, Rinehart and Winston (publisher), 754
"Home to Maryland," 1081
Homer (Chapman's translation), 1224
Hon-No-Tomosha, 670
"Honor of the Goon, The," 1006
Honoring the Researchers of Carolina, 1072
Hoople, William C., 983
Hopkins, John R., 511–12
Hornby, Lester G., 1513
Hosokoshi, K., 457
"Hot & Cold Blood," 911
"Hotel Child, The," 954
Houghton Mifflin (publisher), 701, 707, 716
Hound and Horn (magazine), 1379
"How They Head the Chapters," 863
"How to Live on Practically Nothing a Year," 918
How to Marry Super Rich (Graham), 1628
"How to Waste Material: A Note on My Generation," 929
How To Write (Stein), 1353
How to Write Short Stories (Lardner), 1056, 1377
Howard, Sidney, 816
Howard, William K., 1493
Hoyem, Andrew, 254
"Huckleberry Finn Took the First Journey Back," 1084
Hudson River Editions, 47, 104, 219, 334, 384, 392, 445
Hume, Cyril, 1375
Husband Hunter, The (movie), 1299, 1453

"I Didn't Get Over," 999
"I Got Shoes," 973
I Should Have Stayed Home (McCoy), 1404
"Ice Palace, The," 782, 898
Ice Palace and Absolution, The, 631
Ice Palace and Magnetism, The, 608
Ice Palace and Other Stories, The, 674
Ideas for Writing (Knickerbocker), 717
Iggulden, John, 1067
"Image on the Heart," 1699

"Imagination—and a Few Mothers," 730
In Memoriam Princeton 1917, 1517
"In the Darkest Hour," 978, 1082
"In the Holidays," 1012
In Their Time, 805–6
"Indecision," 956
Indispensable F. Scott Fitzgerald, The (ed. Parker), 582
"Infidelity," 1107–14, 1193, 1416–21
"Infidelity: A Screenplay," 1036
Information Handling Services (publisher), 797
Innocent Merriment (ed. Adams), 708
inscriptions. *See under* Fitzgerald, Francis Scott Key
"Inside the House," 995
Institute D'Études Américaines, 779
"Intercollegiate Petting-Cues," 886
Interim (magazine), 1031
Internal Revenue Service, 1238, 1312–13, 1666
International Collectors Library (publisher), 339
International Mark Twain Society, 1165
Intimate Notebooks of George Jean Nathan, The, 1385
"Intimate Strangers, The," 983, 1698
"Invasion of the Sanctuary, The," 717
"I.O.U., The," 777
Irresistable Lover, The (movie), 1491
"It Is Art," 782

Jackson, Katherine Gauss, 733
"Jacob's Ladder," 933
Jakes, John, 1067
James, Henry, 1158
Jazz Age, The, 432
Jazz Age Stories (ed. O'Donnell), 675
"Jelly-Bean, The," 123
"Jemina," 873
Jenkins, Oliver, 1152
"John Jackson's Arcady," 917
John Jackson's Arcady (ed. Strack), 304
John Player Special Collection (publisher), 238
John, Roland, 638
Johns Hopkins University Press, 706
Johnson, Nunnally, 1435–36
Johnson, Samuel (publisher), 352
Johnston, William, 688
Jones, Henry Festing, 1366
Jones, Jennifer, 1481–82
Joseph, Michael (publisher), 1633–35
Josephson, Matthew, 781
Joy Ride (Taylor), 737
Joyce, James, 1347–48, 1376
Jurgen (Cabell), 1339

Kairyudo (publisher), 220
Kaleta, Kenneth Charles, 1257
Kalman, Oscar and Xandra, 797
Kasahara, M., 631

Kataoka, Akira, 608
Kawanishii, Susumu, 156
Kazin, Alfred, 1068
Keats, John, 1224
Keeley, Edmund, 1068
Kelley, A. M. (publisher), 152
Kenkyusha (publisher), 586, 606
Kenkyusha Pocket English Series, 606
Kennerley, Mitchell (publisher), 1393
Kent State University Press, 478, 1051, 1291
Kenyon Review, 1027
Kerr, Deborah, 1479–80
Kerr, Joan P., 785–87
Kerr, Robert, 797
Kerry, Norman, 1491
Key, Francis Scott, 1233
Key, Philip, 1292
Kiley, Jed, 846
King, Ginevra, 1284, 1294
King, Henry, 1488–89
"Kingdom in the Dark," 986, 1083
Kiuchi, Nobuyuki, 220
Knickerbocker, Kenneth L., 717
Knight, Richard, 1033
Knopf, Alfred A., Inc. (publisher), 683–84, 722, 1149, 1335, 1351, 1355–57, 1363, 1373, 1384–85, 1395, 1404, 1656
Knopf, Edwin, 1466
Kōbunsha (publisher), 631
Kodansha (publisher), 665
Koyama, T., 457
Koyama, Toshisaburo, 589, 605
Kroll, Ernest, 573
Kuchi, Naotaro Tatsuno, 220
Kuehl, John, 470–72, 480–84, 493–97, 760–61
Kunitz, Stanley, 840
Kyioku Tosho, 635

La Gatta, John, 943, 947, 1596
Ladd, Alan, 186, 1471
Ladies and Gentlemen (Cabell), 1341
Ladies' Home Journal, The, 730
Ladies' Home Journal Treasury, The (ed. Brown), 730
Lalli, Biancamaria Tedeschini, 632
Lanahan, Eleanor Anne, 1567
Lanahan, Frances Fitzgerald. *See* Fitzgerald, Scottie
Landesman, Jay Irving, 749
Landon, Seland Whitney, 693
Lane, J. (publisher), 1378
Langhorne, Nora, 833
Langhorne Sisters, The (Fox), 833
Larbaud, Valery, 1376
Lardner, Ring, Jr. 1672
Lardner, Ring W., 573, 1056, 1164, 1239–40, 1281, 1377
Large Type Books, 283

Lasky, Jesse, 1305
"Last Kiss," 728, 1028
Last Kiss & Other Stories, 642
"Last of the Belles, The," 943
Last of the Novelists, The (Bruccoli), 801–4, 1646
Last Time I Saw Paris, The (movie), 1477–78
Last Tycoon: Manuscript and Revised Typescript . . . , The, 565
Last Tycoon, The, 243, 385–405, 414–15, 565, 585, 590, 633, 640, 660–61, 666–67, 753, 1062, 1227, 1282, 1323, 1578, 1641. *See also Love of the Last Tycoon, The*
"Last Tycoon, The" (screenplay by Shaw), 415
"Last Will and Testament," 1319
Late Lily Shiel, The (Graham), 1631–32
Latham, Aaron, 773–74
Laughlin, James, 416
Laurel Edition, 467
Layman, Richard, 797, 807, 814–15, 1056
Lazy Laughter (Boyd), 1653
le Carré, John, 1067
Le Vot, A., 634
Leacock, Stephen, 1378
Leake, Gerald, 977
Learning to Write (Stevenson), 1352
Left Bank Revisited, The (ed. Ford), 781
Legman, Gershon, 749
Leighton, Lawrence, 1379
Leland Hayward Agency, 1322
Lemmon, Elizabeth, 1172
Lenz, Susanne, 256
Lescanne, Dominique, 650
Leslie, Shane, 86, 883–84, 1135–39, 1151, 1265–66, 1380–82, 1673, 1676, 1690
Letters of F. Scott Fitzgerald, The (ed. Turnbull), 460–69, 1046, 1690
Letters of Thomas Wolfe, The (ed. Nowell), 729
Letters on Literature and Politics (Wilson), 799
Letters to His Daughter (ed. Turnbull), 627–28
Levy et Neurdein Reunis (publisher), 1140
Lewis, Sinclair, 726
Liberty (magazine), 984, 1017, 16969
Library of America, 677–78
Liebert, Herman W., 734
"Life Begins at Eight-Thirty" (Johnson), 1435–36
"Light of Heart, The" (Johnson), 1435
Lillian Gish: The Movies, Mr. Griffith, and Me (Gish), 768
Lily-Iron (Biggs), 1654
Limited Editions Club, 247, 343
Lindley, Clara Hill, 1367
Lion Library Editions (publisher), 725, 728, 732
Lippincott (publisher), 488–89, 756
"Lipstick," 814
"Litany of Slang, A," 877
Literary Guild, 548, 633

Literary Review of the New York Evening Post, The, 1653
"Literature of Despair" (Heller), 1333
Little, Brown (publisher), 411–12, 783, 796, 847, 1401, 1513, 1563
"Little Minnie Mccloskey," 876
Litz, A. Walton, 245
Liveright (publisher), 694
Lives of Eighteen from Princeton, The (ed. Thorp), 712
Living Authors (Tante [Kunitz]), 840
Livre de Poche (publisher), 459
"Lo, The Poor Peacock!" 1089
Locke, Jesse Albert, 1447
Loew's, 1477
Long Kickline, The (Marsden), 1530
"Long Way Out, The," 1009
Longman (publisher), 258, 638
Longman Structural Readers, 638
"Looking Back on Fitzgerald," (Turnbull et al.), 1648
Loos, Anita, 798
"Lost and Unpublished Stories of F. Scott Fitzgerald, The" (Atkinson), 777
"Lost Decade, The," 1016
Lost Decade and Other Stories, The, 620–22
"Lost Lover, The," 870
Lost Summer, The (Buttitta), 849
Louisville Free Public Library, 1297
Love and Revolution (Eastman), 752
"Love Boat, The," 934
"Love in the Night," 920
Love in the Night, 671
Love of the Last Tycoon: A Western, The, 406–13, 1064, 1088. See also *Last Tycoon, The*
"Love to All of You, of All Generations," 1033
Low-Down, The (Shaw), 839
Lower Depths, The (Gorky), 1661
"Luckless Santa Claus, A," 858
Lyceum Editions, 485
Lyons, Margareta F., 785–87
Lythway Press, 241–42

MacArthur, Charles, 843, 1260
MacCubin-Waters, Zack, 1267
MacLeish, Archibald, 1269, 1350
Macmillan (publisher), 11, 80, 348, 394, 448, 458, 496, 601
Macpherson, Orison, 960
Mad Anthony Wayne (Boyd), 1655
Madame Curie (movie), 1430–34
"Magnetism," 937
Mailer, Norman, 1067
Making of Americans, The (Stein), 1405
"Mama-Quotes" (Scottie Fitzgerald), 1610
"Man in the Way, A," 1019
Man without a Country, The (Hale), 1401
Mankiewicz, Joseph, 1415

Manners, J. Hartley, 1349
Maplethorpe, Robert, 1035
"Marching Streets," 682, 888
Margolies, Alan, 122, 534, 561
"Marie Antoinette" (screenplay), 1470
Mark Twain Journal, 1084
Markfield, Wallace, 804
Markle, Fletcher, 450, 1270
Marquis, A. N. (publisher), 837
Marquis, Don, 573
Marsden, Donald, 1530
Marshall Cavendish (publisher), 255
"Martin's Thoughts," 1074
Martin's Thoughts, 1043
Massachusetts Institute of Technology (publisher), 731
Matin, Richard, 253
Mattock, Katherine, 279
Matz, Charles, 753
Max Perkins: Editor of Genius (Berg), 813
Maxwell Macmillan (publisher), 266, 568–69, 1562, 1564
Maxwell, William, 1067
"May Day," 902
May Day, 589
"May Small Talk," 862
Mayer, Louis B., 1134
Mayfield, Sara, 775–76
Mayo, Frank, 661
McBride, Robert M. (publisher), 703, 1339–41, 1654
McCall's (magazine), 916, 924, 983, 1698–99
McFarlane, Leslie, 1663
McGraw-Hill (publisher), 708
Mckenzie, Vernon, 703
McLaglen, Victor, 1493
McPhee, John, 1068
McPherson, James Alan, 1068
McQuillan, Clara, 1232
McQuillan, Lorena and Phil, 1146, 1190, 1401
Meeker, Chris Marie, 946, 1597
Memorial Day keepsake, 1044
Men Who Make Our Novels, The (Baldwin), 838, 1155
Men Without Women (Hemingway), 762
Mencken, H. L., 307, 683, 692, 762, 1033, 1271, 1326, 1351, 1384
Meredith Press, 761
Merker, K. K., 511
Merrill, Charles E., Inc. (publisher), 772
Metro Motion Pictures (studio), 1300, 1452, 1456–59
Metropolitan (magazine), 904, 906
Meyer, Fred, 247, 263, 343, 661
Meyers, Jeffrey, 274
M-G-M (Metro-Goldwyn-Mayer studio), 415, 1064, note preceding 1092, 1185, 1245, 1406–36, 1467–69, 1478

Milford, Nancy, 770–71, 1272, 1679
Millar, Kenneth, 578, 1268
Miller, Arthur, 1068
Miller Music Corporation (publisher), 1484
Millett, Fred B., 841
"Millionaire's Girl, A" (ZF), 725, 1598
Mind and Face of Bolshevism, The (Fülöp-Miller, René), 1373
Mirror of the Sea, The (Conrad), 1368
"Miss Ella" (ZF), 1599
Mitchell, Charles D., 892, 912, 1695
Mitchell, Margaret, 816
Mitchell, Ted, 835
Miyata, Hitoshi, 426
Miyauchi, Kayoko, 629
Mizener, Arthur, 440–48, 623–26, 712, 716, 1263, 1648
MJB (publisher), 1057, 1062, 1072
M.J.B., C.S. III, and P.S. (publisher), 1061
MJF Books (publisher), 543
Modern American Prose (ed. Van Doren), 1390
Modern Library (publisher), 63, 176–77, 695
Modern Reading: Number Eight (ed. Moore), 709
Modern Standard Authors, 228, 585
Montgomery Independent, 1543
Monthly Letters of the Limited Editions Club, The, 343
Moore, Harry T., 1549–59
Moore, Martha, 1017
Moore, Reginald, 709
Moran, Lois, 28, 1273, 1487–1500, 1680
"More than Just a House," 1438
Mossir, Edwin Mark, 1513
Motada, Shuichi, 608
Motion Picture (magazine), 1499
Motion Picture Classic (magazine), 1458
Moveable Feast, A (Hemingway), 1362
Movie Star Composition Book: Lois Moran, 1494
Moving Image, The (Gessner), 763–64
Mowat, H. J., 920, 957
"Mr. Ickey," 893
Mumford, L. Quincy, 1440
Murakami, Haruki, 629
Murfin, Jane, 1133
Murphy, Gerald, 1274–75, 1674–75
"My First Love," 682, 888
"My Generation," 772, 1034, 1050
My Hollywood (Graham), 1633–36
"My Old New England Homestead on the Erie," 691, 921
"My Ten Favorite Plays," 814
"My Trip Abroad" (ZF), 1569
"My Wedding" (Mary M. Fitzgerald), 1533
Myers, Carmel, 27, 1607
"Myra Meets His Family," 894, 1299, 1453–55
"Mystery of the Raymond Mortgage, The," 743, 851
Mystery of the Raymond Mortgage, The, 1042

Nagai, Makoto, 53
Namba, Totsuo, 636
Nan'un-do (publisher), 426, 589, 591
"Narcissus off Duty," 53
Nassau Herald Class of Nineteen Hundred and Eighteen, The, 1521
Nassau Herald Class of Nineteen Hundred and Seventeen, The, 1512
Nassau Literary Magazine, 871–875, 878–85, 887–88, 1288, 1526
Nardini, Harry, 20, 321, 375
Nathan, George Jean, 683–84, 1385
National Anthem, The (Manners), 1349
National Screen Service (publisher), 1479
NCR/Microcard Editions Books (publisher), 498, 766–77, 769, 777, 782, 784, 791
Neall, Adelaide, 815, 1171
Neurotica (magazine), 1030
New American Credo, The (Nathan), 684
New American Library (publisher), 1554–56, 1558
New Classics Series, 181
New Directions (publisher), 181, 416–25, 432, 1661
"New Leaf," 700, 957
New Republic, The (magazine), 1672
New Republic, The (publisher), 1394
New Republic Anthology, The (ed. Conklin), 704
"New Types," 977
New York Evening Post, 1655
New York Times, The, 1508, 1646
New York Times Magazine, The, 1651
New York World, 688
New Yorker, The (magazine), 1007–8, 1332
New Yorker Scrapbook, The, 698
Newlin, J. V., 826
Newman, Frances D., 694
Newman News (Hackensack, N.J.), 858–60
Newman School (Hackensack, N.J.), 1074, 1264, 1293, 1445, 1447, 1701
Newsweek (magazine), 1287
"News of Paris—Fifteen Years Ago," 1026
Niblo, Fred, 1607
"Nice Quiet Place, A," 951
Night at the Fair and Forging Ahead, The, 594
Night Club Era, The (Walker), 1391
Nijinsky, Vaslav Fomich, 1585
1914 & Other Poems (Brooke), 1397
1917's Fortieth (Durrell et al.), 1528
Nishiyama, Tamotsu, 607
Nissenson, Hugh, 1068
"No Flowers," 976
Nonsense Novels (Leacock), 1378
Norton, W. W. (publisher), 1392
"Not in the Guidebook," 926
Notebooks of F. Scott Fitzgerald, The (ed. Bruccoli), 529–33, 1058, 1682

Note-Books of Samuel Butler, The (ed. Jones), 1366
Notes on Life & Letters (Conrad), 1399
Notes on My Books (Conrad), 1400
Novels and Stories, 1920–1922, 677–78
Nowell, Elizabeth, 729
Noyes, Alfred, 1386

O. Henry Memorial Award Prize Stories (1921), 685
O. Henry Memorial Award Prize Stories (1933), 702
Ober, Anne, 147, 1183–89, 1192, 1194, 1196, 1198–1200, 1204, 1206–8, 1210, 1212, 1241, 1253–56, 1359, 1439, 1576, 1581, 1583
Ober Associates, Harold, 74, 87, 126, 171, 300, 319, 386, 1328, 1606
Ober, Harold, 74, 126, 147, 171, 300, 319, 386, 797, 1086, 1359, 1439, 1582, 1598, 1637, 1667, 1671; correspondence with FSF, 486–91, 1161, 1180, 1189, 1196, 1200, 1202–3, 1207, 1209
"Obit on Parnassus," 708, 1007
O'Brien, Edward J., 686, 696, 701, 707
O'Brien, George, 1496
O'Conor, Herbert R., 705–6
Octopus (publisher), 640
O'Donnell, Patrick, 61–62, 675
Of Making Many Books (Burlingame), 711
"Offshore Pirate, The," 791, 899, 1078
"Off-Shore Pirate, The" (Calhoun), 1458
Off-Shore Pirate, The (movie), 1456–59
"Oh, Sister, Can You Spare Your Heart," 777
O'Hara: A Biography (Farr), 783
O'Hara, Belle, 1278
O'Hara, John, 577–82, 783–84, 1059, 1278, 1387
"Old Frontiersman, The," 877
Olivier, Laurence, 1279
"On a Play Twice Seen," 884
"On Schedule," 972
"On Your Own," 1037, 1081
"One from Penn's Neck," 877
100 Greatest Masterpieces of American Literature, The, 246
"One Hundred False Starts," 971
"One Interne," 376, 970
"One Not-Forgotten Summer Night" (Corso), 797
"One of My Oldest Friends," 688, 922
"One Trip Abroad," 953
O'Neill, Rose, 1697
"Open That Door," 1321
Opfer, Ivan, 1262
Ordeal of Mark Twain, The (Brooks), 1289, 1364
Ordway, Kathryn, 1608
"Original Follies Girl, The" (FSF & ZF), 946
Orion (publisher), 671
"Oui, Le Backfield Est from Paris," 877
"Our American Poets," 886

"Our Next Issue," 872
"Our Young Rich Boys," 924, 1594
Outlook Photoplays, 1304
"Outside the Cabinet-Maker's," 940
Overton, Grant, 689, 695
Owens, Isabel, 1086, 1176–77, 1179, 1222, 1248, 1665
Oxford Library of the World's Great Books, 250
Oxford Progressive English Readers, 279
Oxford University Press, 122, 248, 251, 279, 668, 1503
Oxford World's Classics, 122

Page, Geraldine, 1688
Pages (ed. Bruccoli & Clark), 794
"Pain and the Scientist," 859
Paintings by Zelda Fitzgerald; Photographs by Marion Hines, 1609
Palo Alto Times, 1543
"Pampered Men, The," 785
Pan Books (publisher), 542
Papers of Henry Gauss, The (ed. Jackson & Haydn), 733
Paramore, E. E., 1100, 1104, 1106, 1190, 1410–15, 1468
Paramount Pictures (studio), 183, 186, 1227, 1471, 1473–75, 1485
Parini, Jay, 60, 119
Paris in the Twenties (U.S. Information Service), 742
Paris–New York (Bibliothèque Publique d'Information), 800
Paris Review, 1606
Paris Tribune, 781
Parker, Dorothy, 577–82
"Paroxide Blonde, The," 1085
Parrott, Stephan, 1229
Parrott, Ursula, 1420
Parsons, Ian, 325
Parties (Van Vechten), 1357
Pasquier, Hélène du, 1376
Passing Chapter, The (Leslie), 1382
"Passionate Eskimo, The," 984
"Pasting It Together," 989
Pat Hobby Stories, The, 449–58, 614, 1691
Pat Hobby and Orson Welles and Other Short Stories, 459
"Pat Hobby's Christmas Wish," 723–24, 1018
"Pat Hobby's Preview," 1023
"Pat Hobby's Secret," 1021
Patterson, Russell, 691, 921
"Paul Briggs Is a Cute Little (?) Lad," 856
Paus, Herbert, 919
Peanuts art (Schulz), 1442–44
Pearson Education (publisher), 290, 676
Peck, Gregory, 1479–80
Penguin (publisher), 49, 61–62, 111–15, 121, 195–201, 237, 257, 288, 291, 344, 346–47,

355–56, 363–71, 397–403, 427–31, 453–56, 468, 506–10, 572, 609–22, 646–49, 675–76, 679, 758, 1557, 1559, 1624, 1660
Penguin Authentic Texts, 271
Penguin Book of Modern Verse Translation, The (ed. Steiner), 758
Penguin Classics, 291
Penguin English (publisher), 271, 663–64
Penguin Modern Classics, 198–200, 365–66, 508–10, 609–11
Penguin Poets, The, 758
Penguin Readers, 290, 676
Penguin Twentieth-Century Classics, 61–62, 121, 257, 356, 648, 675
Pennsylvania State University Press, 781
"Penny Spent, A," 925
"Penrod and Sam," 878
Penrod and Sam (Tarkington), 878
Percy, Eileen, 1455
Perfect Behavior (Stewart), 1354
"Perfect Life, The," 734, 942
Perfection Form Company (publisher), 1476
Perkins, Maxwell, 480–85, 715, 1033, 1035, 1046, 1048, 1052, 1057, 1145, 1170, 1242–43, 1280–82, 1301, 1323, 1331, 1578, 1694
Permabooks (publisher), 110
Perosa, Sergio, 753
Peter Whiffle (Van Vechten), 1355
Petrini, G. B., (publisher), 637
Phil Berg–Bert Allenberg, Inc., 1322
Philadelphia Inquirer, 179
Philadelphia Inquirer/Public Ledger, 1005
Philadelphia Record, 1014
Phillipe Reclam (publisher), 256
Phillips, Larry W., 644–45
Phillips, William, 191–92
Phoenix Paperback, 671
Photo Repro Co., Inc. (publisher), 1463
Picador Edition, 542
Picture Show (magazine), 1455
Pieces of Hate and Other Enthusiasms (Broun), 1365
"Pierian Springs and the Last Straw, The," 885
Pilgrimage of Festus, The (Aiken), 1395
Pilgrimage of Henry James, The (Brooks), 1158, 1338
Pinchot, Ann, 768
Pine, Edward, 37
Piper, Henry Dan, 232, 754–55, 1031
Pirie, Ginevra King, 1284
Plain Edition (publisher), 1353
Plath, Sylvia, 182
Plato, 1220
Playbill (magazine), 1688
Plon-nourrit et Cie (publisher), 1376
Pocket Books (publisher), 504
Poe, Edgar A., 1665
Poets, Farewell! (Wilson), 1358

Pohlenz, Dagmar, 253
Polyglot Club, The (publisher), 202
"Pope at Confession, The," 682, 888
Popular Authors (card game), 1535
Popular Library (publisher), 479, 495, 528
"Porcelain and Pink," 890
Portable F. Scott Fitzgerald, The (ed. Parker), 577–82
Portrait of Mr. W. H., The (Wilde), 1393
Portrait of the Artist as a Young Man, A (Joyce), 1347
Portraits: Real and Imaginary (Boyd), 1362
Post, Paula, 310, 380
Potter, Dennis, 349
Potter, Laura, 117
Powell, Anthony, 1283
Pratt, George C., 759
"Preface to *This Side of Paradise*," 777
Prejudices: Fourth Series (Mencken), 1384
Prejudices: Second Series (Mencken), 1351, 1383
Prentice-Hall (publisher), 768
Presses Pocket (publisher), 650
Preston, James, 926
Preston, May Wilson, 894, 897, 972
Prevost, Marie, 1461
Price, Reynolds, 1068
Price, W. T., 1388
Price Was High: The Last Uncollected Stories of F. Scott Fitzgerald, The (ed. Bruccoli), 535–43, 1089
Priestley, J. B., 238, 243, 590
Prigozy, Ruth, 57
Primer for Tomorrow, A (Gauss), 1344
"Princeton," 693, 1528
Princeton (Collins), 1503
Princeton Alumni Club, 1522
Princeton Alumni Weekly, 815
"Princeton and F. Scott Fitzgerald," (Frances Scott Fitzgerald), 1526
Princeton Bric-a-Brac, 1505–6, 1510, 1514, 1516
Princeton in the World War, 1523
Princeton 1916 (calendar), 1507
Princeton Pictorial Review, The, 1509
Princeton Stories (Williams), 1501
"Princeton—The Last Day," 883
Princeton Tiger (magazine), 699, 826, 861–70, 876–77, 886, 1287–88
Princeton Tiger, The (publisher), 826
Princeton University, 1–3, 5–8, 534, 815, 1290, 1501–30
Princeton University Alumni Directory, 1525
Princeton University Library (publisher), 440, 472
Princeton University Library: American Library Association Visit, 1511
Princeton University Library Chronicle, 1029, 1039

Princeton University 1917 Commencement Week, 1515
Princeton University Photo-gravures, 1519
Princeton University Press, 682, 699, 712, 1386, 1512
Princeton University Store, 1519
Pringle, Henry F., 1500
Profile of F. Scott Fitzgerald (ed. Bruccoli), 772
Progress Publishers, 643
Proposed Exhibit of Fitzgeraldiana for Chas. Scribner's Sons, 1053
Proulx, E. Annie, 1068
Prouty, Olive Higgins, 1487
Publications in the Humanities, 731
Publishers' Weekly, 795
Pursuit of Priscilla, The, 2, 6
Pushcart at the Curb, A (Dos Passos), 1342
"Pusher-in-the-Face, The," 689, 919
Putnam (publisher), 735, 737
Putnam's Sons, G. P. (publisher), 687, 1247, 1345

Quality Books, 302
Quality Paperback Book Club, 656
Quartet Books (publisher), 538–40
Quarto of Modern Literature . . . Fifth Edition, A (ed. Brown), 227
Queen, Ellery, 743
Quigley, H. Walton, 298
Quill and Brush (publisher), 1068
Quintero, José, 1688

Raduga Publishers, 345
"Rags Martin-Jones and The Pr-nce of W-les," 916
"Rain before Dawn," 880
Raleigh, Henry, 904, 933, 954, 956, 962, 964, 968, 973, 976, 979, 1598
Ralph, Lester, 930
Random House (publisher), 546–48, 719, 733, 743, 752, 808–9, 1042, 1059, 1657–58
Rappaport, H. A., 1386
Rascoe, Burton, 713
Rau, Rudolph F., 276
Rawlings, Marjorie Kinnan, 312
Raymond, Charles, 230
Raymond, Landon T., 1529
"Reade, Substitute Right Half," 952
Reader's Companion to F. Scott Fitzgerald's Tender Is the Night (Bruccoli & Baughman), 831–32
Real F. Scott Fitzgerald Thirty-Five Years Later, The (Graham), 1629–30
Red Badge of Courage, The (Crane), 1655
Red Book Magazine, The, 923, 927, 930
Redbook Magazine, The, 963, 978, 982, 986–87, 1024, 1082–83
Reid, Margaret, 759
Remarks at the Opening of the F. Scott Fitzgerald Centenary Exhibition . . . , 1069

Remarque, Erich Maria, 517–28, 1409–10, 1413–15
Rennie, Thomas, 818, 1373
Replica Classics, 66, 90
Rest of the Story, The (Graham), 1618–19
Reynard, Grant, 935
Reynaud, Jacques-Paul, 1376
"Rich Boy, The," 927
Richardson, Alice Wootton, 1223
Richardson, Dorothy, 815, 1317, 1677
Richardson Studio, 1472
Richman, Susan, 493
Ridout, Albert K., 221–26
Rimbaud, Arthur, 758
"Ring," 704
Ring, Frances Kroll, 828, 1604
Ring W. Lardner: A Descriptive Bibliography (Bruccoli & Layman), 1056
Ritz, Dorothy Williamson, 169
"River Idyll, A" (Biggs), 1280
River Pirate, The (Coe), 1493
Roaring at One Hundred (Princeton Tiger), 826
Robards, Jason, Jr., 1481–82
Robson (publisher), 849
Rogers, Cameron, 315
Rogers, John William, 1352
Rogers, John W., Jr., 149
Roll River (Boyd), 1336
"Romantic Egoist, The," 753, 1135–37
Romantic Egoists, The (ed. Bruccoli, Smith, & Kerr), 785–89, 1285
"Room Where Scott Died, The" (Graham), 1651
"Room with the Green Blinds, The," 857
Rosenfeld, Paul, 307, 416
Ross, Alan and Jennifer, 584
Ross, Cary, 1244, 1609
Rotograph (publisher), 1457
"Rough Crossing, The," 945
Rowe, Barry, 669
"Rubber Check, The," 967
"Rugged Novel, A," 1653
Rutgers University Press, 470–71
"Ruth Sturtevant and F. Scott Fitzgerald," 815

Safety First, 7–8, 1514, 1516, 1530
St. Martin's Press, 827, 1636
St. Paul Daily Dirge, The, 81–82
Saint Paul Academy, 851–57
Saint Paul Academy Now and Then, 851–57
Sakai, Yoshitaka, 591
Salons of America (publisher), 1602
Samples, 690
Sansyusya (publisher), 457, 629
Saturday Evening Post, The, 815, 892, 894–95, 897–99, 903, 912, 917–18, 920, 925, 928, 933–35, 937–39, 941–45, 948–60, 962, 964–68,

970–74, 976–77, 979, 992, 995, 1002, 1078–80, 1141, 1161, 1171, 1438, 1598, 1695
Save Me the Waltz (ZF), 1544–59
Sayre, Anthony D. (ZF's father), 1392, 1437
Sayre, Mrs. Anthony D. (ZF's mother), 791, 1157, 1228, 1363, 1571, 1572, 1584, 1662
Sayre, Constance, 511
"Scandal Detectives, The," 938
Scandalabra (ZF), 1267, 1560, 1568
Schevill, James Erwin, 718
Schöningh, Ferdinand, (publisher), 253
Schulberg, Budd, 567, 795, 1067–68, 1657–60
Schulberg, Victoria, 807
Schulz, Charles M., 1067, 1442–44
Scott and Ernest (Bruccoli), 808–10, 1057
Scott Fitzgerald (Turnbull), 744–45
Scott Fitzgerald and His World (Mizener), 780
Scott Fitzgerald at La Paix (Turnbull), 731
"Scott Fitzgerald: Considered the Most Beautiful 'Show Girl' . . . ," 1508
Screenplay Library, 523–28
"Screen's New Prodigy—Lois Moran, The," 1490
Scribner, Charles, II, 1135, 1298, 1306, 1311
Scribner, Charles, III, 1327, 1670
Scribner, Charles, III [V], 104, 249, 265, 266, 289, 504, 1061; introductions by, 153–55, 166, 247, 263, 343, 348, 661
Scribner, Charles, Jr. [IV], 297, 1548
Scribner Classics, 48, 54, 58, 80, 105, 116, 119, 155, 265–68, 270, 285, 340, 342, 348, 393–94, 438–39, 448, 458, 496, 600–601
Scribner Library, 79, 100–103, 206–8, 216–18, 239–40, 330–33, 361, 382–83, 436, 442, 485, 592, 595–98
Scribner Library of Contemporary Classics, 141, 602
Scribner Paperback Fiction, 55–56, 282, 351, 409, 497, 603, 659
Scribner Quarto of Modern Literature, The (ed. Litz), 245
Scribner Reprint Editions, 152
Scribner Research Anthologies, 232
Scribner School Edition, 222, 224
Scribner School Paperbacks, 223
Scribners (Charles Scribner's Sons, publisher), 9–25, 28–30, 32–35, 44–48, 64–74, 78–79, 83–87, 89–95, 98–106, 123–32, 138–50, 153–54, 157, 160–71, 180, 203–19, 221–28, 231–32, 239–40, 245, 284–85, 293–300, 302, 306–15, 317–23, 330–34, 340–41, 353, 357–61, 372–82, 385–93, 405, 433–36, 438, 441–45, 449–52, 460–62, 466, 480–83, 485, 493–94, 502–3, 568–69, 570, 585, 587–88, 592, 595–600, 602, 623–28, 630, 633, 644–45, 651–57, 711, 715, 729, 744, 765, 785–87, 795, 1046, 1053, 1086, 1137, 1144, 1151, 1298, 1301–2, 1306, 1310–11, 1315, 1327–28, 1336–37, 1344, 1346, 1346, 1352, 1358, 1360–61, 1377, 1380–82, 1389, 1402, 1501, 1539, 1544–45, 1561–62, 1653, 1655, 1690–91
Scribners (London), 260, 262
Scribner's Bookstore, 166
Scribners Large Type Edition, 231
Scribner's Magazine, 305, 896, 900, 961, 975, 1141, 1599–1600
Secker & Warburg (publisher), 774
Second Empire, The (Guedalla), 1345
Secret Agent, The (Conrad), 1369
See, Carolyn, 1068
Seiter, William, 1460
Seldes, Gilbert, 312, 1164, 1281, 1586
Selected Letters of John O'Hara (Bruccoli), 1059
Selected Short Stories, 637, 643
Selected Stories, 632
Selected Works of F. Scott Fitzgerald, The, 670
"Self-Expression," 818
Seltzer, Thomas (publisher), 1396
Selznick, David O., 1245
"'Send Me In, Coach,'" 710, 1000
Senior English Library, 275
"'Sensible Thing, The,'" 1696
"Sentiment—And the Use of Rouge," 884
Seton-Thompson, Ernest, 1389
Settle, Mary Lee, 1067
Shakespeare & Co. (bookshop), 168
Shakespeare and Company (Beach), 740–41
Shakespeare and Company (publisher), 1348
Shakespeare, William, 1148
Sharp Shooters (movie), 1495
Shaw, Charles G., 839
Shaw, George Bernard, 1220
Shaw, Irwin, 415, 1227
Shearer, Norma, 1470
"She'd Better Be Nice" (Pringle), 1500
Sheffer Card Co., Max B. (publisher), 1459
Shenton, Edward, 306–13, 316–23, 975
Sheridan, Jack, 963
Sherwood Anderson, His Life and Work (Schevill), 718
Shinn, Everett, 911
Shinozaki Shorin (publisher), 642
Shohakusha (publisher), 593
"Short Autobiography (with Acknowledgements to Nathan)," 698
Short Stories / Nouvelles, 650
Short Stories of F. Scott Fitzgerald, The, 607
Short Stories of F. Scott Fitzgerald: A New Collection (ed. Bruccoli), 651–59
Short Stories of F. Scott Fitzgerald Selected and Introduced by Malcolm Cowley and Twelve Short Stories, The, 590
"Short Trip Home, A," 935
"Show Mr. And Mrs. F. to Number—" (FSF & ZF), 1603

Showtime, 1486
Siddons, Anne Rivers, 1068
Sidgwick & Jackson (publisher), 1397
Signet Book, 1554
Signet Classic (publisher), 60, 119
Silent Avenger, The (movie), 1453
Simon & Schuster (publisher), 282, 351, 497, 571, 603, 659, 723, 730, 833
Simpkin, Alfred N., 982, 986
Simply Stories, 663–64
Sinclair, Dr., 1181
"Sitting by the Window" (Conrad), 1498
Sivaramkrishna, M., 248
Six Letters to an Apprentice, 573
"Six of One," 963
"Six Previously Unpublished Fitzgerald Letters to Hunt Stromberg" (Samsell), 782
Six Tales of the Jazz Age and Other Stories, 138–41
Skopan, Martine, 459
"Sleeping and Waking," 980
"Slow Surprise and The Deepening of Art, The" (Dickey), 1067
Small, Maynard (publisher), 686
Smart Set, The (magazine), 889–91, 893, 901–2, 905, 907–8, 1141, 1271, 1694
Smart Set: A History and Anthology, The (Dolmetsch), 757
"Smilers, The," 901
Smith, Frances Scott Fitzgerald. *See* Fitzgerald, Scottie
Smith, Harvey H., 1528
Smith, Newman, 1361, 1390
Smith Press, 6
Smith, Rosalind Sayre, 128, 1080, 1166, 1182, 1195, 1390, 1678
Snyder, Harold E., 178–79
Society of Arts and Sciences, 685
Society of Baltimore Independent Artists, The, 1601
Society of Midland Authors, 1153
Some Letters of Monsignor Louis E. Caillet and August N. Chemidlin (ed. Lindley), 1367
Some Sort of Epic Grandeur (Bruccoli), 817–25, 1060
Some Time in the Sun (Dardis), 795
Song of Kentucky, A, 1498
Sound and the Fury, The (Faulkner), 1371
"Southern Girl" (FSF & ZF), 946, 1596
Southern Illinois University Press, 517–27, 801–3, 810, 1409, 1544, 1548–52
"S.P.A. Men in College Athletics," 854
Spake, Hubert, 1168
Sparks, Richard, 661
Spellbound in Darkness (Pratt), 759
Spencer, Elizabeth, 1068
"Spire and the Gargoyle, The," 879
"Spires and Gargoyles," 53

Sprague, Annabelle Fitzgerald (Mrs. Clifton Sprague; FSF's sister), 1178, 1246, 1531–32, 1534
Spring Salon 1933, 1602
Starrett, Henrietta McCaig, 938–39, 941–42, 944, 955, 965, 992, 995, 1002
Stasollo, Mario, 661
State of California Franchise Tax Commissioner, 1221
State of Heat, A (Graham), 1627
"Staying Up All Night, The," 886
Steele, Frederic Dorr, 910
Steenburgen, Mary, 1486
Stein, Gertrude, 416, 722, 1353, 1405
Steiner, George, 758
Stella Dallas (movie), 1487–90
Stella Dallas (Prouty), 1487
Sten, Anna, 1466
Stephen Leacock, Humorist and Humanist (Curry), 738
Sternberg, Vernon, 524, 804, 808, 1544, 1548
Stevenson, Robert Louis, 1352
Stewart, Donald Ogden, 1354, 1429, 1681
Stewart, Lawrence D., 420
Stivers, Harley Ennis, 928, 951–53, 958
Stokes, Frederick A. (publisher), 1391
Stone, Marland, 1499
Stone & Company, H. S. (publisher), 1372
Stories of F. Scott Fitzgerald, The (ed. Cowley), 433–39, 633, 1327
Stories of F. Scott Fitzgerald, The (Penguin series), 453–56, 612–22
Story of Princeton, The (Mossir), 1513
Strack, Lilian Holmes, 304
Strange, Derek, 271
"Strange Sanctuary," 1017
Stratton, Florence, 1593
Strauss, Peter, 1486
Stromberg, Hunt, 782, 1109, 1114, 1193
Studies in Modern Literature, 829
Sturtevant, Ruth, 815
Sugarman, A. L., 84
Suitt, Burke, 1181
Sun Also Rises, The (Hemingway), 1402
Sun Dial Press, 1659
Sun Within Us, The (Drawbell), 845
Sunday Times Weekly Review (London), 1649–50
Suttle, Preston, 1297
Swann, Don, 705–6, 1169
Swann, Don, Jr., 705–6
Swann, Francis, 1163
Swann, Rita, 1175
Swanson, H. N., 1245, 1321
"Swimmers, The," 671, 793, 948, 1072, 1079

"T. S. Eliot's Copy of *Gatsby*" (Siegel), 777
Tait, D. F., 1373
Takamura, K., 635

Takamura, Katsuji, 641
Talbot, Daniel, 727
Tale of Benjamin Bunny, The (Potter), 1661
Tales of the Jazz Age, 123–36, 661, 670, 1155, 1195, 1302, 1694
Tanner, Tony, 257, 291, 1067
Tante, Dilly (Stanley Kunitz), 840
Taps at Reveille, 372–84, 670, 1315
Tarkington, Booth, 878
Tarner, Margaret, 117, 272, 669
"Tarquin of Cheapside," 905
"Tarquin of Cheepside," 881
Tasaka, T., 631
Tasaka, Takashi, 642
Tattooed Countess, The (Van Vechten), 1356
Tauser Head Press, 1043, 1047
Taylor, Cecilia Delihant, 1162, 1246, 1639
Taylor, Dwight, 737
Taylor, H. Weston, 937, 949
Taylor, Robert H., 734, 1467
Technique of the Drama, The (Price), 1388
Temple, Shirley, 1223
"10 Best Books I Have Read," 782
Ten Years of Princeton '17 (Drorbaugh), 693
Tender Is the Night, 305–56, 420, 563–64, 580, 590, 633, 640, 660–61, 666–67, 670, 737, 783–84, 790, 807, 975, 1041, 1044, 1052, 1059, 1065, 1091, 1279, 1287, 1663, 1699; movie and television versions, 341, 346, 818, 1270, 1481–84, 1486
Tender Is the Night "With the Author's Final Revisions," (ed. Cowley), 357–71, 585, 1671
Tender Is the Night, Autobiographical Pieces, Letters to Frances Scott Fitzgerald and Four Short Stories, 590
Tender Is the Night: The Diver Version, 564
Tender Is the Night: The Melarky and Kelly Versions, 563
"Tender Is the Night" (Webster), 1484
Tepper, Saul, 978
Thalberg, Irving, 1470
Thames and Hudson (publisher), 780
That Summer in Paris (Callaghan), 747
Thaumatrope Press, 573
"There Is a Young Man Who's Not Sour," 856
"There Is an Old Lady Next Door," 856
"There Was a Young Fellow Named Ware," 855
"There Was Once a Second Group Student," 861
These Stories Went to Market (Mckenzie), 703
"Things That Never Change!" 877
"Third Casket, The," 1695
13 Great Stories (ed. Talbot), 727
Thirties, The (Wilson), 850
This Is Where I Came In (Anthony), 844
This Room and This Gin and These Sandwiches, Three Plays (Wilson), 1394
This Side of Paradise, 9–63, 511–12, 560, 590, 630, 633, 640, 660–61, 666–67, 670, 672, 748, 777, 1014, 1051, 1070, 1076, 1152, 1154, 1173–74, 1298, 1304, 1305, 1334, 1365, 1445, 1518, 1690
This Side of Paradise and Six Short Stories, 590
"This Side of Paradise, by F. Scott Fitzgerald" (Gennert), 1518
This Side of Paradise: The Manuscripts and Typescripts, 560
This Side of Paradise 26 March 1920 26 March 1970, 1049
Tibbott, David W., 1528
"Tiger Lillies" (ZF), 1601
Thomas Cooper Library (University of South Carolina), 4, 158, 559, 830, 1062–63, 1066, 1069, 1072
Thomas, Faith, 19
Thomas Wolfe (ed. Mitchell), 835
Thorp, Willard, 712
"Thoughtbook of Francis Scott Key Fitzgerald," 1073
Thoughtbook of Francis Scott Key Fitzgerald, 472
"Three Acts of Music," 735–36, 993
Three "Basil" Stories, 606
Three Comrades (Remarque), 517–28
Three Comrades (movie), 1097–1106, 1190, 1197, 1409–15, 1468–69
"Three Days at Yale," 865
Three Hours Between Planes, 475
Three Novels by F. Scott Fitzgerald, 630
Three Novels of F. Scott Fitzgerald, 585, 587–88
Three Years, 1924–1927 (The American Mercury), 692
Through the Wheat (Boyd), 1337, 1361, 1655
Tiger's Family Album, The, 699
Tilghman, Christopher, 1068
Time (magazine), 809
Times Book Club, 135
Tinling, James, 1496
To Loot My Life Clean (ed. Bruccoli & Bucker), 1331
"To My Unused Greek Book," 871
Today Library, 605
"Too Cute for Words," 992
Tooker Lithography (publisher), 1467
Towne, Charles Hanson, 1247
"Trail of the Duke, The," 860
Transaction Publishers, 674
Transworld (publisher), 1617
"Triangle Club Number," 1509
Triangle Club, Princeton, 1–3, 5–8, 1507–10, 1514, 1516, 1530
"Tribute to Mark Twain," 1084
Trilling, Diana, 12, 67, 181
Trilling, Lionel, 12, 67, 164, 181
"Trimalchio," 1055, 1071
Trimalchio by F. Scott Fitzgerald, 158, 1071, 1155
"Trouble," 1002

Trowe, Chester, 1230
Truex, Ernest, 144, 793
Tsurumi Shoten (publisher), 156
Tudor (publisher), 700
Tulips and Chimneys (cummings), 1396
Turkey Remains and How to Inter Them . . . , 1040
"Turn of the Tables, The" (Scottie Fitzgerald), 1686
Turnbull, Andrew, 460–69, 627–29, 731, 744–45, 1032, 1046, 1648
Turnbull, Margaret, 1690
Turvey, Celia, 290
Tuttle, Frank, 1463
Twain, Mark, 1084, 1165, 1289, 1364, 1579
Twayne Publishers, 748
Twenties, The (Wilson), 792
20th Century–Fox (studio), 1479–81, 1483–84, 1613
"Two for a Cent," 686
"Two New Fitzgerald Letters" (Hemenway), 815
"Two Old-Timers," 709
Two Short Stories of F. Scott Fitzgerald, 593
"Two Wrongs," 949

U. Mursia (publisher), 632
Ueki, Yoshihide, 594
Uemura, Ikuo, 586
Ullman (publisher), 1461
Ulysses (Joyce), 782, 1348
UMI Research Press, 829
Unfinished Woman, An (Hellman), 847
Ungar Publishing Co., Frederick, 526
United Artists (studio), 1466, 1488
United States Army, 1296
Universal Studios, 1321, 1491
University Cottage Club, The, 1527
University of Alabama Press, 1566
University of Denver Press, 718
University of Manchester, 1052
University of Michigan Press, 753
University of Pittsburgh Press, 750–51, 1054
University of South Carolina, 1062–63, 1067, 1155
University of South Carolina Press, 4, 158, 574, 680–81, 830–32, 1066, 1071, 1331, 1693
University of Virginia, 1041
University of Virginia (publisher), 714
University of Virginia Library, 805–6
University Press of Mississippi, 1692
University School of Liberal & Applied Studies, University of Rochester (publisher), 759
"Unreflecting Shield, The" (Dickey), 557–58
Untermeyer, Louis, 583
Updike, John, 1068
USIS (United States Information Service; publisher), 742
"Usual Thing, The," 874

"Valentine was a Saint . . . ," 766
"Vampiest of the Vampires, The," 875
Van Doren, Carl, 1390
Van Dyke, Henry, 682
Van Peet(?), Elizabeth P., 296
Van Vechten, Carl, 746, 1355–57
Vandamm, 1490
Vanderbilt, Kermit, 121
Vanity Fair (magazine), 1490
Vaughan, Courtney Sprague, 1531–32, 1700
Vegetable, The, 142–56, 566, 670, 793, 1306, 1307
Vegetable, Stories, and Articles, The, 566
"Verses in Peace and War," 884
Verses in Peace and War (Leslie), 884, 1381
Viaduct Publications, Ltd., 252
Victory (Conrad), 1370
Viking (publisher), 773, 849
Viking Portable Library, 577–81
Viking Press, 577–81, 848
Viztelly, Frank H., 1150
Vogue Press, 1055
"Voyelles" (Rimbaud), 758

Wagstaff, Joseph, 1498
"Wait Till You Have Children of Your Own!" 915
Wald, Jerry, 1479–80
Walker, Meredith, 1560
Walker, Stanley, 1391
Walker, Susan, 546–48
Walker's (alumnae bulletin), 1038
Wallace, Irving, 322
Waller, Stephen, 663–64, 676
Wanger, Walter, 815
Wann, Elizabeth Clarkson, 797
War Baby, The, 1518
Warner, A., 1303
Warner Books (publisher), 1629
Warner Bros. (studio), 1460–61
Warner, H. M., 1303
Warren, Anne Crawford, 419, 441
Warren, Charles Marquis, 419, 441, 818, 1217, 1248, 1640
Washington Post, 1543
Washington Square Press, 57, 118
Watson, John B., 1392
We Were Interrupted (Rascoe), 713
Wead, Frank, 1094, 1408
Weaks, Dan, 1037
Weatherby, J. W., 1279
Webb, Thomas, 967
Webster, Paul Francis, 1484
Wedding Night, The (movie), 1466
Weidenfeld and Nicolson (publisher), 1622
Weinstein, Henry T., 1481–82
Weisberger, Siegfried, 148
Wells Gardner, Darton (publisher), 709
Wells, H. G., 884

Wescott, Glenway, 416
Wescott, Mrs. Ralph W., 1289
Wesker, Arnold, 1067
West, Nathanael, 777
Westfälische Wilhelms-Universität, 1065
Westover Publishing, 778
Wharton, Edith, 416
"What a Handsome Pair!" 968
"What Became of the Flappers?" (ZF), 924, 1594
"What Becomes of Our Flappers and Sheiks?" 924, 1594
"What 'College of One' Taught Me" (Graham), 1650
"What Happened to Susie," 868
"What I Think and Feel at 25," 909
What Makes Sammy Run? (Schulberg), 1657–60
Wheelock, John Hall, 715
"When Vanity Kissed Vanity," 769
"When You Find a Man Doing a Little More than His Duty," 877
Whitcombe & Tombs (publisher), 21, 65
White Bear Yacht Club, 1608
White, Charles T., 1521
White, Edward, 449
Whittlesey House (publisher), 708
"Who's Who and Why," 903
Who's Who in America, 837
Widdemer, Margaret, 700
Wiggins, Robin, 638
Wilbur, Richard, 1068
Wild Animals I Have Known (Seton-Thompson), 1389
Wilde, Oscar, 1393
Wiley & Sons, John (publisher), 483
Wilkinson, Chuck, 246
Willert, Lady Florence, 311
Willerval, B., 634
Williams, Blanche Colton, 685
Williams, C. D., 923, 948
Williams, Jessie Lynch, 1501
Williams, Tennessee, 1285, 1688
Williamson, Annah, 376
Williamson, Dorothy, 30, 73, 129, 169, 294
Wilson, Edmund, 5, 385–405, 414, 416, 585, 661, 792, 799, 850, 1033, 1053, 1286–91, 1358, 1386, 1394, 1519
Wilson, Elena, 799

Wilson, H. W. (publisher), 840
Windhover Press, 474, 511–12
Winston, Carl W., 1159
Winston Company, John C. (publisher), 1359
"Winter Dreams," 262
Winter, Ella, 1363
With Love from Gracie (Lewis), 726
Wives and Lovers (ed. Austin), 732
Woburn Press, 490–91
Woiwode, Larry, 1068
Wolfe, Thomas, 416, 729, 835, 1331
"Woman from Twenty-One," 719–20
"Woman with a Past, A," 952
Woman's Home Companion (magazine), 915, 919, 922, 926, 932
Women, The (movie), 1116–34, 1422–29
Wootton, Alice, 295, 320, 1167, 1170, 1123, 1167
Wordsworth (publisher), 273, 350
World's Best Short Stories of 1926, The, 688
"World's Fair, The," 727, 1027
Wright, George, 959
Write and Rewrite (Kuehl), 761
Wyatt, J. F., 229
Wyllie, John Cook, 148
Wynn, Wilhelmina and Bob, 798

Yamaguchi Shoten (publisher), 594, 605
Yamamoto, Hiroshi, 604
Yank at Oxford, A (movie), 176, 1092–95, 1406–8, 1467
Yohn, F. C., 900
Yorke, Lane, 1606
Yoshida, Hiroshige, 636
Yoshida, Mitsuo, 593
You—At Twenty, 691
Young, Sean, 1486
Young, Waldemar, 1458
"Your Way & Mine," 932
Youth (Conrad), 814

Zaid, Barry, 1036
Zelda: A Biography (Milford), 770–71
"Zelda: A Worksheet" (ed. Yorke), 1606
Zelda: An Illustrated Life (ed. Lanahan), 1567
Zelda Fitzgerald: The Collected Writings (ed. Bruccoli), 1561–66
"Zone of Accident," 985